HOUSING AND URBAN DEVELOPMENT IN THE USSR

The explicit acknowledgement by Soviet writers of a housing shortage invites the following questions. Why, almost seventy years after the Revolution, is housing still regarded as a 'problem'? What are the consequences of shortages? How has the state sought to alleviate the situation? Who should be responsible for providing accommodation? In approaching these questions, certain other issues involving urban development systematically come to the fore, revealing the interconnectedness of housing and urban development generally. This book is thus concerned with these two intricately related subjects: housing and the urban environment in a socialist society.

The first part of the book deals with *who* builds and controls accommodation in the Soviet Union and speculates on whether particular types of tenure might be associated with specific social groups.

The second part asks: *What sort of* housing is considered to be most appropriate for the new Soviet person living in a socialist society?

The third part, in focusing on *where* housing is built, not only sheds light on the source of the discrepancy between plan and reality in urban development, but also pursues a suggestion advanced earlier that certain forces operating in Soviet cities may be giving rise to spatial patterns of social segregation.

Both metaphorically and literally, the architects of the Revolution were the architects and town-planners who, in their designs of dwellings and juxtapositioning of crèches, kindergartens and social facilities, were to provide a setting for a cultural revolution. Paradoxically, whilst a half a century ago these conceptualisations of the environment most conducive for engendering a 'new way of life' ran too far ahead of the level of development of Soviet society for them to be implemented, today these ideas have been rendered largely redundant by the development of Soviet society. New social structures have created new norms, values and demands, particularly in the visible form of a more privatised, consumer-orientated, home-centred, car-ownership-seeking, nuclear family with segregated role-playing. (Thus, while the USA and USSR diverge over the question of house-ownership, they converge in terms of the privatised lifestyle that the type of accommodation being built encourages.) None the less, the Party has turned its back on the peasant, his wooden hut, private plot and innate conservatism: the worker of tomorrow will be housed in high-rise blocks of flats which are being produced like any other mass-produced commodity using assembly-line techniques. However, this goal is far from being realised; huge areas in Soviet cities remain dominated by low-rise housing, a fact responsible for making urban renewal a central issue in Soviet town-planning policy.

Dr Gregory D. Andrusz is Senior Lecturer in Sociology at Middlesex Polytechnic. He was an undergraduate and then postgraduate student at the Centre for Russian and East European Studies of the University of Birmingham. As a British Council scholar he studied urbanisation and social change in Poland at the University of Warsaw, 1965–6. After a brief spell in industry exporting heavy engineering equipment to the USSR and Eastern Europe, he joined the staff of Middlesex Polytechnic in 1968. He spent the academic year 1975–6 in Kiev and Moscow, researching into Soviet housing and urban development policy. He has contributed to several books.

SUNY Series in Urban Public Policy
Mark Schneider and Richard Rich, Editors

HOUSING AND URBAN DEVELOPMENT IN THE USSR

Gregory D. Andrusz

State University of New York Press
Albany

© Gregory D. Andrusz, 1984

First published in U.S.A. by
State University of New York Press, Albany

For information, address State University of New York Press,
State University Plaza, Albany, N.Y., 12246

Printed in Hong Kong

Library of Congress Cataloging in Publication Data

Andrusz, Gregory D.
　Housing and urban development in the USSR.

　Bibliography: p.
　Includes index.
　1. Housing—Soviet Union.　2. Housing policy—Soviet
Union.　3. City planning—Soviet Union.　I. Title.
HD7345. A3A68　1984　　　363.5'0947　　　83–24258
ISBN 0–87395–911–6
ISBN 0–87395–912–4 (pbk.)

To my parents and Katya

Contents

Part III Housing and Urban Growth

Acknowledgements

A number of close friends have cheered me from the sidelines as I plodded through *Pravda* and *Postanovleniya* and throughout the short lifetime that it has taken to write this book. They encouraged me but without exhortation and in 'bidding me take life easy' saved me from atrophying in a waste of six by fours.

I am particularly indebted to Professor Bob Davies for his detailed, painstaking comments and skilful editing, especially of the first section of the book, and to Dr Denis Shaw for his patient reading of the whole manuscript in its different phases and the critical advice he offered. I would also like to thank Dennis Hardy of Middlesex Polytechnic for suggestions on Chapter 3, and Jenny Brine, the librarian at the Centre for Russian and East European Studies, for all her assistance over many years.

London   G. A.

Glossary

gorispolkom	Executive Committee of the City Soviet
gorkom	City Party Committee
gorsovet	City Soviet ('Local Authority')
gosgrazhdanstroi	State Committee for Civil Construction & Architecture
gosplan	State Planning Committee
gosstroi	State Committee for Construction
krai	Krai; Territory (Administrative Subdivision of the RSFSR)
mikroraion	Micro-district ('neighbourhood unit')
NKVD	People's Commissariat of Internal Affairs
oblast'	Oblast' (Administrative Subdivision of a Union Republic)
oblispolkom	Executive Committee of the Oblast' Soviet
RSFSR	Russian Soviet Federal Socialist Republic
Sovnarkom (SNK)	Council of People's Commissars
SSR	Soviet Socialist Republic
Sovet Ministrov	Council of Ministers
TsIK	Central Executive Committee (of the Congress of Soviets)
vedomstvo	Central Government Department
Sobranie Postanovlenii (SP)	A Collection of Decrees (normally by the Council of Ministers and/or the Central Committee of the CPSU) at the All-Union level (*SP SSSR*) or Republican level (e.g. *SP RSFSR*)
Sobranie Uzakonenii (SU)	A Collection of Enactments for Soviet Russia until 1923, for the RSFSR from 1924 onwards (from 1917 to 1938)
Sobranie Zakonov (SZ)	A Collection of Laws for the USSR (from 1924 to 1938)

TsK KPSS	Central Committee of the Communist Party of the Soviet Union
ZhEK(y)	House-management Office(s)
ZhSK(y)	House-building Co-operative(s)

The Russian word *predpriyatie* has been translated throughout the book, with few exceptions, as *enterprise*. R. E. F. Smith (*A Russian–English Dictionary of Social Science Terms*, Butterworth, 1962) gives a number of alternative translations: 1. an undertaking; 2. works; plant; enterprise; production organisation; a production unit (factory, mine, quarry, etc.) administratively identified mainly by having a final balance sheet of its own; a firm; concern.

Preface

Ever since the stimulating debates on history as a science at the end of the nineteenth century, scholars have been conscious of the tensions and difficulties of striving to remain ideologically neutral in their analyses. The self-designated empiricist, adamant that ideological bias has been banished like Satan from his study, would do well to remember Alfred Marshall's trenchant admonition that the most reckless and treacherous of all theorists is he who professes to let facts and figures speak for themselves. He is treacherous because a social-scientific work has a moral and political content; research is not a detached intellectual activity set apart from the rest of the researcher's life.

Since one has either a basic sympathy with or antipathy towards the Soviet Union which is an aggregate of positive and negative attitudes towards specific institutions, aspects of the nation's past and its goals, some theories about the USSR are accepted fairly readily as convincing and others are rejected as unconvincing. It is impossible to have no value orientation towards the events surrounding those 'ten days that shook the world', the setting up of the revolutionary workers' state, Stalinism, the Great Purges of the 1930s, and today, détente and dissidents and the origins of the 'new' Cold War. Behind our explicitly formulated assumptions lie a set of 'background assumptions' (about these and other topics) as a result of which some theories are 'intuitively' convincing because their background assumptions coincide with those of the reader. Thus, for example, a reference-point in the polemic between Isaiah Berlin and E. H. Carr over particular philosophies of history and judgements on the moral qualities of different social and political systems is the Soviet Union, and the reader of these two scholars has a greater affinity either for the essentially liberal and individualistic view of history of Berlin or for Carr's Marxian interpretation.[1]

The Russian revolution of 1917 saw the setting up, for the first time in history, of an alternative system to capitalism, and whatever the successes and failures of the Soviet system over the last sixty years might have been, Western capitalism has reacted to them.[2] The crassest vilification of experiments carried out to devise new forms of political representation, to plan the industrialisation of a backward economy and to find specifically socialist designs for living have been matched by ridiculous panegyrics on all facets of Soviet society. And it is not just the practices of institutions that are applauded or challenged but the body of ideas which are evoked to justify the practices. The significance of ideational systems was questioned in 1953 by Dahl and Lindblohm who, foreshadowing the 'convergence' and 'end of ideology' debates of the 1960s, contended that 'Techniques and not "isms" are the kernel of rational action in the real world. Both socialism and capitalism are dead.' This is a proposition vigorously rejected by Hayek, for whom 'it is ideas which rule the world and its events', and for whom 'the most important political [or "ideological"] differences of our time rest ultimately in certain basic philosophical differences between two schools of thought, of which the one that holds change by design to be possible can be shown to be mistaken'.[3] The deduction drawn from the premise that because the millions of facts and actions which constitute society cannot in their totality be known to any single person is that decisions are best left to the market. However, the truism that there is no single 'grand designer' (neither deity nor dictator) does not justify the conclusion that reliance should therefore be placed on a 'hidden hand'. On the contrary, it has led many to believe in the inevitability of an expansion of bureaucratisation – on the ground that, as Max Weber discerned, in modern societies the choice as far as administration is concerned is between bureaucracy and dilettantism.

However, not only do relationships within bureaucracies represent the interplay between particular strategies which culminate in the manipulation of information and other resources to serve the private career and power ambitions of individuals and rival bureaucratic cliques, but, as Marx observed, a crucial characteristic of bureaucracies is that they behave like private owners *vis-à-vis* public resources.[4] Such behaviour is readily evident in Soviet society where, Taubman rightly notes, bureaucracies (i.e. ministries, departments, planning institutes, etc.) 'develop parochial perspectives from information gathered from their own sources and processed through their own channels', and adopt strategies which promote their own self-interests and guard against attempts to reduce the importance of their functions, or to decrease the resources allocated to them.[5]

These negative features of 'bureaucratic politics' which are recognised and criticised by Soviet politicians and other commentators come clearly to the fore when political leaders try to rectify the imbalance between 'productive' and 'non-productive' (i.e. housing, schools, etc.) investment. Then

> they find that old evils have a powerful inertia, that institutional arrangements devised to implement one set of priorities resist efforts to set new goals, that bureaucratic interests that gain from an old order fight to perpetuate their position, that even a powerful central leadership may find it difficult to overcome these obstacles, especially when the leaders cannot bring themselves to break fully with the assumptions of an earlier era of which they themselves are a product.[6]

That the Soviet Party leadership recognises this fact is evident, for instance, in Mr Brezhnev's statement at the XXVI Party Congress that 'The practice of downward plan revision has become widespread. Such a practice disorganises the economy, demoralises personnel and accustoms them to irresponsibility.'[7]

But because bureaucracies have a marked tendency to act in their own particularistic interests, sometimes circumventing the procedures and goals set for them, this does not mean that they should be dismantled or abolished. They have to be made both more efficient and representative, which means being more responsive to the demands of their mandators. In the Soviet Union the government strives to achieve this second objective by increasing the role of mass participation in the administration of society; and, arguably, in meeting this democratic imperative, the actual process of goal achievement of bureaucracies is improved.[8] However, this Leninist ideal, encapsulated in his tract, *State and Revolution*, envisaging the gradual supplanting of the professional administrator by mobilising citizens, is succumbing to its antithesis, scientific management, with its stress on 'administration as a science' which does not always value citizen participation very highly. Overall, the trend in the USSR, as in other European and North American countries, towards greater participation in the political and decision-making processes is counterposed by the attempt by bureaucracies (particularly, perhaps, the apparatuses of the central state) to extend their control over resources and through artifice to reduce their accountability.

The question which arises from the foregoing is this: does dogma really determine social and economic development of advanced industrial societies in the last quarter of the twentieth century? In 1982, certainly in the UK and the USA, the current credo of political economy favouring a 'market solution' to the problems facing these countries may be no more congruent with the nature of the difficulties that they are experiencing than is the alternative 'centrally planned' solution. The gravity of the difficulties facing these societies notwithstanding, adherents to the monetarist doctrine are as unswerving in their demands to see their ideas on market determination applied as is the Soviet government in its reiteration of the necessity to improve planning. The plan is law 'not just because it is approved by the Supreme Soviet' but also 'because its observance assures the harmonious functioning of the national economy ... The time has come to tighten requirements as to plan fulfilment and the quality of the plans themselves.'[9]

The political leaders of these two schools appear equally inquisitorial, challenging anyone who has the temerity to suggest that these countries face common problems, whose causes have a certain commonality and whose alleviation requires the making of similar political choices.

This book, in looking at certain aspects of housing and urban development in the Soviet Union, deals with a subject that is the source of grievance to the majority of citizens in all societies at some time in their life and is one that perplexes all governments.

GREGORY D. ANDRUSZ

List of Tables

Introduction

'The first premise of all human existence,' wrote Marx in *The German Ideology*, 'is ... that man must be in a position to live in order to make history. But life involves before anything else eating and drinking, a habitation, clothing and many other things.'[1] No national government has yet succeeded in providing for all its citizens accommodation of a required standard at a cost which absorbs a small proportion of a family's income. This present work takes as its central problematic the provision of 'habitation' in the Soviet Union. From the very foundation of the Soviet state, the country's leaders have acknowledged in their speeches and promulgations the existence of a housing problem.

Among the purposes of the Party and government, reaffirmed at the XXII Party Congress held in 1961 and published as the Communist Party Programme in that year (and not yet superseded by any other Programme), was a section entitled: 'Solving the Housing Problem and Conditions of Daily Life'. In this document the Party leadership noted that the most acute problem to be solved, if the standard of living of the population were to be raised, was housing. It declared that by 1971 (the end of the first decade of building communism) the housing shortage would have come to an end, and that those families who were still living in overcrowded and generally poor living conditions in 1961 would have received new flats. By 1980 (by which date 'the material basis of communism will have been created, providing an abundance of material and cultural wealth for the whole population') every family would have its own fully-equipped flat; peasant houses 'of the old type' would largely have been replaced by new buildings or, where this was not possible, would have been renovated and fitted with basic amenities. In the course of the second decade people would gradually cease to pay rent. The same section of the Programme also drew attention to environmental improvement measures ranging from higher standards in architecture and city layouts to pollution control.[2]

The summary documents of the XXV and XXVI Party Congresses, published in 1976 and 1981, had little to say on the subject of housing[3]

1

and the references which were made differed scarcely at all from those contained in the Directives of the previous XXIV Congress (1971) – except that, in the latter, the Prime Minister had noted that: 'We still cannot say that the whole population is being provided with housing at the required standard. This will continue to be a serious problem'.[4] It is perhaps significant that Mr Brezhnev in his Report to the XXVI Party Congress should draw attention to the related issues of housing shortage, and distribution. Because of the shortage manifested by 'many families still sharing flats and many newly-weds waiting years for accommodation', public authorities were called upon to show particular care in ensuring fairness in distribution.[5]

The explicit acknowledgement of a housing shortage invites the following questions: Why, over sixty years after the socialist revolution, is housing still regarded as a problem? For whom does a shortage of accommodation constitute a problem? What are the consequences of shortages? How has the state sought to alleviate the situation? In approaching these questions, certain other issues involving urban development systematically come to the fore to reveal the interconnectedness of housing and the exploitation of the environment. This book is thus concerned with these two intricately related subjects: housing and the urban environment in a socialist society. Although the scale of research, supervision and resource allocation differs depending on the 'environment' – ranging from the prevention of water pollution occurring over thousands of square miles to tidying up a couple of acres of wasteland in an urban area – there appears to be an almost endemic conflict between so-called environmentalists on the one hand, and on the other groups who have production, directly or indirectly, as their prime objective. To put it another way, whereas the former are concerned with the long-run and/or non-revenue generating issues, the latter recognise, as did J. M. Keynes, that in the long run we are all dead politicians and producers as well as economists. This raises the question of whether 'environmentalists' are any more likely to prevail in Angarsk than in Aberdeen, on Tayside than in the Tyumen'. The long-run interest may tentatively be regarded as being represented by the local soviet while economic organisations – principally those of manufacturing, mining and other natural resource exploitation – are primarily concerned with the short run (that is, with their 'branch' interests).

The conflict between local soviets and enterprises finds expression at urban and regional planning levels as a contradiction between spatial and sectoral planning. One manifestation of this contradiction is the continuing population increase of the largest cities beyond the projected maximum sizes and the emergence of agglomerations. An historical analysis of the reasons for the rise to prominence of the agglomeration and urban renewal as policy issues reveals the influence of earlier housing policies which are themselves the outcome, in terms of tenure type and physical design, of the form industrialisation has taken. Such an analysis of urbanisation and urban form may usefully be viewed in the context of a much broader debate on the objective laws of social development.

In 1882 Vorontsov put forward the notion that countries which are latecomers to the arena of history have a great advantage over their predecessors because of the accumulated historical experience of these predecessors. This advantage enables them to work out a relatively true image of their own next step and to strive for what others have already achieved – not groping in the dark but knowing what should be avoided on the way.[6] On the other hand, Marx had written in *Capital* that 'a society can neither clear by bold leaps nor remove by legal enactments the obstacles offered by the successive phases of its normal development'.[7] The laws of social development push their way with 'iron necessity' and the less developed nations have to pass through the same phases of economic development which the developed ones have already completed. This poses the question: do the urban spatial forms characterising the industrially advanced capitalist societies represent a necessary pattern for settlements in the Soviet Union?[8]

Discussion of this issue has to take into account that urban planning (and planning in general) took form in a specific historical situation whose principal characteristics, according to Soviet commentators, were: (1) the need to build socialism in one country; (2) the economic backwardness of the first socialist state; (3) the low level of education and shortage of qualified workers; (4) an external threat which necessitated a high level of expenditure on defence. These historical parameters – and not government caprice – forced architects and urban planners in the 1930s to modify their visions. Today, despite the quantitative and qualitative changes that have taken place in the society, these constraints remain and have been supplemented by five others: (a) a declining birth rate; (b) a rising domestic demand for consumer goods; (c) the need to raise labour productivity; (d) the shift to using energy resources in Siberia; (e) an agricultural sector which despite vast inputs of capital is thwarted in its development by climatic variability.

It has also to take into account the special role assigned to cities which Lenin referred to as the centres of the 'economic, political and spiritual life of the nation ... and the main motors of progress'.[9] Even today they are described as being 'the basis for the communist transformation of production, culture and the way of life; the city is the centre for directing the communist transformation of the village, the school for moulding the new man, the seat of the high communist ideal, the frontier of science.'[10] Such a bold, encomiastic definition of the city stands as a twentieth century reminder of the nineteenth-century urbanist's rebuke to rural romanticism. It firstly echoes the objection raised by Marx and Engels to the 'idiocy' of rural life and to those who were seeking an answer to the depravity and inhumanity of nascent urban–industrial society by turning their gaze to an earlier bucolic era and, secondly, reaffirms Lenin's position in his polemicising with the Russian Populists (*narodniki*).

Such was the importance of the nineteenth-century Populist–Marxist debate – reflected in Mikhailovsky's search for an alternative path to capitalism, envisaging development through a socially transformed agrarian commune and Marx's own vacillation on the possibility of 'an alternative path to socialism'[11] – that Lenin's *The Development of Capitalism in Russia* is first and foremost a documented treatise against the *narodniki* intended to prove that no alternative any longer existed to progress along the evolutionary path marked out by Marx and Engels. Acceptance of the historical role of the proletariat meant acceptance of capitalistic industrialisation and its spatial concomitant, the city.[12] Among the principal questions placed by the October 1917 Revolution on the agenda for the Soviet government and intelligentsia was: what form should urbanisation take? This entailed the posing of more specific questions which constitute the subject matter of this study: who should be responsible for providing accommodation? in what sort of housing should the worker in a socialist society be accommodated? what form should the city itself assume? what should be the spatial relationships between settlements?

Because the policies proposed and the measures adopted had to contend with industrial backwardness in a vast country, the first chapter is principally concerned with outlining the broad contours of housing provision and urban development in tsarist Russia and the ideologically determined legislative enactments of the Soviet government which laid the foundation of all future housing and urban policy. The concluding section summarises some of the main features of the current housing situation and outlines the four main forms of housing tenure. Since an examination of the evolving housing situation in terms of tenure not only answers the question, 'who is responsible for providing and controlling accommodation' but may also shed light on a number of social, political and institutional trends in the Soviet Union, Chapter 2 describes the evolution of the four main forms of housing tenure from 1917 to 1941. Chapters 3, 4 and 5 discuss the individual contributions which the state, co-operative and private sectors have made to meeting accommodation demands in the post-war period. An attempt is made to understand the function each tenure performs and the social and institutional conflicts inherent in each housing category. Chapter 3, in dealing with state housing, examines what may be considered to be one of the main tensions in Soviet society, namely that between local soviets and enterprises. The struggle which takes place at all levels between these two institutional complexes (or bureaucracies) is not confined to housing alone but extends to a wide range of 'objects of collective consumption'.

Although housing co-operatives comprise about 7 per cent of all new house building in towns, compared with 35 – 50 per cent in Poland and Czechoslovakia, it nevertheless represents an important tenure form. The fact that its long term future seems well assured is an indication of the direction of change in Soviet society. The government's categorising of the house-building co-operative as part of the state rather than the private sector is obfuscatory for a flat in a co-operative is, to all intents and purposes, as private as the house belonging to the owner-occupier. Nevertheless, as Chapters 4 and 5 make clear, substantive differences distinguish the private from the co-operative sector.

Since a housing policy invariably involves more than just a consideration of 'bricks and mortar' and economic costs, Chapter 6 directs attention to another aspect of the question: in what sort of housing should people in a socialist society be housed? High-rise, high-density, publicly (or co-operatively) owned housing may be a requisite for the pursuit of some sort of 'collectivist ideal' – an ideal that permeates Soviet Marxism. Yet such an ideal conflicts with a dominant trend in Soviet social life – towards a more privatised way of life arising from increasing personal mobility, rising car ownership, a falling birth rate and nuclearisation of the family.

If it was to embark on a major housing programme to relieve the acute housing shortage, the government recognised that huge resources would have to be committed to the task – and these would have to be used efficiently. Chapter 7 examines the keystone of the house-building programme, namely the widespread application of standard designs and prefabricated methods of construction. Besides reviewing the institutions responsible for housing and city design on the one hand, and the salient features of the organisation and finance of the construction industry on the other, attention is drawn again to the related issues of labour shortages and labour mobility – both particularly evident in the construction industry.

Soviet urban policy-makers are currently preoccupied with two main issues: urban renewal and agglomerations. Chapter 8 describes the extent of low-rise housing development and outlines the policy alternatives facing central and local government. Although the choices between renewal (demolition) and rehabilitation (modernisation) faced by central and local governments in the USSR and UK are broadly similar, their social effects are different. None the less, this chapter raises the issue of the spatial segregation of social groups – a phenomenon closely tied to the class specificity of housing tenures discussed in Chapters 2 to 5. The underdeveloped nature of the Soviet economy presents a contradiction between productive (sector) planning and non-productive (spatial) planning. Chapter 9 describes this contradiction through the continuing growth of large cities and the emergence of agglomerations and commuting. The reasons for these phenomena are explored against a background of less than total success in fostering small town growth.

1 Historical Background and Overview

On the eve of World War I only about 18 per cent of the population (28.5 million) of the Russian Empire lived in towns.[1] Figures available for European Russia reveal the rapid expansion which occurred in the preceding century.

TABLE 1.1 *Urban population of European Russia, 1811–1914*

Year	Millions	% of total
1811	2.77	6.6
1863	6.15	10.0
1897	12.05	12.9
1914	18.60	15.3

SOURCE A. G. Rashin, *Naselenie Rossii za 100 let, 1811–1913*, Moscow, 1956, p. 98.

Towns tended to be small: by 1914 just twenty-one had over 100 000 inhabitants and in only four cities (St. Petersburg, Moscow, Kiev and Odessa) did the population exceed 400 000 which, when aggregated, accounted for some 28 per cent of the total urban population.[2] The capital, St. Petersburg, with over two million inhabitants, had trebled in population since 1870 and with six persons to a room had twice as many occupants in each flat than in any other European capital.[3] This low level of urbanisation may be compared with the rate of urban growth in England during the nineteenth century. In 1801 only one-third of the population lived in towns of any size, but by 1851 half the population lived in towns, over one-third in towns with more than 20 000 inhabitants, and nearly one-third in towns of over 100 000. In 1861 London had a population of 2.8 million and by 1907 had reached 4.5 million, while eight other towns had over 250 000 inhabitants and twenty-four over 100 000.[4]

These societies differed considerably not only in the size of their cities and the proportions of their populations actually living in towns (UK: 1851 (54%); 1881 (68%); 1911 (80%)), but also in their outward appearance. As one French traveller observed, in their external form most Russian towns resembled overgrown villages:

> It is not only by their scarcity, their dispersion over a vast territory, that Russian towns differ from those of Western Europe. With their wooden houses, low and far between, their preposterously wide streets, for which only the fear of fire accounts, streets usually unpaved . . . Instead of standing their houses side by side, instead of heaping tier upon tier up to the sky as in the old cities of France, Italy and Germany and thus forming a little world entirely distinct from the country . . . the Russian towns stretch and sprawl out into the fields into which they merge, leaving between the houses and public buildings areas of waste land that can never be filled or enlivened. To the traveller arriving from Europe, they appear as something huge, deserted, unfinished; they often seem to be their own suburbs and the foreigner expects to enter the city when he is just leaving it behind him. To him they are so many overgrown villages and, in fact, there is less difference here than anywhere else between town and village, as regards the manner of building and living.[5]

This impressionistic account is confirmed by the single most important source on the housing situation before 1917, the government publication, *Towns of Russia in 1910*. Surveying 1228 towns which were either administrative centres or had more than 10 000 inhabitants, it yielded data on little more than twenty-five thousand buildings. 48 per cent of the buildings had wooden walls and about 60 per cent wooden or thatched roofs. 99 per cent of all houses were single-storey and even in Moscow the figure was 91 per cent.[6]

Towns and villages were distinguishable from one another neither by their outward appearance nor by their economic functions. Writing in 1855 a St. Petersburg court official noted how in other countries it was normally the artisans in the towns who supplied the villages with articles, whereas in Russia the villages tended to provide for the needs of the towns.[7] Even after the emancipation of serfs in 1861, the persistence of an estate-like social structure with its legal barriers to peasant mobility meant that by the end of the century over half of all workers in European Russia employed in factories and mines were to be found outside the towns, for since 'the peasant is not allowed to go to the factory, the factory goes to the peasant'.[8] These facts notwithstanding, in the fifty tumultuous years between 1863 and 1914 the nascent Russian urban proletariat was experiencing all the discomforts and degradations associated with the rapid development of capitalism; by the early twentieth century living conditions were similar to those depicted by Engels as existing in England in the 1840s. The housing conditions endured by workers in many weaving mills, the Donbas coalmines and Baku oilfields were worse than those ever experienced by workers in West European countries.[9] The burgeoning growth of Russian towns and the lack of official control over, for instance, building heights, residential densities, building materials, ventilation and so on all contributed to high death rates and eventually led in 1906 to the presentation by the Ministry of Trade and Industry of a plan to encourage the erection of cheap and hygienic dwellings. It never progressed beyond the planning stage. Six years later the government introduced a Bill prescribing sanitation standards in new building projects, requiring that in towns with over 50 000 people the housing stock should be connected to municipal water and sewerage systems. The Bill met considerable opposition from local governments and was never adopted.[10] Other attempts by government officials, voluntary organisations and capitalist employers, especially in the Ukrainian industrial regions and the Baku oilfields, to ameliorate matters were also largely unsuccessful.

Nevertheless, by 1900 the majority of large enterprises in the Donbas and Krivoi Rog mining districts had erected accommodation for their workers. Similarly, in the Baku oilfields, where labour had drifted in search of work, employers partly under pressure from the work force had provided company dwellings.[11] Here by 1913 58 per cent of workers lived in company owned accommodation, which usually meant in a factory barracks with plank beds arranged in two tiers,[12] akin to the early nineteenth century Scottish 'bothy'.[13] Analogous conditions prevailed in the traditional industrial regions: for example, in the textile centres living conditions were frequently cited as being particularly bad, with up to 40 persons of both sexes sleeping on plank beds arranged in two or three tiers occupying one room at densities of 1.5–2.5 square metres per person.[14] In St. Petersburg, Moscow, Odessa and other large cities, the 'bunk and closet' formed a common type of accommodation. It consisted of a room divided by less than ceiling height partitions into as many closets (*kamorka*) as could possibly be fitted into the space. Such flats allowed their further categorisation into: closets, corners, beds, and beds let for a set number of hours which were shared by individuals on different shifts.[15] In St. Petersburg in the early 1900s, 400 000 people (35 per cent of the population) lived in bunk and closet accommodation, basements and attics; by 1912, 155 000 people were renting just the corner of a room, and the average 'closet tenant' enjoyed just 1.8 square metres of floor space.[16]

In the absence of summary statistics giving a breakdown of the housing standards of different social groups on a nation-wide basis, it is difficult to calculate accurately the average amount of living space occupied by a working class family in the years prior to 1917. But, from figures collated for a large number of cities, it has been estimated that, in 1913, each person in a workers' district had on average 2.0–2.5 square metres of actual dwelling area, as against 4.4 square metres for the urban population as a whole.[17] Yet even in such overcrowded, insanitary conditions the rate of return from capital invested in housing for the working class was higher than that from middle class dwellings. Whereas the latter yielded about 1.90 roubles per cubic metre of space per year, the cost of renting one cubic metre in a worker's flat, which was many times smaller in area and volume and lacked services, exceeded 3.60 roubles a year.[18] Despite all this, in a list of nearly all strikes that took place in the mining and metallurgical industries during the revolutionary crisis of 1905–6, not once were demands for improved housing put forward[19] – a finding which could perhaps be contested.

Municipal facilities were also relatively primitive. In 1916, a public water-supply system existed in only 200 of the country's 1084 towns with a bare 10 per cent of the houses in these towns actually being connected up to the system. Twenty-three towns possessed a central-ised sewerage system, to which a mere 2–3 per cent of the houses were connected. 5 per cent of all urban dwellings were supplied with electricity, whilst only 134 towns had electric street lighting (with, on average, 105 street lamps per town), basically because the low generating capacity of the electricity stations meant that their output was mainly consumed by industrial users. As to gas, only 3000 flats (about 2 per cent of the total) in St. Petersburg were connected to a supply-line. And, of course, none of these facilities extended to the workers' districts.[20]

As towns were established and expanded, limited rights of self-government were slowly and grudgingly extended to them. Until the latter part of the nineteenth century the rights exercised by local governments differed scarcely at all from those laid down in Catherine the Great's 'Charter to Cities' granted in 1785. Under this Charter, by dividing the urban population into six categories, each to be represented in the city council, almost all townsmen became entitled to take an active part in the conduct of municipal affairs. However, liberal legislation of this nature was incongruent with the existing rigid, estate-like social structure which thwarted such attempts at change.[21] Furthermore, the municipal bodies created by the reform were hampered in their functioning by their 'complicated machinery, their lack of independence from the central government and, above all, the denial to them of the power to levy taxes.'[22]

However, following the emancipation of the serfs in 1861, the central authorities began directing more attention to the need for towns to assume a greater degree of responsibility for securing their own interests and needs. Local committees, specifically established to advise the Minister of the Interior, recommended that cities be given a definite degree of independence in the management of municipal affairs and that restrictions should be placed on the rights of central government to interfere. The ensuing legislation of 1870 went some way towards meeting these demands. According to the 1870 Municipal Statute, the right of municipal suffrage depended on the payment of local taxes: all citizens who paid city taxes or fees (perhaps as little as one rouble for a licence to set up a stall in a street market) were entitled to vote in municipal elections and were eligible for service on local government boards. The real merit of the Act resided in its establishing for the first time that municipal governments were allowed to function to a certain extent without central government intervention; its greatest drawback, in the view of a former mayor of Moscow, was that it entrusted the management of local affairs almost exclusively to the commercial class.[23]

During the course of the next decade the movement along the path of reform was reversed and culminated in the Municipal Act of 1892, which converted the municipalities from self-governing, relatively autonomous units of administration responsive to local needs and demands into integral parts of the central state bureaucracy. This was partly achieved by replacing the old franchise, which depended on the payment of taxes, by one based on the ownership of real estate.[24] Thus, in the capital, whereas the extended franchise of 1870 had placed 3 per cent of the city's population on the electoral roll (of which only 8 per cent bothered to vote), the 1892 statute reduced the size of the electorate by one-third so that of the more than one million inhabitants only 0.6 per cent were eligible to vote. The figure for Moscow was 0.7

and for Odessa 0.4 per cent; while the average electorate for all Russian towns was less than 1 per cent, and of those still franchised less than one half exercised their right to vote.[25]

Despite its incompatibility with the vast social changes taking place associated with the pace and direction of the country's economic development, the 1892 statute continued in force until the Decree of the Provisional Government of 9 June 1917. The long overdue reform introduced a dramatic change in the system of municipal government on the basis of universal suffrage.[26] The gross failure of the tsarist state to adopt a system of local administration more consonant with the rapidly changing circumstances remains an underexamined contributory factor to the forces which dealt the final blow to the tsarist autocracy.[27] Equally important is the fact that the absence of a political culture of local self-government imposed an additional burden on the local soviets when they came to power. Seen from another perspective, the historically established structure of local and central government relationships which existed in pre-revolutionary Russia furnished the new Soviet government with a paradigm for determining the nature of the relationship between the central state and local authorities.

Again, by contrast, not only had the British government by the end of the nineteenth century created a system of almost full male suffrage, but to cope with the manifold problems of the growing towns, local government during the course of the century had been reorganised and changed from a largely amateur to a professional basis. Although political scientists might point out that local governments in England at the end of the century were far from being models of open participatory democracy[28] and that councils were controlled by employers, 'professionals' and shopkeepers whose ethos was often paternalistic, none the less they did exercise authority independently of central government and could respond to local public needs if the electorate was willing to bear the financial cost of doing so and did thereby create a basis for local democracy. This point of comparison may serve as a foundation for future research on the relationship between local and central government in the UK and USSR.

THE WAR YEARS, 1914–17

It was not until World War I that the tsarist government intervened dramatically in the housing sector for the first time. In 1914 it issued a moratorium exempting soldiers on active service and their families from paying rent for the duration of the war. In August 1915 the Moscow prefect of police issued a decree 'prohibiting landlords and house-agents as well as hoteliers or the owners of furnished rooms and the owners or tenants of dwellings who sublet rooms, from increasing the annual, monthly or annual rent above the amount fixed by agreement'. Other towns soon followed the Moscow example. Twelve months later, on 27 August 1916, a Tenants' Protection Act applying to the whole Empire was promulgated. The Act abolished all previous regulations and authorised landlords to raise rents only in proportion to any increase in expenditure on housing maintenance.[29] The Provisional Government (March–November 1917), like the Imperial Government preceding it, made no major modification to the laws affecting the private ownership of buildings, construction law or sanitary conditions.[30] The wide ranging and lengthy decree of June 1917 on municipal administration did however charge local authorities with a number of duties including: the preparation of the town plan; the organisation of the city in accordance with the plan and the supervision of proper construction; the organisation and maintenance of municipal lighting, water supply, sewerage, transportation and communications as well as other public utilities; and the organisation and maintenance of houses with low-rent flats.[31]

FIRST STEPS OF THE SOVIET GOVERNMENT, 1917–20

The second decree issued by the new Soviet government on the day after the revolution abolished the private ownership of land.[32] In towns with over 10 000 people the government abrogated the right of private ownership of buildings whose value or income exceeded a certain limit set by the local organs of power and so before the end of 1917 large residential buildings had been nationalised.[33] But in the midst of civil war and economic dislocation the government paid little attention to housing policy and of course made no attempt to restore or construct new dwellings. Housing policy consisted of redistributing the existing stock by sequestering and requisitioning houses belonging to the nobility and bourgeoisie. According to Lenin, a rich man's flat was 'one in which the number of rooms is equal to or exceeds the number of persons permanently living there'.[34] And as early as 30 October 1917 the NKVD issued an order granting municipalities the right to sequester empty buildings suitable for habitation and to use them for people living in overcrowded or unsanitary conditions and also entitling them to set up housing inspectorates, tenants' committees and courts for settling disputes arising out of the lettings of buildings.[35] According to the Programme of the VIII Party Congress (March 1919) 'Soviet power, in order to solve the housing problem, has expropriated completely all housing belonging to capitalists and has handed these over to city soviets; it has brought about a large-scale resettlement of workers from the outskirts of cities into the houses of the bourgeoisie; it has transferred the best of these houses to workers' organisations'.[36] This policy, however, was not intended to affect smaller property owners, for the Party had explicitly stated that it had 'no intention of interfering with the interests of the non-capitalist owners'.[37] Nevertheless some local soviets and individuals, acting independently, did seize property belonging to 'small house-owners'. But such 'attempts to effect a general nationalisation of the small houses (as in the provinces) had as their only result that the nationalised houses, large and small, had no one to care for them properly'.[38] Furthermore, the nationalisation of residential property was far from being even throughout the country. While over three-quarters of all buildings in the capital cities were nationalised, this figure fell to one-quarter in towns with between 100 000 and 200 000 people and 12 per cent in Ivanovo-Voznesensk (the 'Russian Manchester'). Ironically, a significant proportion of these were not then used as domestic residences, for with an expansion in the number of administrative bodies the more solidly built structures – which generally speaking were those that had been nationalised – had to be designated for non-residential purposes. In so far as this withdrew 34 per cent of the nationalised residential space from the housing sector, it only exacerbated the critical accommodation shortage.[39]

The sharp decrease in industrial production during the revolution and civil war saw the inauguration of an economic policy referred to as 'War Communism'. Although initially the government planned to nationalise only certain sectors of the economy, the exigencies of war compelled it constantly to extend its sphere of direct control and management. Since it was geared to military and political survival, the government could not expend valuable resources on consumer goods and as a result had nothing to offer the peasantry in exchange for agricultural produce. In response to the emergence of a primitive system of barter, increased speculation and declining deliveries of grain to the market, the government introduced in May 1918 an order compelling the peasants to supply their products to the state without compensation, which often meant armed detachments from the towns and army forcibly requisitioning foodstuffs. It was during this period that housing policy was transformed and the steps taken then have never been reversed. Land was nationalised. Housing space was redistributed according to need and to a definition of a minimum requirement[40] and a maximum entitlement of space per person. Two new sectors of housing tenure were created – the municipalised and nationalised sectors (see below). Immediately after the revolution rent and service payments for specific categories of tenants and accommodation were suspended;[41] in July 1919 rents in Moscow and Petrograd were frozen at the 1 July level[42] and then on 27 January 1921 rents were abolished altogether.[43]

THE NEW ECONOMIC POLICY (NEP), 1921–28

After its victory in the civil war, the Bolshevik government was still faced with outbreaks of rebellion including that of the Kronstadt sailors in March 1921 and the uprisings which spread from the Tambov province. In order to save the new system, consolidate political power and have its authority recognised and legitimised both at home and in the world at large, Lenin proclaimed the introduction of the New Economic Policy which he defended against opposition within the Party in terms of 'one step backward, two steps forward'. The essence of NEP – a form of mixed economy tolerating a certain amount of private trading and small-scale private manufacture – was the coexistence of a state sector in industry and a private sector in agriculture. Its main political objective was to restore the alliance between the peasantry and the urban working class and this could only be achieved by abolishing the system of requisitioning agricultural produce and by reviving the market exchange of products between town and country. Concessions to private enterprise were also made in the housing sector.

The introduction of NEP led to three main changes in housing policy. Firstly, the state divested itself of the function of administering small houses which were either being used by individual families or which, because of their small overall living area, were of little interest to the local soviets. Secondly, an administrative system was set up whereby the tenants bore responsibility for the upkeep of their dwellings. Thirdly, rent and payment for communal services were reintroduced with the charges being directly related to the worker's income. The experiment in, or flirtation with, providing rent-free accommodation was short-lived for on 20 April 1922 the payment of rent was restored.[44] However, rents remained low and the notion of low-rent accommodation has never been publicly challenged (see p. 28). The government regarded its policy in this respect to be correct in principle and one moreover which had enormous propaganda value, both internally and externally.

But it was evident that funds had to be found from alternative sources to prevent further deterioration of the existing stock and to finance new construction. The first step was a decree issued on 23 May 1921, one of whose main objectives was to raise the level of tenants' responsibility for the maintenance of dwellings.[45] Shortly afterwards a more precise decree of 18 July 1921 made it compulsory for residents to maintain their accommodation, providing their own resources – in money, labour or materials – in proportion to the amount of space they were occupying.[46] In enforcing these obligations on tenants, the government relied on a combination of moral imperative and a rather rudimentary system of administration, involving housing committees or tenants' associations set up by the local soviets. Yet no amount of moral appeal or the application of legal sanctions could overcome the customs and traditions which the mass of the population brought with them across the great divide marked by the October revolution. The former tsarist regime had known only one form of public property – state or 'Treasury' (*kazennoe*) property, to which the population had long ago adopted a carefree, negligent and even hostile attitude. This attitude did not change when property was nationalised after the revolution.[47] This partly explains why, in addition to the nationalised and municipalised tenures – forms established under War Communism – NEP witnessed the creation of a new tenure type, the co-operative, and resuscitated the pre-revolutionary individual builder/owner-occupier. But of greater importance than cultural factors as impediments to the maintenance and restoration of accommodation was the sheer difficulty of procuring the necessary materials.

The inadequate housing stock and underdeveloped city infrastructure which existed in 1913 were made much worse by events during the period 1914–21, when the number of urban dwellings either destroyed or rendered completely unfit for habitation amounted to almost one-fifth of the total with living space in Moscow declining by 29 per cent between 1915 and 1924.[48] The urban population which had stood at 28.5 million in 1914 fell to 20.9 million in 1920. But after 1922, with the revival of industrial activity, people began to return to the towns from the countryside so that by 1923 the urban population had recovered to 21.6 million and in 1926 it reached 26.3 million. The house-building industry was unable to keep pace with this growth and as a result the average per capita urban living space[49] fell from 6.4 square metres in 1923 to 5.8 in 1926 as compared with 6.3 square metres in 1913.[50]

The redistribution and equalisation of housing space which had taken place, although important in many respects, did not affect the average level of living space provision which in 1926 remained extremely low, as Table 1.2 shows.

TABLE 1.2   *Actual dwelling area of workers in 1926*

Dwelling area per person (m²)	Proportion of the working population and their families in each group (%)
less than 3	29.4
3–4	18.7
4.1–6	27.0
6.1–8	12.7
8.1–10	6.1
more than 10	6.1
	100.00

SOURCE   The Housing Census for 1926, cited by D. L. Broner, *Zhilishchnoe stroitel'stvo i demograficheskie protsessy*, Moscow, 1980, p. 15.

The figure of 5.8 square metres for 1926 conceals social class variations. Manual workers on average occupied 4.8 square metres and white collar employees 7.0 square metres.[51] These figures remained stable for the economic year 1927–28.[52] The 1926 housing census also revealed variations in per capita urban living space between republics,[53] between towns within republics[54] and within towns depending on the type of industry (metallurgy, mining, transport) providing accommodation for its workers. As in pre-revolutionary Russia, textile workers occupying enterprise-controlled accommodation fared particularly badly. Surveys of factory housing in Ivanovo-Voznesensk revealed that the buildings were so dilapidated as to be unfit for human habitation – whole families were living in corridors, storerooms, bathrooms and sheds.[55] In one spinning mill in Moscow, workers had a meagre 1.1 square metres per person, while a report on the chemical industry in 1924 found that 80 per cent of workers in the industry lived in unhygienic conditions and commented: '60 per cent do not live but drag out a miserable existence'.[56] Living conditions were graphically portrayed in the press during the 1920s. A correspondent on one newspaper described the housing of bricklayers employed at an electricity generating station:

> Most of the workers live in unsatisfactory huts, each occupying from 2.6 to 5.2 square metres. The atmosphere is made even more unhealthy by the fumes and smoke from the stoves which heat the buildings. Ventilation is considered a luxury and does not exist. The huts are very dirty, the floors are scarcely ever washed. They are infested with vermin. Two or three people sleep on the same wooden bench, which also serves as a table and a seat. The lighting is very inadequate and a man with normal sight can barely see to read. The sanitary inspectors have frequently demanded that steps be taken to improve matters, but the authorities have always turned a deaf ear.[57]

Although new building had a mitigating effect on the severity of these living conditions, the structures being erected were to prove only a short-term solution. In the period 1923–26, in the private sector, the proportion of all newly erected housing space with wooden walls ranged from 61.7 per cent in the Ukraine and 76.2 per cent in the RSFSR to 99.3 per cent in Belorussia. The corresponding percentage figures for the state and co-operative sectors combined in these three republics were 18.4, 51.0, and 68.1. In the RSFSR, just under 40 per cent of the new housing in the state sector had stone walls compared with 2 per cent in the private sector. As a proportion of *all* new housing erected during these three years in the RSFSR, those with stone walls amounted to just 14.1 per cent.[58] The heavy reliance placed on the individual builder throughout the twenties (see pp. 42–4) changed with the beginning of the five year planning period in 1929.

BRIEF SURVEY OF HOUSING DEVELOPMENT SINCE 1929

After 1928 the contribution of the private sector declined both absolutely and relatively, with the state assuming responsibility for the erection of most new accommodation. This shift to concentrating resources in the hands of the state was probably motivated as much by economic, organisational and technological factors as by ideological and political considerations. The decision to industrialise rapidly in accordance with a centrally co-ordinated investment plan made it logical to transfer resources directly to the state agencies responsible for implementing the plan, so as to enable enterprises and institutions to provide accommodation for their new workforce. Resources for house building were also channelled through local urban soviets, themselves large employers of labour, whose constituencies were rapidly expanding as the society urbanised at a tempo unprecedented in world history (see pp. 119–20). The concentration of house-building resources in this way was considered to be not only economically and administratively more efficient but also a technological necessity, since a central objective of the government's housing strategy was to industrialise the construction industry and to make widespread use of standardised, prefabricated components in house building (see Chapter 7).

During the war (1941–45) 1710 towns and settlements were destroyed, amounting to a loss of 70 million square metres of living space equivalent to one-sixth of the country's urban housing stock and at least another one-sixth damaged. In the RSFSR, for instance, Voronezh lost 96 per cent of its housing, and in Leningrad, three million square metres of living space were destroyed (about 17 per cent of all housing in the city). The Ukraine suffered especially severely: in Sevastopol' only 3 per cent of the pre-war housing stock remained standing; in Kremenchug and Kramatorsk 80 per cent of the socialised (and hence more solid) housing was destroyed; between 40 and 60 per cent of the housing stock in Donetsk, Zaporozh'e and Poltava was in ruins, and 25–40 per cent of the housing in Kiev, Khar'kov and Odessa.[59]

The destruction caused by the war only served to compound the drastic shortage of accommodation which urbanisation and investment priorities in the 1930s had created. The government responded by substantially increasing state investment in housing; by strengthening its resolve to industrialise construction, thereby accelerating house building (at reduced unit cost) and rationalising the construction industry as a whole; and by granting greater scope, at least until 1960, to the private sector to meet the demand for accommodation.

Investment in housing during the fifth five-year plan (1951–55) was, in ruble terms, almost double that in the preceding planning period, and it more than doubled in the next period (1956–60), when it reached 23.5 per cent of total capital investment (see Table 1.3).

TABLE 1.3   *Capital investment in housing in the USSR, 1918–80 (in comparable prices)*

Year	Capital investment in housing	
	Actual investment (million roubles)	As a percentage of total capital investment
1918–28	2835	64.3
1st FYP (1929–32)	1346	15.4
2nd FYP (1933–37)	2516	12.8
3rd FYP (1938–June 1941)	3470	17.0
1 July 1941–1 Jan 1946	3073	15.0
4th FYP (1946–50)	9206	19.4
5th FYP (1951–55)	17794	19.8
6th FYP (1956–60)	39454	23.5
7th FYP (1961–65)	45218	18.6
8th FYP (1966–70)	59696	17.2
9th FYP (1971–75)	75354	15.3
10th FYP (1976–80)	86305	13.6
1976	16504	14.0
1977	17013	13.9
1978	17522	13.5
1979	17332	13.3
1980	17934	13.4

SOURCES
Narodnoe khozyaistvo SSSR v 1978g., pp. 342–3.
N. kh. SSSR v 1979g., pp. 366–7.
N. kh. SSSR v 1980g., pp. 336–7.

Since 1960 the absolute sums directed towards the housing sector have continued to increase but the proportion of all capital flowing into house building has steadily declined, falling to an average of 13.6 per cent during 1976–80. As a result of this investment programme the amount of living space per person has risen from 8.8 square metres per person in 1960 to 13.2 square metres in 1981, which means that the 'sanitary norm' of nine square metres of 'actual dwelling area' set in 1926 has now on average been achieved (see note 40).

The private sector received an initial (and understandable) stimulus in the aftermath of the war. But especially since 1960, as tables 1.4 and 1.5 clearly show, there has been a general decline in its contribution to the house building programme,[60] although the amount of floor space erected by owner-occupiers remains proportionately higher in some republics, reflecting different cultural traditions[61] (see Tables 4 and 5

TABLE 1.4 *Construction of urban housing by sector, 1960–81 (end of year)*

Year	Overall total (million m² overall living space)	local Soviets, state enterprises, etc. mln. m²	%	house-building co-operatives mln. m²	%	private individuals mln. m²	%
1950	20.7	14.3	69.1	—	—	6.4	30.9
1951–55	129.8	91.0	70.1	—	—	38.8	29.9
1956–60	241.7	181.0	74.9	—	—	60.7	25.1
1960	59.0	44.6	75.6	—	—	14.4	24.4
1961	56.1	43.7	77.9	—	—	12.4	22.1
1962	58.9	47.5	80.6	—	—	11.4	19.4
1963	58.4	46.8	80.1	1.8	3.1	9.8	16.8
1964	57.5	43.5	75.7	4.8	8.3	9.2	16.0
1965	60.7	46.2	76.1	6.5	10.7	8.0	13.2
1966	63.4	49.0	77.3	6.7	10.6	7.7	12.1
1967	66.1	51.8	78.4	6.5	9.8	7.8	11.8
1968	66.1	52.5	79.4	6.4	9.7	7.2	10.0
1969	68.6	55.3	80.6	6.2	9.0	7.1	10.4
1970	71.3	57.0	79.9	7.7	10.8	6.6	9.3
1971	72.9	60.1	82.5	6.8	9.3	6.0	8.2
1972	73.5	61.0	83.0	6.5	8.8	6.0	8.2
1973	77.6	63.6	82.0	7.1	9.1	6.9	8.9
1974	77.1	64.0	83.0	6.3	8.2	6.8	8.8
1975*	76.3	63.8	83.6	5.8	7.6	6.7	8.8
1976	75.9	69.5**	91.6	N.A.	N.A.	6.4	8.4
1977	77.2	70.9**	91.8	N.A.	N.A.	6.3	8.2
1978	76.6	70.4**	91.9	N.A.	N.A.	6.2	8.1
1979	72.7***	65.8**	90.5	N.A.	N.A.	6.3	8.7
1980	76.3***	69.3**	90.8	N.A.	N.A.	6.0	7.9
1981	76.1***	69.0**	90.7	N.A.	N.A.	6.1	8.0

SOURCES

1950, 1951–55, 1956–60: *Narodnoe khozyaistvo SSSR v 1980g.* p. 387.

1960–67: *N. kh. SSSR v 1967g.* pp. 675, 681.

1968–69: *N. kh. SSSR v 1969g.* pp. 562, 565.

1970–75: *N. kh. SSSR v 1975g.* pp. 570, 575.

1976–81: *N. kh. SSSR 1922–1982, Yubileinyi statisticheskii yezhegodnik,* 1982, p. 426.

Notes:

 * Statistical handbooks since 1975 have not cited figures for co-operative housing construction.

 ** These figures include building by housing co-operatives.

 *** The totals for 1979, 1980 and 1981 include 0.6 million, 1.0 and 1.0 million square metres of overall (useful) living space erected in these respective years by 'collective farms, collective farmers and the rural intelligentsia' in urban settlements.

TABLE 1.5 *Ownership of urban housing stock by sector and per capita living space, 1913–81 (end of year)*

Sector/ Indicator	1913	1926	1940	1950	1955	1960	1961	1962	1963	1964	1965	1966	1967	1968
Total urban housing: million m² overall living space	180	216	421	513	640	958	1017	1074	1130	1182	1238	1290	1350	1410
of which:														
Socialised (million m²)	—	103	267	340	432	583	626	670	716	759	806	854	906	959
(%)	—	47.7	63.4	66.3	67.5	60.9	61.6	62.4	63.4	64.2	65.1	66.2	67.1	68.0
Private (million m²)	180	113	154	173	208	375	391	404	414	423	432	436	444	451
(%)	100	52.3	36.6	33.7	32.5	39.1	38.4	37.6	36.6	35.8	34.9	33.8	32.9	32.0
Urban Population (million)	28.5	26.3	64.9	73.0	88.2	108.3	111.8	115.1	118.5	121.7	123.8	126.9	130.9	134.2
Per Capita overall living space (m²)	6.3	8.2	6.5	7.0	7.3	8.8	9.1	9.3	9.5	9.7	10.0	10.2	10.3	10.5

Sector/Indicator	1969	1970	1971	1972	1973	1974	1975	1976	1977	1978	1979	1980	1981
Total urban housing: million m² overall living space	1469	1529 (1542)	1594	1661	1730	1800	1867 (1875)	1932	2001	2070	2134	2200 (2202)	2270
of which:													
Socialised (million m²)	1014	1072 (1046)	1132	1193	1257	1322	1385 (1352)	1446	1510	1574	1634	1696 (1655)	1715
(%)	69.0	70.1 (67.8)	71.0	71.8	72.7	73.4	74.2 (72.1)	74.3	75.5	76.0	76.6	77.1 (75.2)	75.5
Private (million m²)	455	457 (496)	462	468	473	478	482 (523)	486	491	496	500	504 (547)	555
(%)	31.0	29.9 (32.2)	29.0	28.2	27.3	26.6	25.8 (27.9)	25.2	24.5	24.0	23.4	22.9 (24.8)	24.4
Urban Population (million)	136.0	138.8	142.0	145.4	148.6	151.9	155.1	157.9	160.6	163.6	166.2	168.9	171.7
Per Capita overall living space (m²)	10.8	11.1	11.2	11.4	11.6	11.8	12.0	12.2	12.5	12.7	12.8	13.0	13.2

SOURCES

Narodnoe khozyaistvo SSSR v 1958g, p. 641; *Narodnoe khozyaistvo SSSR v 1962g*, p. 499
Narodnoe khozyaistvo SSSR v 1963g, p. 515; *Narodnoe khozyaistvo SSSR v 1964g*, p. 610
Narodnoe khozyaistvo SSSR v 1967g, p. 7; *Narodnoe khozyaistvo SSSR v 1968g*, p. 580
Narodnoe khozyaistvo SSSR v 1969g, p. 569; *Narodnoe khozyaistvo SSSR v 1975g*, p. 577
Narodnoe khozyaistvo SSSR v 1978g, pp. 7, 399
Narodnoe khozyaistvo SSSR v 1979g, pp. 7, 418–19
Narodnoe khozyaistvo SSSR v 1980g, pp. 7, 392
Narodnoe khozyaistvo SSSR 1922–1982, p. 431

Note: The statistical handbook for 1982 revised the figures for 1970, 1975 and 1980 cited in the 1980 Handbook. The revised figures are given in parentheses. The numerically larger 1982 figures, especially the higher proportion classified as 'private', may be due to the incorporation of rural settlements within revised urban boundaries.

in Appendix A, and also Chapter 5). The diminution in the proportion of urban dwellings that are privately owned from 39.1 per cent in 1960 to 24.4 per cent in 1981 and the absolute and relative decline in new private house building (from 14.4 million square metres in 1960 – 24.4 per cent of all new accommodation in towns) to 6.1 million square metres in 1981 (8.0 per cent) has not been compensated by a commensurate increase in co-operative house building.

Despite frequent reiterations by government officials on the importance they attach to co-operatives since 1962, when the co-operative tenure-form was resuscitated after its demise in 1937, its annual contribution to the housing stock has fallen below expectations (see Table 1.4). Moreover, in 1976 the main statistical handbook ceased publishing figures on co-operative house construction. The decline in the private sector and modest size of the co-operative sector means that the state is responsible for over four-fifths of all new house building in towns. The first section of the book examines in detail the pre-war development of the main tenure types and their subsequent histories.

By the beginning of 1982, the vast majority of the country's 172 million city dwellers (comprising 64 per cent of the total population) lived in state accommodation. Housing standards, measured in terms of per capita living space and level of amenity provision, are improving steadily. And now the average urban Soviet family, consisting of 3.3 persons,[62] lives in a self-contained unit in a high-rise, prefabricated block of flats. The second section of the book explores the historical and contemporary debates on the type of accommodation appropriate for the 'new Soviet man' and on how to provide housing in the most economical and efficient manner.

Part I
Forms of Housing Tenure

Introduction

The study of housing tenure (that is, of the individuals and agencies who own and have responsibility for financing and managing accommodation), taken in conjunction with an examination of the changing roles and importance of each type of tenure, sheds light on a number of social, political and institutional trends in a society. In the USA, only 3 per cent of the housing stock is publicly owned. In the USSR, on the other hand, in 1980 the public sector accounted for 77 per cent of all urban accommodation. Historical factors, customs and political ideologies help to explain this difference between the USA and USSR and the greater balance which exists between the public, quasi-public and private sectors in other societies. In the UK for instance, in 1979, 32 per cent of the total housing stock belonged to, and (coincidentally) 32 per cent of all new construction was undertaken by, local authorities (although this sector has been in decline over the past two decades). At the same time, in Poland and Czechoslovakia house building by co-operatives has in recent years accounted for between 35 and 50 per cent of all new construction.

The ownership of housing in the Soviet Union falls into two broad categories: socialised and private. The former is divided among the local soviets, state enterprises, institutions, central agencies and local organisations. It is also regarded as including houses belonging to house building co-operatives, other co-operative organisations and trade unions. The private sector has had a very chequered history, although, except for an interlude in the 1930s, it has made a valuable contribution to increasing the housing stock. In Soviet terminology, housing in this last category belongs to individuals on the basis of their right to 'personal' property, and is never referred to as 'private' property. (Only sources of unearned income, which are inconsistent with a socialist society, are placed in the 'private' category.)

While most statistical handbooks employ this basic division of the housing stock, administrators operate with four categories of ownership: (1) local soviets; (2) state institutions, enterprises, organisations,

26

trade unions and other co-operative bodies (the so-called 'departmental fund'); (3) house-building (and dacha building) co-operatives; and (4) individuals (as personal property). Unfortunately, statistical data on these categories are not published systematically.

The differences between accommodation belonging to trade unions and other co-operative organisations (in category 2) and that belonging to house-building co-operatives (in category 3) is a legal one. In the case of the former, housing is set aside for members of these particular organisations (for instance, Unions of composers, writers, consumer co-operatives etc.). A house building co-operative, on the other hand, is set up by a number of individuals who may work in different occupations and in different plants or organisations, for the specific purpose of providing themselves with accommodation. The principal reason for bracketting various sorts of house-owners (tenure types) together in category 2 as parts of the 'departmental fund' is that housing in all these cases is provided by the owners for those with whom the 'owners have productive relationships'. Functionally, the departmental housing tenure-type is clearly distinguished from housing belonging to local soviets, whose task it is to allocate housing to individuals living within their administrative jurisdiction, irrespective of where they work.

The historical factors which gave rise to the distinction between the local soviet and departmental housing stocks are regarded as no longer operative by many Soviet authors who therefore argue that all state housing should be transferred into the hands of local soviets. This demand, emanating from the soviets themselves, continues to face resistance from the 'departmental' owners. The tug-of-war taking place between these institutional bodies for possession of a set of property rights constitutes one of the central issues of present day Soviet housing policy and reflects a much broader debate in Soviet politics. Although at the end of 1980 the state sector as a whole controlled 77 per cent of the total urban housing stock and is responsible for 91 per cent of all new building, the private and co-operative sectors continue to fulfil important functions in meeting the demand for accommodation and in determining the spatial distribution of social groups.

As a general proposition, housing differs from other consumer goods and services in several ways. In particular, because its capital cost is high relative to family income, it can rarely be purchased directly out of income nor, in most cases, can it be wholly financed from an individual's savings. Thus, housing falls into two main categories: (1) housing which individuals wish to purchase and own, and therefore borrow money in order to do so; or, (2) housing in which public or private agents (landlords) invest capital, with the intention of renting to others. Co-operative and private tenures obviously fall into category (1) above. In the state (local soviet and departmental) sector, the amount of rent to be paid was laid down as long ago as 1926 in a decree 'On rent and measures to regulate use of housing in urban settlements'[1] which was later supplemented by decrees of 4 January 1928, 'On housing policy',[2] and 14 May 1928, 'On payment for residential premises in cities and workers' settlements'.[3] These long-established rental rates are based on a fixed tariff which varies from 3 to 4.4 kopeks for each square metre of actual dwelling space, with the highest charge occurring in cities with over 40 000 people. Small adjustments are made to the charge depending on the distance from the centre of the town and whether or not the accommodation is supplied with a full range of amenities, is damp, below pavement level and so on. There is then a further small addition which rises with the wage of the highest paid member of the family – but this is quite insignificant for the scale of charges is related to 1926–29 wage levels. In any case, the total rental charge cannot by law exceed 13.2 kopeks per square metre of dwelling space a month.[4] As a result of this policy, the Soviet Union claims to have the lowest rents in the world. Even when the costs of gas, electricity, hot water and heating are included, the total rent in 1979 amounted on average to no more than 4–5 per cent of a family's budget[5] and by 1981 to just 3 per cent.[6]

The fact that the method of rent assessment has not changed since the 1920s, despite a continuous building programme, means that rent and service charges paid by tenants cover only one-third of the overall running and maintenance costs of state housing, which requires an annual subsidy of five milliard roubles – a figure that does not include state expenditure on capital investment in new housing projects.[7] If rents are not to rise (for ideological and political reasons)[8] and yet construction, maintenance and running costs continue to increase, then deficits in the state sector will be reduced mainly by improving housing management and by cutting unit costs of construction by encouraging further standardisation of components and techniques. The first method is discussed in Chapter 3 and the second is the subject of Chapter 7. A third way of reducing the subsidy to housing is to encourage the growth of the self-financing co-operative and private sectors, which are examined in Chapters 4 and 5.

2 The Development of the Four Housing Tenures, 1917–41

THE STATE SECTOR

Municipalised (local soviet) housing

On 28 December 1917 a decree banned any transactions harmful to the proletariat by owners of houses and land. No reference was made in the decree to either municipalisation or nationalisation of housing which remained the property of landlords.[1] However, some local soviets, acting on their own initiative, had already taken over the larger houses.[2] And so just eight months later, on 20 August 1918, these actions were sanctioned by a law which, while abolishing all private ownership of land in urban communities, largely left the municipalisation of buildings to the discretion of local soviets.[3] Since the government lacked the power to stipulate which houses should or should not be taken over by the local soviets, a confused situation developed as regards smaller houses. A combination of pressure from the masses and an absence of clearly defined criteria often resulted in extensive municipalisation by the local soviets, including even small wooden houses. Little was done to change this situation until a decree of 8 August 1921, which attempted to rationalise the municipalised sector by requiring local soviet departments to revise their lists of municipalised housing so as to transfer to individuals or groups (including the former owners of the property) those houses too small or unsuitable for use by local soviet departments.[4]

The legal enactments on housing passed during 1921 and 1922 were directly associated with the introduction of the New Economic Policy and reflected an attempt to systematise, encodify and, in some cases, reverse the actions taken by individuals, *ad hoc* groups and organised

29

bodies in sequestering accommodation during the period of War Communism. Many buildings had fallen into disrepair during the previous tumultuous years and it was now imperative to formalise their management in order to ensure their adequate maintenance and repair. The legislation had an aura of 'back to normalcy' about it: the revolution was over, the expropriators had been expropriated and now evictions should cease, or at least be carried out properly. So, for instance, in April 1922 a decree forbade the eviction of tenants from residential premises without following the due process of law, when it had to be proven that the tenant had a 'predatory relationship to the accommodation' manifested in his wrecking it or failing to pay rent.[5] And a month later, on 22 May, the law consolidated the rights of the individual to own and dispose of property that had not been municipalised.[6] The next logical step taken by the government was to stipulate what in fact constituted 'municipalised property'. This it did in a decree of 14 May 1923 'On municipalised buildings',[7] which defined as 'municipalised': buildings taken over by local soviets before 22 May 1922; buildings which were, wholly or in part, leased from their former owners for use by central government and local soviet enterprises and institutions; buildings confiscated from their owners before 22 May 1922; and buildings whose maintenance was neglected and which were not being used economically.

However, in the following year, on 12 January 1924, the government decreed the cessation of further municipalisation and required the local soviets to compile lists of municipalised buildings within their administrative jurisdiction. Henceforth, this sector could only expand in specific cases laid down in the 1922 Civil Code of the RSFSR.[8] These included: new building specifically carried out by local soviets, accommodation inherited or confiscated by the state where no landlord existed or was known, or where one of the parties to a housing transaction was seeking to make an unjustified gain. The actual compilation of these lists by the local authorities evidently did not proceed very quickly, as a series of rulings subsequently called for their completion by a definite date.[9]

The preceding catalogue of legislation might give an impression of widespread if not total socialisation of residential properties. In fact, this was not the case. Only 17 per cent of residential buildings listed in the 1923 Housing Census were classified as state property, a figure which rose to just 18 per cent in 1926.[10] On the other hand, because the state had socialised the largest and most valuable buildings, in 1923 it housed 38 per cent of the urban population and accounted for 60 per cent of the value of the total urban housing stock.[11] As table 2.1 shows,

TABLE 2.1 *Structure of the urban housing stock in 1926*

Tenure	Number of houses ('000)	(%)	Dwelling area ('000m²)	(% of Total)	Residents ('000)	(% of Total)	Dwelling area per person (m²)	Value of 1m² of dwelling area (in roubles)	Average size of building (m² of overall living space)
Socialised	523.5	18.12	72,300	47.0	11,309	43.4	6.4	340	230
Individual Ownership	2358.6	81.88	81,700	53.0	14,882	56.6	5.4	102,8	42
Total	2882.1	100.0	154,000	100.0	26,191	100.0	5.8	—	—

SOURCE 1926 Census, cited by D. L. Broner, *Zhilishchnoe stroitel'stvo i demograficheskie protsessy*, Moscow, 1980, p. 16.

although only 18 per cent of all residential buildings were classified as part of the public domain, they were much larger in size (230 square metres compared with an average sized dwelling of 42 square metres in the private sector) and contained 47 per cent of the living space.

The fact that local soviets had gained control over a high proportion of the structurally more sound housing placed them in a strategically important position in the housing sector; whether or not they would be able in future years to extend their activities in this sphere would depend on the state's changing ideological attitude to the private and co-operative sectors and on the strength of the bargaining power of the local soviets compared with that of industry and transport, the other main providers of state accommodation. Their position was consolidated in a decree of October 1925 when they were formally declared to be the 'highest organs of state power in the territory of a given city or settlement'.[12] The decree specified the wide range of activities for which the local soviet bore responsibility, including the 'construction of housing and managing housing affairs'. A month later the government made a clear distinction between the nationalised and municipalised sectors.[13] All buildings forming part of the socialised sector but not part of the 'departmental stock' (industry, transport, ministries etc.) were now regarded as municipalised. Henceforth, any transfer of buildings from the municipal to departmental sector (or the reverse) had to be sanctioned by the Council of People's Commissars (*Sovnarkom*).

Legislation passed in the 1920s did little to expand the role which the local soviets were expected to play in the upsurge in house construction; in fact, they tended to shed responsibility both for the creation of new housing and its maintenance. The 1926 census revealed that the local soviets controlled 42.9 million square metres of dwelling area representing 59.4 per cent of the overall state sector.[14] Then an enactment of July 1927 allowed urban soviets to sell off certain properties (essentially smaller buildings) at public auction.[15] Despite the apparent undermining of the theoretical primacy of local soviets in housing affairs consequent upon this legislation, the government continued to reaffirm their importance as providers of accommodation. A decree of 4 January 1928, 'On housing policy', stipulated a role for both departmental and local soviet housing construction, declaring that 'industrial enterprises, transport organisations and local soviets should be the main builders of workers' dwellings'. It added that in large cities, house construction should be predominantly by local soviets.[16] But lacking finance and manpower to fulfill the demands placed upon them, the cajolery and exhortations to build more, to which the local soviets were subjected, can be seen to have been misdirected. Moreover, local soviets relinquished control of a substantial proportion of the housing for which they were formally responsible. Following a decree of 19 August 1924, which permitted the transfer of municipalised housing stock to house-leasing co-operatives (*ZhAKTy*), local soviets had by 1937 lost control of over 84 per cent of their housing (see pp. 39–40).

Nevertheless, as the volume of house building carried out by industry increased (see table 2.2) – and this was given a fillip by a decree on the 'director's fund' which specified that no less than fifty per cent of the total fund was to be spent on housing[17] – the role of the local soviet as provider of housing became more closely circumscribed. It came to occupy a place somewhat similar to the role envisaged by some politicians for local authorities in the UK, namely, as the supplier of accommodation for the poor, the weak and the invalid. By 1937, the local soviets controlled just under half of the state-owned dwelling space. Even the decree of October 1937 which reformed the whole system of house ownership and management and charged the soviets with the task of supervising the physical state of the whole housing stock, ensuring it was kept in good repair and complied with sanitary standards – irrespective of to whom it belonged – had a limited impact in practice.[18]

The impending war, increased pressures on industry to expand as rapidly as possible, continued migration into the towns on a large scale and shortage of resources for housing militated against the performance of these functions. Furthermore, although it is difficult to assign any weight to this argument, the fact that no historical precedent existed in pre-revolutionary Russia for local government to act as a supplier of accommodation must partly explain why the local soviets' role in this sphere remained so modest.

Nationalised ('departmental') housing

The close relationship that existed before 1917 between manufacturing industry and the ownership of dwellings continued after the October revolution when housing belonging to factory owners was nationalised at the same time as the manufacturing plant. Thus, after the revolution, one set of reciprocal relationships within a fairly closely defined social system was replaced by another. Enactments affecting tenants in housing belonging to employers in the post-revolutionary

TABLE 2.2 *Capital investment of public sector agencies in housing, 1924–37 (percentage of total)*

Agency	Date		
	1924/25–1927/28	*1928–32*	*1933–37*
Industry	42.6	63.0	59.0
Transport	9.7	7.9	17.2
Local soviets	26.7	14.8	11.3
House-building co-operatives	13.7	6.3	4.0
Government departments	7.3	8.0	8.5
Total	100.0	100.0	100.0

SOURCE N. N. Belkovich, V. A. Shavrin, *Mestnoe khozyaistvo i mestnye byudzhety SSSR*, Moscow, 1938, p. 144.

years, while radically transforming property relations and thereby abolishing the exploitative nature of the landlord and tenant nexus, none the less preserved the association which linked (and later bonded) the tenant to the employer through the workplace.

The composition of the departmental housing stock, initially formed when industry was nationalised after the revolution, was specified in a circular issued by the NKVD in July 1922.[19] It included houses belonging to transport organisations and to enterprises under the control of the commissariat responsible for state industry, the so-called Supreme Council of the National Economy (*VSNKh*), and its subordinate organs, as well as accommodation regarded as being of a more national than local character such as army barracks, and accommodation belonging to state museums, art galleries and theatres. The publication of the circular did not, of course, bring to an end the dispute as to whether certain buildings belonged to the nationalised or municipalised sector and subsequently the government found it necessary to define what constituted 'nationalised housing' in a decree of 30 November 1925. According to the new legislation, it included buildings belonging to the state prior to 7 November 1917 and used by the 'Soviet state and its constituent bodies' after the revolution. It also embraced: buildings nationalised for the use of central departments and those institutions and enterprises of national importance, so long as they continued wholly or in part to use these premises for residential purposes; property that was regarded as a necessary appurtenance of nationalised enterprises; and property specially constructed to meet the needs of departments of war. All other buildings belonging to the state, the decree assigned to the municipal fund.[20]

While in the 1920s, industrial and other economic organisations were, in the main, reluctant to construct housing,[21] matters changed with the introduction of the five-year plans. House building by industrial enterprises accelerated rapidly, especially in the most heavily industrialised regions, including the Donbas, the Urals and the Baku district,[22] with the result that industry and transport increased their share of public housing investment from about 52 per cent during the period 1924–28 to 76 per cent during 1933–37. Some housing earlier transferred to local soviets was now handed back to manufacturing and mining organisations.[23] By the end of 1937, the nationalised sector had risen to account for over half the total socialised housing stock, compared with 24.2 per cent in 1926.[24]

The 'tied-cottage' element associated with the departmental sector was not strictly observed during the 1920s, although powers of eviction were clearly embodied in existing legislation.[25] With the introduction of the five-year plans, evictions became more commonplace. A characteristic decree of February 1931 granted the Commissariats of Communications and Water Transport the right to evict from their premises 'at any time of the year' anybody no longer connected with them. This decree not only freed these organisations of any responsibility for providing alternative accommodation for the evicted persons, but imposed a new function on local soviets by making it incumbent on them to offer accommodation. Housing had been converted into a direct reward for services rendered to a specific employer.

On the other hand, an individual had the right to be provided with living space by the local soviet. However, such a 'harmonious' solution would have defeated another purpose of the government, which was to tie workers to their work-place and to 'raise labour discipline'. In order to achieve these aims, a further clause was added to the effect that local soviets were not obliged to offer accommodation to those who were evicted either because they had terminated their employment without the consent of the management or because they had been dismissed for 'violating labour discipline' or committing a crime.[26] The policy of evicting people from housing reached its apogee with a decree of August 1943 which stipulated that individuals occupying living space without authorisation were subject to eviction by the militia and did not have to be offered alternative accommodation.[27]

The departmental stock also included housing built for 'creative unions' such as the Union of Artists, Union of Writers etc., so catering for some of the most privileged groups in Soviet society. Decrees issued during the 1930s increased the housing norm to which certain categories of workers and functionaries were entitled.[28] Thus a decree of 5 April 1933 granted scientific workers (*nauchnye rabotniki*) the right to an additional separate room for working in or, in the absence of a separate room, additional floor-space of not less than twenty square metres – the total living area to be paid for at the 'normal rate'.[29] Moreover, the Central Housing and Municipal Bank (*Tsekombank*) was required to set aside special credit funds for scientific workers to erect co-operative dwellings.[30]

The decree of October 1937 which virtually abolished the co-operative sector (see p. 40) led to an increase in the size of the departmental housing stock. Houses, cottages and other property belonging to dissolved co-operatives had to be transferred by 15 December 1937 into the hands of housing managers appointed by a housing administration under the control of the local soviet or enterprise (institution or other organisation) which had supplied the necessary finance in the first place.[31] In keeping with their enlarged role as providers of housing, commissariats and departments financed through the Industry Bank (*Prombank*) were to receive extra funds through this channel to finance the construction of housing and public utilities.[32] Even the rise in individual house building (from 9.1 per cent of all house construction in 1933–37 to 16.5 per cent during the third five-year plan) was also largely administered through the departmental sector.[33] Thus by the end of the 1930s most of the funds for capital investment in housing were being chanelled through the departmental sector. In fact it was logical, given the set of choices it had made, for the government to choose to direct resources allocated for housing through ministries and central departments. For if an economic planning organisation determined a new factory's requirements in terms of workshops, equipment and manpower, then it could simultaneously calculate the sum of money and materials necessary to accommodate the workforce. In this fashion the autarchy that was a feature of the manufacturing sector became extended to the field of housing and amenity provision: not only did enterprises provide accommodation, but also public utilities and social amenities such as shops, public baths and cinemas. The lack of uniformity of standards – in terms of the quality of accommodation and the range of social facilities – is to a large extent explained by the fact that many enterprises diverted resources assigned specifically for these purposes to other uses.

THE RISE AND DECLINE OF THE HOUSING CO-OPERATIVE, 1924–39

The development of housing co-operatives in the Soviet Union should properly be viewed both as a pragmatic response to a particular historical situation and as part of the history of the larger co-operative movement. Its Proudhonist overtones and the fact that co-operatives as such had been subjected to criticism by Marx meant that a section of the party membership regarded their growth with suspicion. In Marx's view, workers' co-operatives could never succeed in transforming capitalist society. Whilst theoretically and practically beneficial to workers, co-operatives could not, according to Marx, arrest the movement towards monopoly capitalism. They could never bring freedom to the masses nor even adequately alleviate their poverty so long as co-operative membership remained confined to a more privileged section of the working class. Moreover, in so far as co-operation was a movement of opposition to capitalism, it was only a transitory form of economic organisation. Its fate was bound up with that of capitalism: it had its origins under capitalism and was destined to die with it since, under socialism, the co-operative form was superfluous. In the words of an early Soviet commentator:

> The co-operative movement, which arose in capitalist society, does not create new relations in the world of labour. It takes as its starting point the conditions created by capital, which is omnipotent in society. The idea that co-operation could rescue any considerable number of the working class from the domination of capital is one of the illusions of the co-operative movement, an illusion as hampering and dangerous as other reformist delusions.[34]

The Bolshevik attitude towards co-operatives under the dictatorship of the proletariat was outlined in the Programme adopted by the VIII Party Congress (1919). This stated, in essence, that the co-operative movement should be encouraged during the transitional period, and that Party members should take an active part in their formation and co-ordination.[35] With the introduction of NEP, the authorities began to offer both practical and ideological assistance to co-operatives. In fact, in Lenin's view, now that the working class controlled the means of production, the broad, popular development of co-operatives had become a 'positive necessity'.[36] On the assumption that the only thing needed to achieve socialism was a demonstration to the masses of the advantages of co-operation, Lenin threw his weight behind the advocates of the co-operative movement and in doing so gave an undoubted fillip to the decision to set up housing co-operatives. Nevertheless, widespread antipathy within the Party to the co-operative movement in general had a dampening effect on the development of housing co-operatives. Its semi-autonomous status, the fact that it had traditionally attracted a more privileged section of the population (under capitalism – the working class aristocracy; under NEP – the intelligentsia and members of the so-called 'unproductive classes') called forth a certain hostility from a section of the Party hierarchy who viewed the co-operative as a heretical form of housing tenure.

Doubts and hostility notwithstanding, on 16 May 1924 the XIII Party Congress passed a resolution which, in stressing the need to pay greater attention to the housing question and the necessity of drawing upon the 'independent activity of the population', proposed the creation of co-operatives.[37] Subsequently, on 19 August 1924, two quite distinct forms of co-operative association were established: the house-leasing co-operative association (*zhilishchno-arendnoe kooperativnoe tovarishchestvo* – the *ZhAKT*) and the house-building co-operative association (*zhilishchno-stroitel'noe kooperativnoe tovarishchestvo* – the *ZhSKT*).[38]

The house-leasing co-operative

A government resolution of December 1917 had empowered tenants' committees (formed by general meetings of tenants in each building and supervised by the housing committee of the local soviet to which they were subordinate) to collect rent, let vacant dwellings and other premises, carry out necessary repairs, entrust management to paid functionaries and prosecute and have evicted tenants who failed to pay rent. The August 1924 decree gave leasing co-operatives priority in renting municipalised houses.[39] It was the failure of departments of municipal economy satisfactorily to maintain their properties that led to the gradual transfer of the municipalised stock into the hands of the ZhAKTy, which by the late 1920s were widely regarded as the most efficient means of running local soviet controlled accommodation.[40] By the end of 1926, two-thirds of the housing stock of the local soviets, representing almost 40 per cent of the total state sector, had been leased to the ZhAKTy.[41] A decade later, these associations were administering 53 million square metres of living space, equivalent to 42 per cent of the socialised sector and 84 per cent of the municipalised stock.[42]

For a number of years the government was willing to encourage leasing co-operatives, for they fulfilled a variety of useful purposes. As one contemporary protagonist of the co-operative declared: 'the main functions of the leasing co-operative are to maintain the existing housing stock and to increase living space by carrying out structural repairs'.[43] In addition, co-operatives were to organise kindergartens, crèches, communal dining-rooms, laundries, clubs and recreation rooms and also to tackle the problem of illiteracy – although there is little evidence that their activities in practice were so wide-ranging. Then, from a more theoretical and ideological standpoint, they were regarded as a means for drawing the 'broad masses' into the field of administration. This not only complied with Lenin's injunction on 'the need to involve the general public in creative organisational work'[44] but also served as a way of 'drawing us out of the petit-bourgeois swamp of the individual economy and leading us to a collectivised way of life on a socialist basis'.[45]

As late as 1935, local soviets were still being required by the XVI Congress of Soviets (RSFSR) to 'provide practical assistance to the ZhAKTy'.[46] However, the demise of the co-operatives was in sight. The reason given by present-day Soviet commentators for the change in official policy at the time towards this sector was that 'the housing co-operative was becoming redundant and unable to cope with the new problems thrown up as a consequence of large-scale construction and the use of industrialised building techniques'.[47] In the words of the October 1937 decree which liquidated them:

> The existing system of management ... does not ensure the preservation of the state housing stock as state property and its maintenance, but hinders further improvement in housing. The system of house management and the laws regulating the building of houses and the distribution and use of dwellings contain harmful survivals of that period when local soviets, because of their organisational and economic weakness, were forced to transfer their rights to individual collectives of tenants ...
>
> The stock of fifty-three million square metres administered by the ZhAKTy is in an unsatisfactory condition. The overwhelming majority of the ZhAKTy do not, in fact, manage the houses, do not look after repair work and do not keep the houses in a civilised condition. Lack of management frequently reduces the housing to a state of semi-ruin. A great deal of irresponsible rebuilding is taking place, especially the transformation of kitchens for general use into dwellings; kitchen ranges for preparing food have been installed in bedrooms – a practice which only worsens living conditions and increases the fire risk. Furthermore, not a few ZhAKTy are encouraging speculation in living space. The co-operative housing societies' associations or unions, with their numerous branches, are spending some forty million roubles each year on maintaining their administrative apparatus without ensuring proper management.

But, technical factors apart, the ZhAKTy had not been able to achieve certain of the other goals set for them. On a simple, practical level they had failed to prevent the deterioration of housing standards, while, on an ideological plane their objectives of 'educating the mass of the population to participate in the democratic administration of housing' was no longer congruent with the new political policy which emphasised administrative and political centralisation at the expense of individual and institutional autonomy, to which the leasing co-operative had given rise and encouraged.

The house-building co-operative

These co-operatives – directly contributing to the housing stock by erecting new dwellings – fell into two categories: workers' co-operatives (*RZhSKT*) and general citizens' co-operatives (*OZhSKT*). Only employees in state, co-operative and other public organisations (or individuals equal to them in rights, such as invalids) could be members of the former, whereas any citizen could join the latter. This meant that although the OZhSKTy were able to attract individuals with private capital, they could not claim the same access to state credit and building materials as could workers' co-operatives.[48]

Despite labour costs being relatively high, building materials expensive, work always behind schedule and building organisations tending to treat workers' co-operatives in a high-handed fashion,[49] the ZhSK was alleged to be 'very popular'.[50] Yet as early as 1925 voices of doom could already be heard. The newspaper *Ekonomicheskaya zhizn'* prophetically announced that 'it is justifiable to say that workers' housing co-operatives are not yet effective means for dealing with the accommodation shortage and never will be of any real importance'.[51] At this date, however, the government was aiming to make the co-operative a valuable vehicle for meeting the housing crisis and, in 1927, laid down that for the RZhSKTy the share contribution should be reduced to 13 per cent of the estimated cost of construction with the balance repayable over a period extended to 60 years, at interest rates varying between 0.25 and 2 per cent a year, thereby going some way to countering earlier charges that monthly payments were too high. A decree of 1928 considered that the role of the co-operative should be expanded still further since it was 'necessary to attract substantial sums of private capital for the construction of large houses'.[52] Partly as a consequence of this policy, the amount of living space erected by ZhSKy during the period 1928–32 was almost three times greater than in the preceding five-year period (1923–27). However, this absolute increase cannot conceal the fact that the ZhSK's contribution relative to other sectors was halved between 1929 and 1937, from 14.6 per cent to 6.8 per cent. And yet, it was during the Second Five-Year Plan that the XVI RSFSR Congress of Soviets (15–23 January 1935) passed a resolution to the effect that 'urban soviets must cease their unhealthy practice of undermining the role of the housing co-operative'. Instead, they should 'ensure that the co-operative fulfills its obligations to the shareholders by erecting and then efficiently managing their dwellings, organise the sale of building materials to co-operatives and refrain from taking space from them'.[53] Then in October 1937 the government decreed the abolition of all co-operatives, ostensibly because houses built by ZhSKy were effectively becoming the private property of their individual members even though up to 90 per cent of the cost of construction was financed by the state.

Lenin had given his stamp of approval to the co-operative movement as a necessary form of social organisation in the period of transition to socialism. Protagonists of house-building co-operatives argued that they not only helped satisfy real needs for shelter but also introduced individuals to a whole series of new relationships including the emancipation of women.[54] In terms of the amount of housing built, they were only moderately successful in the brief period when they flourished, for by 1931 the ZhSKy had only about 400 000 members, that is approximately 4 per cent of the workforce.[55] The charge levelled against them that they were both inefficient and riddled with corruption and nepotism may have been well-founded but the other housing sectors were hardly paragons of efficiency and virtue. In the final analysis, the paramount cause for the housing co-operative's abolition was ideological in origin: in 1936 Stalin declared that socialism had been achieved; the co-operative – which Lenin had defended as a form of organisation well suited to the period of transition to socialism – was abolished in the following year. It is difficult to interpret Soviet policy, whether in the realm of domestic or external affairs, without careful regard to ideology. In the view of the government, the housing co-operative had been 'dialectically' superseded by more strictly socialist forms of organising house building and management, namely the local soviets and state undertakings and departments.

THE PRIVATE SECTOR

During the first three years of Soviet power the housing stock as a whole diminished in size and fell into a state of disrepair. With the introduction of NEP, the government set out to deal with both these problems by seeking to enlist the assistance of the urban population at large. A decree of May 1921 which sought to involve tenants in the management of housing[56] was shortly followed by one allowing groups of people or separate individuals to erect dwellings on plots of land which the soviet did not invisage requiring in the near future.[57] A further decree recommended that local soviets transfer to groups of residents, or individuals, municipalised buildings containing only one or two flats (or up to five flats in Moscow and Leningrad), with a total living space not exceeding 94 square metres.[58] This system of transference was not as successful as anticipated, for housing associations and private individuals proved powerless to carry out the necessary repairs. The size of the housing stock continued to decline because, as one journal observed, 'the situation with the production of building materials is such that new building has had to be given up altogether and work confined to absolutely essential repairs to the existing stock'.[59]

When the worst crisis was over and new building began again, it was the private sector which took the initiative and which was counted upon to provide additional housing. Its contribution in the form of new or restored buildings to the total urban stock declined from a high of 80.8 per cent in 1923 to 54.3 per cent in 1928.[60] This reliance on private citizens was clearly acknowledged: 'the demand for housing in 1924 was 91 million square metres and the ten-year house building programme envisages increasing the average per capita living space to eight metres. A programme of this magnitude would entail a total expenditure of 3000 million rubles. Yet, neither the state nor local authorities possess the necessary funds; thus it is crucial that we fall back on the general public'.[61]

This fall-back position was to have deleterious consequences for the future because, as Table 2.3 shows, housing erected in the private sector was from the very beginning of a very low standard in terms of amenity provision. Furthermore, with less than 7 per cent of all houses in this sector having stone or brick walls, the country was laying the foundation for future urban renewal programmes (see Chapter 8).

In order to attract private capital into housing, individual builders were

TABLE 2.3   *Distribution of newly built housing by wall materials and amenity provision (as a percentage of housing built in each housing tenure, in 1926–8)*

Builder	Proportion of Housing with:				
	brick walls	running water	sewerage disposal	central heating	electric lighting
state	55.6	76.0	73.0	50.0	75.0
co-operatives	53.1	60.1	50.0	50.0	75.0
individuals	7.5	2.3	2.3	none	18.0

SOURCE   D. L. Broner, *Zhilishchnoe stroitel'stvo i demograficheskie protsessy*, Moscow, 1980, p. 18.

granted permission to build and lease residential and non-residential premises and charge a rent agreed by landlord and tenant.[62] Thus legislation passed during the 1920s anticipated attracting both the savings of individual workers into building houses for themselves and the larger resources of 'Nepmen' (private traders or private entrepreneurs) and members of the liberal professions for building to rent. Demunicipalisation comprised an integral part of this policy and was intended both to demonstrate that the state was not hostile to house ownership *per se* and to enlist the support of the tenants themselves in the maintenance of the property they occupied.

However, Nepmen preferred to engage in trading activities in order to benefit from the rapid turnover of money rather than tie up their capital in an investment where the yield was lower and recoupment periods spread over a greater number of years. The reluctance of those with capital to invest was not misplaced, for after 1929 the government's attitude towards the use of private capital in house construction came to approximate that expressed by the slogan 'elimination of the *kulaks* [rich peasants] as a class' in agriculture.[63] In 1930 the state ceased to provide credit, the acquisition of building plots became difficult and building materials were no longer made available to private builders. The small amount of private building for rent stopped altogether. Private construction by urban residents of their own dwellings continued but the amount they erected during the first five-year plan declined in absolute terms from 5.1 million square metres in 1927–28 to 4.6 million in 1929–32, and in relative terms from 54.2 per cent to 16.4 per cent of the total.[64] The decline accelerated during the second five-year plan (1933–37) to 2.7 million square metres (9.1 per cent of all urban house building) when the private sector came under increasing political pressure. Unlike the housing co-operative however, the private builder was not abolished by the October 1937 decree; on the contrary, during the period of the third five-year plan (1938–June 1941), this sector was given a fresh lease of life. Consistent with the policy of enhancing the role in housing provision of the 'departmental' sector, the compilation of lists of workers to whom loans were to be granted for house construction, and the size of the loan were made the prerogative of the enterprise director, subject to the agreement of the factory trade union committee (*Fabzavkom*). A loan was repayable over five years at 2 per cent interest and was paid by the bank to a worker through his place of employment. The borrower had to contribute 30 per cent of the cost of construction, which could be in the form of cash, materials or his own (and his family's) labour. In cases where the borrower ceased to be employed by the enterprise for any reason, he was allowed to retain the property so long as he had paid at least half the cost of construction, otherwise the house became the property of the enterprise.[65]

CONCLUSION

The Russian revolution, which caused the rapid and fundamental transformation of the state and class structure, also resulted in the emergence of new political forms of housing control and management. The confiscation of housing belonging to the rich, the redistribution of housing space to reduce overcrowding, the setting up of house committees composed of elected tenants, and the abolition of rent, were all features of the initial revolutionary phase: they were symptoms of the radical change that had occurred and indicated the direction in which the society was moving.

This was followed by the New Economic Policy which Lenin described and justified as a temporary retreat. Rent was reintroduced, some housing was demunicipalised, and housing co-operatives were created both to manage the existing stock and to enlist the assistance of the population, including those with 'large private capital', in helping to provide accommodation.

Then, when the government embarked in 1929 on its rapid industrialisation policy, it was obliged to reassess its housing strategy.[66] Towards the end of the pre-war period the already mentioned decree of October 1937,[67] regarded by contemporary Soviet writers as the principal law on housing, created a system of housing management which, with few modifications, continues in force to the present day.[68] Among other things, it abolished the housing co-operatives, and severely curtailed the role assigned to personal building for owner occupation, thereby placing the main responsibility for house building and administration on the state.

3 The State Housing Sector

INTRODUCTION

This chapter focusses on the relationship, since 1945, between the local soviet (municipalised) housing sector and the departmental (nationalised) sector. A considerable amount of discussion on housing policy in the Soviet Union revolves around the question of who controls the housing stock and investment in new home construction. Yet the debate on this institutional relationship is not confined to housing, for it embraces the broader issues of control over the whole infrastructure.

Whereas, generally speaking, the local soviets are concerned with the conditions of life for the population living within their administrative jurisdiction, economic organisations, concerned directly or indirectly with production, have as their principal objective the satisfaction of national demands. Enterprises, apart from those catering chiefly or totally for the local economy, are part of a production network contributing to the national economy and hence their interests (meeting planned input and output targets, increasing efficiency etc.) are not necessarily congruent with local interests. In order to chart the debate on the contradiction between these so-called 'territorial' and 'branch' (sector) interests since the war, the chapter has been divided into four sections. The first documents the demands made by local soviets over the last thirty years and the main legislative acts in this field and also questions the extent of their autonomy. The second describes the degree to which local soviets have increased their 'property rights' against other public bodies, while the third analyses the cases for and against a transfer of housing from the departments to local soviets. The fourth section deals with the broader context of the local soviet – department conflict.

LOCAL SOVIET DEMAND FOR CONTROL OF HOUSING

The extensive and rapid development of the economy during the 1930s was accompanied by waste, inefficiency, a rapacious attitude towards the environment and falling and low standards of living: high costs had to be paid for the benefits gained from joining the ranks of the advanced industrial nations. The government often declared that 'the city soviet is the master of the city' but at the time such statements were often devoid of practical significance, principally because planning was essentially on a sector basis, whereas the soviets were organised territorially. In other words it was easier to channel resources through ministries than through the soviets. The exhortation to local soviets was made when the government had embarked on a policy of rapid industrialisation, of transforming an agrarian society into an industrial power. With notable exceptions, little time and effort were devoted to the question of aesthetics in town lay-outs or even to providing surfaced roads, social facilities and an urban infrastracture. Municipal investment in housing was, therefore, of a low priority in government planning. However, while the tangible effects of pronouncements in favour of the local soviets were minimal, they retained an important political value as affirmations that the soviets of workers' deputies were the foundations of political power in the Soviet state. This element in Soviet political–constitutional doctrine would gradually be translated into reality as the economy expanded. The power to control spatial planning and development was exercised only when the tempo of industrialisation slowed down. Only then did the state enjoy the luxury of both contemplating the social costs of its policies and the opportunity of trying to reduce them. Only then were resources (including managerial cadres) diverted from investment in heavy industry to consumer goods and to other low-priority sectors, including homes and social facilities.

Throughout these upheavals of industrialisation and war, the maxim remained unchanged that although the local soviets lacked the means to carry out their statutory obligations, their role as 'master of the city' had in principle been established, and was strongly insisted on by local planners in discussions on housing and social amenities in the last years of the Stalin period. The chairman of an Ukrainian *oblast'* planning committee firmly stated in April 1951, 'In every town in our country, the master is the urban soviet of workers' deputies. The Constitution makes this body responsible for the "guidance" of the provision of local services and of the urban economy'.[1] However, he went on to add that 'for a variety of reasons, many urban soviets do not always exercise their rights as master', citing the example of Zaporozh'e to illustrate why soviets so often failed in their role as city master.

This planning official pointed out that the major builders of Zaporozh'e were enterprises and building organisations of Union and Republican industrial ministries. Each year, the Executive of the local soviet (*gorispolkom*) called a meeting with representatives of industrial organisations and together with them drew up the annual plan for housing construction and public service provision. Since the city soviet's contribution to the construction of housing and municipal services was only 2 – 5 per cent of the total expenditure, it had to rely on the goodwill of these other agencies. One way of doing so was to involve them in the planning process. In this particular instance, a large-scale housing programme had left a serious shortage of water conduits, an incomplete sewerage system and a poor transportation network. In order to rectify the shortage of water conduits, the central government allocated funds to the Ministries of ferrous metallurgy, agricultural machinery, communications and food. The construction work itself was to be undertaken by the building trust belonging to the Ukrainian Ministry of Housing and Civil Construction and, when completed, handed over to the 'client', the Zaporozh'e trust (*Vodokanal*). As so often happened the ministries only remitted a fraction of the money allocated to them to supply the necessary pipes. The 'narrow departmental approach to housing and amenity provision and the unco-ordinated departmental planning and distribution of financial and material resources for municipal purposes reflected negatively on the city's development and meant that participation by the heads of enterprises in planning was not always effective'.[2]

Clearly, managements controlling resources were willing to take part in discussion on a comprehensive development plan but withdrew support as soon as their own particular interests were affected. The conclusion drawn by the chairman, repeated time and again over the next 30 years, was that 'financial and material resources for general city construction allocated to Union and Republican ministries should be concentrated in the hands of the city's soviet'. At this date, the demand was restricted to a limited number of public amenities: 'first of all funds for urban transport, roads, water, sewerage and electricity networks and environmental improvements. We consider that enterprises of industrial ministries should retain control of the housing stock and some cultural and domestic amenities'.

This was by no means an isolated instance of complaints made by local soviets on this topic, in the last years of the Stalin period. Two months later, in June 1951, the chairman of the Kirov District soviet of Leningrad claimed that enterprises and other institutions of Union-Republican subordination[3] were guided by one over-riding objective – to lay their hands on as much housing as possible. They paid no attention whatsoever to the building of schools, hospitals, pre-school facilities, landscaping and the laying of gas pipelines and telephone cables. The industrial authorities did not even consult the local soviets over the planning and carrying out of their housing schemes. And so this soviet official argued that the city soviet should be given the right to regulate both the amount and type of construction carried out by departments, and that further resources for constructing municipal utilities in new residential areas should be transferred to the urban soviets.[4]

In September of the same year the Chairman of the Minsk City soviet drew attention to another problem confronting many local soviets. Not only did the latter receive inadequate resources, but enterprises operating in the city were often allocated sums of money for housing sufficient only for small-scale construction, with the result that effort and resources were being 'dissipated'. Instead of large blocks of flats being erected in the centre of the city, buildings with as few as eight flats, lacking even the most elementary amenities such as piped water or sewage disposal, were built on the city outskirts. Since this system of allocation made it impossible to use industrialised building methods, construction costs could not be reduced. The Minsk chairman proposed that the resources of industrial enterprises should be pooled so that bigger and better housing units might be erected.[5]

During the early 1950s the claims of officials in the local soviets were fairly modest. And it was not until July 1957 that the government was moved to enact the first post-war legislation specifically designed to promote an increase in the proportion of the housing stock belonging to local soviets. The decree made it obligatory for local soviets to enter into contracts with builders who would construct houses for them, thereby making the local soviets the principal clients for urban housing construction within the state sector.[6] Then, following innovations in the country's system of economic organisation introduced in 1965 and the housing decree of 1967,[7] both housing and enterprises of municipal economy began to be transferred to local soviets.[8] Yet, for all the legislation and institutional changes, the 'greater part of the housing stock and municipal enterprises still did not belong to local soviets but to numerous enterprises and organisations',[9] and there was no decline in the flow of examples critical of the irrationality of the existing system nor in the demands made by the local soviets to manage objects of 'collective consumption'.

In 1970 the chairman of the Vorkuta City soviet, for instance, complained about the wide range of activities the city's main enterprise, *Vorkutaugol* (a coal-mining trust), was engaged in. They included the running of 200 shops, a railway, six state farms and a dairy; furthermore it controlled the telephone network of the city and surrounding workers' settlements as well as water and sewerage systems and housing. Other organisations, like the Department of the Northern Railway, also possessed their own retail outlets, medical-centres and housing and social amenities, while seven departments (*vedomstva*) maintained over 300 km of water mains, 140 km of gas mains and 210 km of central-heating piping (which was becoming obsolescent and in need of major repair). After citing examples to demonstrate the sort of difficulties created when control over housing and social services are vested in different departments, the chairman concluded that if the local soviet became the city's sole master then decisions could be arrived at and executed much more quickly and efficiently.[10] Until Stalin's death Vorkuta was a centre of a large labour camp area in the extreme north-east of European Russia, so it could be contended that the concentration of such variegated functions in the hands of a few principal organisations may well be typical of former penal colonies, but is unrepresentative of the organisation of city services in the society as a whole. We lack precise information on the ownership, control and administration of municipal services in all cities, but it is significant that the overwhelming majority (52 out of 57) of senior officials of the executive committees of large city soviets interviewed in a survey conducted between 1976 and 1979 were unanimous in their opinion that the absence of a single unified system of enterprises of communal economy under the direct administrative control of the *gorispolkom* only adds to the difficulties of running the urban economy.[11]

In the same year (1970), the chairman of the Omsk executive committee pointed to another matter of central concern to the local soviet, one affecting its ability to control the environment in which its citizens live. In drawing up the city's long term (25–30 year) plan, it was predicted that its population would rise to 1.2 million, on the assumption that no new large factories would be built in the city since it was more expedient to locate them in smaller, less industrialised towns in the *oblast'*. Yet within two years the figures had to be revised upwards, because ministries insisted on erecting new plant in the *oblast'* centre (Omsk) instead of in the nearby smaller towns, even though the latter possessed all the requisite conditions for developing as industrial centres.

The *gorispolkom* always exercised its right to examine and comment on the construction plans drawn up in the departmental sector and was often forced to make amendments because industrial managers and planners had allowed building norms and rules to be infringed, but agreements between ministries and local soviets on the nature and location of new projects were often broken by enterprise managements without any explanation for doing so.[12] The agreements broken normally related to the responsibility of enterprises for providing accommodation and the attendant municipal amenities. Sometimes, as in the case of one ministry in Omsk, estates to house employees of their three new factories had been erected but not the school, polytechnic or social club, even though they were included in the plans and financial estimates for the erection of the factories. The remedy suggested by the Omsk *gorispolkom* was a familiar one: when the design institutes and planning organisations have produced their final building plans and estimates, the capital assignments should be transferred to the main client, whom the local soviet firmly believed should be itself.

In spite of all these criticisms and calls for more local autonomy, the government did relatively little before 1970 to enhance the powers of the local soviets. Instead it remained content to exhort them to use the legal powers already bestowed upon them.[13] The fact that cities were lacking in basic amenities and developing in an amorphous, unplanned fashion was attributed to the inefficiency and incompetence of local soviets, the 'urban managers', who were allegedly far too faint-hearted in dealing with enterprises and ministries. In 1957, a resolution to improve the working of local soviets was severe in its rebuke: 'The facts show that the daily needs of the masses are ill-met, not because the material resources and conditions are lacking in the local soviets, but because of bureaucracy and voluntarism and the irresponsibility of some functionaries in the soviets who have lost contact with the masses'.[14] Although in some cases such charges were undoubtedly quite justified, the main problem lay in the subordinate status of the local soviets in their institutional relationship with industry; local soviet personnel were being made the scapegoat for a set of problems created by the state's own priority system.

After Khrushchev's removal from power in 1964, the more strongly worded criticisms of local soviets characteristic of his period of office were dropped. Then, in 1970, the government issued a decree roundly condemning the practice of not providing essential services. The attack centred on the fact that 'in many cities, especially Republican capitals, *krai* and *oblast'* centres, instead of concentrating financial and material resources on building schools, houses, hospitals and children's facilities, funds are spent on administrative buildings, purpose-built entertainment and sports complexes'.[15] In many cases construction plans for the latter were being overfulfilled by a large margin, at the expense, needless to say, of housing, socio-cultural amenities and public utilities.[16] The decree went on to stipulate, *inter alia*, that Party and Soviet Executive Committees were to call to account individuals found guilty of diverting resources to unnecessary and unplanned for projects.

Furthermore, the All-Union Bank for Construction (*Stroibank* USSR) and the State Bank (*Gosbank* USSR) were instructed not to finance unplanned construction and the building of administrative offices, entertainment facilities and so on above quarterly and annual plan and budgetary assignments. The intention was to avoid, on the one hand, spending money on what in the government's view amounted to less important construction and, on the other, wasteful duplication. Although this criticism was directed more at enterprises and ministries, the local soviets were also implicated. Some of them unquestionably do display excessive civic consciousness and devote far too high a proportion of limited resources to the erection of monuments or to lavish expenditure on town halls, and also demolish thoroughly good housing on the ground that it constitutes an eyesore (see Chapters 7 and 8). Nevertheless, the incontrovertible fact is that the greater proportion of resources for infrastructural construction have been channelled through the departmental sector which must bear responsibility for their misuse.[17]

From the point of view of the government, by the early 1970s the time had come for a stop to be called to the misuse of funds caused by directors of enterprises and institutions acting in their particularistic interests. The local soviets, it was thought, could at least be expected to refrain from unnecessary duplication of services and to devise a programme of resource allocation more consonant with the needs of the whole population residing within their administrative areas.[18] As a handbook on local soviets put it, the enhanced role envisaged for the soviets was a function of the 'rise in the level of economic and cultural development, changes in the social structure, the growth of democracy, greater efficiency in the management of economic and social processes and changes in the system and methods of running the economy'.[19] These macro social and economic changes were said to be 'exercising an ever increasing influence on the organisation and activity of local soviets' and this required a further increase in the role the latter played 'in the management of social production, social and cultural construction and in servicing the population'.[20] This expanded range of functions attributed to local soviets could not possibly be carried out without improvements in the legal foundations on which their organisation and activities are based. If the local economy was to be developed as a single complex, then local soviets had to be given effective power to co-ordinate the various economic and service sectors within their administrative jurisdiction and to supervise the operations of all enterprises, organisations and institutions.[21]

There is an important exception to this general enhancement of the local soviets' powers. In cases where all the inhabitants in a town or new district are 'engaged in the same production activity', then a *prima facie* case exists for the ministry which is responsible for constructing a new factory (or HEP station or industrial complex) to retain the functions that it was initially required to fulfil, including running the municipal economy. This also applies in rapidly growing cities such as Tol'yatti (533 000) and Naberezhnye Chelny (346 000) when the functions of 'single client' for both industrial and civil construction are fulfilled not by the *gorispolkom* but by the administrations for the capital construction (*UKS*) of large industrial organisations. In the case of Cherepovets (279 000), the city soviet has succeeded in controlling only 10 per cent of all capital investment for house construction leaving the metallurgical *kombinat* as the main client for both accommodation and all other municipal facilities.[22] A list of towns where the function of single client for the construction of accommodation, cultural and social facilities and infrastructural amenities devolves on enterprises is determined by the Council of Ministers of Union Republics.[23] Evidently, therefore, it is really only when a city becomes industrially diversified that all non-industrial building is placed in the hands of the local soviet, with the ministries and enterprises contributing their share of expenses.[24]

In order to deal with the general problem of local soviet control, on 14 March 1971 the Council of Ministers promulgated a decree 'On Measures for the Further Improvement of the Work of the District and City Soviets'[25] which was followed a few days later by a decree of the Presidium of the Supreme Soviet 'On the Basic Rights and Duties of City and District Soviets'.[26] In essence, these decrees asserted the

categorical necessity for enterprises and agencies providing services
primarily for the local population to be placed under the jurisdiction of
district and city soviets. Indicative of the elevated importance now
attached to local soviets is the description of their rights and duties
contained in the 1977 Constitution. Article 146 states among other
things that: they 'shall direct state, economic, social and cultural
development within their territory; endorse plans for economic and
social development and the local budget; exercise general guidance
over the state bodies, enterprises, institutions and organisations subordinate to them...'. Article 147 further adds that: 'local soviets of
people's deputies shall ensure the comprehensive, all-round economic
and social development of their area; exercise control over and
observance of legislation by enterprises, institutions and organisations
subordinated to higher authorities and located in their area; and
co-ordinate and supervise their activity regarding land-use, nature
conservation, building, employment of manpower, production of consumer goods and social cultural, communal and other services and
amenities for the public'.[27]

To enable local soviets to fulfil their newly acquired functions, the
government took steps to increase the financial resources placed at
their disposal.[28] It allowed the soviets to use part of the profits made by
enterprises subordinated to them and to have transferred to their
budgets a proportion of the profits earned by enterprises and economic
agencies of republican, *krai* and *oblast'* subordination.[29] As a result, in
Moscow for example, during the period 1971–75, 8.8 milliard rubles
(66.2 per cent of all capital investment in the city) was spent on the
urban economy – which was over 4 milliard roubles more than a
decade earlier (1961–65).[30]

This increased expenditure on the urban economy is a result of a
rising standard of living – reflected in more and better services and
higher wage rates for those working in the municipal and retail sector –
the growing urban population and the overall increase in the number
of workers employed in this sector.[31] The larger budgetary allocations
for the municipal economy beg the question of whether local soviets
are becoming financially more independent of central state authorities. An answer must be deferred until a survey has been completed of the ways in which local soviets generate their own revenue
and the extent to which they decide on its allocation for different
purposes. However, it can be said that, given the tendency for production to become more concentrated and to be organised in industrial
combines, some enterprises, at present supplying the local economy,

are being transferred into the jurisdiction of higher ranking administrative bodies. This is particularly evident in the case of the transfer of urban objects (*gorodskie ob"ekty*) to authorities at the oblast' level.[32] This means a reduction in the size and value of the property base belonging to the local soviets and thus also a fall in their budgetary revenue. Furthermore the expansion in public services together with a general rise in the wage level of employees working in this sector together with a general rise in the wage level of employees working in this sector has led to an increase in running costs. At the same time, since the price paid by the consumers for these services does not increase, the local economy declines in profitability.[33] Although these tendencies and outcomes are partly offset by the policy to strengthen the role of local soviets by transferring to them enterprises and institutions comprising the community's social and technical infrastructure, thereby increasing the soviets' income, on balance the decline in the local revenue-generating base necessitates a proportionate increase in the contribution from the central state's budget.[34] This will probably have the effect of restricting the growth in local government autonomy. At the same time, any discussion of power or 'legitimate authority' wielded by an organisation (for instance, a local soviet) has to take into account not only its relationship to the generation and disposal of 'new resources', but also its relationship to existing stocks of resources. In the present context, this refers to the question of the extent to which local soviets have increased their property rights *vis-à-vis* other institutions.

THE EXTENT OF TRANSFER OF DEPARTMENTAL HOUSING TO LOCAL SOVIETS

In the RSFSR local soviet control over the public housing sector declined from 45.6 per cent of overall living space in 1940 to 34.8 per cent in 1950 and 26.8 per cent in 1956.[35] The decree of July 1957 began to reverse this decline and initiated the transfer of housing from state enterprises and institutions to local soviets. By the end of 1960, local soviets in the RSFSR controlled 32.4 per cent of the socialised housing stock.[36] By January 1965 they had increased their holding to about 34 per cent.[37] Yet a decade later the deputy minister for Housing and Communal Economy in the RSFSR could only affirm that 'at present only 35 per cent of the socialised housing stock is in the hands of local soviets in the Russian Federal Republic'.[38]

A decree of September 1978[39] noted that over the 'past few years' there had been a slackening of interest in the transfer of housing to the soviets. In the period 1976–78, the proportion of *state* housing (in terms of living space) controlled by local soviets in the RSFSR rose by a mere 1 per cent, from 34 to 35 per cent.[40] In other words, in the Russian Federal Republic, the local soviets' share of the socialised urban housing stock remained virtually constant between 1965 and 1980. (And, as far as the *total* urban housing stock is concerned in the mid-1970s, in the RSFSR the local soviet share amounted to 24 per cent.)[41] In the country at large the housing stock of the local soviet sector rose from 543.2 million square metres in 1975 to 623.2 million in January 1979, which increased its proportion of the state housing stock from 39.2 per cent to 39.6 per cent.[42] These global figures mask, however, vast variations existing between cities, regions and republics in the extent to which local soviets control housing.

Historical factors play an important role in determining the size of the different housing sectors (private, departmental, local soviet). The local soviets in the largest administrative centres, where the more solidly built housing was concentrated and municipalised after the October revolution, tend to control a high proportion of the residential buildings.[43] For instance, by 1974 the Moscow borough soviets controlled two-thirds of the total city housing stock.[44] In the mid-1960s the Leningrad and Kiev city soviets administered 78.1 per cent and 67.0 per cent of the public sector respectively (77.1 per cent and 58.2 per cent of the total stock within their jurisdictions). In two other Republican capitals, Tallinn and Yerevan, the figures for housing controlled by local soviets was equally high: in the former it stood at 66.9 per cent in 1970 (lower than in some previous years) and in the Armenian capital it was already 91.2 per cent in 1966. These figures are, however, considerably lower when housing controlled by local soviets is calculated in terms of the total city stock: the Tallin figure falls to 56.6 per cent and in Yerevan to 50.1 per cent.[45] In Kemerovo (486 000) three-quarters of the total housing stock is controlled by the local soviets,[46] in contrast to Perm' (1 018 000) where in 1973 the figure was 19.9 per cent.[47]

In general these statistics certainly do not substantiate statements made by Western scholars that 'since then [the expropriation of privately-owned property by the decree of 8 August 1918] the fund [of housing held by soviets] has been greatly increased by building and by the transfer of accommodation from state undertakings',[48] and that, 'since 1957 the bulk of housing funds have been controlled by local

soviets'.[49] The comment of a Soviet author in 1970 that 'the transfer of
the departmental housing stock to the local soviets is still proceeding
slowly'[50] has not been invalidated by events in the following decade.

PROBLEMS CONCERNING THE TRANSFER OF HOUSING TO LOCAL SOVIETS

The Soviet Case

There is no single uniform structure whereby local soviets manage
their housing, nor does a unified system exist in the departmental
housing sector. The fragmented system which has evolved is administratively (and hence, economically) highly inefficient and some form of
rationalisation has become inevitable. One of the main ways of reducing cost is through administrative reorganisation. To this end, a
Resolution of the Council of Ministers RSFSR of July 1959 'On
Measures to Improve the Running and Maintenance of the State
Housing stock'[51] required the setting up of a larger housing administrative unit, the 'house-management office' (*zhilishchno-
eksploatatsionnaya kontora- ZhEK*) which has gradually become the
system of administration adopted in most large cities in the RSFSR. [52]
More recently another type of organisation has appeared in Moscow,
Leningrad and several other large cities – the 'housing industrial
operational trust' (or 'Association') (*ZhPET* or *ZhEO*). Servicing
600 000–700 000 square metres of living space and combining from
six to eight former *ZhEKy*, they embrace departments which undertake current repair work. The first one established in the Ukraine,
where they are becoming the basic administrative unit of the housing
economy, covers the newly built Darnitsa estate in Kiev where it
services 82 modern multi-storey blocks accommodating 40 000
people.[53] One benefit gained from this reorganisation has been to
place housing management on a firmer financial basis. In contrast to
the smaller housing managements which were constantly in debt to
other organisations that had carried out repair work and provided
materials and transport, the larger offices (ZhEKy), by cutting administrative staff expenditure, began to operate profitably. Previously
the lack of funds on current account meant that work was periodically
paralysed, since at times the housing management was unable to
purchase the necessary materials or settle with building contractors for
the work they had undertaken. The process of rationalisation taking

place in this sphere has produced advantages normally associated with economies of scale (larger liquid assets, availability of material resources, personnel and equipment) and is also alleged to confer important benefits on the tenants serviced by these enlarged units. Whereas local soviet housing management offices take care of all blocks of flats in one particular ward, housing owned and controlled by enterprises is sometimes distributed throughout the city and sometimes even in different settlements.

In general, the housing managements of local soviets administer housing space five or six times greater than that of the equivalent organisations responsible for the departmental housing stock. Survey data for the mid-1960s revealed that in Kemerovo *oblast'* departmental housing was in the hands of 376 enterprises and organisations, which together had set up 600 housing departments to administer it. In the area around one Chelyabinsk factory about 20 000 m^2 of dwelling space belonged to five different organisations.[54] Along one of Chelyabinsk's main thoroughfares, one-quarter of the five-storey houses had seven owners, while in Vologda, the 30 buildings connected up to one heating system belong to 12 different organisations,[55] and in Stavropol' and elsewhere it was not uncommon to find one building belonging to several departments.[56] By 1980, in the RSFSR as a whole, the local soviets had just over 3000 housing offices (*domoupravlenie* or *ZhEKy*) overseeing 'their property', whereas the departmental sector with *twice* as much living space to run and maintain had seven times as many (almost 21 000) house-management departments.[57]

If statistics cited by Broner are still roughly applicable – that the losses incurred by housing managements in Leningrad with less than 5000 m^2 of dwelling space were 16.5 roubles per square metre, whilst those with over 25 000 m^2 ran at a profit – then it might reasonably be concluded firstly that running costs could be partially reduced by increasing the unit size of housing managements and secondly that this might be most feasible if all state housing were to be controlled by local soviets.[58] That this disparity in running costs still exists is confirmed by one author who comments that 'running the departmental stock is very expensive and annually brings losses of hundreds of millions of rubles'.[59] Another author is more specific: 'In 1974, in housing administrations and *ZhEKy* run by local soviets, revenue exceeded expenditure (excluding capital repairs) by 11.1 million rubles, whereas in the departmental sector expenditure exceeded revenue by 1.65 milliard rubles – 95 million rubles more than in 1975'.[60]

The transfer of control over housing to the local soviets is also viewed as a basic precondition for substantially increasing the amount of repair work carried out.[61] At present over 15 per cent of all resources allocated to housing are spent on maintenance. Figures for current repairs have risen steadily over the last few years both absolutely and relative to total running costs: from 0.62 roubles per square metre of living space in 1965 (24 per cent of total outlay on running costs) to 1.19 roubles (41 per cent) in 1971. Forecasters estimate that 'in the future the size of funds allocated to current repairs may reach 50 per cent'.[62] For the country at large, the annual outlay on repair work amounts to one-fifth of the average annual capital investment on new house construction.[63] Nevertheless, since enterprise directorates fail to assign the necessary and planned resources to repair work, the buildings they control continue to deteriorate. In 1978, for instance, not a single ministry or department fulfilled its capital repair plan and overall in that year the plan was only 88 per cent fulfilled.[64]

One explanation offered by Soviet officials for the slow transfer of housing into their jurisdiction is that they refuse to accept enterprise accommodation which is in a poor state of repair and insist that properties will be taken ever when fully renovated. Indeed, in contrast to the contention by one Western author that 'housing belonging to local soviets is generally considered to be worse than that provided by specific enterprises',[65] a Soviet correspondent considers it to be common knowledge that many 'departmental' controlled buildings are both badly maintained and lacking in basic amenities. The following figures for the country at large are seen as indicative of the higher standard of amenity provision in soviet controlled housing.

TABLE 3.1 *Proportion of housing in the two state tenure-types provided with amenities, 1979 (%)**

Amenity	Form of Tenure	
	Local soviet	Departmental
water	90	85
sewerage	89	82
central heating	85	83
gas	88	83
hot water	58	47
bath or shower	81	73

* for further details on amenity provision, see Chapter 8.
SOURCE   T. Fetisov *op. cit.* p. 56.

Ever increasing maintenance costs, the continued existence of a large number of small housing departments and the relative inefficiency of the departmental sector occasioned the issuing in September 1978 of a decree 'On measures to improve the running and repair of the housing stock'.[66] In its preamble the decree referred to the persistence of too many small, unprofitable housing management offices, to the inefficient use of resources and to the poor quality of repair work carried out. In order to deal with these problems the Republican Councils of Ministers were to adopt by 1980 new methods for administering the housing economy. In the first instance these should entail the setting up in the large cities of a single building repair service which would contract to carry out current and capital repairs for both the state and the co-operative sectors. The decree reiterated the government's policy on the transfer of departmental housing to the local soviets, expounded in 1967, and pointed out that the accommodation to be transferred first of all should be that which the departmental sector is unable to service properly and which in the main is owned by small organisations.

An account of the transfer process in the Saratov oblast' and the oblast' capital itself illustrates, as the RSFSR ministry of Housing and Communal Economy observed, the difficulties faced by the majority of oblasts and cities in seeking to effect the transfer.[67] The city of Saratov (873 000) lies 858 km south-east of Moscow. Three-quarters of the population in the oblast' is urban. In 1979, local soviets in the oblast' controlled 34 per cent of the state housing stock. Three years previously the oblast' soviet had ratified a time-table for taking control of 452 residential buildings with 320 000 square metres of living space (equivalent to 3 per cent of the departmental housing stock) during the period 1976–80. Although the schedule was basically being adhered to, a number of extremely difficult problems remained to be settled. For example, in the workers' settlement of Stepnoe, which predominantly comprised employees in the oil industry, the local soviet owned only a small proportion of the housing stock and the transfer of departmental housing onto its books was proceeding very slowly. Apparently, a high proportion of the eight-apartment houses (normally of two or three storeys) were obsolescent and the four-storey blocks required major repair work. And yet it was the declared policy of the district soviet only to take over buildings in perfect condition; after all, since they received a fraction of the resources available to the departments, the latter should first of all complete the repairs before discussing the transfer.

The representative of the largest 'landlord' in Stepnoe (the Trans-Volga Oil and Gas Extractive Administration) countered the charge by producing a large dossier of documents concerning the transfer going back over 10 years. He pointed out that in 1978 a special committee composed of both parties had drawn up a detailed list of all the defects in the houses subject to transfer. After the 'landlord' had rectified all the faults, the local soviet then unearthed a mass of additional problems and refused to take the buildings. This led the landlord's representative to comment that 'We do not see "our" soviet as being very interested in the whole affair. It is always possible to find excuses and fault-find and always much easier for the "organs of power" to give orders and pressurise us to do this or that than to take over the housing and run it themselves'. And so far as material and financial resources and equipment for servicing the accommodation were concerned, the landlord again referred to the dossier to show how funds, personnel and materials (including a construction gang, three house-management offices, a transport workshop, heating-supply plant, warehouse and stores) would be transferred to the local soviet. But in defence of the soviet's procrastination, since it controlled just 7 per cent of all living space in the settlement it was perhaps not unnatural that it should be apprehensive about taking on the responsibility for so much more housing. However in the end, as the district soviet chairman acknowledged, the 'oilmen' would hand over their housing and related resources, and the soviet would have to 'overcome its faintheartedness and become psychologically prepared' to undertake the enlarged commitment.

According to the director-general of the Trans-Volga Productive Association, when questioned on the matter of the housing transfers in other settlements in the oblast' (apart from Stepnoe) where they owned accommodation, the transfer was proceeding satisfactorily. As far as Stepnoe was concerned, the Association was quite helpless to do anything in face of an obstinate (*upryami*) soviet executive committee. The problem was that the oblast' authorities were not being persistent enough in ensuring that their subordinate (district) soviet implement the transfer. He conceded, however, that in general enterprises still remain in a better position than the local soviets to allocate labour, materials and equipment for housing maintenance – adding that 'it is another matter altogether whether they do so'. Therefore, 'changes will have to be made in order to strengthen the material–technical base of the local organs of power'.

An examination of the problems of transferring housing in the city of

Saratov itself brings to the fore the specific and serious difficulty facing most old, large cities, namely the presence of a 'considerable number of low-rise houses, erected prior to 1917, which are ill-provided with amenities and even rely on the traditional Russian stove (*pech*') for heating'. In 1979 a report prepared by the standing committee on the city's housing economy concluded that the housing stock controlled by small enterprises and organisations was in a sorely neglected state and ought to be taken over by the local soviet as soon as possible. The same applied to some large factories. In one instance, an enterprise with 160 000 square metres of living space, much of which had been constructed during the 1920s, found itself unable to maintain it properly and as a result presented a case for accelerated transfer. On the other hand, the productive association responsible for the manufacture of the well-known 'Saratov' refrigerator presented a completely different picture. Here the management had set up a special repair and operating service to take care of its 270 000 square metres of living space. Because of this and the fact that the hot water and energy supply lines to the houses were also linked into the factory supply network, a transfer of housing, which would necessitate changing this linkage, would be too expensive and was not recommended. In this and similar cases, the deputies reasoned, it would be better to wait a while before proceeding with the transfer.

A session of the Saratov soviet held in 1979 to review the general issue of housing, especially its maintenance and operation, decided that to date progress on the transfer had been slow. At the same time it recognised that, in order to be successful, the whole procedure for handing over staff, material and financial resources and equipment would have to be simplified for, according to a ministerial circular issued in 1969, all documentation relating to the transfer has to be ratified by two people: the deputy chairman of the oblast' soviet executive committee and the appropriate deputy minister or head of a central department. Since the latter are usually located in Moscow the volumes of paper work involved in each house and 'object of communal economy' transfer have to be taken (*vezti*) to Moscow and then returned – which in the case of Magadan or Khabarovsk means a round trip of over 21 000 and 17000 km respectively.

This ostensibly cumbersome, bureaucratic procedure is an unfortunate example of the limitations of a highly centralised administrative system. To remedy this particular defect (overcentralisation) in this particular instance (housing transfer) requires not only decentralisation of decision-making (to, for example, the directorate of a more local subdivision of the ministry), but also a strengthening of the resource base of the local soviets. After all, the success of any housing transfer depends to a considerable extent on the ability of housing organisations to carry out repair work. Yet the soviets still lack the requisite material and technical base to meet this desideratum. In Saratov, which is not unique in this regard, the house-management sections do not even have premises for workshops; the most basic materials such as pipes, glass, paint and nails 'are allocated to us literally as crumbs (*po krokham*)'; even old hands in the house-building and repair trusts could not recall when they had last received, for example, radiators, boilers (the present ones have been in use for over 30 years – well above their intended life-times), water-supply fittings and toilet fixtures. The chairman of the Voroshilovgrad executive committee produced a similar catalogue of shortages which included: of 158 tons of bitumen requested, only 23 tons had been delivered and, of an equivalent of 3900 metres of central heating radiators requested, only 315 had been received. Related to this and associated with delivery difficulties, is the fact that 'equipment and spare parts for the housing economy are manufactured by thousands of enterprises belonging to a dozen ministries'.[68] In itself this need not be a problem – this lies elsewhere 'in the whole system of planning and supplying of equipment and fittings for housing'.[69]

At first sight the transfer of housing from one state body to another might be thought to be a straightforward book-keeping exercise. However, not only is the transfer itself beset with problems and complexities, but the factors and agencies involved have brought to prominence the inefficiency and inadequacy of the existing system of planning with its command structures, organisational linkages, and time-consuming procedures, which both regulate the powers of local authorities to take decisions on matters of purely local concern and also unnecessarily limit direct contacts between 'customers' for resources for the urban economy and 'suppliers'.

The paradox is that the extent to which the structural reform can be pursued is contingent upon the willingness and ability of those at the end of the planning and decision-making chain to assume greater responsibility. Yet local officials may be reluctant to show more 'initiative' given current wage structures, which do not take into consideration either the amount of housing being serviced or the quality of the management. For example, whereas the Voroshilovgrad soviet controls 2.5 million square metres of living space, and the Kommunarsk and Severdonetsk soviets oversee 429 000 and 471 800 square metres respectively, the salaries of the personnel involved in each operation are the same.[70]

Thus, in order to reduce the cost of the state housing sector without raising rental payments, research and policy on the housing (and urban) economy are moving along two paths: the first explores and seeks to change the formal, hierarchical and horizontal linkages between organisations and, the second 'studies the human factor in urban management' by examining 'the socio-demographic characteristics of personnel, their personal motivations and their value orientations to the population and their sensitivity to public opinion'.[71] Evidently the impact of psychology, social psychology, communication and information theory on Soviet urban studies is increasing, as the following quotation testifies:[72]

> One must take into account that in large cities, individuals are constantly perceiving and processing a large quantity of information and their interaction with the administrative system is characterised by a certain distancing and anonymity. That is why there is a growing interest in the social-psychological aspects of public participation in urban management – especially because these issues have not yet been studied by Soviet psychologists.

At the research level then, the social sciences are 'fragmenting' with the emergence of more specialised (sub-) disciplines, including management science which looks not only at the gamut of motivational factors influencing managers, but also how the latter interact with the managed and the amateur public participant (the 'activist'). This interest in public participation – a concept central to the socialist ethos – is a manifestation of the leadership's concern with 'a certain distancing and anonymity' that exists in so far as such attitudes or psychological states can be symptomatic of alienation from the political system at large. At the same time, larger housing management departments are being formed in the anticipation that these will become managerially more professional and also economically more efficient.These two tendencies reflect a tension or contradiction, common to all advanced industrial societies, between professionalism and dilettantism, and between centralisation and democratic control. As was mentioned in the Preface, the 'systemic choice' between centralisation (associated with 'the plan') and democratic control (associated with decentralisation) depends on political and ideological factors, as the following comparative example with recent changes in the Greater London Council's housing policy suggests.

At the height of its powers the GLC 'as one of the largest single landlords in the world' owned over 230 000 homes.[73] But the general policy hitherto accepted by both main political parties was fundamentally changed by the Conservative party after it came to power in 1977. The latter considered the GLC to be too large and remote and that the 32 London boroughs were the best size to undertake new house building and the management of the existing stock. Negotiations were then initiated by the GLC with the borough councils on the transfer of the GLC-controlled properties. The concept was accepted in principle by some Labour- and by all the Conservative-controlled local authorities, but the eight Inner London Labour-controlled councils rejected the proposal. The first major transfer involving 125 000 properties took place on 1 April 1980; because of the refusal of the Inner London boroughs to co-operate, the GLC turned to central government – with the result that the minister responsible issued an Order in Council requiring the transfer of their 53 000 properties on 1 April 1982. On completion of the transfer, in 1985, the GLC will be left with about 10 000 dwellings.

This abrupt change and rapid implementation of policy is more a consequence of compliance with political doctrine than of the pursuit of administrative efficiency, which might have been achieved through a partial decentralisation of control. One of the effects of this policy will be to increase the number of staff employed in housing management, which will, given political proclivities, have to be compensated for by rent increases.

It is also worth noting that studies undertaken by the Department of the Environment have demonstrated that the savings made by setting up local management offices on all housing estates with over 300 houses more than offset the cost of the local office. The reasons for this cost saving – a reduction in vandalism and the virtual elimination of empty units – are not to be found in the Soviet Union. Of greater comparability with Soviet developments is the finding that local councils in England which had decentralised their maintenance services as well as their management, had achieved even larger savings. One study revealed that neighbourhood repair teams were 57 per cent more productive than centrally controlled teams.[74]

The different housing management strategies being pursued in the two societies suggest the need for studies comparing the housing economies of, say, Moscow and London (and other large cities in both countries). At this point all that can be said is that for the Soviet Union, where anything like a rent increase sufficient to cover the cost of running and maintaining housing (let alone the costs of new construction) lies outside the boundaries of political options, the method chosen to reduce the size of the subsidy (or at least contain its growth) is greater administrative efficiency. And, this is to be achieved through the formation of larger management units.

The 'Departmental' Case

Despite all the well-reasoned arguments for transferring control over housing (and other objects of communal economy) to the city soviets, 'departments' continue to press their case for retaining control over 'their' housing. One argument repeatedly advanced by enterprises is the significant role played by housing in enabling them to fulfil their plan targets. Lack of housing appears to be one of the main causes of high labour turnover. The chairman of the Dnepropetrovsk city soviet executive committee cited sociological research conducted to examine the reasons for high labour mobility rates, and noted that only a small proportion of those changing jobs were 'drifters' and 'money-chasers'. The majority of people leaving one job for another were doing so for the first or second time in five years and, when they did, the primary reason for changing was undeniably the hope of finding better living conditions at the new job. Thus, if labour mobility is to be reduced, then according to this official the central objective of a city's long-run development plan must be to raise the standard of social amenity and housing provision of the more backward enterprises to that found in the advanced ones.[75]

A long article on the city of Omsk (1 044 000) entitled 'Town and Factory' described how a large new district had grown up around an oil-processing complex set up in 1955.[76] The various ministries involved in the project supplied houses, hospitals and polyclinics, sporting facilities, shops and restaurants for the local work force. Every year a large number of ministries and central departments applied to the city soviet for permission to erect new undertakings in the city. The request was quite understandable since 'the infrastructure and housing are already in existence here. . . . This last factor is especially important. The success of an enterprise is closely tied to the living conditions of its workers. Those enterprises which pay greater attention to the building of houses, cultural facilities and various services achieve higher rates of production and have the lowest rates of labour turnover'. This is forcefully illustrated by the low levels of output in Ul'yanovsk (485 000), where a newly opened shoe factory could only operate at half capacity in the leather-treating section and two-thirds capacity for shoe output. The principal reason advanced for this was the labour shortage. The article parabolically recounted how, although during the course of building the factory the city soviet had drawn the ministry's attention to the inadequacy of the financial resources being provided for housing and the social infrastructure, the ministry had taken no notice. As a result, the shortage of accommodation (and pre-school places) had served as a major impediment to labour recruitment.[77]

As might be expected, lack of housing and social amenities leading to high labour turnover is especially acutely felt in the 'frontier' towns in Siberia and the Far North. The town of Surgut, in the Tyumen' oblast'[78] which grew from 6000 inhabitants in 1959 to 34 000 in 1970 and 137 000 in 1981 was already in 1966 'stretching twelve kilometres along the banks of the Ob' river, built without plans and mainly of wooden houses'. With an average of only 2–3 square metres of dwelling area per person, only 50 school places per thousand population against the norm of 160, an inadequate water supply system and non-existent sewage disposal system, 80 per cent of families moving to the region left within a year.[79] Ten years later the same complaints were being raised. For although house-building in the region was taking place at double the national average rate, the average amount of living space per person was still 6 square metres and the norm for polyclinics had been only 32 per cent fulfilled; for schools and hospitals the figure was 50 per cent and for kindergartens, 33 per cent.[80] 'It would be wrong', wrote one correspondent, 'to think that people are attracted to these areas only by the high wage rates. These help in drawing them to the Priob'e but are in themselves not enough to keep them there – what does, in the main, is housing. If they do not receive a flat, the newcomers often leave for no higher wage coefficient can induce them to stay'.[81] Mr Brezhnev at the XXVI Party Congress in 1981 reiterated this point almost word for word: 'More often than not a person leaves Siberia not because the climate is harsh or the pay too little but because it is more difficult to obtain housing and to put a child in a kindergarten and because cultural centres are few and far between'.[82] The problem is indeed a serious one. A survey of 12 new communities in the Tyumen' revealed that 46 per cent of people leaving the region cited dissatisfaction with housing as one of their three main motives for migrating. 38 per cent gave the lack of availability of food and consumer goods and 35 per cent, cultural and everyday services, as the reason for their departure. Only 18 per cent mentioned wages and 17 per cent the climate.[83]

Because of its proximity to the Samotlor oil-field – which in the period 1971–75 contributed over 50 per cent of the oil extracted in Siberia – the town of Nizhnevartovsk grew from 16 000 people in 1970 to 76,000 in 1976, when it was estimated that if the town's population continued to grow at the existing rate, there could be less housing available per person in 1980 than at the time.[84] By the end of the decade, despite a concerted building programme, the director of one Chief Administration in the Tyumen' bemoaned the fact that of his organisation's 90 000 employees only one-third lived with their families in their own accommodation; the remainder were housed in hostels, caravans and in other people's flats.[85] No doubt the dual problem of labour supply and the cost of providing the infrastructure has been instrumental in the decision to increase the proportion of oil produced by fully automated fields to 85–90 per cent by 1985.[86] But yet, such is the housing situation that employers find difficulties in attracting and holding on to specialists. As a consequence, despite a high level of automation in the oil-field, the number of inactive wells has been rising.[87] In those towns where improvements in living conditions have occurred, as in the city of Rubtsovsk (158 000) in the Altai Territory, labour mobility declined from 28.3 per cent in 1966 to 16 per cent in 1976.[88] In the East Siberian town of Bratsk (population in 1959: 43 000; in 1981: 222 000) annual labour turnover stands at 14 per cent. When interviewed three-quarters of those leaving, most of whom are highly skilled and with five to seven years' experience, cited the impossibility of obtaining a flat as the main reason for their departure.[89] In order to counter this problem, at the end of 1979 the government issued a long decree on 'The further strengthening of labour discipline and reduction in labour turnover in the economy', noting in the preamble that 25 million labour days fewer were lost in 1978 than in 1970 and that during the same period labour turnover had declined from 21.2 per cent to 18.2 per cent.[90]

There can be little doubt that labour turnover is a cause for serious concern to Soviet planners. According to the 1970 Census, 13.9 million people changed their places of residence in the year 1968–69,[91] whilst during the ninth five-year plan 14–15 million people migrated each year,[92] with no more than 10–12 per cent of all migrants constituting part of planned and organised movement.[93] Even the more optimistic estimates on the extent to which the movement of labour takes place under the aegis of centralised organising agency do not put the figure higher than 20–25 per cent.[94] It is precisely because the migration rate (and by definition labour turnover) is not only high but also 'unorganised' or unplanned that considerable attention is paid to factors responsible for this phenomenon. Although, as already mentioned, press commentary in the main stresses housing and general living conditions as predominantly responsible for high mobility rates, researchers conducting more detailed studies on mobility tend to be divided on whether or not strong correlations exist between housing supply and mobility.[95] For example, Vilnius (503 000), where at the end of 1980 the per capita living space of 13.4 square metres was above the national average (13.0 square metres), also suffers from a labour shortage. So in order to recruit labour, Lithuanian Ministries have offered workers a variety of incentives including higher wages and the early provision of accommodation. However, particularly among the younger workers, labour turnover continues to increase. Similarly in the industrially developed Ukraine with its higher per capita earnings, 28 per cent of those changing jobs and their places of residence were doing so because they were dissatisfied with the housing situation and provision of social and cultural facilities. The implication of these findings is that even in cities and regions comparatively better off in terms of housing, the local population still feels itself to be suffering from an accommodation shortage.[96]

In other words, individual perceptions of relative deprivation and unfulfilled expectations may be just as likely to induce labour turnover as might the persistence of severe housing deprivation. This fact and other caveats notwithstanding, the overall tenor of the argument advanced by a number of commentators is that in order to achieve national economic and social objectives, including increased production through improved productivity rates, not only must more housing be built, but ministries and enterprises rather than local soviets must assume responsibility for providing accommodation. It is difficult to see how this role-relationship between ministries and local soviets can be wholly reversed. The devolution of economic decision-making to enterprise level, stemming from a decree of 1965, will make more (decentralised) resources available for house building. This decree, part of the package of economic reforms initiated in that year, stated that: 'in order to raise the material interestedness of the enterprise collective in the fulfilment of the enterprise plan, deductions can be made from profits for the improvement of the cultural and living conditions of its employees . . . Resources are to be spent on new technology, housing and cultural services, rest homes and sanatoria, personal bonuses and repairs to the housing stock'.[97] Furthermore, all newly-erected dwelling space commissioned by and employing resources from this so-called 'enterprise fund' are to be used solely for housing individuals included on a list drawn up by both the enterprise management and the shop floor committee. Other clauses in the decree allow enterprises to divert a proportion of the resources allocated by the central authorities for house building to the construction of pre-school facilities, which are also regarded as a way of attracting labour.[98] And then in 1979, enterprise managements were given the right to allocate a proportion of the incentive fund to partly repay bank loans on co-operative and 'private' homes of workers with over five years of service (or two years in the case of young people).[99]

The 1965 decree referred not only to the right of enterprises to allocate dwelling-space in housing built using their own profits, but to their right to distribute space in other accommodation under their control. This last point is very closely associated with what remains a thorny legal issue, namely, who has the right to allocate accommodation which has fallen vacant? An earlier decree of 21 September 1945 stipulated that ministries and central state organs had to transfer to the local soviets 10 per cent of dwelling space in their newly-built and restored buildings for allocation to demobilised members of the armed forces, war invalids and families of servicemen.[100] Since then, the government has issued a number of circulars, rulings and decrees specifying which organisations were exempted from this '10 per cent rule'[101] But because local soviets were deducting from enterprises newly erected dwelling space above the legally defined limit, the government found it necessary in 1970 to remind them that apart from the 10 per cent laid down in the 1945 decree they were only entitled to 6 per cent of newly erected space for people made homeless when their property was demolished and another 2 per cent for individuals servicing and running the housing stock.[102] Even this issue of 10 per cent, though, has not been definitely settled. For while some Soviet legal authorities consider that local soviets have a right to allocate this 10 per cent transferred to them each time the property falls vacant,[103] others have pointed out that there is nothing to suggest that space is allocated on a permanent basis; when departmental accommodation allocated to someone under an order of the local soviet falls vacant, then it reverts back to the original departmental owner.[104] However, a Ruling by the Presidium of the Supreme Court RSFSR in 1971 has tipped the balance of the case in favour of the local soviet possessing the right to reallocate the accommodation when it falls vacant.[105]

None the less, the issue cannot be considered closed: the transfer of housing to the local soviet is one thing, the right to allocate or at least to participate in the allocation, is another. For instance, in Sumgait (201 000) all newly-erected housing is handed over to the local soviet which takes responsibility for managing the city's total housing stock. However, the right to reallocate accommodation already leased to workers of a particular enterprise is reserved for that factory.[106] Sometimes industrial enterprises, supported by their administrative superiors and also by appeals and complaints from their workforce, are led to make claims on the local soviets to be allowed to retain for their own use that part of the housing stock built using the enterprise's resources.[107] (Interestingly it is not only housing which is reserved in this fashion. When pre-school places fall vacant they too have to be reallocated in the first instance to children of workers in the enterprise which has contributed funds for this purpose.[108]) The situation in Vilnius is somewhat different. A rationalisation of the design of housing estates and their construction has been achieved by creating one client (the *gorispolkom*), one housing planning office (Institute for the Planning of Urban Construction) and one general contractor (a residential construction combine (*domostroitel'nyi kombinat*)). Enterprises transfer to the Executive Committee all funds allocated for house construction and then 'a short time later pick up the keys to the newly built flats'.[109] Clearly such organisational innovations, allegedly improving the whole planning, construction and management process, do not affect the enterprises' housing domain.

As long as industrial enterprises continue to have considerable resources for housing construction and the provision of ancillary services channelled through them, they will probably only consent to the soviets administering 'their' housing provided that they retain a substantial say in its distribution.[110] The housing may be seen to be 'theirs' not only because resources are channelled through them but also because a proportion of new house-building is directly financed from the surplus produced in the individual enterprise. In fact, 'one of the features of building during the period 1966–1970 has been the increase in the volume of house-construction undertaken using the resources of enterprises and organisations. The plan for 1966–70 envisaged that the amount of living space being financed from this source would be 2.8 times greater than in the previous five-year period'.[111]

Any examination of housing policy has to bear in mind the two important precepts which underlie Soviet housing policy: firstly housing, a much sought-after good in short supply, is offered by some of those who control it as an inducement to attract and hold labour; secondly, a person's accommodation need is not seen by the Soviet government as independent of that person's contribution to society. Khrushchev made this quite clear in a 1957 statement: 'In building and allocating dwellings, we must not simply think – because a man is alive, give him a good apartment. You have to take a look at what he is doing, what he is giving to society. In our socialist society, each must give something to the general welfare of the people, each must carry a certain load. Only then does he get the right to use the fruits of his labour which are created by society'.[112] This precept was reiterated a decade later by one writer who regarded the state housing stock as being created by the labour of the whole society and distributed like other material wealth – 'according to his work'. This principle, he maintained, combines in the best possible fashion the interests of the individual and the collective and serves as a powerful stimulus to the growth of production.[113] However, this principle does not always operate in practice.[114] Stated as boldly as this, with housing treated as a reward for work, there would appear on the surface to be good reason for not transferring control from the enterprises to the soviets. And it is because managers of the departmental stock fear they will lose their right to reallocate dwellings when they fall vacant that they are reluctant to surrender their control over housing.

Although the relationship between local soviets and the industrial sector is changing as a consequence of structural changes in the society, there is no reason to believe that the claims made in 1964 by the First Secretary of the Khabarovsk *gorkom* and the chairman of the city's *gorispolkom*, that the present system of housing distribution is unjust, are no longer valid. The major social disadvantage of allowing enterprises to determine who should have new housing was, according to these officials, that an enterprise's definition of which individuals found themselves in most need did not necessarily mean those still living in barrack accommodation. As a result of enterprise managements sending pleading letters to *Gosplan* (no doubt justifying their claims for more housing in terms of the beneficial impact more housing will have on production) they sometimes 'receive for each employee many times more living space than, for example, teachers, doctors and other categories of workers'.[115] The officials, acknowledging as justifiable the principle of offering rewards to certain workers in the form of higher wages, bonuses, holidays etc., were adamant that housing should not be part of the reward structure. In order to lend force to their case they quoted the 1961 Party Programme which stated that 'during the first decade of the building of communism (1961–70) the housing shortage will be eliminated, with those families still living in overcrowded and poor housing receiving new flats',[116] adding that the decade was wearing on so new flats must first of all be allocated to those in the worst housing conditions.

Their article clearly illustrates the different interests represented by local soviets and enterprises: the former regard housing as a social asset to be distributed according to need (in a sense to those who are weak in the economic market place), whilst the enterprise treats it as a reward or inducement. It is tempting, though not necessarily correct, to simplify and polarise these two institutional groups and see the enterprises as expressing the socialist maxim 'from each according to his ability, to each according to his work', and local soviets the communist maxim 'from each according to his ability, to each according to his need'.

THE BROADER CONTEXT OF THE LOCAL SOVIET–DEPARTMENT INSTITUTIONAL CONFLICT

The press continues to carry a steady stream of articles and commentaries blaming the parochial attitudes held by enterprise managements for the slow transfer of housing to local soviets. The lack of attention paid by the former to maintaining their properties has meant their falling into an increasing state of disrepair.[117] Another subject of complaint is the poor quality of workmanship; in Kemerovo (486 000) for example, during the last few years not a single block of flats has been rated 'excellent' by the body responsible for commissioning them. This was attributed to the fact that there were too many clients with the results that men, materials and equipment were distributed among an excessive number of unco-ordinated projects.[118] Time and again the call has been for the setting up of 'one client' as in, for instance, Vilnius.[119] But even in this city, although departmental tendencies have been overcome in house building, they continue to flourish in the provision of public utilities, cinemas, libraries, social centres and medical facilities.[120] This problem which represents a broad institutional conflict is not confined within a spatial object, the city.

In the case of vast tracts of Siberia no coherent planning strategy exists for the development of the region's mineral wealth and energy sources. No single planning agency has powers to oversee, for example, the development of the Nizhnevartovsk oil-mining complex. In 1976 a *Pravda* correspondent reported that, when questioned, ministerial and departmental executives and senior Party and economic officials both in Moscow and in Tyumen' were unanimous in their opinion that the West Siberian mining complex needed a wider, more uniform and centralised programme for housing and the provision of a range of socio-cultural services.[121] The Secretary of the Krasnoyarsk *krai* Party committee went a stage further, averring that the Angara complex was not an independent object of long-range planning at all. Although it is referred to as a 'complex', each industrial sector compiles its own development plan objectives without being supervised or constrained by some overall co-ordinating authority.

What is happening in Angarsk is being replicated in many ways in other parts of the country presently being industrialised. The example of Surgut of the mid-1960s, cited above, finds its mid-1970s equivalent in Lesosibirsk whose population of 50 000 inhabitants sprawls along 30 km of the Yenisei river without any organised network of underground utility lines.[122] Moreover this chaotic system of urban development is not confined to Siberia and the Far North. Apart from Moscow, Leningrad and a few other major centres, cities have not been regarded as independent objects of economic planning. This is primarily because of the dominant role played in a city's development by ministries and departments whose subordinate enterprises seek to provide their own accommodation by building spatially separate settlements alongside their factories, with the largest industrial enterprises sometimes running their own tramways as in Nizhnii Tagil (404 000). In fact, of the 68 cities in the RSFSR with tramways, in 13 of them they belonged to industrial enterprises.[123] The industrial city of Novokuznetsk (551 000) has been built by 30 separate government departments, each of which has followed the dictates of its needs. Furthermore, 4 000 enterprises have their own water conduits with a daily capacity of 20.2 million cubic metres; 2 660 enterprises 'own' their sewerage systems; 1 966 enterprises run 2 695 hotels with over 100 000 beds. In all these cases, their overall economic efficiency is lower than that found in local soviet-run concerns.[124]

As a result of this pattern of investment control, the parallels with the 1930s are startling, especially where industrial managers continue the autarchic policies of an earlier generation. In seeking to develop their own 'natural economies' they render almost impossible the co-ordination of land use, infrastructure and sector planning.[125] And, as in the 1930s, there are those writers who, whilst critical of the waste and misuse of resources, recite laws in order to demonstrate the powers already available to local soviets. They then criticise the soviets for failing to take a determined stand against large industrial enterprises, either to prevent them from contravening aspects of the city's development plan in the first place or to take requisite action after violations of regulations have occurred. Others argue that the soviets' rights are still too limited for them to be able to face ministries; only when all funds earmarked for housing and municipal services are in the hands of the local soviets, and when the ministries divest themselves of responsibility for these non-productive sectors (and direct their energies to improving the quality of their products etc.), will the city be developed as an integral whole in the interests of all its inhabitants. Despite the legislative changes of recent years, soviets still have little control over the plans and performance of factories on whose profits municipal budgets depend and over the construction of housing and other services operated by industrial enterprises.[126] So one can only accept with qualification the statement made at the XXVI Party Congress in February 1981, that 'the local soviets are increasingly coordinating and controlling the work of enterprises and organisations on their territory'.[127]

Although the issue of building maintenance alone presents a strong justification for the transfer of departmental housing into the administrative jurisdiction of the local soviets, it is not only housing which is at stake, for 'in general, the development of the urban communal economy lags behind even the rate of housing construction'.[128] The reason for this is not unfamiliar; enterprises neither erect nor provide new 'objects of collective consumption' nor do they maintain those they already control.[129] Even in the nation's capital, 'considerable disproportions continue to exist in the construction of accommodation and related public facilities'. One correspondent, highly critical of the fact that throughout the city over 400 servicing facilities (dining rooms, shops, cinemas, clubs, laundries etc) were not yet ready for use, attributed this state of affairs to 'the absence of a single, comprehensive plan for financing, designing and erecting buildings in Moscow'.[130] Such disproportions are not, however, unique to Moscow or other Soviet cities. Even before the cuts in public expenditure in Britain, which began in earnest in the latter part of the 1970s, in Crawley New Town (England) – to quote just one example – the erection of two permanent community centres had to be deferred for two years because of financial restrictions.[131] In general, however, the low priority accorded to non-production activities by the departmental sector, in conjunction with the small-scale nature of many of their projects, leads to duplication, inefficiency and an overall lack of co-ordination which makes administrative reorganisation a functional imperative for the system.

The government and planning authorities are fully aware of the tensions and conflicts between and within organisational structures, which are conceptualised as representing 'general state' and 'local' interests respectively. In order to find a means of reconciling these needs and interests, a system of *dual subordination* has been devised whereby departments of urban administration (for example, the parks' department, housing department) are responsible on the one hand to the 'centre' (in the form of the corresponding department of the oblast' executive committee or the ministry) and, on the other, to 'territorial bodies' (in the form of the executive committee of local soviets). This administrative mechanism of dual subordination is regarded as a useful device in so far as it is difficult, in theory and practice, to define clearly and precisely the boundary between those 'objects' which are the proper concern of territorial administration and those which are controlled along branch or functional lines. (The advantages of the so-called branch principle allegedly are that it ensures a unified policy throughout the branch and the balanced development of all branches throughout the economy). The key problem is in trying to combine these two 'forces' in the best way possible.[132] Of course, not all 'objects' have equal status in the eyes of planners and are for the most part grouped into two categories. The first refers to enterprises and organisations whose production and customers are determined 'vertically' by central agencies. Since these come within the jurisdiction of All-Union and republican organisations, city authorities only have the legal right to influence their activities within well-defined parameters. As to the second group of 'objects', the centre ('vertically') restricts its authority to specifying, for example, the general principles of 'socialist production and the rules of economic and labour law' and to issues affecting further technological development as defined by the policy for that particular branch. All other matters concerning the functioning and development of these enterprises – including the drawing up of production and economic plans – are dealt with by local administrative bodies; in other words, objects in this second category are organised 'horizontally'.

However, relations between soviets at different levels are themselves fraught with tension. In cities which are of oblast' subordination, such as Murmansk, Pskov, Novgorod, Yaroslavl', Vologda, Kaluga and Kostroma (all with populations ranging from 180 000 to over 600 000), local industry, urban transport, communications, daily service undertakings, public eating places, water and electricity supply and a variety of other services forming part of the urban economy, together with control over the distribution and use of labour, have all been transferred from the city to the oblast' executive committee.[133] (see p. 55). Soviet researchers conclude that from the evidence available there are no clearly defined criteria for subordinating enterprises and organisations to different administrative levels – although it would seem that the inadequacy of financial, material and labour resources at the disposal of the city managers is a prime determining factor.

The fact that the city may not have its own transport office (as in Murmansk) of daily services department (as in Novgorod), for example, and that it is unable to redistribute resources to those sectors which the *gorispolkom* regards as more important, has given rise to a complex of time-consuming organisational structures which have to reconcile the needs and interests of the town with those of the oblast' authorities.[134] And the reason why a town might be lacking this or that department lies in the fact that existing legislation, perhaps understandably, does not prescribe a binding list of offices or directorates to be included in any local government structure. Instead, the decision on what departments to create is left to the local soviets themselves. This, in turn, begs the question – why do city soviets not furnish their executive committees with a full complement of offices to cover the whole range of services that make up the urban economy? The answer, which a student of British local government might have expected, is that there are financial limits on what local soviets are permitted to spend on administration. Unfortunately these limits frequently fail to be raised in conjunction with expansions in the range of tasks that large and rapidly growing cities have to perform. Indeed, since the population of a number of large cities has doubled over the last decade and yet the number of employees in the *gorispolkom* has remained constant, the consequence has been to overload the present staff, the majority of whom have to work overtime. Possibly because of this, city soviet departments still have restricted legal authority to manage their affairs. For instance, the department of trade (*otdel torgovli*) of the Yaroslavl' *gorispolkom* has limited powers over the type and location of shops; in fact, it is only empowered to set their working hours, supervise the observance of trading regulations and carry out the day-to-day administration of the network of retailing and other trading enterprises. As a result of this limited competence, the population suffers because the oblast' organisations 'are not in a position to know the real demands for services' at the neighbourhood level.[135]

Urban government might well become more responsive to local needs and become more efficient if some of the resources and power at present lodged with the oblast' authorities were transferred to them. They would also benefit from divesting themselves of a whole variety of mundane daily tasks which could be undertaken solely by borough (*raion*) soviets. (Towns are divided into districts (boroughs) each with its own local soviet when the population reaches 200 000.) These would include, for instance, decisions on the sale or decoration of a house or garage, the demolition of a house, reducing or abolishing altogether maintenance payments for children attending boarding schools or opening an extra class in one of these schools, and a whole array of decisions relating to the allocation of housing space to 'young specialists', war veterans or retired members of the armed forces.[136] In fact, matters such as these need not even be the concern of the executive committee of the city or district soviet: is it truly necessary to have a collective discussion at a session of the city council on child adoptions, the appointment of guardians or the payment of compensation to someone who, through urban redevelopment, has lost their garden – questions which comprise about one half of the total dealt with by the soviets and which could be left to the relevant local government departments?[137]

CONCLUSION

The relationship between the two institutional complexes discussed in this chapter is defined by the contradictory demands which emerge and are associated with industrial society. At a particular stage in the society's development the conflict of interests between these complexes seems to be almost irreconcilable, since the complex concerned with expanding the sphere of collective consumption is wholly dependent on the other which is developing the means by which the objects of consumption can be produced. The formal rejection in the Soviet Union of private ownership of the means of production initially created a tendency for those possessing a set of property rights in the productive sphere to extend their range of activities to embrace the production (and maintenance) of objects of collective consumption in order to ensure the reproduction of their labour needs. During the 1920s and 1930s there was no reason for individual units within the industrial sector to surrender their property rights over housing and services to another institutional complex, namely, the local soviets. If there had been a case for doing so, then it would have to be proven that in Stalin's Russia of the 1930s the Party could not, even though it wanted to, make the soviets 'masters of the city'. This would be a difficult task since the party permeates all institutions and at any Party organisational level (city, region) it represents the points of view of, among others, Chairmen of local soviets and directors of the most important enterprises.

Without going into detail, this point needs a little elaboration. The activities of all state administrative agencies take place under the auspices of the Communist Party, which has its own 'apparatus' coincident with every level of government and administration. Its power to operate effectively in government is enhanced by the interlacing of government and Party personnel. At the very apex of local government stands the chairman of the executive committee of a city soviet, who is invariably a member of the city Party committee (*gorkom*). At the city level, the fact that Party cells are formed in municipal and industrial bodies means that the Party is able to co-ordinate the activities of a diverse range of organisations and institutions and to resolve conflicts between them without the case being referred to superior authorities for a final decision.[138]

In other words, the case of the local soviets have every chance of being expressed and heard within the Party. If the arguments of local soviets are beginning to prevail it is because the point has been reached when it is necessary to supplement verbal genuflection to the slogan of 'all power to the soviets' by actually transferring resources to the latter. And it has become necessary either on account of the enhanced influence of what might be designated the soviet-Party group, or because the industry-Party group now believes that maintaining its property rights is of diminishing importance to the (short or long term) interests of industry. If the first is correct, the implication is that the local soviets are a social and political force independent of and standing against industry whenever the latter violate certain presumptions on the nature of socialist society. The second implies that the increased property rights accruing to local soviets have been granted to them by industry which regards the transfer of resources (rights) and accompanying administrative responsibilities as advantageous from its own point of view. Enterprises are coming to recognise that they stand to gain economically from the more co-ordinated spatial planning policy which local soviets could implement if they controlled these resources. This is a more likely interpretation for, as Vladimir Anderle and others have noted, enterprise managers have greater opportunity than most other occupational and sectional groups to articulate their interests and, moreover, have the advantage of direct access to Party and government officials. In other words, it will be their wishes which will normally prevail.[139]. The declaration made at the 1981 Party Congress – to the effect that Party organisations should firmly implement the Party line and not take their cue from enterprise managements when the latter are in the wrong – is unlikely to have a great impact.[140]

At present, then, the situation may be summarised as follows: the overwhelming majority of enterprises not under the control of the local soviets are unwilling to relinquish their title to the infrastructure. Sometimes this reticence on their part concerns only specific objects, sometimes large parts of the social and technical infrastructure. To some extent, the enterprise directorates evince a certain 'individualism' in wishing to maintain their independent right to dispose of their 'assets'. This applies particularly to enterprises possessing substantial property rights, particularly in the housing sphere, and to those who exercise these rights to attract and hold on to labour. From the point of view of the city soviets, they themselves are not always able to receive on to their books various components of the infrastructure, primarily because they simply lack the resources to do so – especially when compared with the equipment, personnel, materials and workshops at the disposal of the larger enterprises. Lastly, the growing scale of operations of enterprises and organisations comprising the infrastructure means that their 'markets' or catchment areas are no longer confined within the town boundaries and hence become integrated into the administrative apparatus of the oblast'.

The factors involved in the transfer are highly complex; there is evidence of indecisiveness, inertia and fear on the part of some senior officials in the local soviets to take on a vastly expanded administrative responsibility. In most cases, they are unqualified, lacking the professional managerial training which would enable them to undertake the organisation and operation of such a composite entity as the modern city.[141]

An important question remains: is this albeit slow movement towards concentrating control over housing (and other resources constituting the municipal economy) in the hands of the local soviet a move towards the achievement of an ideologically defined objective – is it an end in itself? Or, is it motivated by purely practical economic, cost-saving considerations? For not a few people the local soviets, with their historical association with workers' control and a new form of democratic state, retain their romantic aura. From this perspective, it is possible to discern in the renewed attention being accorded by the government to the local soviets, which were born in revolution and interred in the 'Thermidor', a revitalisation of the society's moribund political culture. There can be little doubt that the legislation, dealing with housing and the role of the local soviets in providing and maintaining it (1957, 1967, 1978), and the decrees of 1971 concerned with enhancing the general prerogatives, duties and funds of the soviets, will be seen in the future as milestones in the emergence of more autonomous local governments. At present however, the powers of the local soviets remain closely circumscribed and the movement that we are witnessing has to be seen more prosaically as an attempt to 'properly run, preserve and extend the life span of housing – one of the nation's principal assets'.[142]

4 The House-building Co-operative

In the aftermath of Stalin's death, modifications to the goals and *modus operandi* of the system that had evolved under his leadership were inevitable. Although by 1953 the output of consumer goods and services were beginning to increase, more drastic improvements were necessary. Stalin's successors realised that their goals could be effectively achieved by using means which did not entail compromising the ideological presuppositions on which the whole state apparatus was founded. One need, whether articulated or not, was acknowledged by everyone in the society – the desire by all for better accommodation. The government responded and investment in housing as a proportion of total capital investment in the country at large rose. In order to build more houses, the government continued to stress the necessity of industrialising construction techniques. At the same time, it was compelled to utilise the 'financial and material resources' of the population, thereby sanctioning the continuing contribution of the private sector. Both these aspects of the response were pragmatic and realistic; to mechanise, modernise and rationalise the production of dwelling-units had long been the goal of the Soviet government. It was equally reasonable to rely on a contribution from individuals.

The July 1957 decree, in proclaiming the intention of eliminating the housing shortage within ten to twelve years, and in revising the house construction programme upwards, prepared the ground for re-establishing the house-building co-operative as a tenure form. The decree itself made no mention of the co-operative, but chastised local soviets and heads of enterprises and institutions for not 'organising builders into house-building collectives (*kollektivy*)'.[1] The collective, it has to be stressed, is completely different from the co-operative (*kooperativ*), although Western authors do sometimes confuse the two.[2] In contrast to house-building co-operatives, which are regarded as part of the socialised housing sector, houses and flats belonging to collectives are included in the private housing stock. This means that the house-building collective, which represents an association of individual builders, does not constitute a specific property form known as co-operative ownership (*kooperativnaya sobstvennost'*), for each member of the collective acquires a *right of personal ownership* to a flat in a building consisting of a number of flats, or to a separate house.

The collective was none the less a first step away from the unadulterated individualism of the private sector, encouraging individuals to join together to provide mutual assistance for meeting their accommodation needs. But, whilst it was intended to serve a political and moral educative function by demonstrating the advantages of collective activity, its major drawback lay in its property form. The absence of any reference in the 1957 decree recommending the formation of co-operatives was rectified less than a year later when the government announced that co-operative building activity could parallel the work being carried out by individual builders.[3] The significance of this lies in its resuscitating and giving a preliminary stamp of approval to a form of housing tenure whose demise prior to the outbreak of war has been referred to earlier. However, in practice, individual (private) builders continued to receive preferential treatment over the co-operative; the former were granted credit for a seven- to ten-year period, whereas co-operative members remained deprived of any state assistance, having to deposit the full cost of construction in the bank before they could start building. As a result of the financial unattractiveness of the co-operative form, the 1958 decree failed to attract an influx of would-be co-operative members.

This impediment to *ZhSK* formation gave rise to a discussion in Soviet legal journals and elsewhere on the need to stimulate co-operatives, primarily by granting them long-term credit.[4] Since the State was not prepared to take upon its shoulders the full burden of providing accommodation it had to adopt measures to encourage people to spend a larger proportion of their income and savings on meeting their housing needs. The outcome was a decision taken at the XXII Party Congress (1961)[5] and the issuing in June 1962 of a decree 'On Individual and Co-operative Housing Construction'. According to this new legislation, co-operatives could receive state loans covering up to 60 per cent of the estimated cost of construction, repayable over a 10 to 15 year period.[6] Just two years later, a decree of November 1964 'On Further Development of Co-operative Housing Construction' introduced a number of amendments.[7] Co-operatives could now also be set up on state farms and in rural areas, instead of being restricted to capitals of Union and Autonomous Republics, *krai* and *oblast'* centres and other smaller urban settlements, so long as these places possessed the necessary building materials and other requisite resources. It also increased the credit facility from 60 to 70 per cent in rural areas, the Far North, Kazakhstan and 'other remote areas' and at the same time extended the repayment period to 20 years. The loan bears an annual interest charge of 0.5 per cent.[8] Although the government had come to accept the principle of co-operatives and to accept that when private, wooden dwellings were demolished they should be replaced by co-operatively owned multi-apartment buildings, they resisted suggestions that the initial deposit be reduced from 40 per cent to 20 or 25 per cent, or that the repayment period be extended up to 25 years.[9] 18 years later, in August 1982, the government accepted the suggestions by allowing the initial deposit to be reduced to 30 per cent of the estimated construction cost for the country at large, and to 20 per cent for Kazakhstan, Siberia, the Far East, the Far North and 'similar regions'. The repayment period for these 70 and 80 per cent loans has also been extended to 25 years.[10]

In urban areas the basic criterion for setting up a co-operative, which may consist of a number of blocks of flats, some even in different parts of the city, is that there should be as many potential members as there are flats in the standard block. Restrictions on the numerical composition of co-operatives vary; the Ukraine places no restrictions, the RSFSR requires that a co-operative should have no fewer than 60 members in Moscow and Leningrad, 48 members in *oblast'* centres and other cities with over 100 000 inhabitants, and 24 in other towns and settlements.[11] Since the authorities envisage that co-operative houses should be multi-storey blocks of five or more floors, with up to 300 flats, clearly the number of shareholders will normally exceed the required minimum membership. Moreover, the co-operative has a positive interest in increasing the number of members, for this lowers the contribution which each member has to make to the running and upkeep of the building.[12]

The *ZhSK* may be organised either at the work-place or in the district of residence or intended residence. A group of individuals wanting to form a co-operative approach the housing department either of the local soviet or of the enterprise (institution), which then convokes a general meeting of the applicants. A list of all prospective members and their families who will live with them in the co-operative is sent to the *gorispolkom* for examination. After each individual applicant's tenant's book, containing details of his existing living conditions, has been checked and the local housing department has issued a certificate confirming the authenticity of the application form, another general meeting of members is held for the purpose of drawing up the co-operative's charter which, when completed, is registered with the local soviet. From the moment of registration, the *ZhSK* becomes a juridical person: a symbol of this status is the possession of property. Thus, houses built by the *ZhSK* belong to the co-operative 'as a right of co-operative property'. This means that it has the exclusive right of disposing of the property belonging to it. In other words, members of the co-operative do not acquire a 'right of personal property' to the co-operative, but a right, corresponding to their share, to the ownership and use of specific parts of the property. The body of rights accruing to a co-operative member differ from the rights of personal property provided by Article 25 of the Principles of Civil Law (USSR). Legally speaking, since the co-operative member does not possess the right of ownership to a flat, he cannot sell it, give it away as a gift or bequeath it. The right of disposal is lodged with the highest administrative body, namely, the *general assembly* of the co-operative membership. In fact, an indicator of the legal vagueness and ambiguity of certain issues affecting members is that the right of former family members to continue using space in the co-operative on the dissolution of family relations has not been defined. As a consequence, 'family members of a co-operative shareholder find themselves in an unequal position compared with the family members of a tenant in a state owned flat'.[13]

Where a co-operative has more than 100 members, the general meeting of all the members is replaced by a meeting of delegates elected by at least two-thirds of all members for a two-year period. A general or delegates' meeting has to be convoked at least twice a year and extraordinary meetings can be summoned at the request of one-third of the membership. The meeting elects an executive governing body with a minimum number of three and an unspecified maximum depending, *inter alia*, on the floor space and number of shareholders. In order to 'promote the election to the leading organ of individuals who, by their actions and political qualities, are capable of ensuring the fulfilment of the social obligations placed upon them', potential members of the governing body are selected in the first instance by the *gorispolkom* and 'presented' to the general meeting.[14] Although all members of the governing body are unpaid functionaries, the general meeting may decide to award its members a bonus or prize for their 'good work'. The award should not, however, become a regular feature for it would then be converted into a scantily veiled form of salary; in fact, the bonus received by the chairman of the governing body must not exceed the monthly salary paid to a housing manager in the state sector.[15]

The governing body is assisted in its work by a number of public committees (*obshchestvennye komissiya*), regarded as manifestations of the principle of self-government. This aspect of the co-operative is reminiscent of its 1920s antecedent. Of far greater importance than these committees is the auditing commission whose three members, again chosen by the *gorispolkom* and usually selected for their knowledge of accounting, are responsible for supervising and auditing the work of the governing body from which, by its very nature, it has to be independent. The functions of the executive governing body, auditing committee and general meeting are extensive and in many respects the co-operative does operate as a self-governing entity. This does not mean, however, that 'it falls outside the state leadership and supervision', a function fulfilled by the *gorispolkom*.[16]

The supervisory role of the *gorispolkom* does not differ in substance from that played by English local authorities, which also have to ensure that by-laws are not infringed by organisations (including housing associations) operating within their administrative jurisdiction. Depending on the specific legal form of the housing co-operative in England,[17] differences in the exercise of power by local soviets and by English local authorities are essentially ones of degree. Suffice it to say that there are English parallels with the Soviet practice of allowing the *gorispolkom* to vet applicants for membership of the co-operative, to appoint officials to the co-operative's administrative staff and to recommend the expulsion of members from the co-operative and from the governing body and auditing committee. Similarly, a dispute over a flat exchange, with a co-operative member wanting to live elsewhere, and the co-operative general meeting having to agree to accept as a member the other party to the exchange, becomes a matter for the courts to decide when the *gorispolkom* has refused permission for the exchange to take place.[18]

The government has established certain minimum conditions for applicants wishing to join a co-operative and so not everybody is eligible for membership. Normally, they must be registered with the police as a permanent resident in the district where the co-operative is being formed.[19] The principal criterion for offering a place in a *ZhSK* is that the applicant's living space falls below the average amount of living space found in that locality. Since large numbers of people find themselves in this situation and, since co-operative membership is regarded as a privilege, other factors are taken into account when the *gorispolkom* examines the list of potential members submitted to it. Preference is given to certain groups. Those living in private houses subject to demolition as a consequence of urban planning policy and choosing monetary compensation instead of state accommodation, do not have to join a waiting list for *ZhSK* membership.[20] Other groups to which preference is given include: young specialists who on graduation are given specific work assignments and for whom their employers or local soviets have to find accommodation; those on municipal or departmental housing lists;[21] young workers living in hostels or as tenants in the private sector;[22] war invalids, family members of those killed during the war, families with three or more children, people living in basements and dilapidated houses and barracks which are unsuitable for modernisation, heroes of the Soviet Union and heroes of Socialist labour;[23] people who have worked for a long time (normally a minimum of 10 years) in the Far North and other equally inaccessible (and inhospitable) areas;[24] generals, admirals and officers in the armed forces (and officers of the same ranking in the KGB) who have volunteered to prolong their period of service and who have served abroad, in the Far North (and other comparable regions), in garrison towns away from the large cities.

This is little more than an outline of the ground rules. Those given preferential treatment reflect the general social ethos of Soviet society, namely one which is essentially meritocratic whilst protecting the weak. It rewards those whom it deems to have 'sacrificed' by working (or serving) in harsh climatic conditions where, moreover, cultural and living standards are lower than in the industrialised European parts of the Soviet Union,[25] and also those whose past efforts have been recognised by some honorific rewards. It also seeks to provide for those who, through no fault of their own, have become disadvantaged: invalids and people whose houses are to be demolished or are beyond repair. Although this is a reasonably accurate description of the broad parameters of social policy, especially those defining the allocation of accommodation, it may be a misleading representation of reality. Apart from the problem of defining 'meritocratic' and the associated vexing issue of the 'validity' of the criteria used in ranking different occupations in a social hierarchy, there is the fact that those who are well rewarded financially and given preferential opportunity to join co-operatives (because they have worked under arduous conditions), may choose not to become members of the *ZhSK*. Then again, citizens

TABLE 4.1 Housing space constructed by house-building co-operatives, by republic, 1963–1975 (thousand square metres of overall (useful) living space)

Republic	Year														
	1963	1964	1965	1966	1967	1968	1969	1970	1971	1972	1973	1974	1975	1966–70	1971–5
USSR	1864	4791	6513	6743	6538	6442	6245	7711	6858	6459	7088	6294	5798	33679	32497
RSFSR	1277	3493	4487	4505	4222	4196	3945	4785	4039	3580	3862	3345	3142	21653	17968
Ukraine	286	659	916	1141	1093	1108	1235	1496	1413	1418	1542	1478	1307	6073	7158
Belorussia	89	154	288	285	316	302	287	388	408	461	435	393	344	1578	2041
Uzbekistan	9	43	89	90	96	67	40	58	74	41	72	74	55	351	316
Kazakhstan	35	64	118	129	115	109	110	114	108	109	146	90	107	577	560
Georgia	34	103	87	111	134	85	113	192	105	187	211	186	171	635	860
Azerbaidzhan	—	23	65	49	65	66	13	35	42	13	32	66	53	228	206
Lithuania	54	94	158	170	191	153	208	280	261	271	299	243	238	1002	1312
Moldavia	17	38	46	57	85	66	61	83	83	90	96	94	84	352	447
Latvia	23	49	75	95	87	77	73	84	74	68	91	94	87	416	414
Kirgizia	8	14	23	18	18	38	21	44	48	46	53	35	28	139	210
Tadzhikstan	3	1	19	4	26	19	12	31	22	27	50	38	32	92	169
Armenia	—	26	96	46	37	90	68	51	97	71	103	92	73	292	436
Turkmenia	—	0.4	1	2	3	4	1	3	5	5	12	1	10	13	33
Estonia	5	30	45	41	50	62	58	67	79	72	84	65	67	278	367

SOURCES
1963–1967: Narodnoe khozyaistvo SSSR v 1967g. p. 681.
1968–1969: Narodnoe khozyaistvo SSSR v 1969g. p. 567.
1970–1975: Narodnoe khozyaistvo SSSR v 1975g. p. 575.

TABLE 4.2 Housing space constructed in towns and rural places excluding collective farms, by republic, 1963–1975 (million square metres of overall (useful) living space)

Republic	Year														
	1963	1964	1965	1966	1967	1968	1969	1970	1971	1972	1973	1974	1975	1966–70	1971–5
USSR	79.3	75.1	79.3	81.8	84.3	83.5	86.1	89.6	91.7	91.9	96.1	96.0	95.9	425.3	471.6
RSFSR	47.8	45.4	47.5	48.4	49.4	49.5	51.4	53.0	54.1	54.7	56.5	56.8	56.9	251.7	279.0
Ukraine	13.9	12.8	13.4	13.9	13.8	13.4	14.4	14.4	14.7	14.9	15.8	16.2	16.1	69.9	77.7
Belorussia	2.3	2.2	2.5	2.7	2.9	3.1	3.2	3.4	3.5	3.5	3.9	3.7	3.6	15.3	18.2
Uzbekistan	1.8	2.1	2.3	3.1	3.6	3.4	3.5	3.4	3.7	3.4	3.4	3.3	3.5	17.0	17.3
Kazakhstan	6.1	5.3	5.8	5.6	6.0	5.6	5.0	5.6	5.6	5.5	5.9	5.8	5.7	27.8	28.5
Georgia	1.2	1.0	1.1	1.2	1.3	1.1	1.2	1.4	1.2	1.4	1.6	1.5	1.4	6.2	7.1
Azerbaidzhan	1.2	1.1	1.2	1.2	1.1	1.2	0.8	1.0	1.2	0.9	1.0	1.1	1.3	5.3	5.5
Lithuania	0.9	0.9	1.0	1.1	1.1	1.2	1.4	1.5	1.5	1.6	1.6	1.5	1.6	6.3	7.8
Moldavia	0.6	0.6	0.6	0.7	0.8	0.8	0.7	0.9	1.0	1.0	1.2	1.1	1.0	3.9	5.3
Latvia	0.7	0.7	0.7	0.8	0.8	0.8	0.8	0.9	0.9	0.9	1.0	1.0	1.0	4.1	4.8
Kirgizia	0.6	0.6	0.7	0.7	0.8	0.8	0.8	0.8	0.9	1.0	0.9	0.8	0.7	3.9	4.3
Tadzhikstan	0.5	0.5	0.6	0.5	0.6	0.6	0.6	0.7	0.7	0.7	0.8	0.8	0.7	3.0	3.7
Armenia	0.8	0.9	1.1	1.0	1.0	0.8	1.0	1.1	1.3	1.0	1.2	1.1	1.1	4.9	5.7
Turkmenia	0.5	0.5	0.5	0.6	0.6	0.6	0.5	0.7	0.6	0.6	0.7	0.6	0.6	3.0	3.1
Estonia	0.6	0.6	0.5	0.5	0.5	0.6	0.6	0.7	0.7	0.7	0.6	0.6	0.6	2.9	3.2

SOURCES
1963–1964: Narodnoe khozyaistvo SSSR v 1964g. pp. 610, 612.
1965–1967: Narodnoe khozyaistvo SSSR v 1967g. pp. 678, 680.
1968–1969: Narodnoe khozyaistvo SSSR v 1969g. pp. 565, 566.
1970–1975: Narodnoe khozyaistvo SSSR v 1975g. pp. 572, 573.

belonging to other privileged categories (for instance, invalids and young workers living in hostels) frequently will be unable to pay the required deposit, or find that the monthly loan repayments would consume a high proportion of their income, thus making the housing co-operative an unattractive choice.

Although there is no published data on the ratio of locality-based co-operatives to work-based ones, it is likely that the majority are formed around the place of work. And without detailed information on the geographical location of *ZhSKs* and on whether in general they are work-based, any assumption can only be tentative. The evidence does suggest that whilst co-operatives can now be set up in rural areas, the *ZhSK* remains an essentially urban tenure-form. Indeed, one Soviet source calculated that in the period 1971–75 only 0.6 per cent of co-operative building took place in the countryside.[26] By the end of the 1970s, 700 co-operatives, embracing 5000 houses with half-a-million square metres of living space had been set up in rural areas, this representing less than 3 per cent of all co-operatives.[27] For this reason, Table 4.3 has been calculated to show the development of the co-operative sector in relationship to the growth of the total housing stock, excluding collective farm construction. There can be little doubt that this sector has not developed as rapidly as the Soviet leadership anticipated. Moreover, the figures reveal a steady decline from an All-Union peak of 8.6 per cent in 1970 to 6.0 per cent in 1975. And yet, in both years, in four republics the proportion exceeded 10 per cent, reaching almost 20 per cent in Lithuania. In the RSFSR, if housing erected by house-building co-operatives is calculated as a percentage of all house building in towns and urban settlements, then the decline in the contribution of the co-operative sector is remarkable: from 12.9 per cent in 1965 to 11.1 per cent in 1970 and to 5.4 per cent in 1981; from 7.8 per cent during the ninth five-year plan (1970–75) to 6.0 per cent during the period 1976–80.[28] In light of these statistics it is difficult to see how one Western author derived a figure of 'about 15 per cent of new housing in Soviet cities involves co-operative apartments'.[29]

Not only are there tremendous variations between republics and *oblasts* in terms of the contribution made by co-operatives to new house construction,[30] but from the few statistics available it would appear that co-operatives are to a very considerable degree concentrated in the largest cities; for example, in 1970 Moscow and Leningrad accounted for 33.4 per cent of all co-operative house building in the RSFSR;[31] Yerevan for 93.9 per cent of co-operatives in Armenia[32]

TABLE 4.3 Housing space constructed by house-building co-operatives as a proportion of all construction, excluding collective farms, by republic, 1963–1975

Republic	1963	1964	1965	1966	1967	1968	1969	1970	1971	1972	1973	1974	1975	1966–70	1971–5
USSR	2.4	6.4	8.2	8.2	7.8	7.7	7.3	8.6	7.5	7.0	7.4	6.6	6.0	7.9	6.9
RSFSR	2.6	7.7	9.4	9.3	8.5	8.5	7.7	9.0	7.5	6.5	6.8	5.9	5.5	8.6	6.4
Ukraine	2.1	5.1	6.8	8.2	7.9	8.3	8.6	10.4	9.6	9.5	9.8	9.1	8.1	8.6	9.2
Belorussia	3.9	7.0	11.5	10.5	10.8	9.7	9.0	11.4	11.7	13.2	11.2	10.6	9.6	10.3	11.2
Uzbekistan	0.5	2.0	3.9	2.9	2.7	2.0	1.1	1.7	2.0	1.2	2.1	2.2	1.6	2.1	1.1
Kazakhstan	0.6	1.2	2.0	2.3	1.9	1.9	2.2	2.0	1.9	2.0	2.5	1.6	1.9	2.0	2.0
Georgia	2.8	10.3	7.9	9.2	10.3	7.7	9.4	13.7	8.8	13.4	13.2	12.4	12.2	10.2	12.1
Azerbaidzhan	0	2.1	5.4	4.1	5.9	5.5	1.6	3.5	3.5	1.4	3.2	6.0	4.1	4.3	3.7
Lithuania	6.0	10.4	15.8	15.5	17.4	12.8	14.9	18.7	17.4	16.9	18.7	16.2	14.9	15.9	16.8
Moldavia	2.8	6.3	7.7	8.1	10.6	8.2	8.7	9.2	8.3	9.0	8.0	8.5	8.4	9.0	8.4
Latvia	3.3	7.0	10.7	11.9	10.9	9.6	9.1	9.3	8.2	7.6	9.1	9.4	8.7	10.1	8.6
Kirgizia	0.2	2.3	3.3	2.6	2.3	4.8	2.6	5.5	5.3	4.6	5.9	4.4	4.0	3.6	4.9
Tadzhikstan	0.6	0.2	3.2	0.8	4.3	3.2	2.0	4.4	3.1	3.9	6.3	4.8	4.6	3.1	4.5
Armenia	0	2.9	8.7	4.6	3.7	11.3	6.8	4.6	7.5	7.1	8.6	8.4	6.6	6.0	7.6
Turkmenia	0	0.1	0.2	0.4	0.5	0.7	0.2	0.6	0.7	0.8	2.0	0.2	1.7	0.4	1.1
Estonia	0.8	5.0	9.0	8.2	10.0	10.3	9.7	9.6	11.3	10.3	14.0	10.8	11.2	9.6	11.5

SOURCE Derived from Tables 4.1 and 4.2.

and the city of Perm' for 88.1 per cent of co-operatives built in the Perm' *oblast'* [33] By the beginning of 1979, 650 000 Muscovites (8.3 per cent of the population) were living in co-operative flats with a total floor space of seven million square metres. [34]

One reason for such concentration is that it enables the *ZhSK* to make use of standard designs, preferably of high-rise blocks constructed from pre-fabricated panels. And such buildings can only be erected in the vicinity of an existing major construction base. However, technical factors, such as the presence in the industrially advanced regions and largest cities of well-organised house-construction combines (see Chapter 7) capable of erecting multi-storey blocks, have not been the only reason that in the five years 1971–75, of all co-operative house building carried out in the 10 regions into which the RSFSR is divided, 36 per cent was in the Central Region. [35] For such has been the attraction of the metropolitan centres to scientific, cultural and administrative organisations, that the state has been compelled to make provision for its young, talented elites, who can appreciate, and tend to avail themselves of, the right accorded to the *ZhSK* to introduce modifications to the accommodation design and furnishings of their apartment block. [36] Whereas in the 1930s the departmental sector (Academy of Sciences, Gosplan etc.) helped to meet their (elite) members' accommodation needs, it is possible that today this function is to a certain extent being transferred to the house-building co-operative. This shift bears a slight resemblance to the suggestion in the UK that the mortgage subsidy should be discontinued. The effect of the removal of mortgage subsidy, and the substitution of the *ZhSK* for rent-subsidised accommodation in well-situated and better provided housing in the Soviet Union, would be to make the higher paid social groups in both societies spend a larger proportion of their income on accommodation.

The co-operative housing system has considerable advantages to the state, which has to bear the enormous costs of all other public housing. The high price of initial membership and the large monthly outlays [37] absorb purchasing power. Equally important, this price is much closer to 'true' construction costs. Furthermore the co-operative, not the state, is responsible for bearing the costs of running and maintaining its property. Fully in keeping with general trends, 'the most expedient form' of servicing the *ZhSK* is for the latter to enter into a contract with building contractors who provide a comprehensive maintenance service, including – current repairs (excluding interior repairs in flats which are carried out at the individual shareholder's own expense);

refuse disposal; servicing the hot and cold water supply and the sewerage and central heating systems; calculating and collecting payments for the building maintenance they undertake. These and a variety of other administrative functions have to be paid for by the co-operative membership.[38] Whilst it is not uncommon for members to work out a rota system for cleaning the stairs, for instance, as a way of reducing costs (and, arguably, as a means of raising the level of civic consciousness), the underlying premise of the co-operative that it should be self-financing, underlines the state's concern to transfer a higher proportion of the costs of accommodation and servicing the immediate environment on to the individual citizen. Whether they service it themselves or pay others to do so is immaterial.

In return for a high initial deposit and a monthly outlay which is about two-and-a-half times greater than the rent paid for state accommodation, the government is obliged to allow a co-operative member to regard his monetary outlay as an 'investment'. That some people are clearly inclined to treat it in this fashion is reflected in the legal stipulation that the only serious misdemeanour justifying expulsion occurs when the rent charged by a member subleasing part (or all) of his flat far exceeds the specified maximum.[39] Such an offence is bound up with regulations prohibiting the use of unearned income (that is, income earned unlawfully) for purchasing a share in a co-operative. If a person circumvents this rule and is later found out, he may be expelled from the co-operative. It should be remembered, however, that not all unearned income is unlawful. In Soviet law, it does not include money which is received as a gift or as an inheritance, won in a lottery, derived from the sale of produce grown on the garden plot (even though this might be at speculative prices), or rent from property leased out at the 'established rate'. As far as co-operatives are concerned, since the rent for subletting can only cover the shareholder's portion of the co-operative's running expenses,[40] charges exceeding the 'established rate' must be quite common. The government may justifiably reason that if the lessor were to receive a payment greater than this, he would be receiving a return on a capital investment.

Since, in effect, the state is appealing to an individualistic trait in the population, the attitude of the Soviet government to the *ZhSK* is broadly equivalent to the British social-democratic attitude towards home ownership and a property-owning democracy. The desirability of 'owning one's own home' becomes a valued goal. Possession is accorded a higher status compared with a tenancy in public (municipal) accommodation in the UK and local soviet housing in the USSR.

Governments in the UK, as in the Soviet Union, have deliberately fostered the idea that such accommodation is more desirable, primarily because the state finds it too expensive to meet everyone's demand for accommodation and, further, considers that giving individuals a vested interest in the property – which means that they are held responsible for the property's repair and upkeep – will encourage them to take greater care of the places where they live. In contrast to the UK, the ideological basis of a preference for 'home-ownership' in the Soviet Union is more difficult to comprehend.

In order to enlist a proportion of the population in this 'conspiracy', the housing co-operative (mortgaged house) must appear to have certain desirable features which confer a higher status on the resident. Frequently, an object becomes esteemed and desired not solely on account of any positive objective features inhering in it, but because of its social meaning. This is true of the housing co-operative: the co-operative member will first of all consider himself to be lucky in having been accepted into a co-operative since more people want to join than there are places available. Secondly, he will regard being a member as a privilege in the sense that he is a member of a minority housing-tenure group and thereby distinguished from people living in other housing-tenures. (Membership of a house-building co-operative might have the same social significance as living on a particular private housing estate or in a postal district in England.) Thirdly, his privileged status will be regarded as such by large numbers of non-members.

The government may well be enthusiastic about the future of house-building co-operatives both from the point of view of the economic benefit to the state and in terms of their introducing an element of flexibility into the housing system by creating a tenure-form advantageous to different elite groups. And the Prime Minister's references to the need to increase the amount of building carried out on behalf of *ZhSKy* should be regarded as a definite statement of intent. Despite demand for membership allegedly exceeding the number of co-operatives being built, the actual contribution of this sector during the ninth five-year plan (1971–75) fell below that for the previous five-year period. As table 4.3 shows, the *ZhSKy* were responsible for 7.9 per cent of all new house building (excluding collective farms) in the period 1966–70 and 6.9 per cent during 1971–5. In spite of the prediction made in 1971 by O. A. Beyul, head of USSR Stroibank's House Building Department, that during the ninth five-year plan co-operative housing construction was to rise by 85 per cent,[41] the number of square metres of living space built for

ZhSKy between the two periods fell from 33.7 million to 32.5 million, that is by 3.7 per cent.

It is difficult to account for the singular lack of success in this sector as whole, for it is quite clear that co-operatives have not developed as rapidly as the state has intended. No credence can be given to the suggestion by Cattell that people fear co-operative flats might, at a future date, be confiscated as they were in 1937.[42] Apart from the fact that the system of financing co-operatives is quite different from that in the 1930s, it is highly unlikely that the political environment will revert to its 1937 condition. Moreover, it is frequently stated that the number of people applying to join a *ZhSK* is constantly growing.[43] The overriding factor responsible for this discrepancy between policy and practice is the shortage of resources to satisfy the needs of the huge house building programme in the state sector. Those applying for membership are often office workers and members of other social groups who are not well placed on the priority list for new accommodation. For such people the only way of improving their living conditions is to pay for it, which means joining a co-operative. They are thwarted in this attempt because resources have to be diverted to the state sector; if an upsurge occurred in the number of manual workers, particularly skilled labour, applying for membership, then, possibly, larger supplies of materials, equipment and manpower would be made available to the *ZhSK*. But the majority of workers, accustomed to paying low rents and knowing that flats in co-operatives do not differ so significantly from those built by the state, are simply unwilling to pay the much higher charges for accommodation required by the *ZhSK*.[44] In some cases where groups of people have been successful in their petition to set up a co-operative, the local bureaucracy has 'retaliated' by allocating land in 'marshy areas' and districts lacking an infrastructure. On the other hand, members of certain social groups are not subjected to the same degree of petty-foggery and their housing will tend to be 'in the better districts' of the city.

In order to deal with the problem of low priority which has tradition-ally been accorded to the *ZhSK* by building contractors, the co-operative membership can now provide in the original building documentation for a fund for making bonus payments to the contractors.[45] As far as repair work is concerned, because co-operative properties tend to be dispersed throughout the city repair organisa-tions show little interest in undertaking work on them – a situation further exacerbated by the fact that co-operatives appear merely as 'other work' on the repair organisation's work-schedule, which relegates them to the end of the queue. The setting up in Moscow of an Administration for the Co-operative Economy in March 1978 has as one of its objectives 'to represent the interests of co-operatives, champion them with builders and take responsibility for the financing, design and estimate documentation etc'.[46] Such an administrative and organisational reform, perhaps entailing increased centralisation of co-operative management, might offer a partial solution to one set of problems that have hampered the development of house-building co-operatives since their inception in 1962.

Unfortunately there does not appear to be a satisfactory explanation for the 'underperformance' of this sector. A recent statement that 'in a number of cases in the localities, this method of increasing the housing stock has been underestimated',[47] reveals nothing. And, by themselves, the facts that the house-building plan for 1976–80 was 'only' 98 per cent fulfilled, and that capital investment in housing as a proportion of total capital investment has continued to fall, do not explain why the *ZhSK* is not contributing to new building as much as offical statements would lead one to anticipate.

Again, a comparison with a particular strand of current housing policy in the UK might be instructive, namely, the sale of council housing. So far, this strategy has met with little success, for during 1974–76 only 0.1 per cent of the existing local authority stock was sold or leased, a figure rising to 0.8 in 1979, still below the record of 1.3 per cent in 1972.[48] Among the reasons why sales failed to reach expectations, two are of particular relevance. Firstly, council tenants, when fully appraised of the fact that on purchasing the property they become wholly responsible for all current and capital repair work and insurance, realise that the costs of 'ownership' outweigh any benefits attached to it. Secondly, many, particularly Labour-controlled, Councils with a strong ideological commitment to public housing, are averse to the selling off of council homes and have refused to co-operate, with the result that the Conservative government has felt compelled to introduce further legislation to ensure that its policy is implemented.

As far as the Soviet Union is concerned, it is possible that the co-operative scheme has faced similar objections for similar reasons. A tentative proposal that Muscovites should bear the cost for current repairs to their homes received a hostile reception marked by thousands of letters of protest to the Moscow Soviet.[49] And, of course, the co-operative represents just another way of foisting this responsibility on individuals. Perhaps on account of this attitude, in 1964 a decree issued by the Soviet equivalent of the British TUC, the VTsSPS (the All-Union Central Council of Trade Unions), aimed at explaining more clearly 'the advantages offered by the state to house-building co-operatives'.[50]

From the demand side then, the evidence is less than conclusive that the mass of the Soviet population is any more anxious to rush and join a co-operative than are the mass of British council tenants to buy their council-rented homes. From the supply side, perhaps as a consequence of the social characteristics of would-be co-operative members, local soviets appear to be unwilling to furnish them with the requisite resources.

CONCLUSION

The extension of the right to form and join house-building co-operatives to people living in rural areas is unlikely to lead there to a sudden upsurge in co-operative building. In the medium and long term, the *ZhSK* will remain an urban phenomenon. Its high cost will ensure that membership of co-operatives is restricted to better-paid occupational groups; but income will not be the sole determinant of membership. One need not subscribe to the Davis and Moore functionalist analysis of stratification to assert that, with few exceptions, all social systems are stratified; that certain occupations are accorded higher status than others and that there are certain symbols associated with status. When a good is in short supply and yet in demand, then its possession tends to confer a certain status on its possessor. Further, when that good is not homogenous, then prestige will be associated with the ownership of one of its forms. In all industrialised societies, for whatever reason, although a large number of people (perhaps the majority of the population) are aware of the degrees of prestige accruing to possession of different goods (or access to services), normally not all those who are objectively able by virtue of income or political power to command access to that prestigious symbol will do so. In other words, it is not only power (economic or political) which determines whether a person will seek to possess a symbol of prestige. To put it crudely, not all those in the UK who could own Rolls Royce cars actually choose to do so; on the other hand, there are very many for whom, although ownership of such a car must forever remain within the realm of fantasy, it is a much desired object. In the case of the Soviet Union, membership of a house-building co-operative is recognised by most as a symbol of status; not all who want to join a co-operative can, and some of those who could, choose not to. For many unskilled workers fresh from the countryside, the co-operative has little or no significance; for the low status, poorly paid office worker and employees in the service industries, the co-operative is something to be aspired to; for the high status coal-miners and well-paid construction workers the prestige attached by others (and recognised by them as attached by others) is an irrelevance. Hence, just as there is no unitary value system for housing in the UK, so that not everyone can be said to be 'pursuing a suburban deal', so in the USSR perceptions of the desirability of co-operative membership varies between individuals and social groups.

As in the 1920s and 1930s, the co-operative form of house owner-ship caters for a proportion of the society's different elites. Further-more, just as 50 years ago, if the public statements made by the country's leadership are not pure window-dressing, the housing co-operative is regarded as a necessary component in an overall strategy for meeting the nation's demand for accommodation. On a practical level, it brings cost advantages to the state; ideologically, involving collective activity, it represents a step away from the inherent indi-vidualism of the private sector. Yet even this 'ideological' dimension of the co-operative is not devoid of its practical benefit, for the self-management function devolving on to the co-operative releases labour otherwise employed in the administration of local soviet and enter-prise housing.

The fact that co-operative houses are concentrated in the main industrial and administrative centres and cater for high status groups will influence the pattern of urban development and the spatial distribution of social groups. One Soviet housing specialist rightly drew attention to the fact that 'the co-operative should not expand at the expense of the private sector since the former caters, in the main, for well-provided citizens, specialists and highly qualified workers'.[51] Because private houses can with few exceptions only be built in smaller towns or on the urban periphery, and because, moreover, it is usually those who have recently moved from the agricultural to industrial sector and low-paid unskilled workers who prefer to own their home and have a garden plot to tend, it may justifiably be assumed that it is members of these social groups who will live in the badly provided outlying suburbs and settlements. This association of housing tenure form, social group and spatial location, a *leitmotiv* of this book, is readily identifiable in the private housing sector.

5 The Private Housing Sector

As a result of the devastation and loss of the urban housing stock during the World War II, legislation was passed to stimulate private house-building by individuals.[1] This was followed by a further decree in 1948[2] which required soviet executive committees at *krai, oblast'*, city and district levels to allot plots of land both inside and outside city boundaries to any individual wishing to erect a single or two-storey house with up to five rooms. Depending on local factors, the size of the plot could range between 300 and 600 square metres in towns and 700 to 1200 square metres outside the town boundaries. Until the publication of this decree, plots within towns were normally 800 to 1200 square metres, and in some Ukrainian towns a house and garden might occupy an area of 2000–3000, and sometimes up to 5000 square metres. A combination of accommodation shortage and propitious legislation resulted in individual house construction accounting for about 30 per cent of all newly erected and renovated housing space in towns and urban settlements in the period 1946–49. In Voroshilovgrad (Lugansk), it reached over 70 per cent and even in Kiev it was 43 per cent.[3] In Stalingrad (Volgograd), between 1945 and 1957 individual builders erected about 40 000 houses, equivalent to 40 per cent of the city's total housing space. Because of the large amount of unauthorised building that was taking place, the Stalingrad city soviet even set up an inspectorate to control individual builders; but 'it was of no practical use whatsoever since it had no powers; the inspectorate's members could only monitor the numerical growth of such unauthorised construction'.[4] In 1950 the individual owner-occupier sector was still contributing 30.9 per cent of all new house building in towns. In the light of these figures, it is difficult to agree with one Western specialist's comment that 'private housing has never played an important role in Soviet cities'.[5]

A further impetus to the private sector came in the decree of July

99

1957[6] which criticised local soviets and industrial enterprises for not helping to provide public services and amenities in those settlements and districts mainly given over to private dwelling units. Then, in the general upward revision of the plan for house construction for the period 1956–60, the government set the amount to be erected by individuals at 113 million square metres of total housing area (as against 84 million in the Directives issued by the XX Party Congress). This meant that the private sector would be responsible for 34 per cent of all new housing. Since people would be taking an active part in house building and would be drawing on finance and resources channelled through and distributed by employers, the government regarded its encouragement of building for private ownership as a symbol of a 'high level of socialist consciousness'. In fact, it was no more than a method of appealing to the individual's self-interest and of enabling employers to add another item to their reward structure. The government's boldly declared objective of 'solving the housing problem in the next ten to twelve years' had a greater chance of being achieved (although it never was) if the labour and savings of the population could be harnessed to the task. The outcome of this policy was that the private sector contributed one-quarter of all new housing brought into use in towns in the period 1956–60, with its share of the total urban stock reaching a post-war peak of 39.1 per cent in 1960 (see Tables 1.4 and 1.5).

In 1962, five years after the 1957 decree, the government acted again to remind local soviets and enterprise managements of their obligation to provide individual builders with plots of land and to help them obtain and transport the building materials they required.[7] At the same time the 1962 decree revealed a striking change in emphasis. It did not conceal the fact that the private builder/owner had no long term future. The government's stated aim was to bring about a gradual shift from individual single-dwelling construction in urban areas to multi-dwelling, co-operatively built blocks of flats. One sign of this intention was the decision to prohibit the allocation of land and credit for private house construction in Union Republic capitals and to give the Council of Ministers of Union Republics the right to lease land and credit allocations to individual builders in other cities and urban settlements. In the following year (1963), private housing construction was banned in all cities with over 100 000 inhabitants.[8] In 1961–65, urban private house construction slowed down dramatically, declining to 17 per cent for the five-year period.

However, the 1962 decree should be viewed as part of the

'Khrushchev interlude' – one tinted by visions of the proximity of the transition from socialism to communism and thus one particularly inimical to the private sector. Under the present leadership, in the face of a continuing housing shortage, wishful thinking has been replaced by a more pragmatic attitude towards the private sector, which is reflected in the increased encouragement being shown to it. For instance, in 1973 a commentator on the legal aspects of Soviet housing pointed out that one indication of the government's genuine concern for the individual builder is to be found in the variety of forms of assistance, including credit facilities, which it makes available to him.[9] Elsewhere mention was made of the positive impact that the increase in individual and co-operative house construction, encouraged by a decree of October 1964, and XXIII Party Congress (1965), could have on meeting the demand for accommodation.[10]

But, according to the head of the Department for Long-term Credit at *Stroibank*, local soviets paid no attention whatsoever to housing in this sector and tended to act obstructively in regard to private owners or prospective builders. For instance, even where no official ban existed on private house building, local soviets allocated land in areas quite unsuitable for building, failed to provide them with public services and amenities and did not fulfill their obligations to supply building materials.[11] Then in 1967 the government intervened in the private sector again, this time requiring local soviets to set aside funds for improving areas of private housing and to enlist the support of local residents in keeping their neighbourhoods neat and tidy. The main intention of the measure was to prevent the physical deterioration of buildings and to combat the general run-down appearance which, in the absence of a system of state supervision of maintenance in the private sector, these areas frequently tended to assume.[12] The government was also seeking to counteract another tendency which was adversely affecting the private sector. In some cases local soviets were deliberately depriving areas of resources, thus hastening their deterioration and justifying the demolition of tracts of of one-storey dwellings (see Chapter 8).

But even without this, the private sector continued to decline: from 113.8 million square metres of newly commissioned housing in 1956–60, to 94 million in 1961–65 and 64.3 million during the ninth five-year plan (1971–75), which represented a proportionate decrease over the 20-year period from 33.6 per cent in 1956–60 to 13.6 per cent in 1971–75. And, for the urban sector alone, private builders in 1980 contributed 7.9 per cent of all new building, compared with

24.9 per cent in 1960 – although the magnitude of the absolute decline was smaller (from 14.4 million to 6.0 million square metres).

Until 1958, the law allowed an individual to build or buy a one- or two-storey house with up to five rooms without laying down a limit on its overall size in square metres. Then, in July 1958 an edict of the Presidium of the Supreme Soviet stipulated that as from that date private dwellings could not exceed 60 square metres.[13] However, this restriction was not to (and does not) apply if the house-builder (owner) has a large family, or is a member of certain social and occupational groups. These include 'personal pensioners' of the Soviet Union, republic or locality,[14] heroes of the Soviet Union, heroes of socialist labour, individuals awarded Orders of Honour of the Third Degree,[15] employees with responsible jobs (*otvetstvennye rabotniki*) needing a spare room to work in, those suffering from an illness requiring isolation, and officers with rank of colonel and above. The extra entitlement actually amounts to an additional room or space of up to 13.65 square metres above the norm applying in that region. Other groups are even more privileged. Legislation passed during the 1930s granted scientific workers, including those on pensions, those with a higher degree or specialist qualification and their coevals in the creative arts (writers, composers, architects, artists, sculptors) a right to an additional room or at least 20 square metres of living space.[16] Others recently elevated to this privileged status include 'innovators and rationalisers whose contributions to the economy have been especially notable'.[17] On application to the executive committee of the local soviet, they are allowed to build, buy or keep additional space, the maximum being set at the norm of living space provided in accommodation belonging to local soviets. Furthermore, the 60 square metres limitation does not apply to those who came into possession of a dwelling prior to the Supreme Soviet's ruling in 1958.[18] The proportion of the private housing stock falling into this category is, of course, continually declining as a result of the normal process of physical deterioration and demolition taking place as part of urban renewal programmes.

The private sector has been tolerated because it has served several vital functions. It has augmented the housing supply, absorbed purchasing power in the economy, and provided an incentive to individuals to keep their dwellings in a good state of repair. Furthermore, it has given hope to those who would otherwise stand little chance of receiving more than the minimum of living space and to those low down on the state's housing waiting list. Then, since it makes private builders purchase materials at retail prices (whilst state repairs continue to be carried out at wholesale prices) and insists on the principle that private owners be responsible for the upkeep of the areas in which they live, it serves to subsidise the public sector in a minor way. Lastly, it is an attractive form of accommodation for those newly arrived from the countryside. For the migrant who is normally not highly qualified, and as a result tends to be in low-paid occupations, is interested not just in a roof over his head but also in having a garden plot to provide the family with food. As the family frequently takes part in building the house, it is able to economise on the financial outlay.[19]

None the less, there would appear to be four main objections to private house building from the point of view of the Soviet authorities. Firstly, it is uneconomic in terms of land requirements. Secondly, it is said to require 'unproductive expenditure of resources' in providing the infrastructure. Thirdly, small houses are thought to damage the architectural unity of a district composed mostly of multi-storey blocks of flats. And lastly, it helps to perpetuate a psychology of private ownership. Evidently, there is no unitary view on the private sector: at the local level of policy execution, as within central government decision-making agencies and academic circles, opinions differ on the costs and benefits of private housing. Housing policies pursued by British governments again provide a useful point of comparison. Differences clearly exist *within* the Labour and Conservative Parties (as well as between the parties) on the proper or best balance between council housing, owner-occupancy and privately rented accommodation; however, intra-party disagreements receive far less attention than the outcome of the debate which forms 'government policy'. The long-term secular decline in the privately rented sector in England and the decline in private housing in the Soviet Union are both consequent on policies affecting all types of tenure.

Different Soviet specialists and interest groups vary in the emphasis they place on the objections listed above: architects will tend to be more interested in the aesthetic aspects of private house development; land and agricultural economists in land use; engineers and urban economists in the cost of the infrastructure. While the first two objections can be 'quantified' and subjected to a 'scientific' evaluation, the third and fourth are essentially based on value judgements. The animosity felt towards this sector was expressed by one author who urged his readers 'do not forget that the acquisition of private homes with their private plots gives rise among a certain section of the population to private property tendencies, to a striving to "expand the auxiliary economy" and sell produce at speculative prices'.[20]

The Soviet government has always regarded private housing as a necessary evil which performs a useful social function during a transitional phase when the state cannot itself meet the demands of its citizens for accommodation. One of the greatest anomalies, from the point of view of Soviet ideology, is that the private house-owner has the right to sub-let his property. This right is legally granted in articles 298, 299 and 302 of the Civil Code of the RSFSR. The period of lease is formally set out in a contract between landlord and tenant, and the law formally gives the tenant very clear rights. Thus, the 'transfer of the property rights' on the house by the owner to a third party does not affect the tenant, for the new owner has to accept all the rights and obligations entered into between the former owner and the tenant. Moreover, a tenant who has strictly observed the duties contained in his contractual lease has a right to renew that lease except when the contract was for less than one year and stated that he would vacate the premises on the expiry of the period. The tenant may also lose his right to renewal where the court has established that the accommodation is necessary for the personal use of the owner and his family.[21]

Rents are also regulated in law. A decree of 1963 set the maximum monthly rent at 16 kopeks per square metre of actual dwelling area[22] and Article 25 of the RSFSR Civil Code states that charges above this level are 'a form of using personal property for the extraction of unearned income and therefore forbidden by law'.[23] In the absence of statistics on the number of tenants living in furnished or unfurnished private property it is impossible to gauge the extent to which this may occur. Space in a private house, perhaps no more than a corner in a room, tends to be rented by single or married students or young workers who cannot or prefer not to live in a hostel at a density of four to six persons per room. In some cases, a worker who has found a job in the town may have been offered a place in the hostel belonging to his employer. He duly registers there and then seeks out a private room so that his family can come and join him. As has already been mentioned, not only is there considerable geographical and occupational mobility in the Soviet Union, but most of it occurs in response to a 'market demand for labour'. The unplanned and unco-ordinated nature of labour movements in a situation of general accommodation shortage provides a basis for the continued existence of a landlord 'stratum' able to ensure the necessary flexibility in the housing system to meet a variable demand for accommodation.[24]

In practice, as a result of the acute accommodation shortage, the regulations are often breached by private owners, so much so that in the late 1950s one Soviet jurist claimed that tenant protection was difficult to uphold in practice.[25] An authoritative juridicial statement issued by the USSR Supreme Court in 1962 admitted that lower courts 'rarely pass judgement on violations of legality on the part of individual citizens and officials;'[26] and a further statement in the following year enjoined lower courts to make use of their legal powers to confiscate (without compensation) houses used to gain unearned income, houses acquired with unearned income or built with materials illegally taken from state enterprises and other public organisations, or houses built without permission or deviating from the submitted and accepted architect's drawing.[27]

Some extraordinary examples of private landlordism are reported in Soviet publications. In one case, a person who had been allocated a plot of land in a small urban area in the Moscow *oblast'* erected a five-roomed house with a kitchen and two verandas, the total area amounting to 185 square metres (of overall living space). Over a period of years he also erected next to it another building of 65 square metres into which he moved, adapting and letting the larger building as a kindergarten. This, a Moscow judge concluded, constituted the reaping of unearned income; he duly confiscated the property. But the authors of the book citing this case stressed that such a harsh measure as confiscation is only resorted to when the house is 'systematically used for the purpose of deriving unearned income'. They went on to point out that even when a rate above the maximum is charged – as long as it is not systematically charged – a less severe measure than outright confiscation should be meted out.[28]

In 1979, a long article in *Pravda* illustrated some of the pernicious aspects of the privately rented sector with an example from the industrial town of Gorkii (1 367 000).[29] A Mrs Kizlova, who had come to Gorkii as a girl in 1966, was, at the time the article was written, a 28-year-old widow with a seven-year-old daughter. She worked in the cold-rolling strip shop of the Red Etna plant and had always had to rent a room in a private house; her present room was always cold and there was nowhere to do the laundry. She approached the shop's Trade Union committee for assistance since it had erected its own 215-apartment building – but they could not help for others had been waiting even longer. On asking the TU committee and the personnel department how many people were currently renting private flats, the *Pravda* correspondent was told that they did not know. The correspondent then asked the director's assistant for domestic affairs whether he had given any thought to the question of the availability of space in private houses and to the possibility of providing better accommodation in such houses for those in greatest need, especially mothers with children. Had he been of any help to families who rent rooms in private houses? Not in the least. In general, the correspondent concluded, plant officials pretended that no problem existed, even though in the settlements surrounding Gorkii, there was not a single street where private landlords were not letting out space.

The room rented by Kizlova and her child was in an outbuilding which had been partitioned into cubicles and let out to a total of four families. Each family paid the landlady 35 roubles a month and an extra two roubles for electricity. Her attitude was: 'If you do not like the price, you can leave because there are plenty of other people who would like to live here'. So, without expending any effort, she received more money than some skilled workers. Although the radiators had burst and were not yet repaired, in the yard stood a white brick garage protecting a car belonging to her son-in-law, a Communist. What did he think of his mother-in-law's enterprise? He grinned and replied that 'with the housing shortage, she could get even more out of them'. And as to the fact that she did not register her lodgers or draw up contracts with them, well, other people were doing the same thing. In fact, when Kizlova replied to an advertisement offering a room in a four-roomed flat not only was the rent for the room set at 40 roubles a month, but it had to be paid three years in advance.

When confronted, the deputy chairman of the district soviet executive committee could only parry by saying 'If a property owner demands such an amount, what can we do? It is his own home so he has the right'. The correspondent's comment on this whole state of affairs was to remind his readers that although the terms of the rental and the payment are mutually agreed upon, this does not mean that the size of the payment can be arbitrary: Article 304 of the RSFR Civil Code states that payments for the use of living space in private houses, while determined by both the parties, cannot exceed the maximum rates set for these houses by the Republican Council of Ministers. Despite the fact that the Supreme Court had 15 years earlier called upon the courts to prosecute in cases of 'profiteering', the correspondent was forced to recall that the Civil Code stipulated that a privately owned residence which was systematically used to derive unearned income was subject to confiscation without compensation when an action was brought to the local soviet.

Almost concurrently with the publishing of another article on unauthorised private building and using 'illegally procured materials' (the other two main cases for confiscation without compensation), corruption, cover-up and bureaucratic delays,[30] the RSFSR Supreme

Court issued a 'guiding explanation' on the power vested in the courts to condemn and/or confiscate unauthorised house construction.[31] Then, in the following year (1976) in a review of cases where building had taken place without planning permission or without proper drawings, the RSFSR Supreme Court found that, in the main, such buildings 'tended to exceed the permitted plot size, living space norm and the number of floors', or they included features such as large basements and attics not provided for in the plan, and 'ambitious subsidiary structures that could be converted into a living area'.[32] Newspaper articles and letters to the press dealing with specific cases of abuse in the private sector, and judicial responses, probably reflect fairly widespread popular discontent. It is at least likely that the private landlord in the Soviet Union bears a stigma as does his counterpart in the UK.

Private house ownership could be given a fillip not only by the government's stated policy to encourage this type of tenure in small towns, but also by its pursuance of a set of recommendations which urge treatment of the 'historically created network of small settlements as gigantic reserves of second homes (*vtoroe zhilishche*)'. The number of potential second homes in the Moscow region alone amounts to over three million. As the number of people engaged in agricultural production declines, the number of dwellings actually converted into second homes – either for the former rural migrant to the towns or for acquisition by urban dwellers – increases.[33] This particular viewpoint is almost certainly held by only a small minority of housing and planning specialists. Even more heretical is their suggestion that it is impossible by egalitarian means (*egalitarnym obrazom*) to reconcile the many contradictory demands placed upon housing – that it should be close to nature and to centres of activity, isolated and yet rendering possible intense interpersonal communication.[34]

An extension of this argument is that the thousands of settlements designated as 'having no future' as far as agricultural production is concerned could adjust to another role, that of serving as places of leisure for city dwellers, more and more of whom are spending their spare time in the country. This development has reached such proportions that 'dacha construction, "second homes" and recreation, in the broadest sense of the term, have become a major national problem'. Because of this, even if only a small proportion of the houses, inherited, bought or 'taken into temporary usage' by urban residents, in these futureless villages are occupied, then these places – instead of 'dying out' – will boost the local economy.[35]

While these represent attempts to grapple with the very real phenomena of village and small settlement depopulation and the consequent rise in the number of empty properties, to talk of second homes in a situation of continuing overall housing shortage could be a cause of resentment. Furthermore, the reference to the inefficacy of 'egalitarian means' as a way of resolving the competing demands inherent in their housing policy, is a significant breach of ideological orthodoxy. Nevertheless, these political impediments notwithstanding, rather than municipalise these properties (because of the additional cost to the state for the buildings' renovation and upkeep), the government might introduce schemes to help individuals buy building materials to repair 'second homes' owned outside the main cities.

CONCLUSION

While the history of the Soviet state has been punctuated by periods of explicable schizophrenic repression and reform, at a less dramatic level the history of the private housing sector in towns is one of concessions and encouragement accompanied by the curtailment of privileges and restrictions on its size. It would be extremely difficult for the authorities to regulate this market and, in any case, it is doubtful whether they are really interested in doing so. It creates a certain slack in the system, enabling a section of the population to reveal its preferences, a privilege for which they have to pay. Moreover, the government is able to appear to be adhering to its policy of restricting the growth of large cities while at the same time meeting the demand for accommodation from essential workers required to work in the city. The private sector provides an important point of entry through the city gates.

The government is grateful that part of the burden of providing and maintaining accommodation is borne by a section of the population. However, nothing in this sector's history to date or in the statistics on new house building in urban areas permits the conclusion that the state will substantially expand private house construction in towns. Although circumstances, ideas and policies might be changing, whether the direction of change will favour an expansion of the private sector is a matter of speculation. At present, however, the urban private housing sector is widely regarded as a vestigial form; those owning their own homes constitute a pariah or low caste group – tolerated temporarily because of its important function in society. To the extent that the government wants to transfer a fraction of the cost of accommodation from the public purse to the private pocket, it will seek to do so by cultivating the housing co-operative. Nevertheless, a decree of December 1976 'On the furnishing of credit for individual construction in rural communities'[36] followed 18 months later by another, indicates not only that the government believes there to be a positive correlation between the construction of individual houses and successfully curbing the emigration of labour from the countryside,[37] but also that the state sees private (personal) ownership as a means of motivating individuals to higher levels of economic activity, including maintaining their property in good repair.[38] The fact that the decree on furnishing credit to individual builders in the countryside was in 1979 extended to workers, employees and engineers in towns and workers' settlements[39] could suggest that the government might be in a process of revising its current policy, which so strongly favours multi-dwelling unit accommodation both in rural settlements and in small towns. The significance of any further encouragement of private home ownership in small towns lies in the fact that a principal component of Soviet urban and regional policy centres on a belief in the desirability of expanding the manufacturing base of small towns as part of its policy to contain the growth of its largest cities and to decentralise (see Chapter 9). This change in attitude and direction has been given an extra impetus by the latest in the current sequence of recent laws designed explicitly to assist the 'home-ownership' sector (both the individual and co-operative types of tenure) as a way of reducing labour turnover, by empowering associations (*ob"edineniya*), enterprises etc. to draw on bank credit specifically to build detached houses for their employees for home ownership.[40] Their effects however, go far beyond labour stabilisation.

Recent legislation and judicial statements on the private sector neither signify an ideological hostility towards it nor represent a stamp of ideological approval. Just as 'quality' has become a crucial desideratum for public housing, so in the private sector the state is aiming to curb unregulated private building because it creates eyesores, 'prevents the rational use of land and the rational construction and organisation of public amenities'.[41] Associated as it is with extensive, low-rise development, this sector has made a strong visible imprint both on the internal structure of cities, and on the emergence of agglomerations (see Chapters 8 and 9). This sprawl effect in itself might be deemed sufficient reason for prohibiting any major shift of resources to the private sector. Already mentioned social and economic factors also militate against further expansion of owner-occupation. On the other hand, apart from the obvious economic attractiveness of transferring the cost of housing directly on to the individual family, a number of less quantifiable variables may also influence the outcome of this sector in the long term – especially the rise of the private car and 'consumer demand'. The issue of the private sector cannot be considered closed.

Part II

Housing: Social, Economic and Spatial Dimensions

Introduction

Whereas the previous section, in focusing on tenure forms, was primarily concerned with the ownership and control of housing, the three chapters in this section take as their central theme the physical structure of the housing in which the new Soviet citizen is to be accommodated. Of course, an ideological intent has always underlain the Soviet government's attempts to expand the public and co-operative sectors: housing, a basic human need, should be provided by the state for all its citizens at a low rent. But the provision of low rental, well-equipped accommodation was not the sole objective. The new relations of production characterising a socialist society had to find expression in other spheres of social life, including the workers' state's *control* over the means of social reproduction (accommodation, education, health).

Any examination of the social and spatial dimensions of housing policy involves considering both the way in which physical forms (dwelling units) may be vehicles for encouraging what are, allegedly, desirable patterns of social relationships and the broader spatial context within which house-building takes place. After all, the single family dwelling is but the smallest sub-system within an urban system and it is impossible to discuss urban planning in isolation from the social functions architects consider housing to serve or from the architectural form housing has taken. Neither can housing be considered in total isolation from urban planning, as was so clearly revealed in the debate between the *urbanists* and *deurbanists* in 1929–30 (see below).[1] To suggest that dwelling-units and other buildings may be viewed as sub-systems implies that the city cannot be considered merely as an ensemble of structures.[2] By the same token, a region (or republic) is not a simple ensemble of unrelated cities or smaller settlements.[3] The nature of these linkages and the forms of larger spatial systems are discussed in Part III.

The first part of Chapter 6 looks at some of the key features of Soviet town planning theory and the type of housing envisaged by the avant

112

garde as being most congruous with life in the 'new' socialist society prior to the outbreak of the World War II. The second part examines what ostensibly constitute the principal social reasons justifying current housing and town planning forms. The following chapter deals with the 'bricks and mortar' and organisational aspects of housing construction policy. If Chapters 2–5 on tenure may be categorised as presenting a 'political' perspective of housing policy, and Chapter 6 seen as highlighting a 'social' perspective of housing policy, then Chapter 7 points to some of the 'economic' and 'technological' determinants which have helped to shape the physical environment and thereby influence types of social relations and patterns of interaction.

Much of the argument and content of both Chapters 6 and 7 may be seen as constituting a 'dialogue' with the continued existence of a private housing sector. The possessive individualistic quality of owner-occupied housing (often with its private plot) stands diametrically opposed to the publicly owned residential block providing a whole range of facilities for communal use. Yet the single detached house is not necessarily a sign of private ownership since a high proportion of low-rise housing belongs to state agencies. Chapter 8 discusses the extent and significance of such low-rise developments.

Whilst at one level there is a qualitative difference in the nature of social relations depending on whether single- or two-storey houses are privately or publicly owned, at another level the privatised nature of domestic arrangements and familial relations in both tenure forms cannot be said to differ at all. This raises the question of whether or not it is possible to distinguish significant differences in the structure of relations found in low- and high-rise buildings. Although there are differences, it is a moot point whether they are significant. And the reason why so little variation exists may be traced to the importance attached by the government to the nuclear family as the 'primary cell' in society.

The phenomenon of the nuclear family constitutes part of what might be described as a general privatisation or individualisation syndrome. Among its main features are the home-centredness of the small, two-generational family, interested in accumulating consumer durables and, relatedly, striving towards possession of a private car. Depending on one's view point these tendencies, which are exercising such a dramatic influence on housing, town planning, transport and recreational policies, may appear as another sign either of the 'counterrevolution' or of socio-technical and social-structural convergence between industrial systems.

6 The Social and Spatial Dimensions of Soviet Housing Policy

THE SOCIAL DIMENSIONS OF HOUSING POLICY BEFORE 1941

As early as 1919 the Programme of the VIII Congress of the Russian Communist Party (Bolshevik) adopted a resolution to the effect that the emancipation of women should not be limited to the achievement of formal (i.e. political and economic) equality with men. Emancipation was taken to mean much more than this; it referred in particular to their being freed from the burden of domestic work, including childminding, both by building communal blocks of flats (*doma-kommuny*) with public dining-rooms, laundries and crèches and also by establishing a system of pre-school facilities.[1] Female emancipation had two very closely related goals: one was to liberate women from household drudgery and the other to draw them into productive labour, thereby offering them economic independence.[2] Translating intent into reality required changes in the physical and cultural environments.

Both metaphorically and literally, the architects of the Revolution were architects and town-planners who in their designs of dwellings and juxtapositioning of kindergartens, schools, social and cultural facilities and work-places would provide a setting for a cultural revolution. They maintained a belief in the power of design to shape the course of historical events in more than just a minor way.

The years immediately after the October Revolution saw the working out of the theoretical and practical difficulties of constructing *doma-kommuny* as part of an altogether new settlement form, with its emphasis on a collectivised way of life. But it was not until the mid-1920s that these ideas found a concrete expression when, towards the end of 1925, the Moscow Soviet arranged a competition for the

114

design of a communal block of flats.[3] There was little in this or many of the other blue-prints for the communal blocks which appears to us today as in any way 'revolutionary'. For instance, the communal block built for the Commissariat of Finance (*Narkomfin*) between 1928 and 1929 which consisted of one- and three-roomed flats each with its own bathroom and kitchennette, connected to another building that provided a variety of communal services, had limited influence on the creation of a collectivised way of life. On the other hand, plans of a more radical flavour were being advanced. In 1930 a complex of flats designed to accommodate 2000 people was to consist of eight main blocks, a social centre and children's sector. In each five-storey block the first floor was reserved for services. The remaining floors were given over to living and sleeping quarters (*kabina*), each unit of which had a living area of 6.3 square metres and was intended solely for sleeping and relaxing. The standard unit was designed for a single person, but it could be expanded by removing a partition wall to cater for families. Each of these eight blocks was to be connected to the social centre where there were to be facilities for education and training, leisure and recreation.[4] The Commissar for Education, Lunacharskii, was another advocate of the *doma-kommuny*, recommending that they should accommodate from 1000 to 3000 people and form the basic city unit. Children were to be brought up mainly outside the nuclear family, the younger ones in crèches and kindergartens near the block itself, the older ones in boarding schools where they would be given technical education and practical training.[5] In S. G. Strumilin's proposal for the combination of towns and villages into agro-industrial complexes of 10 000 to 20 000 people, traditional household activities would be socialised and 'factory kitchens' established.[6]

On the other hand N. A. Milyutin, though sharing the views expressed by Strumilin on the way social life ought to be organised, considered it would be premature and unrealistic to try to put them into practice at the time; it was necessary, first of all, to create appropriate conditions for the public upbringing of children and only gradually to supplant the individual domestic households with a system of social institutions.[7] Four years earlier, a housing specialist and staunch supporter of the housing co-operative had made a similar observation: 'The separate kitchen will continue to occupy a place in each flat for a long time. The collectivisation of domestic work is a long process and it will only be completed through a series of intermediate forms; therefore, at present, it is necessary to provide a separate kitchen in small flats. The transformation of domestic life will take decades and will be no easy matter.'[8] This interpretation was based on and revealed an awareness of the backwardness of the population and the paramount importance attached to raising their general level of culture. One way of doing this and simultaneously inculcating a sense of responsibility towards property[9] was through encouraging the housing co-operative movement – which, of course, has only the most tenuous connection with a 'collectivised way of life'. But if there were those like Milyutin who argued for the transition from capitalist individualism to socialist collectivism to be carried out 'at a snail's pace', there were others who wanted the new way of life to begin immediately. The most famous and zealous of this more important group was L. Sabsovich who, writing in 1929, wanted child-rearing to be completely socialised; there were to be no kitchens or shops selling food products; adults would live in communal blocks consisting of 2000 to 3000 people, each individual having five square metres 'of his own' for sleeping and relaxing, the remainder of his time being spent in common rooms.[10] Elsewhere, Sabsovich was to argue the need for a cultural revolution to accompany the political and economic changes taking place.

> The material and social preconditions (in the form of a very high level of development of the productive forces, the elimination of classes and the socialisation of all instruments and means of production) are still not sufficient for the construction of a socialist society. There is a need for a cultural revolution; it is necessary to completely re-educate the individual, and to do this, it is imperative to totally alter his living conditions and forms of existence.[11]

At the heart of this intense debate on housing forms and collectivised provision of services lay the issue of the family unit. In one design proposed by Sabsovich, a family unit could be formed simply by opening a communicating door or sliding partition between one unit and an adjoining one; separation could be obtained by closing the door again. Those who preferred to keep their children by them rather than entrust them to 'educational specialists' could open a third door, thereby creating 'something resembling a three-roomed flat'.[12] The new Soviet person was one who would divide his time between productive labour, study, cultural recreation and sport; a person for whom marriage did not signify the enforced submission of one partner to the other, but a free and deliberate association based on mutual esteem and devoid of any ties anchored in a sense of ownership.[13]

It is here perhaps more than anywhere else that Chernyshevsky's vision of the new woman and the way couples should live – a vision encapsulated in his novel, *What Is To Be Done?* (1864) – anticipated and formed the views held by the Bolsheviks and their supporters. In it, Vera Pavlovna Rozalsky tells Lopukhov, following his proposal of marriage, that just as he and his friend live in separate rooms, so will they. 'We have two rooms, one for you and one for me and a little parlour where we will take breakfast, dine and receive our visitors – those who come to see both of us.'[14]

Whatever the differences existing between radical architects, they were bound by this common, fundamental belief – that architecture and town planning ought to create structures which could liberate women and allow them to participate in social production. It was thought that by providing collectivised dining rooms, pre-school facilities, dormitories, laundries, a range of repair shops and centres for hiring whatever might be required to meet temporary needs, conditions would be created for a radical break with existing attitudes maintained by the familial structure towards property. In the eyes of the architects of the revolution, the socialist transformation of society involved, among other things, the collectivisation of services and, with the liberation of women, the demise of the existing patriarchal family and the extinction of its function as an economic unit. Then, gradually, it would be possible to move towards 'the ending of man's present enslavement to possessions'.[15] This debate closely mirrored similar discussions at this time on the rate and nature of economic development, urbanisation and the physical form of the new socialist city.

Having rejected the capitalist city which had been inherited from the nineteenth century, Soviet architects and planners divided into two main camps: the *urbanists* and *deurbanists*.[16] Their main objective was not just to prevent uncontrolled urban growth through restrictive legislation, but to construct cities which would be representative of a society no longer riven by class antagonisms, and which would erase contrasts between centre and periphery, between slums and fashionable districts and, in the final analysis, between town and country.

One author, L. Vygodskii, writing in 1927, recommended breaking up the largest cities and relocating the population and industry in a number of independent settlements. Each settlement would have an industrial or administrative nucleus surrounded by spatially separate residential areas linked by a good communication system. In his view, 'life in the settlements of such a federative city would be scarcely distinguishable from the healthy natural conditions of rural living'.[17] Although this writer's ideas bear a fairly close resemblance to those expressed by Ebenezer Howard in his design for a 'Garden City', he differed from Howard in that he saw each settlement as a specifically functional unit; the division of labour found in factories or administrative organisations was to be reproduced in a functional division of labour between settlements. Like both the urbanists and deurbanists he agreed on the need to restrict the growth of towns to about 50 000 inhabitants and to disperse the population of larger industrial and administrative centres by relocating industry and services.

Okhitovich, one of the most ardent deurbanists, rejected the very idea of the city and dreamed of a Russia dotted with individual family homes consisting of lightweight structures located in rural Arcadian surroundings. This return to nature depended on the development of an intricate transportation system which for Okhitovich, who had been caught up with the revolution ushered in by the internal combustion engine, meant in some cases considerable reliance on mass ownership of the private car.[18] The two concepts fundamental to the *deurbanists'* philosophy were prefabrication and mobility. Houses should be of prefabricated components, easily assembled, combinable into larger units and equally easily dismantled. Flexible, variable, light and low cost structures would deal, in the eyes of one deurbanist, another blow against urbanism, 'against the frozen mould of petit bourgeois city life. The bourgeois is chained to his house and the house is chained for hundreds of years to a spot where it was, perhaps justifiably, built. And it will stand there for centuries, frozen, an anachronism, apathetic and out of place, no longer an active participant in a fast moving and changing life'.[19] This vision of a decentralised society could be realised through the extension of the electricity power grid to cover the whole country, thus making it theoretically possible to set up a factory anywhere and thereby achieve rapidly what for Engels would have been the culmination of a long, historical process; the elimination of differences between town and country.[20] Suffice it to say that, as far as the *urbanists* were concerned, the position the *deurbanists* most clearly and definitely allied themselves against was the one adopted by Sabsovich whose 'communal houses, those enormous, heavy monumental colossi, permanently encumbering the landscape' could not solve the problem of socialist settlement.[21]

The government's decision to industrialise rapidly furnished the basis for an attack on one of the principal proposals of the *deurbanists*, namely, that towns be broken up into smaller units. One critic, writing in 1929, pointed to a number of factors inhibiting the pursuit of a 'deurbanising' policy: firstly, work had already begun on the construction of hundreds of industrial units in existing towns and thousands of others had already been projected – to put a stop to work in either case would be highly unprofitable; secondly, not all new construction could take place outside already-established centres since some projects were merely additions to existing production units whilst others were able to use the waste or by-products of nearby plants and thus, in effect, combined to form an integrated manufacturing complex; and, thirdly, old cities exerted a cultural magnetic force which did not diminish quickly with the building of new socialist cities.[22] Similar arguments are still employed today (see Chapter 9). Some writers and politicians acknowledged early on that the debate was embodied in a contradiction: only by first of all raising the productive capacity of the large manufacturing cities could a more efficient settlement pattern be established, for an ideal pattern could not be created out of a void.[23] Thus the rebuke to the visionaries of the urban forms they thought to be appropriate to a socialist society was not without foundation.

The words 'be realistic and face the facts' were inscribed on the banner held up to town planners, who were admonished not to dream up plans for individual settlements or systems of settlements of the future, but to work within the confines of an underdeveloped society embarking on a policy of industrialisation. A society in which, moreover, according to United Nations' data, the rate of urbanisation during one ten-year period (1930–40) was perhaps the highest rate ever achieved in history.[24] Table 6.1 shows the overall growth of the population living in towns increasing by 50.9 per cent in the seven years, 1926–33 then falling to 40.8 per cent in the six-year period 1933–39.

The advocates of the individual detached house and dispersed settlement rested their arguments on one solid foundation; the mass of the population was in fact living in one-storey houses under private ownership. But the manner in which reality was presenting itself in the 1920s – low-rise, low-density housing development – was no ground for encouraging it further. The whole concept of small settlements composed of owner-occupiers carried strong Proudhonist overtones with a tendency to espouse the virtues of decentralised authority and a property-owning democracy. Given the propensities of the political leadership in the 1930s there certainly could be no capitulation on this ideological front; the compromise made during NEP to the private builder had been accepted on purely practical grounds, but in the long term the latter could not and would not be allowed to shape the physical pattern of the new socialist society. In 1934 the government

TABLE 6.1   *Urban population growth in the Soviet Union, 1897–1940*

| | | of which: | | | |
| | | Urban | | Rural | |
Year	Total Population (millions)	(mln)	(%)	(mln)	(%)
1897 (9/2)	106.4	15.8	14.8	90.6	85.2
1914 (1/1)	139.3	24.7	17.7	114.6	82.3
1920 (28/8)	130.9	20.8	15.9	110.1	84.1
1923 (15/3)	133.5	21.6	16.1	111.9	83.9
1926 (17/12)	147.0	26.3	17.9	120.7	82.1
1929 (1/1)	154.3	27.6	17.9	126.7	82.1
1931 (1/7)	162.1	32.6	20.7	128.5	79.3
1933 (1/1)	165.7	39.7	24.0	126.0	76.0
1939 (15/1)	170.5	55.9	32.8	114.6	67.2

SOURCES   *Narodnoe khozyaistvo SSSR: statisticheskii sbornik*, Moscow, 1932, p. 404; *Sotsialisticheskoe stroitel'stvo SSSR: statisticheskii ezhegodnik*, Moscow, 1936, p. 542; F. Lorimer, *The Population of the Soviet Union, History and Prospects*, League of Nations, Geneva, 1946, p. 241.

defined its position on the owner-occupied, single-storey house when it declared that 'Since the existing practice of house construction does not, in many cases, correspond to the growth of the cultural level and needs of the broad mass of the population ... houses in towns and workers' settlements must be four and five storeys and more'.[25]

As a result, by the mid-1930s, the government had effectively turned its back on the Anglo-American tradition in town planning (Ebenezer Howard, Clarence Stein, Frank Lloyd Wright) in favour of the European tradition[26] (whose most celebrated exponent was Le Corbusier). With judicious exceptions the 'cottage type' of dwelling was to give way permanently, at least in town planning theory, to high-rise, high-density living and to large cities.

THE DEBATE ASSESSED

Writing in 1929, Lissitsky summed up the feeling of the architect-planners of this period. In the West, he wrote, it was simply a matter of resuming construction activities where they had been laid off before World War I, though under changed economic and technological conditions. In Russia, this became a question of solving a new social problem of fundamental cultural significance. The Soviet architect was given the task of establishing a new standard of housing by devising a new type of housing unit, not intended for single individuals in conflict with one another, as in the West, but for the masses.[27] The Party's interpretation of the task which architects had set themselves found expression in a decree published in May 1930. The Central Committee noted that:

Parallel with the movement for a socialist way of life, highly unsound, semi-fantastical, and hence extremely harmful attempts are being made by certain comrades (Sabsovich, Larin, *et al.*) to surmount in one leap the obstacles that lie along the path to a socialist transformation of the way of life, obstacles rooted in the economic and cultural backwardness of the country and in the need at the present level of development to concentrate most of our resources on the rapid industrialisation which alone will create the necessary material basis for a radical transformation of the way of life. These attempts on the part of certain militants, who conceal their opportunism behind left-wing phrases, are linked with ... the immediate collectivisation of every aspect of the worker's life: feeding, housing, education of children in isolation from their parents, abolition of normal family life and an administrative ban on the private preparation of meals, etc. The implementation of these harmful and utopian proposals which disregard both the actual resources of the country and the degree of preparation of the population, would lead to vast expenditures of money and would seriously discredit the very idea of a socialist transformation of the way of life.[28]

The following year the government again denounced these proposals as 'ultraradical' on the grounds that they espoused 'gigantism' in the form of costly and grandiose projects[29] and demanded that a decisive struggle was required, directed against both the 'right opportunists' who were acting against the Bolsheviks' decision on the appropriate rate of development for the economy, and the 'left opportunists' who were operating with all sorts of 'hare-brained proposals' such as the need to eliminate individual kitchens.[30] Another resolution, this time passed in June 1932 at a plenary session of the Executive Committee of the Moscow City Soviet, was indicative of the new direction house construction was to take: 'each flat with its own bath or shower will, as a rule, accommodate one family.'[31]

Overall, the experiments of the 1920s made an impact little greater than such utopian designs for living as those drawn up by Robert Owen, Fourier and Campanello in the previous century. Nevertheless, the period up to 1930 was indeed remarkable in the history of socialist architecture and town planning, and one Soviet writer has retrospectively depicted it in the following manner:

> In the first years after the October Revolution, we did very little building but we did a lot of designing (leaving most of it, it is true, on paper) and even more talking. Whatever was old was swept out as having outlived itself. A new system, a new regime also means a new style. Recall the poster of those years; a half-naked worker in an apron, hammer in hand, standing against a background of some sort of construction site. This was the concept of architecture of the new — if not a factory, if not a fly wheel, at least something industrial.[32]

It was precisely this search for 'newness' under a new social formation and a pervading spirit of adventurousness amongst Soviet architects that attracted Le Corbusier to the USSR and led him to comment on his return from Moscow in 1929, in a letter to the Soviet architect Alexander Vesnin, that 'at the present moment, Moscow is the most vibrant architectural centre'.[33]

A characteristic of the 1920s was the open discussion taking place between individuals putting forward different ideas and offering divergent interpretations and policies in all spheres of cultural, social and economic development. Those involved in the debates and discussions were neither consciously nor unconsciously in favour of policies inimical to the interests of the working class. On the positive side, an abundance of expressed views reflects and generates creative energy. And ideas for example about art, aesthetics, architecture, city layouts, city size, relationships between men and women, though not the prime movers in the social process, are important.[34] However, on the negative side, at specific historical conjunctures, the potentially anarchic quality of a profusion of viewpoints can eventuate in a cardiac arrest in the body politic.[35] For Kautsky and those who held that a socialist revolution was only possible in the most advanced industrial countries, it seemed that, since the objective economic premises for socialism did not exist in Russia, there could be no political or cultural revolution in that country. Lenin, however, viewed the situation differently. He admitted that the development of the productive forces in Russia had not attained the level that made socialism possible but then added:

What if the complete hopelessness of the situation, by stimulating the efforts of the workers and peasants tenfold, offered us the opportunity to create the fundamental requisities of civilisation in a different way from that of the West European countries?. .... If a definite level of culture is required for the building of socialism ... why cannot we begin by first achieving the prerequisites for that definite level of culture in a revolutionary way and then, with the aid of the workers' and peasants' government and the Soviet system, proceed to overtake the other nations?[36]

For Lenin the visionaries, those who viewed the cultural transformation of Russia not just as a possibility but as a necessity, were not fantasists but important agents in the construction of socialism. Their conceptions, in focusing on social relationships and on providing the institutional forms, especially those propitious to the breaking down of traditional patterns of division of labour between the sexes, could be instrumental in releasing the creative potential of the masses, which in turn would have a positive effect on the pace of economic develop- ment. Yet, by 1934 the death-knell of the 'building for the new way of life' (*dom novogo byta*) had been rung; research was channelled into developing ways of supplying accommodation as quickly and cheaply as possible. And as in Germany, where there had been a decline towards the end of the 1920s in innovation in the architectural and artistic design of housing, primarily because the new flats were too expensive for working class families, rationalisation of construction and the use of prefabrication compelled architects to adopt designs employing identical standardised parts.

It is against a background of squalid living conditions and the dominance of the private sector that one has to assess the judgement, expressed in the decree mentioned above, that the schemes put forward to create a more collectivised way of life by erecting *dom kommuna* were 'hare-brained proposals'. An expansion in housing and municipal services was acknowledged by Kuibyshev in the Report on the second five-year plan as 'a precondition for safeguarding the health of workers, raising labour-productivity and freeing female workers from the slavery of the domestic economy'.[37] Although it would be wrong to regard the aims of 'safeguarding the health of workers' and the 'emancipation of women' as being solely concerned with increasing the size of the workforce and ensuring its fitness for the labour process, there was a clear tendency for policy speeches during the latter part of the 1920s and throughout the 1930s to lay stress on the social engineering aspects of housing in the state's strategy for raising labour-productivity. Certainly by the mid-1930s, the notion of housing as a consciously created environment designed to help bring about a change in cultural values had essentially been replaced by a cost-efficiency concept of housing which postulated a simple linear relationship between an improvement in the standard of accommodation and industrial output. The new property relations established by the political revolution of October 1917 gave rise at the objective level to new social relations; but, at the level of individual consciousness, the revolution could do no more than create the conditions for new social relations.

Almost a century and a half earlier the overseer of the French Revolution, the Committee of Public Safety, had noted that: 'You must entirely refashion a people whom you wish to make free, destroy its prejudices, alter its habits, limit its necessities, root up its vices, purify its desires'.[38] It was in the faith that people may, in a historically short period of time, be refashioned that the 'leaders' of the French and Russian Revolutions built their hopes and it was on this faith, in part, that they foundered. For many of the Party's intelligentsia, if the new socialist Soviet Republic was really to make a successful radical break with capitalist society, it had to do more than replace one particular apparatus of coercion with another, hopefully 'representing the true interests of the working class'. They were recognising, as was Gramsci at this time,[39] that the structure of power depended on a kind of hegemony or 'authority in depth' through which different elements in the social fabric lent themselves to the state's design. Thus, any strategy aimed at a real social revolution had to contest the influence of the old guard, the usurped hegemonic class, at every level or culture including its institutions, art and architectural forms.

THE OUTCOME OF THE THIRTIES

At conferences and congresses throughout the 15-year period preceding the outbreak of war in 1941, delegates never failed to point out that, despite the tremendous progress which had been made, the rates of growth of housing, public amenities and local transportation services were failing to keep pace with industrialisation, and that this uneven development was having detrimental effects on the structure and form of cities.[40] At the root of the government's problem in every sphere of policy was the society's low level of economic development and the high priority given to heavy industry. Skilled manpower was scarce; and would-be cartographers, surveyors, architects and civil engineers were shifted from urban affairs into the more important field of industrial development. The shortage or absence of materials and manpower[41] gave little scope for manoeuvre to the government in the type of policies it could pursue. It seems spurious to argue that these problems could have been overcome if spatial planning, public amenities and housing has been accorded a higher status, since the dominant priority – a high rate of industrial production – was a steadfast and necessary objective; thus qualified manpower, particularly specialists and people of keen organisational ability, could not be released from the manufacturing sector (primarily heavy industry) and transferred to housing and urban development.

In the field of town planning theory, the basic parameters of post-war architects and planners had been sketched out. One way in which the city would come to epitomise the industrial era was through the application of industrial technology to construction. The Bauhaus had exerted its influence; the Constructivists had had some success; neo-classicism had been championed and electicism triumphed. Their total imprint on urban form and development before the war and for a decade after its ending was limited, but they all pointed in the direction of the European tradition, with its emphasis on flat-dwelling in multi-storey apartment blocks. The doctrinaire approach to problems which came to hold sway in the 1930s, combined with very real economic constraints, stifled creativity and nurtured bureaucratic solutions to overcoming the acute shortage of accommodation and to urban layout design. As already mentioned, in one case, the government decreed (somewhat arbitrarily) that houses in towns and workers' settlements must be of four or five storeys and over,[42] adding further that individual low-rise dwellings were to comprise only 10 per cent of the total volume of new construction. As a result of such dogmatically established objectives, which bore little relationship to the resources available, city plans drawn up in conformity with this injunction quickly became obsolete.[43]

The massive migration to the towns and the underdeveloped house-building industry meant a decline in per capita living space[44] and the growth of huge urban areas consisting of low-rise, ill-equipped housing (see Chapter 8). Furthermore, instead of the futuristic 'communal house', envisaged by Sabsovich and Strumilin, it was the 'communal flat' (*kommunal'naya kvartira*), with its shared kitchen and bathroom and housing several families, which emerged as the typical purpose-built flat found in towns. The ideals of the Russian Revolution were laid to rest in the processes of industrialisation. Stalin's state liquidated the radical tendencies and at the same time consolidated the economic consequences of the revolution – one of which was an unprecedented rate of urbanisation.

PARAMETERS STRUCTURING THE HOUSING DEBATE SINCE THE 1960s

Planners after the war inherited far more than a set of principles, concepts, methodologies, administrative machinery and experience: their legacy included everything that had been created on the ground, together with a set of institutional conflicts. They have gradually come to acknowledge and become preoccupied with three main problems facing their Western counterparts: (1) urban renewal; (2) the growth of large towns and the formation of urban agglomerations; (3) the relationship between territorial–administrative organisations dealing with spatial–environmental planning, on the one hand, and economic bodies concerned with production-planning, on the other. These spatial and institutional problems, conflicts and contradictions, already partly discussed in Chapter 3 and dealt with again in Chapters 8 and 9, are interwoven with changes in the social structure, the government's specifically social objectives (those affecting people's life chances and way of life outside the work situation) and the demands made by individual citizens themselves.

Much has changed over the last 40 years and today, however long housing waiting lists might still be and however cramped living conditions on the whole remain, the housing problem is no longer regarded as acute. As a result, the government considers itself in a position to devote more attention to the issue of quality and comfort. The changed economic and political climate which now exists has led to a freer rein being offered to those with new ideas both in the sphere of architectural design of individual buildings and of systems of buildings at the city and sub-city levels. Ideas put forward and tentatively tested in the first decade of Soviet power began to reappear again in the 1960s: the visions of the nature of socialist society, notably its collective character, have changed little.[45] Paradoxically, whilst half a century ago these conceptualisations of the environment most conducive for producing a 'new way of life' ran too far ahead of the level of development of the society for them to be implemented, today perhaps, these re-vamped ideas lag behind, or have been largely rendered redundant by, the development of Soviet society which has, in the process of developing, created new social structures and new demands amongst the population.

A key question underlying the remainder of this chapter is: has a new socialist way of life been created (or in the process of creation) in the Soviet Union? The construction of socialist society is not completed with the 'expropriation of the expropriators' and the transformation of social relationships in the work place: this revolutionary action should be seen (as it normally is) as the first step, the *sine qua non*, for the creation of socialism. Thereafter, 'the march towards socialism' progresses *pari passu* with a cultural revolution in the norms and mores of individuals expressed in their relationship to one another in all spheres of social activity. A certain faction of the intelligentsia has tended to believe that such a cultural revolution will be associated with particular architectural forms and spatial usages. The three sections into which this second part of the chapter is divided look at some of the factors which act as obstacles to social and cultural transformation and which are also partly responsible for the cultivation of an individualistic ethos. Identifying aspects of this ethos is crucial for an understanding of housing forms and emerging patterns of urban development.

FROM 'DOM KOMMUNA' TO THE 'MIKRORAION' AND THE PRIVATE CAR

The 1950s saw the resuscitation of the concept of the *mikroraion* (neighbourhood unit) – 'a complex of residential buildings combined with a variety of services and retail outlets meeting the population's daily needs' – which has become 'unquestionably accepted as the primary structural planning unit'.[46]

A *mikroraion* is intended as essentially a pedestrian precinct with only access roads, and whose boundaries are normally drawn by main traffic thoroughfares. It should embrace within its boundaries crèches, kindergartens and primary schools, shops to meet the residents' daily requirements, library and club facilities and space for garaging cars. The essence of the *mikroraion* as a planning concept is that it combines housing and a diverse range of services to form a systemic whole within a much larger hierarchically arranged 'stepped system' (*stupenchataya sistema*). The concept of the stepped system of social services is found not only in the theoretical articles and handbooks for planners, but also in government-approved documents which determine town planning in the Soviet Union. Over the past 20 years, during the period of ascendancy of the stepped system concept, a number of decrees have been issued by the government seeking to deal with the need to improve the standard of services. According to one decree the provision of more and better public dining-rooms, laundries, pre-school facilities etc. 'not only leads to economies in material and labour resources but also, in the process of freeing the woman from domestic slavery, radically alters the way of life of the family'.[47]

However, the stepped system, and the *mikroraion* in particular, is more than an organisational device for providing a variety of services conveniently. It also carries a strong normative element. It was and remains a construct directed at achieving specific social objectives, though these are now being questioned. If the *mikroraion* forms a closely knit social whole, then the system of services must be spatially distributed in such a fashion that each member of the community will ideally reduce the time spent outside its boundaries, because to step outside them to satisfy daily needs only serves to damage the integrity and harmony of the whole.[48] In a very real sense, the contemporary notion of the *mikroraion* is an extension of the idea of a communal block (*dom kommuna*) as described by Strumilin in his book *Our World in Twenty Years*. In the section on 'What is the Commune?' he asks how the collectivisation of the workers' way of life can be brought about and how women can be freed from domestic slavery. His answer is that communes with populations of two or three thousand persons be organised along the lines of the modern sanatorium or hotel with public catering facilities and a complete supply of services (laundries, clothing and shoe-repair workshops) for the residents. Complexes of communes in large cities would form *mikroraiony* whose population could meet its daily, basic needs without going beyond the confines of such a 'mikroraion of communes'.[49]

More recently, Gradov has designed a 'productive-residential district' (*proizvodstvenno-zhiloi raion*) for 40 000 people covering an area of 156 hectares. The population is housed in four tower blocks each of 100–120 storeys, which he calls 'housing-neighbourhoods' (*dom-mikroraion*). Each tower block provides a whole range of services, including crèches and school, on the ground and first floor and then at 20-storey intervals. The central part of this district, with an area of 30 hectares, is the main shopping and cultural centre where industry is also located. According to Gradov, 65 per cent of all industrial enterprises can be classified as 'not harmful' and so may be situated in residential areas. His plans are quite consistent with two of the basic goals laid down by the government towards which the society is supposed to be moving: firstly, a reduction in distance between place of work and residence, for in Gradov's scheme the journey to work takes only five minutes; and secondly, automation of the productive process to 'eliminate the difference between mental and manual labour'. This principle is incorporated into Gradov's system by ensuring schools provide practical training and by continuing to improve the 'architectural, artistic form of industrial complexes so that they are comparable to the standards achieved in residential construction'.[50]

Visions of the *mikroraion* as an integrated community such as those held by Strumilin and Gradov are unlikely to leave the architect's drawing-board or the intellectual's drawing room for a very long time. Even the far less dramatically envisaged collectivisation of social life – the formation of associations (*kollektivy*) which were to unite residents in the task of self-government and in the organisation of social life in the *mikroraion* – has never materialised.[51] This 'failure' alone might be sufficient reason for questioning the 'community' aspect of the *mikroraion*. Yet there is also, from a Marxist perspective, a fundamental reason of principle why these visions are unacceptable. The central focus of an individual's life activity is his place of work. Consequently, the locus of his community or collective is to be found in the factory or organisation where he works rather than in the *mikroraion* where he lives. As already mentioned, a goal of socialism is the elimination of differences between mental and manual labour, thereby furnishing the individual with the opportunities to cultivate his inherent creative capabilities. It is therefore at the work-place that he can realise himself as an innovator; it is there that he is part of a 'natural' collective – one formed out of interaction and interest. Furthermore, as barriers between mental and manual labour are reduced, interaction becomes less restricted to those in the same occupation or engaged in analogous tasks and comes to embrace individuals fulfilling other functions within a given productive or administrative unit. In this view, social clubs and recreational activities are best organised around the place of work rather than the place of residence. Similarly, pre-school facilities, which continue to be financed mainly through the work-place, are better associated spatially and socially with the factory or office than with the home (see Chapter 3).

This corporate structure, where the whole life process revolves around the place of work (which not only provides social clubs, pre-school places for workers' children and access to resthomes, but also meets the medical needs of its employees and supplies them with accommodation), tends to involve the individual in a widely embracing micro-system such as is to be found in some Western corporations. Yet, this Durkheimian-like corporation, itself a twentieth century (or industrial) equivalent of the medieval guild, itself contradicts the high levels of geographical mobility increasingly a feature of advanced industrial societies.

Neither the work- nor the home-based community (*kollektiv* or *mikroraion*) seems adequately to take into account the fact that individuals are members of social networks which transcend arbitrarily drawn socio-spatial boundaries. In socially mixed residential units, as the *mikroraiony* normally are, individuals belonging to different (or the same) social groups will have no greater motivation or tendency to interact with their neighbours than residents in an English neighbourhood unit. One reason for the apparent absence of local social interaction is that population mobility is constantly increasing, especially where leisure activities are concerned. Individuals are not finding their source of entertainment 'localised in some sort of rigidly drawn territorial boundary' but more and more on a city-wide basis. This tendency had been commented upon in 1964, when two sociologists noted that on the whole social contacts in towns were widely dispersed, with less than half of all friendships arising out of a common place of residence or work-place or even education. They concluded that the grouping of people together on the basis of ensuring the satisfaction of their basic living needs had no real significance in the establishment of social contacts.[52] A concomitant of greater mobility is increased demand for private car ownership which, in turn, stimulates and intensifies mobility.

In 1960 the contributors to an urban planning conference noted that a widespread assumption that the use of the private car, especially in the USA, has been the most important variable in influencing settlement patterns, was not entirely correct. The extreme separation of place of work from residence in capitalist countries was not so much a consequence of the high rate of car ownership but rather of the high price of land in the cities themselves. After pointing out that land rent does not determine settlement patterns in the Soviet Union they listed a series of reasons why private car ownership would not develop to a high degree in the USSR.[53] A few years later, after Khrushchev's fall from power, the government concluded a contract with Fiat to set up a car assembly plant with an eventual annual output of 700 000 cars. Between 1970 and 1980, annual car production rose from 344 200 to

1 327 000 – an increase of 285 per cent.[54] Although the tenth five-year plan target of an annual output of about 1.3 million cars was achieved, no mention was made of car production in the Guidelines for the National Economy for 1981–85. However, it had been estimated that car output will increase by 1.5 per cent for the next 70 years (i.e. doubling during that period) and thereafter remain constant.[55]

The debate in the Soviet Union on the spread of private motoring, on the implications that the advent of 'mass motorisation' has for the society, the desirability of this development and the ultimate ratio of the number of cars to the population which should be aimed for, reveals the existence (as in Western Europe) of contrasting views on private car ownership. A conference held under the auspices of the Section of the Presidium of the Soviet Sociological Association concerned with the social problems of motorisation, reflected the differing opinions that exist on the extension of private car ownership. There are those who question whether it is neccesary for every citizen to own his own car when public transport, especially in large cities, is improving all the time. However, recognising that even a good public transport system cannot fully satisfy 'the social–psychological need for personal means of transport',[56] they concede that the private car will have to be 'tolerated'–with the caveat that it ought to be used mainly for recreation and that the state should operate a car rental service which will eventually lead to the curtailing or total banning of private cars in cities. In support of their argument, the lobby against mass private car ownership points out that private motoring has a deleterious influence on various spheres of people's lives including their personalities. The growing number of private cars might awaken individualistic, anti-social tendencies ('my' parking place, etc.) and aggravate interpersonal conflicts that are incompatible with the moral standards and principles of Soviet society; furthermore, the car could become a prestige symbol as it has in Western countries.[57] The protagonists of private car ownership on the other hand, think first of all that privately owned cars, despite their as yet limited number, have become a permanent feature of Soviet life and, secondly, that they do not contradict the moral goals of the society, since a passenger car can have no greater negative moral–psychological influence on its owner than anything else he possesses.[58]

Those expressing fears about the spread of car ownership, based on current experience in the Soviet Union (where the car is a prestige symbol), on observations of the negative consequences of mass car ownership in Western countries and on considerations of the benefits of a highly developed public transport system, are unlikely to have a very much greater impact on transportation policy than their counterparts in Western countries. The force of their case is possibly diminished by the fact that the Soviet Union is far from reaching the car-population ratios found in other industrialised societies. However, the fact that in 1975 the UK had 251 cars per thousand people and the USSR only 10[59] is less important than the apparent trend in policy, which is to increase the ratio to between 150 and 200 cars per thousand by the year 2000,[60] for the privatisation of the internal combustion engine, like the ownership of certain consumer durables (say washing machines) is to a large degree a concomitant of privatised family life. To state this is not to pass moral judgement on private car owners or the nuclear family; it is rather to suggest the universality of certain forms of living and possession corresponding to a particular level of development of the forces of production. These two social phenomena have a considerable impact on life styles, attitudes and patterns of interaction. The following two sections focus on the impact of the nuclear family in the USSR on gender role and its relationship to housing design.

GENDER ROLES, THE NUCLEAR FAMILY AND HOUSING POLICY

According to one view, familiar to Western students of urbanisation, the urban way of life has been so diffused throughout society that in the USSR today one can no longer properly speak of a rural way of life at all, except perhaps in rural areas in Central Asia.[61] But just as the urban way of life has in many ways been transported into the countryside, rural mores find expression in the town – partly because the overwhelming majority of adult urban residents have had their origins in the countryside. Although Soviet sociologists recognise that ways of life and means of social control differ between town and country, and that rural migrants transfer aspects of their customary life style into the urban milieu,[62] less appears to have been written about the actual impact of rural social relationships in the dynamic interchange between the spheres of industrial and agricultural production, or on the formation of enclaves of 'urban villagers' (see Chapter 8). This is especially true in a country in which, even in 1981, 97.7 million people were living in rural areas. The 1970 census recorded 105.6 million people as rural, living in 469 253 settlements.[63] Some of these settle-

TABLE 6.2 *Sources of urban population growth, 1926–79*

Source of increase	of which				
	Dec. 1926– Jan. 1970	Dec. 1926– Jan. 1939	Jan. 1939– Jan. 1959	Jan. 1959– Jan. 1970	Jan. 1970– Jan. 1979
Total increase in urban pop. (mln)	105.4	29.8	39.6	36.0	27.6
(% of total)	100.0	100.0	100.0	100.0	100.0
of which, from:					
Natural increase (mln)	27.9	5.3	8.0	14.6	12.0
(% of total)	26.5	17.8	20.2	40.6	43.5
Mechanical increase (mln)	59.7	18.7	24.6	16.4	15.6
(migration) (% of total)	56.6	62.8	62.1	45.5	56.5
Administrative reclassification of formerly rural localities (mln)	17.8	5.8	7.0	5.0	
(%of total)	16.9	19.4	17.7	13.9	

SOURCE *Naselenie SSSR. Spravochnik*, Moscow, 1974, p. 54; V. Kozhurin, S. Pogodin, 'Izmeneniya chislennosti gorodskogo naseleniya SSSR v 1939–1979 godakh', *Istoriya SSSR*, No. 6, 1980, pp. 135.

ments were very small; 90 000 had less than five inhabitants; a further
131 532 had populations of between six and fifty persons. The impact
which the countryside has on the culture and social and political
consciousness of the society at large makes itself felt directly through
the continuing migration from the countryside to the towns: between
1959 and 1970, out of an increase in the urban population of 36
million, 45.5 per cent was accounted for by migration. Between 1971
and 1975 a further 8 million persons left the countryside for the towns.
Marx's view that 'the whole economic history of society is summed up
in the movement of this antithesis' between town and country,[64]
certainly has continued relevance for understanding the development
of the Soviet Union.

The way of life of the present population and of other social classes
living in the countryside has considerably altered over the last 70
years; the October Revolution and subsequent economic policies
transformed social relations on the land, whilst the growth in the gross
domestic product has brought an array of material benefits to the
population. Despite general improvements in the standard of living
which have taken place, 'the difference between town and village is
recognised by all Marxists who are conducting research into social
processes under socialism as remaining a social difference and,
moreover, one of the main social differences continuing to exist at the
present level of development of Soviet society'.[65]

In Soviet Marxist terminology the main factor responsible for the
difference was and remains the unequal levels of development of the
productive forces in manufacturing and agriculture. In spite of this gap,
it is not the case of the village merely existing in the shadow of the
town, trailing behind the latter in the degree of economic development
and in the level of provision of social and cultural services, since its
comparative backwardness has a series of consequences for society at
large. It is at least worth considering the proposition that the 'private
plot', which Mr Brezhnev regarded, unlike Mr Khrushchev, as 'per-
forming a useful role in the economy and meriting state assistance',[66]
helps to perpetuate a set of individualistic propensities amongst a
substantial section of the population. After all, the preservation of
social relationships of an essentially capitalistic nature amongst almost
100 million people cannot but have some implications for the society at
large, most directly in the market relationship between the sellers of
agricultural products and their purchasers. It is also a reminder that
urbanisation – the movement from one particular set of social relationships (in the countryside) to another set (in the town), the movement

from one class (peasant) to another (worker) – although it means a formal substitution of one set of objective class relations for another, does not immediately change the social relationships, the traditions and the world outlook of migrants. And what change does occur is extremely slow.

Individuals can and indeed do adapt to some of the characteristic conditions of urban life, such as the impersonal nature of much social interaction, the need to respond to signs and symbols and to recognise and conform to modes of conduct associated with specific roles. These behavioural changes are essentially changes in form which enable them to function more or less effectively in a complex new social environment. Such changes do not imply a conscious or even unconscious jettisoning by the rural–urban migrant of normative patterns which he has been socialised into in the village. The value system of the former rural environment is instead transferred to the urban milieu in a variety of ways. Firstly, relatives play a crucial role in the rural migrant's acclimatisation. The newcomer may, on arrival in a town, live with relatives or *zemlyaks* (individuals from the same region or republic) who also provide him with assistance in finding work.[67] In other words, the individual is 'cocooned' within the urban environment and, if the friends and relatives themselves form a sub-community, then the newcomer may only slowly assimilate urban values. Secondly, the vast majority of the urban populace have their origins in the countryside, thus ensuring that contact with the private plot is maintained. Thirdly, the tending of private plots is not confined to rural settlements for not only do collective farm peasants operate a 'personal economy',[68] but so also do workers on state farms and manual and office workers employed in state industrial enterprises and institutions living in the countryside,[69] and even members of 'other social strata living in towns and urban-type settlements'.[70] These social facts may well have a bearing on the type of accommodation that many people would choose to live in, if offered the opportunity. They may also influence, if not determine, where this migrant group lives in the city or urban system. This issue of residential segregation by social group membership is discussed in Chapter 8: the point that has to be stressed here is the potential significance of rural background as a cultural determinant of housing preferences.

Among the norms and traditional mores, which Western and Soviet sociologists generally assume peasant migrants to take to the city with far-reaching implications for housing, urban planning policy and the rational use of the labour force, is the unequal division of labour between the sexes found in the countryside. This particular cultural norm may influence the fact that in towns Soviet women from all social groups spend twice as much time on housework as men.[71] (In 1973 one survey of collective farm workers in the Rostov *oblast'* found that on average women spent 3.39 hours every day on housework compared with 0.63 hours for men; in addition they each spent 1.36 and 1.09 hours respectively on tending the private plot).[72] Another study conducted by a research institute attached to USSR *Gosplan* found that 'working women with children spend, on average, 4–5 hours per day on housework, a figure which rises to 8–9 hours on their "days-off"'.[73]

Most urban women, then, have two working days – one spent in production and the other in the home. Two Soviet sociologists, Gordon and Klopov, acknowledge that the inequality between the sexes in carrying out housework constitutes 'one of the most important social problems in the modern city' and suggest that there are two ways of lightening the burden borne by women: firstly, by 'creating the conditions' for involving men in domestic work; and secondly, by cutting down on the overall amount of housework. Whereas the latter is almost entirely a product of better accommodation and domestic equipment and improved services, the former requires changes in 'the cultural climate'. In essence this means trying to overcome those traditions and customs 'forbidding' men to take part in cleaning the flat, washing and food-preparation.[74] Observation, together with correspondence and commentary in the press, provides little ground for believing that any major reorientation of values is imminent. Indeed, an article in the trade union newspaper, *Trud*, in 1982 referred to a sociological study which revealed that on average men spend 1 hour 20 minutes per week on shopping whilst women spend 3 hours 10 minutes. The corresponding figures for this gender division of labour for meal preparation and washing up was 2 hours 10 minutes and 13 hours 10 minutes; for cleaning the home, 40 minutes and 4 hours; for caring for clothing and footwear, 30 minutes and 5 hours 30 minutes.[75]

Although Lenin and some of his contemporaries were probably genuinely concerned about the morality surrounding the unequal nature of the relationship between the sexes, the motive force behind statements and legislation aimed at 'freeing women from domestic slavery' largely derived from considerations of expediency, for the substantial amount of time spent by women on domestic duties negatively affects the contribution which they make to the public sector. The changing structure of the family, with young couples increasingly living apart from the grandparents (who formerly looked after the children, shopped and performed a variety of domestic tasks) and the shortfall in pre-school places means that if the father will not undertake them there is no alternative for mothers but to take responsibility for these functions.[76] Furthermore, a married couple finds it financially difficult to survive (if they wish to dress fashionably and stock their homes with domestic furnishings, a television set etc.) when the woman is not the recipient of a full-time wage. In an acquisitive society in which real incomes remain low, an opportunity cost of material goods is children. That this might indeed be the opportunity cost is shown in the declining birth-rate which in towns fell from 30.5 births per thousand in 1940 to 26.0 in 1950, and to a low point of 15.3 in 1968; since 1968 it has risen to 17.0 in 1980.[77] However, the rate is expected to decline again after 1980.[78] The extent of the decline had certainly not been anticipated: a forecast made in 1965 of the urban population in 1975 put the figure at 262.9 million – the actual population in 1975 was 253.3 million.[79] Of the two factors commonly cited as responsible for this decline – the estimated loss of 15 000 000 males in World War II and the increasing number of women restricting family size – it is the latter which is of decisive importance.[80]

According to one Soviet sociologist[81] the most 'common cause' for the declining birth-rate is the changing economic role of children. In the traditional rural society children were regarded as a guarantee against old age and were, in any case, by the age of 10 valuable contributors to the household. In the towns, on the other hand, there is a sharp increase in the family's expenditure on children who are, on average, consumers until they are 20. Not only do they consume the parents' income, but also their time: 'in towns children require constant attention. Child neglect (*beznadzornost'*) is a purely city problem'.

This demand on the parents' time comes into conflict with the demand for a full-time occupation. This demand, on the part of women, declares the socialist and demographer Perevedentsev, is not just dictated by economic necessity, for it is also a social demand; women prefer to go out to work rather than remain at home with children. There is other evidence that women themselves do not always believe that the separation of mother and child for most of the day during the child's early years is desirable or not harmful. However this may be, given prevailing attitudes on the dual role of women as workers both in the public and domestic sectors and the need for a second family income, their work outside the home is, in many cases, a choice forced by domestic economic necessity. In these circumstances it is difficult to agree with the American economist Grosman that; 'rising incomes are likely to induce more Soviet women to opt for a housewife's role rather than paid employment'.[82]

The changes in the demographic and social structure will have increasingly greater impact on the economy. By 1970, there were already 1.7 million fewer workers than the planners had projected as necessary in that year.[83] Such is the shortage that between 1964 and 1976 the number of people who reached retirement age (over 60 years for males and over 55 for females) but remained in employment increased two and a half times; today one quarter of this age group continues to work in public production,[84] with the XXVI Party Congress commenting that 'more veterans must be attracted back to work, particularly in the service industries'.[85] Studies of family size preferences show that 91.4 per cent of families in Moscow and 83.3 per cent of families in the Central European region as a whole are oriented towards having only one or two children; and current estimated fertility is 2.2 children per woman in the USSR as a whole and 1.9 in the RSFSR.[86] It is not difficult to see why it is necessary to attempt to encourage more retired persons back into work in the public sector. This cannot, however, be a long term solution. Feshbach has calculated that with a possible fertility rate of 1.8, the population of the USSR between the years 2000 and 2050 would fall by 29 million to 272 million (compared with 267 million in 1981).[87] Although the manpower situation did not deteriorate too rapidly during the 1970s, in the 1980s the decline in the rate of growth of the population of working age could create a serious constraint on the fulfilment of economic plans.

One arrangement which could lead to a rise in the birth-rate is the provision of part-time employment for women. A survey conducted in the early 1970s gave the reasons cited by women for wanting to work part-time (four to six hours a day): 24.9 per cent because they had young children, 24.8 per cent because there was too much housework and 28.5 per cent because they wanted to study more.[88] Another survey, conducted in 1977, of women in full-time and part-time work in a wide range of occupations found that 76.1 per cent of those surveyed and employed full-time wanted to switch to part-time work (51 per cent wanted a shorter day and 25.1 per cent a shorter week), the majority for child-rearing reasons.[89] Some economists have been led to argue that 'with our millions of non-working women with children and our increasing labour shortage, the shorter working day and home labour are just the solutions needed'. In contrast to Hungary where 11 per cent of the female labour force work a short day, the figure in the USSR is a mere 0.5 per cent (and this includes old-age pensioners remaining at work, disabled persons and part-time students).[90] But the introduction of flexi-time and part-time working is likely to meet substantial and widespread opposition from managers who are not infrequently prone to regard radical change as disruptive to their established procedures and practices.

Mr Kosygin, in his speech at the XXV Party Congress (1976), stressed the need for a more efficient use of manpower since 'it is necessary to bear in mind that in the 1980s there will be a decline in the natural increase in labour resources'.[91] In one somewhat specious calculation it was argued that since a woman spends on average 30 hours per week on housework, this amounts to 100 milliard labour hours a year for all women, which is equivalent to the labour time of over 40 million people. Therefore, if the time women spend on housework can be halved, this would be the same as drawing 20 million extra people into social production.[92] Such estimates clearly have had some effect on government thinking. The 'Programme for Social Development and Raising the Standard of Living' contained in the Party document for the XXV Party Congress, specified a package of measures designed to 'improve the conditions of work and domestic life (*byt*) of working women', which has as its unstated objective the raising of the birthrate. It intended to:

Introduce for working women a partly-paid leave so that they can take care of their child until it is one year old. Create for women with children broader opportunities to work at home. Expand the network of pre-school and school establishments and all-day nurseries. To build 2.5–2.8 million places in crèches and kindergartens. Special attention to be paid to improving the running of children's institutions. Create conditions for shortening time spent on housework by developing the network of domestic services, public eating places and increase the output and sale of semi-prepared meals (*polufabrikanty*) and kitchen equipment.[93]

These proposals, which are of particular relevance to the almost ten million women raising families on their own,[94] represents one side of what Soviet authors refer to as a 'dialectical contradiction' in housing policy,[95] between the expansion and extension of public services on the one hand, and the provision of a high standard of comfort in the home on the other. Since at present the Soviet Union maintains that it is in the process of building a communist society, the actual working out of this contradiction is of the greatest significance and Soviet writers are right to discuss housing and town planning strategies in terms of it.

The XXVI Party Congress (1981) went still further and propounded a distinctly and explicitly pro-natalist policy; it granted state allowances to mothers in the form of partially-paid leave of one year (later to be extended to eighteen months) and lump sum payments of 50 roubles for the first child and 100 roubles for subsequent births. It also revealed its intention of 'taking steps' to enable women with young children to work for just part of the day (or week) and to be employed on a flexible timetable or at home.[96] Legislation in that year not only adhered fully to these pro-natalist policies, but adopted a regionally differentiated timetable for introducing partly-paid leave in order to discriminate in favour of those regions where the labour shortages are most acute and the birth-rates lower.[97]

Although there is no obvious contradiction between the decisions taken at the last two Party Congresses on family policy, a slight shift in emphasis has occurred. Ideally, the two strategies of extending social care and other facilities and providing state allowances to mothers should complement one another and be developed together. To do so, however, would almost certainly be too costly. The state, in shifting from a form of indirect intervention (creating social care facilities) to direct intervention by offering material incentives to women has set in train a policy the cost of which it is impossible to determine, for it is impossible accurately to predict how many women will avail themselves of the new benefits. And, if large numbers of them are attracted by these inducements, the state may find it difficult to fund its social welfare programmes and may have to 'cut back' its other provisions or raise its charges for, say, the use of pre-school facilities. Speculation on the cost to the government of its social welfare and pronatalist policies, and on the choices open to it on how to finance these programmes has to be based upon a key underlying premise that 'the family is the primary cell (*pervichnaya yacheika*) of society, whose functions under socialism are: the strengthening of conjugal relationships based on equal rights, friendship and common interests; propagating the species and child-rearing, recreation and relaxation and providing basic services for day-to-day living in a common household'.[98]

These assumptions obviously have a profound influence on housing design. The appropriate unit for the nuclear family is assumed to be the 'residential cell' (*zhilaya yacheika*), the flat. This has to satisfy, *inter alia*, the individual's physiological needs (sleep, 'personal hygiene'), and provide an environment for social interaction between family members and between a close circle of friends and other kin and for the pursuit of professional interests and hobbies. As far as the foreseeable future is concerned, the role of the home and the nuclear family will not alter very much. In fact, one Soviet sociologist regards 'one of the most important trends in contemporary life to be an expansion in the functions of the family and home'. He went on to say that under conditions of rigid, formalised, mainly impersonal contacts in large cities, the home is the most important sphere where the individual not only sheds the psychological load of the urban environment, but also where he can engage in free, personal intercourse with people who are psychologically close to him.[99]

It is possible that with improvements both in living space standards (which, ultimately, will mean ensuring that each household has one room more than the number of members in the family) and in the range of domestic appliances available, social life will become more and more privatised with individuals spending more time with the family at home. Of the two alternative methods of 'liberating' people from the 'burden of unproductive domestic work' – the socialisation of essential services (eating out regularly, taking clothes to laundries, having the flat cleaned by specialist agencies, etc.) on the one hand, and the provision of processed food products and domestic gadgetry on the other – it is the latter which will persist into the future. This choice has been ingenuously explained by one housing specialist as being not how a system of state-provided services should completely replace domestic labour, but rather how rationally to use the *time of women* on those types of family services which are necessarily domestic'.[100]

The unwillingness of women to have children may call for another housing arrangement. In 1979, a competition was held to design an apartment layout catering for a three generational family, principally on the grounds that the society is faced with an ageing population. 'Alongside the tendency for extended families to disintegrate, we can see the need to maintain links between family members in order to provide mutual assistance: for instance, grandparents can participate in the upbringing of children and the younger generation help care for the old.'[101] Such a view would undoubtedly find support among certain social workers, sociologists and politicians in the UK where, incidentally, it probably has just as little chance of becoming part of public policy.

What effect are improved housing conditions likely to have on the

Soviet birth-rate in practice? A variety of studies indicate a positive correlation: for instance, in one survey an improvement in living space standards was the most frequently cited factor which would induce women to have children. [102] One leading demographer also mentions housing conditions as the primary cause mentioned by women as inhibiting them from having a second child; the number of abortions after the first birth was twice as high in families where living space was below average than in families where it was above average. [103] However, for others, research has demonstrated that housing conditions are not the sole or determining factor of birth-rate but interact in a complex fashion with a range of variables including the level of education of women, income and availability of children's facilities. [104] One Western specialist considers Soviet analysts as being mistaken in their belief that the low birth-rate is consequent upon poor housing, low income etc., even suggesting that *better* housing may restrict the birth-rate still further. In his view, rather than manipulate demographic variables, the only way to reverse this unwanted decline is to offer women the opportunity to withdraw from the labour force for longer periods. [105] This approach, advocated by one school of Soviet demographers, [106] is now apparently beginning to be shared by the government.

It may be premature to conclude that these developments alone herald a total retreat by women into a traditional mother/housewife role. But the current measures aimed at raising the birth-rate must be considered in conjunction with the alarm of the authorities about the rising incidence of family breakdown. This is seen as a cause of a variety of 'social pathologies' such as alcoholism, sexual promiscuity and a general weakening of social control mechanisms. [107] Moreover, the tendency of women to become 'masculinised' is also sharply criticised in the Soviet press. For all these reasons, the efforts to encourage the traditional mother/housewife role of women are likely to be maintained.

CONCLUSION

In all societies housing is more than a physical structure of bricks and mortar. It reflects and reinforces social relationships and contributes to structuring patterns of interaction. Although a housing shortage still exists, the government's vast house-building programme has meant that millions of families are annually moving into new self-contained flats (see Table 7.5) and so at last leaving behind them the communal flat (*kommunal 'naya kvartira*) which constituted the most common type of urban dwelling unit until 1958[108] (Normally this meant that there was a common entrance to the flat with single, or at the most two, rooms leading off the hallway into the family's private accommodation. The kitchen and bathroom leading off the hall was shared by all the families in the flat.) As in the 1930s, the government was (and is) faced with a choice: to provide traditional single-family dwelling units in blocks of flats or experiment by constructing housing complexes expressing the goals and ideals of a socialist society.

Over the past 20 years designs have been drawn up and submitted by research institutes for 'houses with collectivised services.' One such proposal, for Moscow, the 'House of the New Way of Life' (*dom novogo byta*) actually materialised. Its construction, however, has been the subject of a controversy which revealed the polarity of attitudes towards such residential complexes. Critics pointed to the high costs involved in providing the extensive range of services and leisure facilities (such as a swimming pool, cinema, and theatre) and asserted that it had an elitist flavour and was better suited to certain social groups than others. In fact, one of the blocks was transferred to Moscow State University, on the ground that it coincided more with the needs of students, some of whom were married with small children, than with the needs of workers.[109] Such buildings will always have their sponsors. In 1979, the head of a subdivision of Gosplan argued that in order to meet housing requirements, new flats should be of

one or two rooms in hotel-type buildings. These flats with kitchen and bathroom are suitable not just for young people but also for parents. A building of this nature, providing a variety of facilities catering for daily needs such as eating and pre-school places, is appropriate not only for the European part of the Soviet Union but also for Siberia and the Far North and especially rural areas where they might reduce the outflow of young people from agriculture.[110]

The author then referred back to the experiments introduced during the first five-year plan when hotel-type blocks were erected alongside large factories.

But as in hostels, these hotels always had a single kitchen and bathroom complex on each floor. Naturally, life for families living in such conditions was not comfortable; each small flat must have its own kitchen, bathroom and built-in furniture. A shift towards this type of building will necessarily mean a reduction in the number of new flats consisting of three to five rooms; however, life itself dictates this movement to hotel-type dwellings.

Experiments will continue but housing policy is now firmly geared to building ever larger self-contained family dwellings which then have to be furnished and equipped. The XXII Party Congress held in 1961 effectively turned its back on the 'alternative' of the *dom novogo byta* when it passed a Resolution unequivocally stating that; 'each family, including young couples, will have a well-appointed flat corresponding to the demands of hygiene and the cultural way of life'.[111] Indeed, now some architects even refer to the 'house of the new way of life' as one which will 'assist in achieving parity between the number of people and the number of rooms in the flat. . . . In houses in the experimental new district (Severenoe Chertano in Moscow) the living room will no longer be a bedroom'.[112] Perhaps only a 'left-deviationist' (*levatskii zagibshchik*) would refute that this experimental district is a sign of progress. To invoke this still-used pejorative appellation is to invoke the 1930s. And today, as then, the social engineering dimension of housing policy is clearly in evidence. Writing in 1980, Broner honestly and concisely describes the implications of providing (and the functions of) single family dwellings. 'The importance of the radical change which the separate flat has on family life can scarcely be exaggerated. It creates the conditions conducive for child rearing and leisure and, in the final analysis, has a positive influence on the productivity of labour of the family members engaged in public production.'[113] This 'radical change' embodied in the slogan 'to each family its own flat' may justly be considered to be of historic significance; it represents not only an acknowledgement of the public demand for self-contained dwelling units to house the small nuclear family, but also the government's commitment to the nuclear family.

A combination of propaganda, exhorting women to engage in public production, economic need and the demand by women for employment in the public domain has resulted in a high proportion of women being employed in the public sector.[114] The persistence of a set of attitudes towards domestic work has meant that the burden of cooking and child-rearing rests with women. This disadvantageous status is a contributory factor in the declining birth-rate. The government's reaction has been to improve the provisions of public services and increase the output of consumer durables. In so far as the central concern is not the domestic burden disproportionately borne by women but the low birth-rate, the most important innovation, referred to at the XXV and implemented following the XXVI Party Congress, is extended maternity leave. This measure, together with the building of more nurseries and kindergartens, may have the desired effect in that more children will be born, but it will not affect the male–female segregation that exists at present. The concession allowing working mothers to 'work less than a full working day or less than a full working week and to work at home' will only legitimate and accentuate the existing role segregation. The proposal need not have specified 'women with children' and could have instead referred to 'a parent'. It is a measure of the strength of feeling that child-rearing and looking after the home is 'woman's work' that the statement was worded in this gender-specific way. This attitude is clearly visible in the declaration that it is the design and layout of a flat which creates the best opportunity for freeing the 'mistress'/'housewife' (*khozyaika*) so that she can use her time for leisure and the upbringing of children – a function which cannot be taken on by educational and other institutions, since 'nothing exerts such a strong influence on children and the formation of their personalities as the family'.[115]

The present trend suggests that the working out of the contradiction between individualistic tendencies inherent in the growing home-centredness and collectivist ideals embodied in the widespread use of public services is likely to intensify. Furthermore, it is possible that the set of norms and values which may be imputed to the more privatised, consumer-orientated, home-centred, car-ownership-seeking nuclear family with segregated role-playing that is emerging in the Soviet Union, will articulate with an individualism in the sphere of production. The latter is coming to be expressed in terms of greater autonomy for industrial managers whose behaviour and values are oriented towards a market-type rationality – which finds expression in the industrial location choices that the technocratic, efficiency-oriented manager (and economic planner) is constrained to make (see Chapter 9). Indeed, in its search to overcome its labour shortage, the government may be encouraged to grant greater scope to managers to find ways of using labour more efficiently, and that could well mean a step in the direction of the Hungarian path of economic reform[116] (see Chapter 7).

So not only has the government made a choice between privately and publicly owned housing, but it has apparently opted for a more privatised as opposed to collectivised way of life. In other words, whilst the USA (and to a much lesser extent, the UK) and the USSR diverge over the question of house ownership, they converge in terms of the privatised life-style that the type of accommodation they are building encourages. The following chapter examines some of the basic principles and methods underlying, and problems dictating, the Soviet government's strategy to provide its citizens with accommodation.

7 The Housing Problem: Economic and Technological Aspects

INTRODUCTION

An assessment of the successes and failures, merits and demerits of Soviet housing policy requires some comment on the scale of the housing programme, the keystone of which is the widespread application of standard designs and pre-fabricated methods of construction. The major institutional and organisational changes associated with this policy involve the centralisation of research, design and planning and the concentration of building in fewer and more specialised units. Since one attribute of advanced industrial societies is the high degree of specialisation which exists between units of production, the development of the Soviet economy has been accompanied by a fragmentation of decision-making with more and more functional units being empowered to take decisions affecting important aspects of their mode of operating. As a consequence, in the building industry as elsewhere in the economy, the banking system is coming to assume a greater significance through its monitoring of the performance of production units, assisting them by offering individually negotiated credit and by facilitating transactions between units. As far as the efficient operation of the economy is concerned, an expanded and more sophisticated banking and credit system may be deemed an advantage by making the economy more efficient.

Although the use of standardised components, the mechanisation of the industry, improvements in planning and organisation and the better co-ordination of activities through a system of credit and banking finance all contribute to the enhanced rate at which new dwelling units and other buildings are erected, a main determinant of output, especially its quality, is the labour force. In fact, one of the

147

major driving-forces behind the various organisational changes is the overall shortage of labour throughout the economy (as well as in the building industry). This issue of manpower shortage, discussed here and in other chapters, constitutes an important variable shaping domestic policy as well as the pattern of urban development.

Western specialists have yet to examine the pioneering work carried out by the Soviet Union in developing pre-fabrication technologies and new materials and to evaluate the government's success in meeting the enormous challenge presented by planning construction (including housing and infrastructure) on the scale of the USSR. The problems of planning for the whole economy are formidable and the mistakes legion.[1] Lessons are learnt and future planning can build on past experience; this dialectic is integral to the planning process. So, although in this and other chapters more has been said about the recurring problems discussed by planners, academics and politicians than about the successes, the intention is not to devalue the achievements of the planned economy or in any way to imply that any other means could have been more efficacious in developing the economy and raising the standard of living.

The Report on the tenth five-year plan, delivered in March 1981, spoke of its achievements and failures. Failures include the 'bottlenecks and disproportions' in the economy, unfulfilled production targets, unattained increases in labour productivity and inefficient resource utilisation. These were explained as arising from 'objective factors beyond our control', breaches in discipline, instances of mismanagement, inadequate planning and, 'most importantly, the sluggishness, conventions and habits that arose in the period when the quantitative rather than the qualitative aspect of work loomed large, which have still not been fully overcome'. These all point to the necessity for further changes in the organisation of the economy.[2] However, recent history provides sufficient testimony that, in the advanced industrial societies, attempts made by political leaderships to inaugurate radical policies have had limited success. Intellectually adroit or charismatic politicians can prevail over bureaucracies which they formally control and which they look upon, as did Henry Kissinger, as quagmires absorbing creativity and run by officials lacking imagination and resistant to change.[3] For most of the time, however, the collective decisions arrived at by bureaucrats, who prefer that only minor adjustments be made to the *status quo*, tend to prevail.

Yet political leaders, whether in Parliamentary or Soviet-type democracies, do not face a united force counterpoised to them:

instead, in pursuing their policies governments enter different bureaucratic domains, each with its fief and interests. In a real sense these sometimes constitute principalities nourishing their own local interests – the localism (*mestnichestvo*) tendency. Localism has been countered by the creation of a sector (*otrasl'*, *vedomstvo*) tendency: ministries accumulate property rights which they are unwilling to forefeit. In seeking to institute change a minister can be rebuked publicly and dismissed; a state committee or ministry can be disbanded and then reconstituted in another form of its dismembered parts incorporated into other aggrandising ministries. But since there can be little purpose in the state practising self-flagellation, it tries to remedy weaknesses in the operation of its parts by exhortation and persuasion, by issuing decrees, instructions, rulings and circulars, and by expressing its views through the media.

PLANNING AND THE DESIGN OF HOUSING

The 1920s were years of revolutionary cultural change with new ideas constantly being projected on to the stage for public examination and discussion. Architecture and town planning were no exception. The conceptions of architects and planners may well have been 'exciting'; these men were indeed pregnant with visions of how the proletarian revolution should be symbolically expressed in external form. The realisation of these conceptions and visions was, however, very costly – too costly for the resources available at the time. The Council of People's Commissars (*Sovnarkom*) drew attention to this fact in March 1931 stating that, in many cases, 'building is disproportionately expensive' and called for the construction of simplified types of dwellings, using standard designs.[4] Criticisms were levelled at 'wreckers' who used outdated technology and equipment to put a brake on the development of the urban economy and, as far as planning was concerned, dissipated capital investment on too many projects so that even minor projects, such as the construction of bathhouses (*sic*), were being drawn out over a number of years. As far as construction technology was concerned, the government could draw on respected specialist sources, such as V. Shmidt, to substantiate its claims and criticisms. Writing in 1929, Shmidt suggested that the slow rate of house construction was largely to be explained by the fact that 'we are sluggish and conservative in our search to find ways of rendering construction easier by applying new technology and better organisational forms in the construction industry. . . . We are still using roughly the same techniques and building materials as fifty years ago'.[5] The situation described by Shmidt could hardly be explained, however, by the existence of 'wreckers' – although Stalin was all too ready to use such information to vituperate and then incarcerate large numbers of individuals by imputing to them responsibility for, say, 'sluggishness in applying new technology'.

During the 1930s the government issued a series of decrees emphasising the need for building costs to be reduced and, concomitantly, for the quality of new building to be improved and for all organisations undertaking house-building to erect new dwellings in accordance with standard designs.[6] By the end of the decade, when it set up the first Commissariat for Construction (*Narkomstroi*),[7] the government was still upbraiding officials for the fact that: 'up till now, standard designs have not been worked out for the mass of house-building projects and this has meant that the development of industrial techniques for housing construction has been held up – and this, in turn, only serves to make construction more expensive'.[8] Unfortunately, in the 1930s research on the design and layout of buildings was distributed amongst numerous agencies, with the result that there was an 'absence of unity in the planning of house-building, this function being divided among a plethora of organisations'.[9] 20 years later the government still felt obliged to draw attention to the fact that powerful, specialised regional planning and design organisations had to be set up so as to prevent duplication of work and to eliminate small design offices which were failing to produce designs and plans of the required standard.[10]

Then in 1955 the State Committee for Architectural Affairs[11] was required to examine ways in which firstly, to bring design organisations closer to those areas where large scale construction was in progress and, secondly, to create design organisations specialising in particular types of building work.[12] A few months later another decree returned to the same theme, severely rebuking the most senior state architects and pointing out that there were 40 design offices attached to various ministries and central departments all engaged in working out standard designs for housing and public buildings. To remedy this situation the government called for the concentration of housing and civic construction work in one central institute.[13]

This decree, a harbinger for the imminent attack on Stalin and Stalinism, severely criticised 'the extravagance of architects and planners in their construction of buildings with decorative facades, porticoes and other excessive indulgences which have led, in recent years, to a frittering away of huge state resources'. The decree cited specific cases of waste, for instance, Gor'ky Street and the Leningrad Highway in Moscow and a variety of other structures in Leningrad, Kiev, Khar'kov, Minsk, Voronezh and Tbilisi, indicating that the 'excesses' were perpetrated by a large number of ministries and embraced a diversity of buildings – from sanatoria in Sochi to railway stations in Krasnodar and Bryansk. The root cause was the fact that ministries and departments regarded the working out of standard designs for housing and civic buildings as of second-rank importance. The Executive Committee of the Moscow city soviet came in for a special rebuke, for in 1954 only 18 per cent of all housing and civic construction in Moscow had utilised standard designs. As a result, those formerly rewarded for their work were now penalised: the chief Moscow architect was sacked whilst three winners of the Stalin prize, holding senior positions in the Academy of Architecture and Union of Architects, were deprived of their prizes. All were censured for paying too much attention to external features and the head of the Union of Soviet Architects was criticised for the fact that, in the struggle against constructivism, he only furthered 'the dissemination of these overindulgent ideas'. The Moscow Architectural Institute and other teaching establishments were blamed for inculcating in their students 'a one-sided aesthetic approach to the design of residential, industrial and other public buildings: too much attention was devoted to artistic aspects and not enough to economics'.

Re-organisation with necessary streamlining did take place following this ruling. Poor communication between research institutes was attributed by the government to the fact that 'these organisations have still not overcome the fallacious practice – characteristic of the former ministerial system – whereby each enterprise planned and provided for its own needs separately'.[14] After publicly reprimanding a number of organisations and listing detailed criticisms of architects and design and project agencies, the decree called for the training of more architects, a more widespread use of standard designs and an 'uncompromising struggle against manifestations of formalism in architecture'. This enactment marked an important step in the direction of co-ordinating research in the related fields of building design and land use. It came at a time when the government was beginning to pay greater attention to the question of town planning and to the fact that most cities and urban settlements lacked general development plans.

A government decree as long ago as 1926 made it compulsory for all settlements, legally defined as urban or as workers', dacha or resort settlements, to compile plans detailing the existing settlement layout and outlining proposals for reconstruction and expansion to which they were strictly to adhere.[15] Yet in 1961 a member of the Presidium of the Union of Architects observed that only about half of the 1700 cities in the USSR had approved general plans,[16] whilst one *oblast'* chief architect declared that the majority of the nation's 4600 workers' settlements had no plan at all and continued to grow in a completely haphazard way.'[17] In 1963 the introductory remarks to a decree initiating a large-scale re-organisation of urban planning stated that, 'the drawing up of city general plans is moving slowly. . . . Gor'ky, Khar'kov, Novosibirsk, Sverdlovsk, Kuibyshev, Omsk and a number of other cities do not have ratified plans corresponding to the present level of development, and a further 600 cities possess no plan at all'.[18] The decree then went on to speak of the need to achieve two major objectives which were to improve firstly the quality of design and construction of housing and civic buildings, and secondly the design and layout of towns. These goals were to be achieved by a wider application of standard designs for housing and social facilities and also by ensuring that each urban settlement had a general development plan.

Because of the absence of specialised project institutes, general development plans were being drawn up by a large number of departmental project organisations which rendered virtually impossible the co-ordination of project work and acted as an impediment to successful urban planning. Furthermore, standard designs were being drawn up by numerous, mainly small, planning agencies subordinate to different ministries and departments. This only created more obstacles to the manufacture of standardised building components, thus further hampering the industrialisation of construction. It was this fragmented system which the re-organisation, recommended by the 1963 decree, set out to remedy. Under the new system, the State Committee for Civic Construction and Architecture (*Gosgrazhdanstroi*), established directly subordinate to the State Committee for Construction (*Gosstroi* USSR), was to have overall responsibility for working out standard designs for housing and civic building projects.

The main innovation as regards urban planning was the devolution of responsibility for the compilation of town plans to local design organisations and design institutes for urban and regional planning. A list of cities which were to have such institutes was to be drawn up by the Council of Ministers in each Union Republic in consultation with

Gosgrazhdanstroi. The first to be set up were in Volgograd, Gor'ky, Donetsk, Kuibyshev, Novosibirsk, Odessa, Riga, Rostov-on-Don, Sverdlovsk and Khar'kov.[19] The city, *krai* and *oblast'* project offices already in existence were to be strengthened by transferring them to small design offices controlled by regional economic councils (*sovnarkhozy,*) ministries and central departments. And, in order to raise the overall standard of design work in the Eastern regions of the country, a central institute of city planning was to be established in Sverdlovsk.[20]

The intention behind this move to decentralise urban planning was to encourage a greater responsiveness to local needs on the part of the agencies compiling plans. It would also enhance the interest planners had in their work by offering them the opportunity to be more imaginative in their thinking. Formerly, local planners received instructions and blue-prints from Moscow and other 'central' planning and design agencies, which they were merely required to implement. Not surprisingly, they had little identification with their work and carried out their tasks perfunctorily.

The result of centralised decision-making and local apathy was a 'bureaucratic' approach to urban lay-out, monotonous sky-lines, and uniformity of towns in various parts of the country, whose differing cultures, traditions, climate, landscape and building materials were neglected altogether. The government returned to this theme once more in 1969 when it called for 'the creation of favourable conditions in the design organisations for planners to be given the greatest possible opportunity to display creative initiative'.[21] Devolution in some spheres was accompanied by centralisation in others. So as to ensure a unified technical policy in the field of housing and civic building design, the further development of industrialised techniques, and the elimination of duplication in the work carried out by design offices, the government established under the aegis of *Gosgrazhdanstroi* seven central scientific research and design institutes,[22] whose work was complemented by that of zonal institutes (set up in Leningrad, Kiev, Novosibirsk, Tashkent and Tallinn) concerned with the effects of local geographical and climatic factors on urban development.

The setting up of research institutes is a recognition that policy makers need more and better information on which to make decisions. But frequently a considerable time lag exists between their creation and the production of reports, analyses and recommendations, often because of the unavailability of data in a form necessary for the research. And this certainly applies to the field of urban planning, where 'not only is there a shortage of information, but what does exist reflects the dynamic growth of individual branches of the urban economy: statistical collection is geared primarily to national economic planning'.[23] Consequently the type of data required for devising detailed plans for a city's economic and social development has to be gathered separately. Unfortunately many of the indicators selected to analyse and project city development along these two dimensions are mechanically adopted from the methodologies employed in national economic planning.[24] In these circumstances, where satisfactory urban plans have been drawn up they have relied heavily on the participation of academics and other highly qualified specialists working for other organisations who have been 'co-opted' by the *gorispolkom* into the planning process. A further obstacle to more sophisticated urban planning has been the absence of text-books on the subject; in fact, the first book dealing with the methodology of comprehensive or corporate urban planning was not published until 1977.[25]

The picture which emerges is one of an underdeveloped and underfunded sector within the society's overall planning apparatus. This situation is gradually being rectified. But, as with the laws passed during the early 1970s (and culminating in the new Soviet Constitution)[26] extending the rights of the local soviets to co-ordinate and supervise building, manufacturing and most other activities within their administrative jurisdiction, change in practice has been slow. Instead of the local soviets' own planning committees undertaking to meet their mandate to draw up corporate development plans, the initiative lies with the city and oblast' Party committees. In Leningrad, for example, the oblast' party committee (*obkom*) has set up a Council for Economic and Social Development, whose function is to assist the *obkom* in its organisation and supervision of the development of the city and its region.[27] The involvement of the Communist Party in this major policy area is regarded as 'quite natural' and aptly demonstrates the 'guiding' or 'leading' role assigned to it in the process of social development.

As in so many other cases in the management of specific sectors of the society, the Party is charged with responsibility for certain tasks in order to break through bureaucratic log-jams, especially when a policy has been accorded priority but can only be successfully implemented through the co-ordination of different government departments whose interests are mutually exclusive. In this particular instance, although the law stipulates that enterprises and organisations must submit their draft plans to *krai, oblast'* and city planning committees,[28] the latter find it difficult even to communicate their comments and amendments to the ministries and *vedomstva*. Amendments to draft plans proposed by organisations and enterprises of Union – Republican subordination were found in one survey to be channelled to the appropriate ministry along a number of different routes; 30 per cent went via *oblast'* level administrative departments; 40 per cent via the organisation or institution which had submitted the draft; 10 per cent used the intermediary of the city Party apparatus; and, in one instance, the city's planning committee (*gorplan*) sent its proposals directly to the relevant ministries and departments.[29]

Even Soviet researchers have been unable to find out how often proposals and amendents are acted upon in practice. Once again, organisational structures and lines of command contribute to failures to take into account the planning committees' recommendations, for there is still no established procedure whereby ministries can respond to proposals.[30] On the other hand, one can only speculate on whether matters would improve following the adoption of clearly defined rules and channels for the flow of this information. For, after all, many enterprises and organisations of Union and Republican subordination do *not* present the city planning committees with their draft development plans and other data which would be crucial for devising a co-ordinated citywide plan. To complicate matters further, the preliminary drafts which are submitted have frequently not been ratified by the superior authorities (e.g. a ministry) – who also have a penchant for making important modifications to the draft. (Here, as in other cases, Leningrad is an exception and fares particularly well in so far as it is properly consulted and presented with information on time. An order issued by Gosplan RSFSR in 1977 laid down that branch plans affecting Leningrad and its region have to be drawn up in conjunction with the city's planning departments. Only after the various plans have been fully discussed and amended to take into account the overall strategy for the social and economic development of the region are they presented to the different ministries for their ratification.)[31] All that can safely be said is that the setting up of urban planning research institutes in the 1960s and the introduction of the notion of 'comprehensive social and economic development' a decade later, requiring much more detailed statistical data, are indications of the government's intention to improve city planning.

Administrative changes associated with calls for either more centralised control or for more decentralised decision-making apparently have a limited impact on practice. Construction costs, frequently

exceeding initial estimates, continue to rise, at least in part a consequence of architects' prodigality: 20 years after the previously-
mentioned attack on the profession for its members' extravagance,
architects were again criticised for costing the state millions of roubles
by using marble, granite and aluminium instead of cheaper materials.
Even *Gosgrazhdanstroi* had to bear some responsibility for this waste
since it was failing either to exercise sufficient control over the sorts of
materials chosen by design institutes and architects' workshops or to
ensure that the latter used the most economic methods of building.[32]
The government returned to this theme of design estimates again in
1981, remarking on the substantial amounts of time expended on
design work and on the interminable delays in having specifications
accepted, which only means that the latter are quickly outdated and
the estimates considerably inflated. Moreover, designs sometimes fail
to incorporate the most recent scientific and engineering advances and
do not attempt to economise on materials or seek to raise labour
productivity.[33] The Directives for the eleventh five-year plan also drew
attention to this issue of design estimates.[34]

The functions assigned to *Gosgrazhdanstroi* in the field of housing
and civil construction are very wide-ranging indeed and include:
responsibility for drawing up a single town planning policy for cities
and urban-type settlements; initiating and co-ordinating work on
standard designs for housing and civil construction; developing scientific research in the field of pre-fabricated building; co-operating with
Union Republic *Gosstroi* in the working out of detailed city lay-out
plans; assisting *Gosplan* USSR in working out the national economic
plan for housing and civic construction and agreeing to the 'title lists'
submitted for ratification by union republics and all-union ministries
and departments; establishing in conjunction with *Gosplan* USSR the
average estimated cost of erecting one square metre of living space and
then supervising the observance of these estimates; and working out
and submitting to *Gosstroi* USSR plans for future scientific research
and experimental work in the sphere of housing and civil construction
and city lay-outs.[35] Although *Gosgrazhdanstroi* has a considerable
degree of autonomy to carry out these various functions, *Gosstroi*
USSR is, in the final analysis, responsible for defining what constitute
the main technical and scientific problems in the field of construction
and architecture. It examines the research programmes undertaken at
the All-Union and Union–Republican level by those ministries and
departments engaged in construction and architecture, and determines
what financial resources are to be allocated to the various programmes

and projects within the limits imposed by the government's overall allocation of funds to scientific research.[36]

Over the past decade *Gosgrazhdanstroi* has improved the co-ordination and dissemination of information on new research findings and experience gained in the practice of using new materials and designs, and has thereby assisted chief city architects and planning departments by presenting them with an expanded range of techniques and blueprints from which to choose. At present the 90 series of standard designs are worked out in each union republic in order to take into account variations not only in topographical, climatic and geological conditions but also in, for example 'the existing material–technical basis, national customs and demographic structure of the region. In the "new series of standard designs", attempts are being made to move gradually towards the individualisation of design decisions for blocks of flats, houses and individual apartments in order to satisfy the demands of special social groups'.[37]

The programme of re-organisation, entailing the centralisation of research at the same time as greater responsibility was being delegated to local architects and planners, did not bear immediate fruits and another in the series of decrees issued in May 1969 contained a long list of complaints.[38] Standard designs of houses did not meet the expectations of their new tenants in terms of comforts and conveniences; the layout of flats frequently failed to take into account the composition of families; kitchens, bathrooms and halls were too small, principally because they did not provide sufficient storage space for modern domestic equipment and appliances; the blocks of flats were not designed with additional premises for keeping perambulators, bicycles and the like.[39] Furthermore, the external forms of houses and public buildings were unoriginal and stereotypic, with the result that residential districts in the majority of towns were uniform and unattractive in appearance. There is still scope for improvement here as Mr Brezhnev made clear in his speech to the XXVI Party Congress, confirming that 'urban development stands in need of greater artistic expressiveness and diversity'.[40]

Lastly, it has frequently been remarked, not least by correspondents in the satirical magazine *Krododil*, that the overall quality of housing construction remains below standard; it is commonplace to find deviations from the drawings and for houses to be accepted even with major defects. Nevertheless, it bears noting that in contrast to American practice, where shoddy construction is frequently camouflaged by well-finished walls, floors and ceilings, in the Soviet Union what is, from a structural point of view, excellent construction is made to look shoddy by poor finishing.[41] As so often in other spheres of production, whether of capital or consumer goods, solidity not style serves as the Soviet Union's hallmark.

Some of the problems of Soviet architecture can be related to the lower status accorded to it since the 1930s – a fact that may be partly attributed to the greater importance attached to cost and volume of construction at the expense of aesthetic considerations. A specific aspect of the sort of problem that arises from the application of standard designs (whose primary purpose is cost reduction) was highlighted in 1979 by the chief city architect of the Latvian capital. He pointed out that when an old part of the city is to be renovated, no scope is left for architects to exercise their imagination; construction norms and regulations and departmental instructions stipulate, for instance, the number of staircases and even the number of stairs to be contained in the design. He concluded that 'it is time *Gosstroi* and the Construction Ministries revised their attitudes towards the erection of buildings according to standard designs'.[42]

None of the complaints is new; they have all been raised at one time or another over the past 50 years.[43] The novelty consists in their all being listed in one place (initially in the 1969 decree) and showing a common concern for quality and diversity – words which were to form the catchwords in discussions surrounding the XXV Party Congress in 1976. By the 1970s, then, the emphases were changing; people were requesting, architects wanted to offer, and the government was willing to grant greater scope for 'imagination' in architectural forms, especially housing design. This made new teaching methods and an expanded course content *prima facie* requirements. Architectural students are now to be acquainted with such fields as cybernetics, computing technology, sociology, demography, systems analysis and organisational theory. Acknowledgement of the complexity of social life and its indeterminacy has meant that probability theory is now seen as forming an integral part of planning theory.[44] Whether or not these emergent ideas and attitudes will actually alter the urban landscape will largely depend on the government's ability to overcome major constraints on the economy, which in no small measure is affected by the state of international relations.

RATIONALISATION AND INDUSTRIALISATION OF THE CONSTRUCTION INDUSTRY

The state has been concerned not only with the un-co-ordinated activities of a multitude of design and project organisations, but also with integrating the large number of agencies actually engaged in building. The use of standard designs and industrial techniques went hand in hand with the erection of high rise blocks of flats.[45] These trends necessitated the rationalisation of the building industry by creating fewer and larger units. The advantages of concentrating construction and assembly work in large trusts and combines under the control of special ministries are analogous to those accruing to most other forms of large-scale industrial organisation: big units favour the introduction of new techniques and equipment and the mechanisation of the productive process; they lead to a more efficient utilisation of building machinery, higher labour-productivity, and improved quality of work which has as a corollary a reduction in the amount of repair work that has to be carried out. One of the major savings associated with larger units is a reduction in the number of office workers servicing a given work force by introducing more office equipment, from card index systems to electronic calculating machines and, in those cases where systems-planning is being employed, computers to process all the information at present dealt with manually.[46] However, this optimism stands contradicted, in the eyes of another Soviet author, by the experience of the United States where the widespread use of computers by local authorities has not had the effect of reducing office staff; indeed, the introduction of the new technology has not resulted in any diminution in the number of office workers employed in city administration.[47]

By the end of 1980 building contracting work was being undertaken by eleven All-Union and Union–republican ministries; these embraced 29 ministries of republican subordination, 366 general and specialist building trusts and almost 27 000 primary building organisations, of which 71 per cent were subordinate to USSR ministries and central departments and the remaining 29 per cent to the Council of Ministers of the Union Republics.[48] Numerous changes have taken place in this structure, and even the present system is generally acknowledged to be inefficient, giving rise to duplication of activities amongst the differing building organisations and to the familiar 'narrow departmental approach', especially when it comes to establishing material, equipment and manufacturing bases for the construction industry.

A primary objective of the government has been to reduce costs. In 1950 the government called for a 25 per cent cut in construction costs.[49] One of the surest ways of achieving this goal was to expand the volume of standardised construction; in fact, the use of standard designs in urban housing construction rose from 52 per cent in 1955 to 93.5 per cent in 1970.[50] In 1964 the so-called 'improved standard designs' were introduced and by 1975 these accounted for 70 per cent of the total volume of house construction. Then, in 1971, another 'new standard design' based on requirements stipulated in the new planning norms[51] came into production. In 1975 blocks of flats erected according to these latest designs amounted to 30 per cent of all house-building and by 1980 should have reacheed 60 per cent.[52]

The use of such serialised standard designs has as a logical concomitant the employment of pre-fabricated large-scale units in construction. To date Soviet design engineers have devised a system of standardised, modular building components. With only slight modification, all of the components are interchangeable between different building types – for example, there are standard components of pre-cast concrete beams, columns and slabs. One of the major thrusts of the standard component system is to use each one as much as possible, with the result that fewer decisions are left to civil engineers and buildings are more uniform in structure and appearance.

In terms of overall living space in towns, the proportion of all state and co-operative housing erected using large, four-metre wide panels rose from 1.5 per cent in 1959 to 3.3 per cent in 1960 and 15.1 per cent in 1962. By 1965, the figure had almost doubled to 28.5 per cent; it reached 37 per cent in 1970 and 49.9 per cent in 1975.[53] (See Figure 7.1.) By 1980, large panel construction accounted for about 60 per cent of state house building.[54] Their use, as might be expected, has been concentrated in the largest cities such as Moscow, Leningrad, Kiev, Minsk, Alma-Ata, Omsk and Novosibirsk where, in 1980, they were responsible for over 80 per cent of all new accommodation built.[55] In Moscow, 82 per cent of all housing erected by the city's main building trust, *Glavmosstroi* (see below), consisted of large panels and 18 per cent of brick. The corresponding figures for *Leningradstroi* were 81 and 19 per cent.[56] The number of factories manufacturing large panels increased from 270 with a capacity of 14 mln. square metres of dwelling space in 1965 to 404 (48.7 mln. square metres) in 1976.[57]

The extent to which large panels are used varies considerably between different regions, ranging in 1975 from 60 per cent in Belorussia, Lithuania, Latvia and Tadzhikstan to 24 per cent in Armenia, 31 per cent in Moldavia and 35 per cent in Georgia.[58] The attractiveness of this form of construction arises from the fact that, firstly, labour costs are 35–40 per cent lower than for houses built

FIGURE 7.1.　*Proportion of state and co-operative housing erected using different materials*

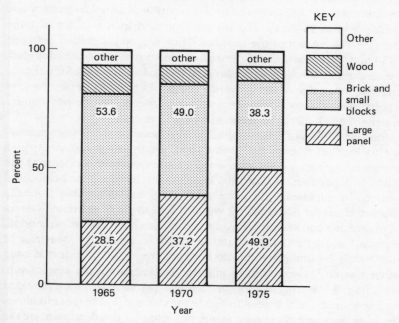

SOURCE　D. S. Meerson, D. G. Tonskii, *Zhilishchnoe stroitel'stve v SSSR v destyatoi pyatiletke*, Moscow, 1977, p. 8.

from bricks; secondly, the prime cost of erecting one square metre of dwelling space using large panels is 10 per cent lower than building with bricks and, thirdly, whereas using traditional building methods it takes 2 to 3 years to erect a 5–6 storey block of flats, when the large panel method is used, the building time is reduced to 3–4 months.[59]

Increased investment in house construction and the development of building technology in the early 1950s was taking place in the context of a visibly chaotic and inefficient building industry, with resources distributed amongst a multitude of ministries and departments. Several building organisations were operating in every town and sometimes side by side, each with its own equipment and stores, on a single street. An important step towards rationalising the industry was taken in April 1954 with the setting up of the Moscow Construction Board (*Glavmosstroi*) which amalgamated under one body 53 building trusts, 225 general and specialist building contractors and over 600 productive and auxiliary enterprises, previously controlled by 44 different ministries and central departments. (In the following year, *Glavlenin-gradstroi* was set up, followed by the creation of *Glavkievgorstroi* and similar boards in Baku, Rostov-on-Don and in a number of large cities).[60] The impact of the reorganisation was considerable: between 1954 and 1958 the volume of work carried out by the board doubled, the amount of dwelling space erected trebled with only a 10 per cent increase in the size of the labour force, thanks to an 81 per cent rise in labour productivity. Furthermore, construction costs per square metres of dwelling space declined by 18.5 per cent.[61]

Rationalisation in this one sphere of economic activity was a precursor to legislation passed in May 1957 when the government, in a sweeping change, sought to counteract the deleterious effects of the 'narrow departmental interests' allegedly fostered by the Ministerial system, by replacing the latter with Regional Economic Councils (*Sovnarkhozy* or *SNKhs*).[62] It was felt that the former branch system of organising construction through ministries had become outmoded, especially since its 'departmental character had led to the formation of small-scale building organisations which frequently duplicated each other's work'.[63] Despite the numerous weaknesses of the new system, including its fostering of a sort of 'localism' (*mestnichestvo*), it revealed a consciousness of the need to tackle the chronic problem of ministries for ever pursuing their own interests, often to the detriment of the government's other goals. As such, the decree setting up the *sovnark-hozy* acted as a tentative step towards countering the inevitable distortions to overall government policy to which the branch system was giving rise. In fact, these opposing departmental–local tendencies represented another dimension of the structural conflict already discussed, namely that between departments (*vedomstva*) and local soviets over the control of housing and the broad spectrum of amenities and resources that comprise the urban infrastructure (*municipal economy*). The abolition of the *Sovnarkhozy*[64] in 1965 did not hinder the major trend which the system had encouraged – the concentration of building materials and construction units and, above all, control over the activities of the permanent construction-and-assembly organisations, into fewer hands.[65] The process of rationalisation has not yet however, been completed.[66]

The tremendous progress made in the use of pre-fabricated building technology and standard designs has been closely associated with the advance, particularly over the last decade, towards the goal where the house-building combine (*domostroitel'nyi kombinat – DSK*) will form the basic production unit for housing. That is to say, it 'not only manufactures all the main components making up a house but also transports them to a building-site using its own custom-built vehicles, then erects them, completes all the necessary interior finishing work and hands the building over to the client'.[67] And, in the case of the most advanced combines, the final product is slowly becoming not just the block of flats but the entire finished *mikroraion*.[68]

The first one was set up in Leningrad in 1959.[69] A decade later there were 133 *DSKs* with a total annual capacity of somewhat over 13 million square metres of living space. By 1980 their number had grown to 188 with an annual output of 27 million square metres.[70] 32 per cent of all *DSKs* possess an annual output capacity of up to 50 000 square metres of living space; 58 per cent with a capacity of 50 000–200 000 square metres and 10 per cent with over 200 000 square metres of living space. The decision to set up a combine depends on the scale of large-panelled housing and civic building construction and also on the presence of a manufacturing base for the production of the required components. In effect, this means that they are mostly to be found where large house-building programmes are being undertaken. After all, with an annual capacity of 100 000 m² of living space, given a norm of 10 square metres per person, they have the potential to house 10 000 people a year.[71] In 1979 *DSKs* in Moscow, Leningrad and Kiev were respectively responsible for 52, 81 and 79 per cent of all house construction undertaken by *Glavmosstroi*, *Leningradstroi* and *Kievgorstroi*.[72] Its advantages are that production and construction can be unified within a single administrative framework; there is greater continuity in house construction; the quality of the materials used and working conditions are improved; building and assembly work come to assume characteristics of ordinary factory production; the quality of the completed building is potentially higher; waste products are better utilised; and it is possible to reduce the amount of paper-work and the number of administrative personnel.

All these improvements have increased the efficiency of building. Nevertheless, the problem of costs remains acute. Between 1970 and 1980 the cost of building new flats rose by 35 per cent because of higher space standards and the quality of building.[73] Yet rental charges for all types of flats remain constant. Currently however, suggestions are being made that differential charges might be introduced to reflect the varying standards and location of accommodation. Any such increases would be small and scarcely affect the proportion of the family income spent on rent and utilities. None the less, this move in conjunction with the government's decision to reduce energy and fuel consumption in the municipal economy sector may, at a later date, lead to a reconsideration of these low service charges, which have been in part kept low by the use of district heat and power stations.[74]

FINANCIAL CONTROLS IN HOUSE-BUILDING AND GENERAL CONSTRUCTION

In discussions on building many authors do not distinguish between house-building and the construction of other objects such as factories, power stations, offices, schools and shopping centres. However, references in decrees and articles to the 'dissipation of resources on a large number of projects', when not specific, apply *mutatis mutandis* to any construction project. The organisational problems besetting the building industry naturally have an impact on house construction and maintenance and on the delivery on time of civic amenities. The strategy chosen by the government to tackle this general problem has been to try to exercise greater financial control over building contractors and other agencies which make up the construction industry.

At present two principal organisational–financial methods are employed in the building industry: the so-called contractor method (*podryadnyi sposob*) and the direct labour method (*khozyaistvennyi sposob*). In the first case, building is carried out by general construction, specialist and assembly trusts subordinate to the construction ministries. Contracts are signed between construction ministries (and their subordinate departments) on the one hand, and their customers, who are often ministries or the capital construction administrations (UKS) of local soviets, on the other. This is regarded as the most 'progressive' form of organising construction and in 1980 accounted for 88 per cent of all building and assembly work in the economy.[75] Where direct labour is employed, the enterprise or institution sets up its own building department. This form is nowadays restricted to what is regarded as technically unsophisticated building (including reconstruction, plant modernisation and repair work) and in 1980 accounted for less than 12 per cent of all construction. Yet the city of Yaroslavl' (608 000), for example, has 25 clients for house building (not including the city soviet itself) most of whom – the Administration of Internal Affairs (UVD) and the Administration of the Northern Railway in particular – employ the direct labour method.[76] However, in general, manufacturing enterprises take on outside building contractors instead of maintaining their own building departments. And in some cities housing management departments dealing with repair work prefer the contract method (the 'customer–client' relationship) on the grounds that, since it means operating on a piece rate system, higher labour productivity is achieved.[77] When it comes to building a whole new town, although a number of specialist building contractors (often belonging to different ministries) are necessarily involved, the role of general contractor is undertaken by a single building organisation specialising in housing and civil construction.[78] As far as industrial trading estates or larger manufacturing complexes are concerned, ideally one principal contractor assumes overall responsibility for providing the infrastructure servicing them. The financial contributions paid by the individual enterprises drawing on the service network are determined by *Gosstroi* when it ratifies the general plan of development for the whole estate or complex, and are calculated in proportion to the demands that each enterprise will place on the network.[79]

The financing of construction falls into five categories: centralised state financing (from the state budget); non-centralised financing (using the resources of enterprises themselves);[80] financing by bank credits; co-operative and collective farm capital construction; financing from the personal resources of members of the public. Financing capital construction through state budgetary allocations has been increasing. *Stroibank*,[81] which is the bank responsible for financing capital construction, providing building contractors with credit and for ensuring that Party and government instructions on the use of resources for capital investment have been carried out, estimated that by 1980 the proportion of capital investment financed by bank credits would rise to 25–30 per cent.[82] It is difficult to tell whether this has been achieved. The intention of legislation over the past 15 years directly dealing with Stroibank, and of specific references to the need to expand the role of credit in construction,[83] is to help to remedy the general lack of co-ordination between planned capital investment and the capacity of the construction industry to meet demand, which has resulted in 'a dissipation of resources on a much larger number of projects than resources permit'.[84] In his summary of the results of the ninth five-year plan in 1976 the then Prime Minister noted that this dissipation of resources was one of the factors why the achievements of the previous five-year plan period, though considerable, were less than they would otherwise have been. Five years later, his successor (N. Tikhonov) re-asserted the same criticism, although the decree of July

1979 'On improving planning and strengthening the impact of the economic mechanism on raising the efficiency of production and quality of workmanship'[85] had taken steps to rectify this chronic systemic problem. Among the measures put forward to increase the efficiency of capital investment was the use of finance and credit as a means of affecting the economic interests of those participating in the construction process.

At the beginning of 1979, the balance of uncompleted construction amounted to 99 milliard roubles, equivalent to 85 per cent of the annual volume of capital investment.[86] Out of 5800 major building projects surveyed by Stroibank in 1978, over 11 per cent had been started prior to 1966 and about 12 per cent in the period 1966–70. Since accelerating the commissioning of uncompleted projects would increase the national income by 2.5–3.0 milliard roubles a year, economists regard it as absolutely essential that action be taken against the dissipation of resources and that buildings already begun should be finished. Not only are there serious delays in delivering commissioned work, but cost estimates are frequently exceeded. *Stroibank* calculated that of 913 construction projects begun during the eighth five-year plan (1966–70), costs had increased in 816 cases by more than 40 per cent over the original estimates.[87] This phenomenon is, of course, not unique to Soviet industry: the (British) *Architects Journal* has reminded us that adjustments to cost-plans are not uncommon in Britain.[88] And housing programmes are no exception to this rule in either society. Although the principle of using credit in capital construction was already accepted by the mid-1960s, the government now intends to increase its role in economic development and to raise the proportionate contribution it makes to the financing of capital investment.[89]

Between 1971 and 1977 the mean annual indebtedness of organisations belonging to one particular construction ministry (*Mintyazhstroi*) to *Stroibank* doubled, as did the payment of default interest and fines for late settlement of accounts. Stroibank and Gosbank have now decided that enterprises failing to deliver completed projects (or stages) on time will have their credit stopped on these particular outlays and will be penalised for loans issued earlier.[90]

Planners have identified a number of advantages deriving from a system of long-term credit financing. For instance, through the use of bank credits the state ensures the availability of 'the necessary resources for capital investment corresponding to plans for developing the national economy'. Also, credit acts as an additional incentive to economic bodies (*khozorgany*) to employ their resources more efficiently, and links capital investment to the future growth of production. Furthermore, in seeking to repay loans within a set period, the borrower has a direct interest in reducing the building time. If a building project is not completed on time then the borrower has to pay a higher rate of interest, which is directly related to the length of the delay in completion. And, lastly, it ensures that resources earmarked for technological re-equipping and reconstruction are not instead employed for erecting new buildings.[91] However, in spite of the benefits which experience has shown to derive from the use of credit, as a form of finance for capital investment its share overall remains small, as Table 7.1 shows.

TABLE 7.1   *Sources of centralised capital investment (in per cent)*

Year	State Budget	Internal Resources	Long Term Credit (Stroibank)
1966	57.9	41.9	0.2
1970	49.3	48.4	2.3
1975	47.7	47.0	5.3
1976	47.7	46.3	6.0
1977	40.0	49.9	10.1
1978	41.2	50.1	8.7

SOURCE   V. Rybin, A. Khachaturyan, 'Sovershenstvovat' kreditovanie kapital'nykh vlozhenii,' *Planovoe khozyaistvo*, No. 3, March 1980, p. 59.

According to Rybin and Khachtauryan, the main reason for the hitherto limited use of credit is the economic system itself, which is not sufficiently oriented to raising the efficiency of capital investment or to hastening the delivery of the finished product. No connection exists between the allocation of resources for capital investment and the results of that investment; organisations are judged on the degree to which they have used their material and financial allocations. Under these circumstances neither clients nor designers nor equipment suppliers are interested in drawing upon credit: builders and clients are more concerned to seek ways of increasing their budgetary allocations for capital construction.[92]

The trend in the eyes of some Soviet writers is away from the earlier system whereby the capital funds allocated to the 'client' (for a building project, for example) by the state came almost entirely from the state budget and essentially did not have to be repaid, and where success was judged in terms not of work completed but of investment expended. The movement now is towards a decline in the proportion of capital investment funded from the central budget and a concomitant increase in the part played by the client's own funds and by bank credit. As already mentioned, this has the effect of enhancing the interest shown by the client in using the resources and its associated with the current practice of evaluating success in terms of completed projects. However, 'the influence of sanctions, such as fines, higher interest charges and other financial penalties which come into operation when either party to the contract fails to meet its obligations, remains limited and in need of improvement'.[93]

The scale of the change and the intricacy of the opposition to which the above and other Soviet writers make reference may be likened to the radical policies initiated in 1979 by the Conservative government in Britain, which have involved a redefining of the local and central government relationship, a re-appraisal of the functions of state bureaucracies and a doctrinal insistence on the dominant role of interest rates in structuring the national economy. Above all, in affecting these 'material' changes the government is seeking fundamentally to alter society's underlying ethos. In both the Soviet Union and the UK the government and various academic and professional authorities maintain that the 'new methods' – in both cases more stringent reliance on financial mechanisms – will lead to greater efficiency in terms of resource utilisation, and *ergo* to higher economic growth and standards of living. In both societies these proposed methods are meeting considerable opposition, the basis of which could be the subject of a detailed political–economic analysis.

Errors in planning not only result in the starting of more projects than can be completed, but also in the prolonging of the construction periods, thus raising overall costs. The main factor responsible for this state of affairs is held to be that 'decisions to erect new buildings are taken solely from departmental and localistic (*mestnicheskie*) considerations'.[94] Local soviets and Party officials, instead of adhering to the policy laid down in the national economic plan, allow resources to be directed into projects which are not listed in the plan, and which therefore have no financial or material allocations. This is possible because, after being informed of the resources which each factory, institute etc. has been allocated, the chief city architect and the *gorispolkom* enter into a bargaining process with enterprises and organisations located within the local soviet's administrative jurisdiction. The latter ask for financial and material assistance for a variety of social projects in return for a building plot in a favoured position and the provision or secondment of specialists employed by the *gorispolkom*. A decree of May 1969 in attempting to deal with this contradiction did not seek to tackle a systemic tendency, but rather to block a loophole – the weak financial position of local soviets. As was discussed in Chapter 3, it is their lack of real economic (rather than juridical) power which has given rise to the symbiotic relationship between enterprises and local soviets, making it possible and inevitable that the national economic plan's investment programme will frequently be infringed. Steps taken to make the soviets financially stronger, and thereby less dependent on enterprises and organisations, appear to be the only way of resolving this particular contradiction. Of course the soviets are not solely to blame. Project-design organisations are also held responsible for the 'dissipation of resources and the rising costs', since often they do not present accurate cost-estimates,[95] with the result that the estimates accepted bear little resemblance to the subsequent real costs of construction.[96]

These organisations have now been brought within the credit-penalty system. The old method of intermediate payments for the completion of specific parts of the design work, or at regular intervals during the preparation of the drawings and estimates, has been abandoned. Expenses incurred by design institutes prior to completion of their contract have to be financed either from internal reserves or from bank loans, the interest on which is raised after the expiry of the loan period.[97] Other bodies, too, have faced rebuke. Building-assembly organisations not only systematically fail to fulfill their production targets, but the buildings they erect are full of defects and the overall standard of their work is low. For instance, in 1977 only 1 per cent of new houses built in Saratov were awarded a rating of 'excellent' and 58 per cent a rating of 'good'. In the following year matters deteriorated further; a mere 0.7 per cent were rated as 'excellent' and 33 per cent as 'good'. The remaining 66.3 per cent were accepted as 'satisfactory' – a category which the author of the article considered 'does not merit comment'.[98] The fact that such a high proportion of buildings received low ratings may be attributed to architects' errors or builders' misreading of the drawings (or a combination of both) or poor workmanship. One example in *Krokodil* showed a photograph of a new block of flats with balconies but no windows. (However, the British construction industry is at times equal match for such excesses: several houses on a

TABLE 7.2 Capital investment plans and construction plans for the city of Kaluga

Objects of planning	Capital Investment plans for Building-Assembly Work (thousands of roubles)		Volume output plans for building contractors (thousands of roubles)		Percentage by which investment plans exceed output plans (%)	
	1978	1979	1978	1979	1978	1979
Total	12683*	11271	11157**	10388	13.6	8.0
of which:						
housing	8428	8928	7898	8582	6.6	4.0
communal economy	1323	609	1069	543	23.8	12.2
education	1946	1221	1550	835	25.5	46.2
health	201	236	152	230	32.2	2.6
culture	186	N.A.	150	N.A.	24.0	—
other	559	277	388	198	44.1	39.9

*The total from the figures given below should be 12643 (G.D.A.).
**The total from the figures given below should be 11207 (G.D.A.).

SOURCE P. N. Lebedev, *Sistema organov gorodskogo upravleniya*, Leningrad, 1980, p. 70.

new estate in Slough (Berkshire) were built without back doors and as a result their occupants had to go out of their front door and climb a fence in order to enter the garden.)[99]

Two main reasons are usually cited for the shortcomings in the work of building-assembly organisations. Firstly, in some regions enterprises producing building materials do not have the capacity to meet the demands of the building industry and, through trying to meet demand, quality standards are lowered. More generally and more importantly, and the 'key to the development of the economy as a whole' is the lack of correspondence between the plans for capital construction and the actual capacity of the building-assembly contractors.[100] The scale of discrepancy between plans of capital investment in construction–assembly work and the planned volume of work by building contractors is clearly depicted in Table 7.2, which reveals the disparity between these plans for Kaluga (276 000) in 1978 and 1979. The reduction in the difference between the plans by over 40 per cent (from 1 526 000 roubles in 1978 to 883 000 roubles in 1979) was largely attributable to lower estimates for capital investment in construction consequent upon a more realistic appraisal of capacity in the building industry. Neither the figures nor the accompanying commentary explained the reason for the greater compatibility of the separate plans for housing.

The second reason given is based on the fact that the building workforce is to a significant extent recruited from migrants from the countryside who lack skills and industrial discipline.

LABOUR AND THE CONSTRUCTION INDUSTRY

A major driving-force behind the organisational changes discussed above is the overall shortage of labour throughout the national economy,[101] with the number of jobs available exceeding by at least 50 per cent the number of people searching for work.[102] The introduction of industrialised building methods and time-and-motion studies ('the scientific study and organisation of manpower') are attempts to raise labour productivity in an industry whose demand for labour continues to grow.

Over the past 40 years the number of workers in the building industry has increased almost sixfold (compared with an increase of 280 per cent for industry and 330 per cent rise in the economy as a whole). Despite this rate of growth, as early as 1966 there were

TABLE 7.3   *Average annual number of persons employed in construction*

Year	Persons employed (thousands)	Index (1940 = 100)
1940	1993	100
1965	7301	366
1970	9052	454
1975	10574	530
1976	10716	538
1977	10880	546
1978	11034	553
1979	11156	560
1980	11240	564

SOURCE   *Narodnoe khozyaistvo SSSR v 1980g.*, Moscow, 1981, pp. 358–9.

230 000 fewer workers in the construction industry than envisaged in the national plan; by December 1967 building and assembly organisations were said to be experiencing a shortfall of 257 000 workers.[103] Between 1970 and 1980 demographic factors caused a further decrease in the possible labour growth rate in the construction industry. Therefore, in the tenth five-year plan (1976–1980) the construction programme was to be achieved not by an increase in the numbers employed, but by a 29–32 per cent rise in labour productivity.[104] In the event, in the tenth five-year plan as in the ninth, the productivity increases failed to reach their planned targets. In fact, the volume output plan for 1976–80 would not have been fulfilled had not about 400 000 extra workers been taken on at building sites.[105] However, the increase in the number of workers (1976–80) was only one-third that of the previous five-year period (1970–75). During the current eleventh five-year plan (1981–85), labour productivity in the industry is planned to rise by a modest 15–17 per cent (compared with 17–20 per cent for the economy as a whole),[106] which will be sufficient to account for the total growth in the volume of building assembly work.[107]

Labour productivity has improved considerably in the industry and the employment of mechanised equipment (bulldozers, cranes, excavators) and pre-fabricated building components has vastly expanded. Nevertheless it seems unlikely that the government's aim of holding the numbers employed in the construction industry constant will be achieved. Some occupations, mainly in the service sector (retail trade, cleaning and catering) and construction, are regarded by townspeople as being low-grade. Consequently, those employed in these occupations, including the building industry, tend to be drawn from the countryside and this has a variety of undesired side-effects. Above all, the standard of workmanship in many instances is poor. This is in part attributed to the 'low level of education' of those working in the industry. In 1962 the government drew attention to this fact and set up additional institutes in order to train and raise the qualifications of workers both on building sites and in factories manufacturing building materials.[108] Seven years later it established 132 vocational–technical schools to provide a three-year course for decorators. The number of places was to rise from 51 800 in 1970 to 100 000 by 1973. The Ministry of Higher and Secondary Specialist Education was instructed to increase substantially the number of students studying architecture.[109]

A decade later serious shortages of skilled labour in the construction industry led to a decree requiring that 600 000 skilled workers be trained during 1979–80.[110] The failure of labour productivity to rise as rapidly as predicted, and as necessary, has been attributed in part to the persistent 'low quality' of labour. One reason for its low level of skill, both manual and managerial,[111] and attendant low productivity is the high labour turnover in the industry – which militates against the development of the requisite skills. In 1968 the Party declared that 'the task of the Party and Komsomol is to raise the level of mass political work amongst construction workers, to inculcate in them a feeling of pride for their profession and to demonstrate a constant concern for improving their living conditions, dining rooms and medical facilities'. The decree further required the application of up-to-date management techniques in order to reduce the amount of labour time lost through poor on-site co-ordination. More places were needed in schools for training building workers, and the Committee on Publishing attached to the Council of Ministers was 'to publish literature on the heroism of builders'.[112] Still, mobility remains high. Thus, a large trust constructing an electrical energy generating station was delayed by labour turnover; over a period of 12 months, 5 145 people had come to work on the project, but 3 330 had left, largely because of unsatisfactory housing conditions.[113] Because of labour turnover, the industry has to draw upon a variety of sources to replenish their supply, including fresh graduates from trade schools, ordinary school leavers, young men who have completed national service (and, it might be added, those still on conscription), workers from other branches of the economy, the non-employed, such as housewives and pensioners, and students on vacation, who tend to be employed in those regions suffering from particularly acute labour shortages. Lastly, employees in industrial enterprises, kolkhoz and sovkhoz workers, can be released on a temporary basis to work on construction sites. If labour turnover could be reduced, it would not be necessary to have recourse to these auxiliary manpower sources.[114]

Four main factors are responsible for difficulties arising from the employment of rural-migrant labour: (1) the difference between industrial and agricultural labour and the way of life of these distinctive environments; (2) migrant labour is normally accommodated in hostels or 'barracks' with four to eight persons to a room;[115] (3) most of them are young and unmarried, or at least separated from their families;[116] (4) employment in the building industry provides a means of entry into the city and registration as a worker with a legal right to reside and work in the city – an important consideration given the operation of a passport system prohibiting the free movement of individuals into the largest cities.

The government has sought to combat these difficulties by improving the living conditions of construction workers. For instance, it has stipulated that 10 per cent of housing erected for clients be retained for the use of the builders themselves.[117] It has also raised wages – which are set by the USSR State Committee for Labour and Social Affairs – and offered other financial incentive schemes.[118] In fact, as Table 7.4 shows, in 1980 the average monthly wage of a manual building worker was 23.1 per cent higher than the national average for all categories of workers. This reverses the relationship which prevailed until 20 years ago, and reflects the acute shortage of building labour.

The main purpose of the wage structure has been to act as a material incentive to attract labour into specific sectors of the economy. Yet the higher rate of remuneration does not appear to have succeeded in reducing labour turnover or in raising productivity to the extent anticipated. In fact, high wages can have a negative effect in certain circumstances. Personal and social disorganisation have not been untypical reactions of rural migrants to their new environments. Without the traditional constraints which a family imposes on a worker, and housed in crowded accommodation with no incentive to save and purchase consumer durables, a substantial proportion of the wage tends to be absorbed by a high level of alcohol consumption.[119] Furthermore, having achieved residential status in the major cities, to which they have been attracted by the opportunity to gain access to a

TABLE 7.4   Average monthly wage of manual workers in the manufacturing and construction industries 1940–80 (roubles)

Category of worker	Year											
	1940	1950	1960	1965	1970	1975	1976	1977	1978	1979	1980
National Average Wage	33.1	63.9	80.1	96.5	122.0	145.8	151.4	155.2	159.9	163.3	168.9
Average Wage of:											
Manual Industrial Worker	32.4	68.7	89.8	101.7	130.6	160.9	168.2	171.8	176.1	180.3	185.5
Manual Construction Worker	31.1	56.5	88.7	108.4	148.5	180.3	185.3	190.3	196.2	202.5	207.9

SOURCE   Narodnoe khozyaistvo SSSR v 1980g., pp. 364–65 Narodnoe khozyaistvo SSSR v 1967g., Moscow, 1968, p. 657.

whole range of products and entertainment unavailable in small towns and villages, rural migrants then seek other forms of employment.

The related problems of low quality, low productivity levels and high labour turnover may be resolvable through a combination of policies. For instance, the government could increase the industry's wage differentials, which since 1969 have been fixed on a six-point scale ranging from a coefficient of 1.0 for those on the lowest grade to 1.8 for those on the top grade, and alter existing piece-rate systems. Secondly, the industry could be made more attractive by improving living and working conditions, including provision for families.

With the present trend being, as the XXVI Party Congress recorded, towards greater independence for associations and enterprises and enhanced power and responsibility for economic managers, it is possible that the latter will try to manipulate wage differentials and piece-rates to a greater extent than at present with the specific objective of improving 'labour discipline' and raising productivity. The second proposal has been partly implemented by setting aside 10 per cent of new housing built for the construction workers themselves.

However, since it is a general rule that once a worker has received a flat in the public sector he cannot be evicted should he move to another industry, this policy is unable to achieve its objective of securing a stable workforce. It is worth noting that, generally speaking, in the Soviet Union a person may not be evicted without a court order and even this has to be accompanied by a certificate offering the individual or family alternative 'well-appointed' accommodation. There are exceptions. Individuals occupying premises illegally or 'systematically damaging the property or regularly breaking the rules of socialist intercourse' may be evicted without receiving alternative accommodation.[120] Also, people living in departmental housing belonging to certain enterprises and institutions may be evicted without being offered other accommodation: if they leave their jobs voluntarily or are dismissed for breach of labour discipline or for having committed a crime. Article 62 of the Principles of Civil Legislation allows the Council of Ministers to draw up lists of enterprises and organisation which can exercise this right.[121] A survey published in 1974 revealed that the number of cases brought before the court in recent years under the provision of Article 62 has increased because the list of organisations allowed to evict under this article has been extended.[122] Neither this fact nor the finding that, in 1973, 64.8 per cent of all suits brought by enterprises to evict were successful, permits the conclusion that eviction is becoming the rule in departmental housing when individuals leave their jobs voluntarily.

And, as far as the building industry is concerned, there is no evidence that workers are being evicted on changing their occupations. Although continued departmental control of 50 per cent of the state housing stock might suggest that enterprises would welcome the opportunity to use the weapon of eviction as a means of reducing mobility, it is scarcely credible that such a retrogressive step towards an extensive form of tied-cottage tenure would receive widespread acceptance within policy-making circles.

THE OUTCOME: LIVING SPACE STANDARDS

Industrialisation of construction has enabled the Soviet Union justifiably to claim to have solved the problem of providing low-cost housing of an acceptable standard for the mass of its population. To this extent, it deserves the applause of the United States Congress, which in 1965 declared that 'the application of modern technology and science could have a profound effect upon both the cost and quality of urban housing and offers perhaps the greatest promise of any of the many areas of urban life to which technology can make a contribution'.[123] This is not to say that everyone is well housed – far from it. But the fact that over the last 20 years (1961–1980) 8.2 million people annually moved into a new flat or private home and a further 2.7 million improved their living conditions is a convincing achievement (see Table 7.5). Although the figures are not strictly comparable, it is worth noting that in contrast to Great Britain where 29.9 per cent of the housing stock was built before 1919, a further 21.3 per cent between 1919 and 1944 and 48.8 per cent between 1945 and 1980, 65.5 per cent of the urban housing stock in the Soviet Union, was erected in the 20-year period 1960–80.[124]

Space standards are constantly rising and in the near future the urban housing norm of nine square metres of actual dwelling area per person defined in Article 59 of the Principles of Civil Legislation should be universally attained. (This norm applies in 12 of the 15 republics, with a higher norm in certain cities; the norm is $12\,m^2$ in Georgia and Azerbaidzhan and $13.5\,m^2$ in the Ukraine).[125] At the beginning of 1981 the all-union average stood at $13.0\,m^2$ of overall useful living space ($9.1\,m^2$ actual dwelling area), having risen from $8.8\,m^2$ ($6.2\,m^2$) in 1961. (See note 49 on page 298 for explanations for these terms). However, as Table A.3 in Appendix A shows, republican variations in the amount of living space per person remain considerable – ranging in 1981 from 9.3 square metres in Uzbekistan to 13.2

TABLE 7.5   *Number of people moving into new or modernised accommodation, 1950–80*

Year	Number of people moving into new accommodation (millions)		Number of people moving into modernised accommodation or expanding their living space (millions)	Total (millions)
1950		4.0	1.3	5.3
1951		4.1	1.4	5.5
1952		4.0	1.4	5.4
1953		4.4	1.7	6.1
1954		4.7	1.8	6.5
1955		5.3	1.8	7.1
(1951–55)	22.5		8.1	30.6
1956		5.7	2.1	7.8
1957		7.6	2.5	10.1
1958		8.8	2.7	11.5
1959		10.0	2.6	12.6
1960		9.6	2.4	12.0
(1956–60)	41.7		12.3	54.0
1961		9.0	2.3	11.3
1962		8.8	2.4	11.2
1963		8.6	2.4	11.0
1964		8.1	2.2	10.3
1965		8.2	2.6	10.8
(1961–65)	42.7		11.9	54.6
1966		8.5	2.4	10.9
1967		8.6	2.5	11.1
1968		8.3	2.5	10.8
1969		8.3	2.6	10.9
1970		8.4	2.8	11.2
(1966–70)	42.1		12.8	54.9
1971		8.5	2.9	11.4
1972		8.2	2.9	11.1
1973		8.4	3.0	11.4
1974		8.2	3.0	11.2
1975		8.2	2.8	11.0
(1971–74)	41.5		14.6	56.1
1976		7.8	2.7	10.5
1977		7.8	2.8	10.6
1978		7.7	2.8	10.5
1979		6.8	2.7	9.5
1980		7.2	2.8	10.0
(1976–80)	37.3		13.8	51.1

SOURCES   *Narodnoe khozyaistvo SSSR v 1967g.*, Moscow, 1968, p. 681;
Narodnoe khozyaistvo SSSR v 1975g., Moscow, 1976, p. 575;
Narodnoe khozyaistvo SSSR v 1980g., Moscow, 1981, p. 391.

square metres in the RSFSR and 16.3 square metres in Estonia. (It may be argued that in overall space terms the urban Uzbek family does not necessarily fare quite so badly as these figures might suggest, given that the much larger families in Uzbekistan – 5.3 persons as against 3.5 for the RSFSR in 1970 – do not require 50 per cent more space.)

Despite the vast building programme, family living continues to be cramped. At the beginning of 1976 two-thirds of all urban families had their own separate flats, and 17 million families and single persons lived in shared accommodation.[126] At this date the average number of persons per room in towns was 1.7, as against 1.9 in 1970 and 2.8 in 1960.[127] By 1981, about 80 per cent of the urban population were living in separate flats.[128]

In addition to increasing the amount of space per person, the authorities have also set a goal of providing each family member with his/her own room, and ultimately providing a further common living room for the whole family. However, the initial objective of one room per family member is unlikely to be achieved in the near future, for it will require a norm of $18-19 \, m^2$ of overall living space ($12-13 \, m^2$ of actual dwelling space) per person.[129] In the mid-1970s over three-quarters of the urban housing stock consisted of one- and two-roomed flats,[130] even though, according to the 1970 Census, the average urban family consisted of 3.5 persons (3.3 persons in 1979), and 74.8 per cent of all urban families had three or more members.[131] This situation is gradually improving, with the proportion of newly built small flats (1–2 rooms) declining from 52 per cent in 1975 to 35 per cent in 1980 with a commensurate increase in 3–5 roomed flats from 48 to 65 per cent.[132] None the less, at the present time, as Table 7.6 shows, room densities are still high. Moreover, the mismatch between family size and flat size (the number of rooms) remains a problem. The figures indicate almost total correspondence between the Census data on the number of households in each size category and the number of flats (columns 2 & 4). Planners used the Census information to plan the construction of their new accommodation. However, there are disparities between the types of flats on the one hand, and households on waiting lists for 'better accommodation' on the other (columns 4 & 5). The supply of one-room flats exceeds by 7 per cent the demand for them by single and two-person households, while there are 10 per cent fewer two-room flats than the number of 3–4 person households seeking them.[133] A serious consequence of this level of overcrowding amidst heightened expectations is a high divorce rate; between 1972 and 1979 the number of divorces in the Volgograd and Astrakhan *oblasts* rose by over 50 per cent, with 72 per cent of newly-weds filing

180

TABLE 7.6 Size of flats and households in one Soviet city

Household size (number of persons)	Household size category as a % of all households	Size of flat		Households on waiting lists for improved accommodation as % of all households
		Number of rooms	% of all flats	
1	7.0 ⎱	1	33	5.5
2	25.6 ⎰			20.2
3	25.4 ⎱	2	48	35.6
4	20.3 ⎰	3	10	22.5
5	12.2	4–5	9	10.0
6 or more	9.5			6.2
Total	100.0	Total	100.0	100.0

SOURCE D. L. Broner, Zhilishchnoe stroitel'stvo i demograficheskie protsessy, Moscow, 1980, p. 57.

for divorce during the first year of marriage, one quarter petitioning on the grounds that they had nowhere to live. This cannot but have a negative effect on the birth-rate.[134] Divorce also tends to create more households.

CONCLUSION

In embarking on a major housing programme to relieve the acute shortage of accommodation, the government recognised that huge resources would have to be committed to the task and that these ought to be used efficiently. Thus, the primary objective of the various organisational changes in the construction industry has been to tackle the problem of the dissipation of resources amongst a plethora of agencies by concentrating material and finance in fewer hands. This rationalisation was further necessitated by the rapid rise in the output of pre-fabricated buildings which occurred simultaneously with the more widespread utilisation of standard designs. Industrialisation of the building process has brought economic and technical advantages. It has also served to alleviate serious labour problems; serious in the dual sense that there are insufficient numbers of building workers (who are, in any case, in demand in other sectors of the economy) and that the workforce, drawn to a significant extent from the countryside, is poorly trained and unaccustomed to the discipline imposed by conditions of industrial employment.

The role assigned to finance and credit as mechanisms for regulating building activity will continue to grow in importance. This change is designed not only to increase the effectiveness of capital investment, but also to raise the standard of building. Housing policy is no longer concerned solely with the volume production of 'shelter'. People are now demanding more space, amenities and comfort. And this shift from quantity to quality requires new methods for organising and controlling production. There is a greater need for 'fine tuning' on the part of the professionals who devise and direct housing policy. And this will require more detailed demographic and behaviour studies and a greater attentiveness to 'consumer demand'.

8 Low-rise Housing, Urban Morphology and Social Structure

LOW-RISE HOUSING: POLICY AND PRACTICE

Two features of urban development in the Soviet Union during the 1930s were firstly, the demolition of low rise, mainly timber houses erected before the Revolution and during the 1920s[1] and secondly, urban sprawl caused by a policy of locating residential areas around new manufacturing plants even if these were some distance from the central city.[2] The destruction caused by World War II posed in a particularly acute fashion the problem of urban reconstruction, which involved both the renewal of existing structures and the erection of new ones. In order to alleviate the housing crisis, concessions were made allowing individuals to build and own their own houses with gardens. But this did not divert the government from its main policy objective established at the end of the 1920s, to increase the proportion of multi-storey structures and thereby raise housing densities. Compactness was, and still is, considered essential if the costs of providing public utilities and amenities are to be reduced. In furtherance of this aim, towns after the war were divided into three zones, depending on building heights and on the existence of private gardens. The first was a multi-storey zone consisting of houses with three, four, five or more storeys; the second, a zone of low-rise dwellings without gardens, which were mainly two- and sometimes three-storey houses divided into flats; and the third, a garden-house zone of one- and two storey dwellings.[3]

In the period 1946–49, individual house-building accounted for about 30 per cent of all newly erected and renovated housing space in towns and urban settlements. Yet this figure grossly underestimates the actual number of low-rise one- and two-storey dwelling units which were built in these years, since local soviets, ministries and departments were also erecting a large proportion of detached houses with gardens. Plans drawn up at the beginning of the 1950s indicated that up to 40 per cent of the total population in many Ukrainian cities would eventually live in such houses, which would occupy up to two-thirds of the total residential area. Inevitably, the overall outcome of such extensive low-rise development was housing densities lower than desired, in the order of 400–800 square metres of living space per hectare; yet even these low densities were regarded as an improvement on the earlier situation.[4]

Even after the recovery from war-time devastation, housing policy after 1945 was far less rigid in its attitude towards the individual sector than it had been in the 1930s. The policy of the 'thirties resulted in the infringement and rapid obsolescence of general city plans as it did not make adequate provision for the individual sector and low-rise build-ing in general. In the post-war period the government learned from that experience and conceded the necessity of involving the builder/owner-occupier in the immense task of reconstruction. It therefore set about planning the growth of low-rise (individual and state) housebuilding. Davidovich, a leading urban economist, re-garded the tendency to construct mainly four- and five-storey build-ings as unwarranted in small and medium sized towns.[5] Single de-tached houses were more popular and common in coal mining regions than in engineering and textile centres, enabling miners in the Kuzbas, Donbas, and other coal basins to cultivate gardens, to grow fruit and vegetables and raise livestock and poultry; and Davidovich considered that 'these preferences should be taken into consideration'.[6] Con-comitantly, the same author considered 'skyscrapers' (buildings of over ten storeys) to be unjustified in a socialist society. This was a view which corresponded closely with government policy at the time for, according to the July 1957 decree, local soviets and *sovnarkhozy* were to operate on the basis of building four- and five-storey blocks in towns (in the main) and two- and three-storeys in small towns and settlements.[7] This particular clause limiting the height of buildings in towns was repealed in 1965, when the government ruled that the number of storeys should be determined 'on the basis of technical and economic calculations'.[8] By the end of the 1960s attitudes towards high-rise buildings had altered considerably with, for example, the chairman of the Kiev city Soviet Executive Committee referring to calculations which demonstrated that 'the most rational distribution of newly built flats by height to be: 15 per cent of five storeys, 75 per cent of nine storeys and 10 per cent of 16–20 storeys'.[9]

As a consequence of, on the one hand, the government's essentially pragmatic response to the housing shortage in the post-war years and, on the other, the form urban development had taken before 1945, urban renewal has, especially since the late 1960s, become a key issue facing Soviet urban planners. For instance, Karaganda had a population of 15 000 in 1930; by 1936 it had grown to 102 000 (the year when its first general plan was drawn up) and to 156 000 in 1939. In 1981 its population stood at 583 000. The urban area of Karaganda, covering 69 000 hectares,[10] was dotted with dozens of scattered pit-head settlements, many of which sprang up during the war when evacuees from the Donbas and other regions were located there. The outcome of this rapid growth was that by 1958 two-thirds of Karaganda's housing stock and 10 per cent of all new house-building consisted of one-storey dwellings.[11] Prokop'evsk, also in Southern Siberia, experienced a similar pattern of development. In 1926 the town had a population of 10 700. By 1939 it had increased almost ten-fold to 107 000. It more than doubled again by 1959 (282 000), but thereafter its population declined slightly to 267 000 in 1981. Here the housing shortage, especially in the pre-war and post-war years, gave rise to a considerable amount of unsupervised individual (private) housing construction and, at the same time, to a form of housing development based on the principle 'to each mine its own settlement'.[12]

However this pattern has not been confined to 'frontier' towns and settlements in Kazakhstan and Siberia. In 1960 the proportion of old, two- three- and four-storey buildings reached 30–40 per cent of the housing stock even in the central districts of such large cities as Gor'ky, Kuibyshev, Perm', Rostov-on-Don, Yaroslavl', Penza, Tula, Ivanovo, Taganrog and Orenburg. In 1959 all these cities had over 200 000 inhabitants and by 1981 the first six of them had populations ranging from 500 000 to 1.3 million. With up to 70–80 per cent of the area of many large cities occupied by individual houses often lacking the most basic amenities, they remained little more than large villages.[13] A decade later, in the majority of towns, buildings of four or more storeys took up less than 10 per cent of the overall residential area,[14] and in major cities such as Arkhangel'sk, Kuibyshev, Gor'ky, and Novosibirsk, the urban area occupied by single-storey buildings accounted for between 55 and 75 per cent of the total land area.[15] Table 8.1 shows the particularly high proportion of single-storey dwellings in some of these cities, while Table 8.2 shows that actual construction in 1958 of low-rise dwellings (one to three storeys) was still high in a number of the largest cities in the country.[16] And surveys summarised

TABLE 8.1 Distribution of housing stock by number of storeys in 10 large cities

City	Year of Survey	Number of buildings of:			Population ('000)	
		1 storey (%)	2–3 storeys (%)	4–5 storeys (%)	1.1.59	1.1.79
Magnitogorsk	1957	34.8	16.7	48.5	311	406
Gor'ky*	1959	41	39.6	19.4	941	1344
Volgograd	1958	46	27	27	591	929
Tula	1958	46	37	17	351	514
Kuibyshev	1959	46	43	11	806	1216
Novokuznetsk	1958	47.4	24	28	382	541
Kemerovo	1957	50	27	23	289	471
Novosibirsk	1959	62	25	13	885	1312
Omsk	1958	68	21	11	581	1014
Kishinev	1965	53	16	31	216	503

* In 1960, 72.4 per cent of the residential area of Gor'ky was taken up by one-storey dwellings, and only 3.6 per cent by 4–5 storeys. In Novokuznetsk, Volgograd, Omsk, Krivoi Rog and Kemerovo, among others, 85 per cent of the residential area was taken up by one-storey houses.

SOURCE *Razmeshchenie zhilishchnogo stroitel'stva v gorodakh, op. cit.* p. 17; A. S. Konstantinov, *Kishinev,* Kishinev, 1966, p. 118.

TABLE 8.2 *New residential building in nine Soviet cities, by number of storeys, in 1958 (per cent)*

City	Total construction		1 storey (%)	of which	
	(thous. m²)	%		*2–3 storeys (%)*	*4–5 storeys (%)*
Magnitogorsk	174	100	5	15	80
Gor'ky	360	100	16	52	32
Volgograd	350	100	17	41	42
Tula	165	100	20	40	40
Kuibyshev	328	100	10	45	45
Novokuznetsk	187	100	15	10	75
Kemerovo	140	100	15	45	40
Novosibirsk	500	100	30	35	35
Omsk	370	100	30	38	32

SOURCE *Razmeschenie zhilishchnogo stroitel'stva v gorodakh, op. cit.* p. 48.

in Table 8.3 disclosed that one-storey housing amounted to as much as 61 per cent of the housing stock (in terms of living space) in 1959 and was still 45 per cent in 1967.

Table 8.4 illustrates the extent to which even in the mid-1960s low rise housing predominated in all groups of towns; virtually all houses (91.6 per cent) in small towns are of one, two and three storeys, while the corresponding figures in medium, big and large cities are 88.1, 84.0 and 78.4 per cent respectively. Only in the very largest do they comprise less than half the total housing stock – although of course the actual number of one-storey dwellings in such cities would contain a total housing space as great as the total housing stock in a small town. What is perhaps most surprising is the fact that 60 per cent of housing space in new towns erected since World War II should be in low rise buildings. While most of these smaller buildings would be of a higher standard than those erected in, say, Prokop'evsk during the war and more likely to have been built in accordance with a general development plan, this has not always been the case. In the new town of Svetlogorsk (58 000) in Belorussia, 'houses with gardens consist, in the main, of huts transported from the nearest village and distributed in a chaotic manner'. The author of this statement pointed out that this was by no means a unique occurrence.[17] In the 13 largest cities in the Ukraine, as Table 8.5 shows, the proportion of single-storey houses ranged from 14.3 per cent to 65.1 per cent, averaging 44.7 per cent.

TABLE 8.3   *Distribution of the urban housing stock by number of storeys in 1959 & 1967 (per cent)*

Number of storeys	Percentage of total living space in towns	
	*1959**	*1967***
1	61	45
2	20	15
3	6	5
4	5 ⎫	31
5+	8 ⎭	
6+		4
Total	100	100

SOURCES
* A. O. Kudryavtsev, *op. cit.* p. 34.
** G. A. Kaplan, A. V. Kochetkov, 'Ekonomicheskie problemy obnovleniya zhilishchnogo fonda gorodov SSSR', *Voprosy ekonomiki gradostroitel'stva i raionnoi planirovki*, Vpusk 4, Kiev, 1970, p. 22.

TABLE 8.4 The distribution of the housing stock in terms of living space in 181 cities by the height of the buildings in the mid-1960s

Category of city by population size	Number of cities	Height of buildings as % of the total living space				Average number of storeys
		9+	4–5	2–3	1	
Small (up to 50 000 people)	19	—	8.4	28.8	62.8	1.4
Medium (50 000–100 000)	20	—	11.9	29.2	58.9	1.37
Big (100 000–250 000)	34	—	16.0	29.8	54.2	1.44
Large* (250 000–500 000)	43	—	21.6	28.4	50.0	1.51
Very large (over 500 000)	38	5.9	45.5	21.6	27.0	2.16
New towns	27	0.1	39.7	31.2	29.0	1.98
Average		4.1	38.4	23.9	33.6	1.98

* In one 'large' city, Penza (1959 – 255 000; 1979 – 483 000), according to a survey carried out in 1960, 89 per cent of the *socialised* housing stock in the city consisted of one- and two-storey houses. Moreover, 61 per cent of the total dwelling space was in wooden houses. (*Penzenskaya oblast' za 50 let sovetskoi vlasti. Statisticheskii sbornik*, Saratov-Penza, 1967, p. 124.)

SOURCE A. O. Kudryavtsev, *op. cit.* p. 34.

TABLE 8.5   The distribution of the housing stock in the 13 largest cities in the Ukraine by the height of the buildings and ownership in the mid-1960s

City	Population in 1979 (thousands)	Storeys (% of living space)			Housing owned by individuals as a % of total living space
		1	2–3	4 +	
Kiev	2144	14.3	17.1	68.6	12.0
L'vov	667	15.5	49.7	34.8	8.5
Odessa	1046	27.8	46.2	26.0	16.5
Zaporozh'e	781	39.0	13.6	47.4	8.5
Khar'kov	1444	39.2	17.4	43.4	31.0
Donetsk	1021	45.7	14.3	40.0	33.0
Krivoi Rog	650	48.5	19.0	32.6	36.5
Nikolaev	441	51.3	18.7	30.0	34.8
Dnepropetrovsk	1066	54.0	20.0	26.0	44.3
Makeevka	436	55.7	21.7	22.9	43.6
Voroshilovgrad	463	59.8	10.4	29.8	53.0
Zhdanov	503	64.8	13.3	21.9	49.5
Gorlovka	337	65.1	23.7	11.2	46.5
Average		44.7	21.9	33.4	32.1

* The data were compiled from the general development plans drawn up in the mid- or early 1960s.

SOURCE V. M. Orekhov, A. D. Ivanova, *Rekonstruktsiya i razvitie krupnykh gorodov UkSSR*, Kiev, 1974, p. 85.

Table 8.5 highlights the fact that even in a city such as Dnepropetrovsk with over one million inhabitants, 54 per cent of the stock
consisted of one-storey buildings. Moreover, in eight of these 13 cities,
while over one-third of the stock belongs to private individuals, the
state also owns a considerable proportion of single-storey units. In
Zaporozh'e, for example, although 39 per cent of all housing consists
of one-storey buildings, only 8.5 per cent of the total living space is in
private hands. Lastly, Gorlovka not only has the highest proportion of
single-storey houses, but also covers the largest area (50 100 hectares),
giving it the lowest population density with 6.8 persons per hectare;
the highest being found in L'vov (88.1 p.p.h.) covering 23 400
hectares.[18]

By the 1990s (the end of the 25–30 year planning period), the
housing skyline should have changed considerably. With a further
expansion in the production of pre-fabricated buildings and general
increase in the capacity of the construction industry, the proportion of
multi-storey blocks of flats (that is, blocks of four or more storeys) is
planned to increase from 42.5 per cent to 85.7 per cent with a
commensurate decrease in low-rise buildings from 57.5 per cent to
14.3 per cent.[19] So whereas in 1965 only about 5 per cent of all state
urban housing units were in blocks with nine or more storeys, by 1970
this figure had reached 20 per cent and in 1975 stood at 35 per cent.
About 80 per cent of these blocks are of nine storeys, although in small
and medium sized towns, five-storey blocks comprise about two-thirds
of all new construction.[20] By 1980 nine-storey buildings accounted for
40 per cent of the total volume of urban housing construction, rising to
65 per cent in the largest cities. For the sake of architectural form, the
proportion of 12–16 (and higher) blocks increased from 6 per cent in
1975 to 12 per cent in 1980 (and in the largest cities, up to 30 per cent).
By the end of the 1970s, in Moscow, Leningrad and Kiev, 12–16
storey blocks represented 40 per cent of new construction.[21] And by
1980, 69 per cent of all new house building in the Moscow region was
planned to be in blocks of flats with nine or more storeys.[22]

As Tables 8.6 and 8.7 demonstrate, besides building high-rise
blocks with a high proportion of 9 to 16 and more storeys, low-rise
dwellings will continue to be built even in the very long term 'particularly in areas which are temporarily without a fully developed
infrastructure'.[23] According to one official at the Central Housing
Research Institute (*TsNIIEP zhilishcha*), 'in the near future, only
10–12 per cent of all urban housing will consist of low-rise units, most
of which will be found in small towns where they will account for about

TABLE 8.6 *The distribution of the housing stock in 181 cities by the number of storeys at two future dates**

Category of city by population size	No. of cities studied	Projected division of the housing stock by number of storeys at two future dates*								Average no. of storeys in the long term
		9 storeys		4–5 storeys		2–3 storeys		1 storey		
		1st stage	long term	1st stage	long term	1st stage	long term	1st stage	long term	
Small	19	—	1.4	42.1	66.8	18.6	11.7	39.3	20.6	2.49
Medium	20	0.2	1.1	52.8	75.5	18.5	11.1	28.5	12.3	2.97
Big	34	1.2	4.3	60.6	78.7	14.8	8.0	23.4	9.0	3.32
Large	43	2.1	10.4	50.2	70.4	18.4	9.5	29.3	9.7	3.30
Very large	38	16.6	34.4	54.0	54.1	14.2	6.5	15.2	5.1	4.20
New towns	27	9.9	16.1	65.0	70.3	16.4	8.7	8.7	4.9	3.88
Average		12.1	24.7	54.0	61.0	15.2	7.5	18.7	6.8	3.84

* Soviet planners forecast for two time periods, the short (5–10 year period) and long term (25–30 year period). Because city plans are drawn up at different dates, it is not possible to specify precisely the years these plans refer to. Since the majority were worked out during the 1960s, they describe in the main building heights in the 1970s and 1990s.

SOURCE A. O. Kudryavtsev, *op. cit.* p. 35.

TABLE 8.7 The distribution of the housing stock in the 13 largest cities in the Ukraine by the number of storeys at two future dates: projected division of the housing stock by number of storeys (as % of total stock)

City	9–16 (or more storeys)		4–5 storeys		2–3 storeys		1 storey	
	1st stage	long term	1st stage	long term	1st stage	long term	1st stage	long term
Kiev	33.4	55.4	48.3	38.0	10.1	4.2	8.2	2.4
Khar'kov	9.6	40.4	53.4	50.4	12.3	5.5	24.7	3.7
Donetsk	9.8	40.3	45.0	51.6	11.7	7.7	33.5	14.9
Dnepropetrovsk	—	—	51.0	68.0	14.0	8.5	35.0	23.5
Odessa	6.4	26.0	42.5	47.6	32.7	18.6	18.4	7.8
Zaporozh'e	—	—	57.2	56.9	10.3	10.9	32.5	32.2
Krivoi Rog	—	11.5	54.4	65.4	17.3	9.5	28.3	13.6
L'vov	5.9	25.0	47.9	54.8	36.4	17.1	10.0	3.1
Makeevka	1.4	18.1	34.9	53.1	18.4	11.8	45.3	17.0
Voroshilovgrad	—	—	45.0	62.2	7.5	3.2	47.5	34.6
Nikolaev	—	—	44.0	82.0	16.6	6.3	39.4	11.7
Gorlovka	1.5	8.7	30.3	53.5	17.0	10.8	51.2	27.0

SOURCE V. M. Orekhov, A. D. Ivanova, *Rekonstruktsiya i razvitie krupnykh gorodov UkSSR*, Kiev, 1974, p. 87. Statistics for the general plans of Dnepropetrovsk, Zaporozh'e, Voroshilovgrad and Nikolaev do not distinguish between 4–5 storey blocks and those of 9–16 storeys.

one-third of all new housing'. To achieve the higher densities regarded as necessary some planners suggest that the individual detached house be replaced by low-rise buildings, each one divided into from two to four flats and surrounded by its own 20–100 square metre courtyard–garden.[24]

The general development plans analysed by Kudryavtsev revealed that housing density of the average *mikroraion* would more than double, from 1070 square metres per hectare in the latter part of the 1960s to 2170 square metres in the 1990s (see Table 8.8).

The new *Building Norms and Rules* published in 1976 revised housing densities operative since the mid-1960s upwards by about 6 per cent over the previous regulations. These higher densities, by reducing expenditure on preparing the site, providing utilities, landscaping and on paying compensation for loss of land and agricultural production, were expected to lower the cost of housing and civil construction by about 0.7 per cent for each square metre of overall living space by 1980.[25] Nevertheless, in 1975 for the country as a whole, housing densities were on average about one-half that envisaged in the norms.[26]

Although current urban planning policy is to build at higher densities and raise the average height of buildings, the figures cited so far belie the image of Soviet cities dominated by multi-storey edifices – a view not dispelled by some contemporary writers.[27] In contrast with a popular image which sees Soviet cities as consisting almost entirely of high-rise blocks of flats, the statistics portray a slightly different picture. Many of the country's most populated centres still have vast tracts of land occupied by low rise, low density housing.[28] None the less, the underlying trend, if existing forecasts are to be relied on, is to accommodate the majority of urban residents in buildings with four or more storeys. This policy is related in the first instance to technological advances and increased economic efficiency in the construction industry. There are grounds for believing, however, that the monotonous skyline resulting from the unimaginative widespread use of four- to five-storey standard designs might lead to a downward revision of the long-term forecasts of the proportionate contribution buildings of this size will make to the total stock.

It is difficult to imagine that the high-rise policy will be abandoned in the next 10–15 years. If the uninspiring uniformity of the urban landscape is to be modified, then this will be by building still higher. Apart from the huge investment in the research and development of pre-fabricated, mass-produced, high-rise dwelling units, housing

TABLE 8.8 *Present and planned housing densities in a Mikroraion*

| Category of city by population size | Number of cities studied | Housing density (m²/hectare) | | |
		Present density	At end of current planning period	Long–term (25–30 yrs)
Small	19	440	540	1000
Medium	20	650	885	1520
Big	34	625	960	1640
Large	43	770	1050	1800
Very large	38	1360	1740	2600
New towns	27	840	1330	1930
Average		1070	1420	2170

SOURCE A. O. Kudryavtsev, *op. cit.* p. 35.

densities are almost certain to rise for two main reasons. Firstly, attitudes towards the way in which land has been used are changing, particularly on the issue of the uneconomic utilisation of good agricultural land. Secondly, there is a growing concern over the deleterious effects of urban sprawl.

THE PROBLEM OF RATIONAL LAND USE

An increase in the size of the urban area is a natural concomitant of urbanisation, yet the growth in land area reserved for towns in the Soviet Union is greater than is generally recognised. At the beginning of 1967 the urban area accounted for 7.7 million hectares, equivalent to 0.35 per cent of the country's surface area. The actual developed urban land amounted to 2.7 million hectares – that is, 35 per cent of all land classified as urban. Between 1950 and 1967, land within city administrative boundaries increased by 1.3 million hectares (20 per cent) and actually built-upon land by almost 1.2 million hectares (77 per cent). At this rate of expansion, by the year 2000 over 10 million hectares would fall within city administrative boundaries.[29] Another leading urban planning authority has calculated that the overall urban area had already exceeded this figure by the early 1970s, adding that the urban area was expanding at a rate of 150 000 hectares per year, with half of this growth being at the expense of agricultural land.[30] These figures may be better grasped when it is remembered that the total surface area of England and Wales is 15 million hectares.

In the 1930s, during a spectacular house-building boom 25 100 hectares of agricultural land were lost to all forms of urban development each year. During the period 1950–74, urban development consumed about 15 400 hectares annually in England and Wales compared with an annual increase of 69 200 hectares in the urban area in the USSR between 1950 and 1967.[31] (Again, these statistics reveal the scope for fruitful cross-national studies; they also warn of the difficulties involved in such research, which has to take into account, for example, the fact that the Soviet population is nearly five times the British, land is much more abundant and the need to expand housing supply without demolition has been much greater than in Britain.)

Urbanisation does not necessarily lead to such a high consumption of land in all societies. However, in the Soviet Union down to the present day, the prevalent attitude amongst most people is that since land is in abundant supply and the property of the state, it can be distributed liberally to any would-be user. None the less, some people have long been concerned with the wasteful way enterprises in particular have used land, and have urged that architects and planners should design more economical factory layouts.[32] The prodigal use of land was commented upon in a decree of 1938 which complained of the 'scattering of workshops over a wide area' and the failure of planners to design compact industrial sites. The normal form of development, the decree noted, 'leads to needless expenditure on providing the necessary infrastructure, to increased distances in intra-factory communications and to rising running costs. Furthermore, industrial enterprises fail to combine with one another to utilise common energy sources, water supplies, transport, depots, warehouse facilities, repair services etc'.[33] 12 years later attention was again drawn to the fact that construction costs were still high because enterprises were wasteful in the use of land, locating their workshops and other buildings over a wide area. Another criticism was that too often building work was begun without the initial production of design plans or cost estimates, and this served to keep construction costs at a higher level than they would otherwise be.[34] A decade later, at the sixth All-Union conference of architects, the chairman returned to this theme, reiterating that 'a major shortcoming in planning and construction is the uneconomic use of land'.[35] Dissertations addressed themselves to the issue of the 'irrational use of urban land' in large cities.[36]

Central to this debate lay the question of whether new housing estates (as well as other buildings) should be located on vacant land or whether sites already built upon should be redeveloped.[37] In general, during the 1960s, planners continued to prefer an extensive form of urban development using new sites, which meant that 'in existing settlements new housing should be located on vacant land, not on sites where buildings have to be demolished'.[38] By the 1970s this extensive growth policy began to be revised, with the new (1976) planning norms stating that:

> In planning and building new towns and settlements, it is imperative that capital investment has a high degree of capital efficiency. This is to be achieved by the most economic use of land, grouping industrial enterprises using common facilities and utilities in industrial estates (*uzly*), employing rational building heights and the further industrialisation of construction . . .
> The territory chosen for the siting of new and expansion of existing

towns and settlements must be on non-agricultural land or on land unsuitable for agriculture or on the least fertile land even if its clearing and development requires special engineering techniques. Land that has not been built upon within the city boundaries must be developed in the first instance. The location of new and the renewal of existing towns and settlements, of industrial enterprises and other installations is prohibited on irrigated and drained land, on arable land and on land which has been under orchards or vineyards for many years.[39]

As a result of this renewed emphasis, during the tenth five-year plan period 61 per cent of all new housing space in the Moscow region (Podmoskov'e) was to be on redeveloped city sites, with the remaining 39 per cent on vacant land.[40]

A principal concern of these planning norms is the need to preserve agricultural land. For a long time, the capital required to open up new land for agricultural purposes was scarcely taken into consideration at all. Only more recently have methods been devised for valuing land taken out of agricultural usage and compensation costs been calculated for land scheduled for urban development.[41] In December 1968 the Supreme Soviet ratified a new set of Principles on Land Legislation which, in seeking to foster the rational use of land, stipulated that all new land allocated for building and other non-agricultural uses has to be generally unsuitable for agriculture. The necessity of preserving land for crops and pasture notwithstanding, in the opinion of a number of commentators some of the largest cities are suffering from an absolute land shortage; the only land available is to be found where for one reason or another the terrain is difficult to build on.[42] Of course, little is gained from talking about an urban land shortage in the absence of any measure of efficient land use or standard for assessing the opportunity cost of a specific land use. For example, there may indeed be a land shortage in so far as land within specified administrative boundaries has already been built upon. But if a proportion of that land is occupied by detached, single-storey houses and by enterprises whose premises are scattered over unnecessarily large tracts, then only in a formal and restricted sense can a shortage be said to exist. Social values and technical–economic costs determine whether urban land is in short supply, whether 'difficult terrain' is brought into use for building, and whether land will be reclaimed for agriculture.

Those who advocate land reclamation, however, face a familiar problem. In 1976, for example, a newspaper editorial suggested the reclamation of some land controlled by electricity generating stations, because the 400–500 hectares each station has which are covered with ash would be extremely fertile and thus suitable for farming. But participants of a discussion group convoked by the Presidium of the Ukrainian Supreme Soviet pointed to an important stumbling block: departmental barriers (*vedomstvennye bar'ery*) invariably prevent the use of this land. One solution, the editorial argued, might lie in demonstrating to, say, the Ministries of Energy and Electrification and of Building Materials that they had a mutual interest in utilising these tracts of land and the products on them.[43] However, beyond establishing the general parameters of the contractual links, it would be best if the ministries did not involve themselves directly in the details of individual contracts between generating stations and manufacturers of building materials. Since in the case referred to the land was said to be very fertile and suitable for agriculture, it would probably be better to farm it (especially if the generating station is in a food-deficit region) than to process the ashes or cinders for the construction industry. Under a planned economy it should be possible for the costs and benefits of alternative land uses to be calculated and the land allocated so as to optimise its usage.

Yet it would seem that even in the absence of a land market the temporary *de jure* owners act in a way similar to public corporations in the UK. Where socialist ministries – and capitalist (public) corporations – lack funds to develop a piece of land, or can see no present use for it, they prefer to 'hoard' it in anticipation of a future use (or, in the UK, a higher market value) rather than release it to some other agency. Since they pay no more than a nominal tax for the land they control, and would receive no material reward for moving to a 'greenfield site' outside the city, there is no incentive to surrender a central location which might then be more intensively (even 'rationally') utilised. Perhaps as a result of this, 30–40 per cent of the inner areas of Soviet cities are occupied by industry compared with 8–11 per cent in American cities. The situation in the USSR is such that one writer has been led to conclude that on the whole industrial enterprises in the Soviet Union do not use land as efficiently as capitalist firms in the West[44] – a severe, and perhaps slightly unjust, indictment of Soviet enterprise management. Leningrad, in many ways a model of a socialist city, stands out and is quoted as an example of efficient land use where 'industrial areas are used at a level of efficiency comparable with land use in England, France and the USA'.[45]

In 1942 a report noted that 'national planning directed to ensuring the best use of land involves the subordination to the public good of the personal interests and wishes of landowners, for a purely individualistic approach to land ownership operates to prevent the proper and effective utilisation of our limited national resources'. But for the term 'land ownership', this quotation could have been drawn from a Soviet document, not, as it is, from a British one.[46] In other words, while land nationalisation may fairly be taken as a *sine qua non* for a rational and planned use of land, it is not itself sufficient to ensure rational use.

During the 1970s the cries for the need to economise in the use of land reached a crescendo. At the heart of these dramatic, sometimes poetical calls is the concern for the loss of good agricultural land, especially arable land. One of the more dramatically worded statements declared that: 'Land is a special type of national wealth. Each hectare of fertile soil taken out of cultivation is food taken from the mouths of a generation. If the population increases rapidly and agricultural land is reduced, then in the final analysis an acute problem of feeding the population will arise'.[47] Another author employs this argument to reject the endorsement given by Peter Self, a leading British academic writer on urban and regional policy, to the 'decision to allocate 800 000 hectares of good land to build low-rise housing in England', and to reaffirm the rectitude of the Soviet decision to 'erect housing to meet the needs of a high density communistic form of living'.[48] In view of the precariousness of the country's agricultural production, subject as it is to climatic vagaries, and of the impact crop failures have on the whole domestic economy, there is every reason why the state should employ this style of language and adopt the stance it does. Paradoxically though, an increase in low-rise, detached housing with gardens is known to be a successful way of helping to meet the population's demand for food products.

After a long period when land was treated as a 'free' natural resource in almost unlimited supply, and as a consequence used extensively and frequently inefficiently, the state has launched a determined campaign preaching the need for a more economic and rational use of space in general and good agricultural land in particular.[49] This reorientation has necessarily been accompanied by a search for ways of calculating the functional value of land, especially in the central districts of cities. This has meant a tentative examination of Western concepts of profit maximisation as ways of determining land use.[50] The theoretical justification for directing research along this path is the Soviet Marxist interpretation of differential rent. In the words of one Soviet economist:

Absolute rent is eliminated with the nationalisation of land. But what about differential rent? Given the existence of commodity–monetary relations, the difference in land quality cannot but give rise to differential rent. Therefore land must have a price. Since, however, land is not a product of labour, it has no value, but its price expresses quite concrete economic realities.[51]

Similarly, according to another economist: 'As is well known, the law of differential rent does not depend on the form of land ownership but operates in all socio–economic formations'.[52]

Since central planners are hardly in a position to devise indicators sophisticated or refined enough to take into account the detailed (micro-economic) decisions on land use in every settlement, this decision-making role could be delegated to the city planning committees. In this case they would assume a mantle similar to that of the 'development control officer' in British local authorities who, under certain conditions of rising land prices, may be able to extract a 'community benefit' in return for planning permission. The question turns on the way in which Soviet planners are able to calculate prices for land at different locations in the absence of a market. At present some sort of land evaluation does take place, for enterprises do make requests ('bids') for specific plots of land which can then be negotiated with the local soviets, often in return for the provision of housing and public amenities. In this particular instance, the Soviet system approximates to the practice found in England, such as in the St. Katharine Dock development in London, where a private developer has built houses for council letting in return for building and development planning permission. The problem of such partnerships between local authority (local soviet) and 'developer' (enterprise) is that the 'private' quality of these negotiations may conflict with comprehensive planning.[53] Overall, however, in so far as the existence of differential rent in the Soviet Union is acknowledged, a double benefit could be gained from operationalising the concept: on the one hand, it could become a source of revenue (land tax) for the local soviets and, on the other, it could lead to more efficient land use.[54]

In summary, the reasoning dominating land use planning policy runs as follows: high-rise housing development is essential because of the rapid rate at which land, not infrequently the most fertile, is being consumed by urban development. The loss of agricultural land is condemned as a matter of national economic waste. Continuing population growth and urbanisation make it impossible on spatial, economic and moral grounds, to sustain in the long run a policy of low-rise 'cottage' development. Socialism recognises this problem and seeks to combat it by containing further urban sprawl (agglomeration formation) and by building high-rise blocks of flats. Urban renewal is one way of achieving this objective, but so far renewal has been taking place without any clear method of assessing optimum land use. It is perhaps on account of this that economists and planners have been unable to deal with the problems created by the reluctance of institutions to surrender land nominally under their control.

URBAN RENEWAL DEFINED

The organic analogy whereby the city is regarded as a living organism[55] can be extended – in a fashion similar to that applied by Herbert Spencer and Bronislaw Malinowski – to view the city as passing through a 'life cycle' with tissues dying and having to be replaced. The replacing of tissues and the phenomenon of the 'cancerous' growth of industrial cities symbolising urban renewal and urban sprawl respectively are, as the metaphor suggests, inter-related.

Urban renewal involves both the replanning and comprehensive redevelopment of land, often through the demolition of existing structures, and also the conservation and rehabilitation of areas threatened by blight and worthy of preservation because of their historical setting and cultural associations. Rehabilitation has at least three distinct advantages over new construction: firstly, it may be cheaper;[56] secondly, it can be carried out in a comparatively shorter period of time; and thirdly, it involves the least disruption to existing social patterns and local networks as long as tenants can be offered temporary accommodation while their own homes are being repaired.

The demolition of housing and other old buildings, the redevelopment of an area and the expansion of city boundaries are hardly a new phenomena, either in the Soviet Union or in world history. The rebuilding of cities *in toto* or in part has been systematically carried out throughout history. And in the twentieth century, successive British governments have included slum clearance programmes as part of their housing and town planning policies. However, only since the 1950s and particularly in the 1960s has the British government turned its attention (and resources) to the issue of urban renewal. This change in direction in housing and urban policy has occurred almost simultaneously in the UK, USA and USSR to the extent that over the last 15 years in all three societies it has attracted substantial funding for academic research.

Although there is a measure of agreement between different professional and political groups in West European states and the Soviet Union on the need to renew and renovate old buildings rather than demolish them, the reasons put forward in support of their case differ in England and the Soviet Union. Beyond doubt, there are important cost benefits to be gained from rehabilitation,[57] but English (and American) planners are often keener to point to the social benefits of these schemes. Firstly, rehabilitation can help to raise the quality of life of low-income groups in these areas. Secondly, it makes it possible to preserve the network of social relations to be found in that spatial community. (On the other hand, urban renewal has become associated with a set of negative phenomena: primarily, the 'gentrification' of inner city districts by members of the professional middle class, which leads to higher house prices and the displacement of low-income, privately-renting tenants.) Soviet writing on the subject distinguishes itself from Western discussions in that the former makes no mention of any benefits arising from the preservation of community structures. Thus, Soviet town planners assume the principal tasks of urban renewal to be: improving the layout of the district, raising the height of buildings, improving the level of provision of services and public transport, raising housing sanitary standards and general environmental amelioration.[58]

However, the situation appears to be changing, for some Soviet sociologists now recognise the existence of 'spatially defined communities'. For instance, one group of authors refers to the fact that 'every form of spatial community (*obshchnost'*) unites people who, despite all their individual and social class differences (socio-professional, socio-demographic etc.) share some common social characteristics'.[59] And the content of a letter published in *Pravda* may be regarded as furnishing evidence on the existence of just such a 'community'. The author of the letter from Belgorod, who lived in a comfortable house with 'decades of life left in it', complained that his own and neighbouring houses were to be demolished in order 'to create an architectural whole'. This prompted him to ask 'who needs such beauty if it is injurious to the interests of a lot of people?'[60]

The local soviet is obliged by law to compensate and rehouse families displaced by redevelopment.[61] However, it is clear that in this case the residents would prefer to remain in their present homes, even though they may have lacked piped water and a connection to the main sewerage system. Moreover, since Belgorod had more than doubled its population in the period 1959–70 (from 72 000 to 151 000) and then risen by a further 104 000 during 1970–81, it is likely that the new accommodation on offer to these citizens of Belgorod was on a new housing estate, still without shops, eating places and general social facilities, some distance from the town centre and/or their places of work and poorly serviced by public transport. It also seems likely that the letter writer's earlier home would have had a large garden and that he would have been able to draw an income from renting part of his premises, especially given the city's rapid population growth. The writer also added that fewer mistakes would occur, particularly the premature demolition of buildings, if renewal plans were first subjected to a broad discussion by the general public: the plans, as they stood, were only explicable in terms of planners' attempts at unnecessary 'beautification' and 'unjustifiable' widening of streets and squares. The letter thus carried a strong suggestion that if there had been 'public participation' in the planning process, urban planners would have found difficulty in justifying their schemes and that in many cases these would have been rejected.[62]

The 'official' response to the sort of complaints and charges raised here is that city soviets, town planning organisations and any other body which could conceivably be regarded as affecting an individual's chances of being given better accommodation, are constantly being inundated with requests from citizens living in 'old', one- or two-storey dwellings to be rehoused in a new state apartment. This is taken as an indication that they would prefer to live in a high-rise flat rather than a small detached house with a garden. The conclusion drawn is, however, not fully warranted, for the choice is not between a new flat and an equally well-built house, but rather between a new flat and a small house, subdivided into flats and supplied with water from a standpipe in the courtyard, an outside water closet and no central heating.

Despite such protestations, and partly because of pressures to economise on land, there was an escalation in housing demolition during the 1960s. In 1969 a group of residents living in Kalinin (422 000) wrote to the editor of *Pravda* asking if it was really necessary to demolish a whole street of structurally sound one-storey dwellings in order to provide space for the erection of one multi-storey block of flats. The same article referred to Sverdlovsk (1 239 000) where, in 1969, the loss to the city's housing stock amounted to over 30 per cent of all new buildings.[63] Another correspondent writing from Podol'sk (205 000) complained that over the previous four years he had witnessed the demolition in the centre of the city of a large number of perfectly good houses which, like his own demolished home, had been equipped with all the basic amenities – gas, water and central heating. And, in Orenburg (482 000) whole rows of streets in the city centre were destined to come under the bulldozer even though 80 per cent of these houses were in need of no repair at all.[64] Moreover, here the housing density was so high that almost one-third of new housing erected had to be allocated to residents whose homes had been demolished. The editor replied that the residents had raised a fundamental question, for if housing conditions for the population were to be improved, it was impossible to rely solely on new building. It was no less important to keep losses to the housing stock to a minimum and ensure good technical management.[65]

During the period of this correspondence, N. Baibakov, the chairman of *Gosplan*, merely reiterated what everyone seemed to be pointing out, namely that in many cities a substantial amount of perfectly good housing was being demolished for no valid reason. To illustrate the point he cited figures for 1968 which revealed that the amount of living space demolished as a proportion of new living space built was 12 per cent in Kishinev, 14 per cent in Tomsk, 11 per cent in Yerevan, 18 per cent in Novosibirsk and 31 per cent in Sverdlovsk.[66] The same point was made in another *Pravda* editorial of 24 February 1970. The issue, however, was not new. The housing decree of July 1957 had also referred to 'the largely unwarranted demolition of housing, leading to a loss in dwelling space'. The loss to the housing stock 'in the long term' was estimated to average about 11.6 per cent of the total housing stock – ranging from 4.6 per cent in new towns (those founded after 1945) to 12.7 per cent in the very largest (those cities with over 500 000 inhabitants).[67]

Following this public debate, in 1970 the government issued an important decree in which it referred, in no uncertain terms, to the great damage wrought by unwarranted large-scale demolition of high-quality (*dobrotnyi*) housing which 'was being carried out simultaneously with premature work on road widening and the building of new major highways and squares'.[68] This policy, it added, only served to impede the solving of the housing problem. And, according to the Party leadership, responsibility for initiating the large-scale demolition of high-quality housing lay with individual heads of Party committees and executive committees of local soviets who 'should be called to account'.[69]

Table 8.9 indicates that losses to the housing stock increased annually from 1960 to 1966 in both absolute and relative terms – in fact, more

TABLE 8.9   *Losses to the urban housing stock, 1960–1980, as a percentage of new construction*

Year	New building	Loss	Loss as % of
	('000m² overall living space)		New Building
1960	59 030	5 833	9.9
1961	56 114	5 595	10.0
1962	58 858	6 519	11.1
1963	58 469	7 326	12.5
1964	57 459	9 470	16.5
1965	60 726	10 956	18.0
1966	63 400	14 040*	22.1
1967	66 108	9 248	14.0
1968	66 039	9 679	14.7
1969	68 570	10 498	15.3
1970	71 195	12 749	17.9
1971	72 743	10 832	14.8
1972	73 368	9 252	12.6
1973	77 524	10 967	14.1
1974	77 060	10 123	13.1
1975	76 240	11 034	14.5
1976	75 920	13 052	17.2
1977	77 120	10 521	13.6
1978	76 530	10 298	13.5
1979	71 890	10 045	14.0
1980	77 473	11 500	14.8

*This high figure might be due to the serious earthquake of 1983 which had Tashkent as its epicentre.

SOURCES   *Narodnoe khozyaistvo SSSR v 1967g., op. cit.* p. 684; *Narodnoe khozyaistvo SSSR v 1974g., op. cit.* p. 588; *Narodnoe khozyaistvo SSSR v 1975g.,* p. 578; *Narodnoe khozyaistvo SSSR v 1978, op. cit.* p. 400; *Narodnoe khozaistvo SSSR v 1980g.,* p. 394.

than doubling in this period (from 9.9 per cent in 1960 to 22.1 per cent in 1966). This figure fell dramatically in 1967, but thereafter rose steadily to peak at 17.9 per cent in 1970, the year in which the government published its decree condemning the practice of 'over zealous' demolition. Although the statistics show a continuing proportionate downward trend from 1971 to 1974, in absolute terms losses have not altered so substantially, for the absolute figure for 1973 is almost exactly the same for 1965. Yet proportionately at the later date this represents 14.1 per cent of all new construction as against 18.0 per cent in 1965. As a point of comparison, when housing demolition was at its peak in Britain (1961–1971), the actual number demolished was equal to about 30 per cent of all new houses built. It declined from a peak of over 105 000 dwellings demolished in 1971 to 42 000 in 1979.[70]

A number of specific factors gave rise to a rate of demolition that assured a momentum unacceptable to the government and called forth a rebuke of town planning practice in the 1960s. Among the most important were the need to provide the population with more living space; the diminution in large cities of suitable undeveloped building land; an increase in road traffic necessitating major road widening and construction schemes; the need to rebuild the centres of cities; and a rise in the proportion of the housing stock considered no longer to be compatible with modern standards.[71] In the mid-1970s, the Central Housing and Town Planning Research Institutes (*TsNIIEP zhilishcha* and *TsNIP gradostroitel'stva*) estimated that the volume of demolition would increase in the future.[72]

In Soviet terminology, buildings are referred to as being 'physically' and 'morally' obsolescent (*fizicheskii i moral'nyi iznos*); the former refers to structurally unsound buildings, whilst the latter implies an absence of what are considered to be basic amenities.[73] Buildings suffering from 'physical and moral' obsolescence (*nekapital'nyi*) are not regarded as part of the country's fixed capital stock. Table 8.10 shows that the vast bulk of *nekapital'nyi* housing stock (85 per cent) consists of one-storey buildings and that 32 per cent of this stock

TABLE 8.10   *The physical condition of the urban housing stock by number storeys*

Physical condition of housing stock	Total living space	Distribution of living space of storey				
		1	2	3	4–5	6 an over
Total living space	100	45.2	15.2	4.8	31.3	3.5
Capital stock	100/59*	16.8	16.0	8.0	53.2	6.0
of which: socialised	100/89**	6.7	17.4	9.1	60.0	6.8
Non-capital stock	100/41*	85.5	14.3	0.2	—	—
of which: socialised	100/32***	60.0	39.4	0.6	—	—

* as a percentage of total housing stock
** as a percentage of total capital stock
*** as a percentage of total non-capital stock

SOURCE   G. A. Kaplan, A. V. Kochetkov, *op. cit.* p. 22.

TABLE 8.11 *The proportion of the total urban housing stock provided with basic amenities on 1 January 1968 and the population of local Soviet housing provided in 1977*

Amenity	Proportion of the total urban living space supplied in 1968*	Proportion of local soviet sector supplied in 1977**
Total housing space:	100	100
piped running water	64	89
sewerage disposal	61	88
central heating	58	82
centralised district heating	31	n.a.
electric lighting	90	c. 100
hot water	23	54
gas	50	88

SOURCES
* G. A. Kaplan, A. V. Kochetkov, *op. cit.* p. 23.
** S. F. Legornev, 'Zhilishchno-kommunal'noe khozyaistvo: tsifry rosta', *Zhilishchnoe i kommunal'noe khozyaistvo*, No. 3, 1979, p. 14.

belongs to the public sector. In Donetsk (1 040 000), Zaporozh'e (812 000) and Gorlovka (338 000) the 'non-capital' stock amounted to 30–45 per cent of all housing.[74]

Apart from the physical obsolescence, as Table 8.11 shows, in 1968, 39 per cent of all urban housing (in terms of living space) was not connected to a central sewerage system and 26 per cent lacked piped water. Although standards could have been expected to improve between 1968 and 1977, the extent of the improvement is exaggerated by the fact that the figures for 1968 include the private sector, traditionally ill-provided with amenities.

The global character of the above figures conceals tremendous variations between cities (both large and small and between towns in each category) and within cities themselves. The scale and rate of reconstruction in any given town depends on the nature of existing buildings, the intensity of land use and availability of land for further expansion. However, the broad parameters of government policy in this field are clearly defined: firstly, buildings of architectural and artistic merit must be preserved;[75] and secondly, as a general rule, housing densities should be increased.

RECONCILIATION OF CONFLICTING OBJECTIVES IN RESIDENTIAL DEVELOPMENT

A number of decrees enacted since the early 1960s have exhorted planners and builders to build higher and not restrict themselves to four- and five-storey blocks. They would thus economise in the use of suitable building land of which a shortage exists in some cities. At the same time however, not only are the unit costs of erecting tower blocks higher, but so are their running costs. Whereas in 1980 in the Ukraine, the revenue from four- and five-storey buildings covered costs, in the case of nine-and ten-storey blocks, costs exceed revenue by 15–20 per cent and those of 16 and 17 storeys by 50–80 per cent.[76]

The land supply factor is not solely responsible for this changed attitude to the building of 'skyscrapers', which Davidovich in 1960 had considered to be unwarranted in a socialist society. There is also the issue of the aesthetic appearance of cities. The outcome of the ever-increasing application of industrialised construction methods and stan-dard designs has been the conversion of large urban tracts into singularly uniform and montonous residential areas. This has led to warnings that the 'soul' of a town or district can be destroyed by constructing 'countless huge boxes'.[77] A number of readers' letters in the weekly, *Literaturnaya gazeta*, have stressed the need for more imaginative architecture and improved urban planning, while others claim that at a time when many people still live in inadequate, crowded conditions, the speed of building and the purely utilitarian aspects of housing should be more important than any aesthetic considerations. The reviewer of the correspondence considered that the issue should not be treated as an 'either or' dilemma, for town development should satisfy both basic needs and yet be aesthetically pleasing.[78]

In 1965 architects and planners were freed from the shackles of the 1957 housing decree; henceforth building heights were to be determined by a city's own unique geographical features and its economic and industrial profile.[79] During the next decade architects, eager to conform with policy indicators, began to seek an optimum combination of three policies. They had to construct houses as economically as possible using standard designs; show imagination and erect higher blocks; and make more rational (efficient) use of urban land, which implied demolition of large tracts of low-rise dwellings. Government and academic comment on building practice has at times echoed the 'dizzy with success' criticism levelled at the over-zealous collectivisers in 1929 – although the terms of rebuke and consequences for those found guilty are in no way comparable. Kudryavtsev simply points out that the 'widespread practice of erecting high, multi-storey blocks without taking into careful consideration local conditions inevitably results in building becoming more expensive'. At the same time, 'in many towns hasty decisions have been taken on the demolition of the existing housing stock; decisions which in a number of cases have paid no attention to the general development plan or to the city's needs.... And moreover, demolition has often been carried out without any close examination of the real physical condition of the housing stock'.[80]

By 1978, studies were revealing that the choice of very high rise buildings could not be justified by 'town planning and technical–economic conditions'. In fact they had been selected by the customer for reasons of prestige or because local officials thought that such buildings improved the appearance of the town. In an attempt to counteract this tendency, which only served to reduce the cost-effectiveness of capital investment, *Gosstroi* and *Gosplan* had in September 1976 issued a set of instructions 'On the rational structure of buildings for 1976–1980'. These stipulated that where large-scale construction programmes were undertaken in large cities, buildings should be of nine storeys, and in other cities of five storeys. And whilst

12 to 16 storey buildings were admissible in a limited number of cases, those of more than sixteen storeys 'were not recommended'.[81] In 1981, the recommendation turned into a decreed guideline: the Council of Ministers of Union Republics were charged with restricting the erection of blocks of flats with more than nine storeys to Moscow, Leningrad and Kiev. Elsewhere, buildings exceeding nine storeys in height are to be permitted only in exceptional cases defined by architectural and town planning desiderata and economic requirements.[82]

Some of the discussions parallel those taking place in the UK, for instance, on the need to assess the relative merits of pursuing a selective policy of combining the renovation of some buildings with the demolition of others, as against a policy of reconstructing an entire *mikroraion.* Unfortunately, the spending of considerable sums on renovating individual buildings (selective rehabilitation) only to discover that, when the city or district plan is published, the renovated houses were scheduled for demolition, is to be found in Soviet practice as well as in the United Kingdom.[83] The straightforward explanation for this sort of occurrence is that communication channels between different bodies responsible for ratifying urban plans and then financing their implementation are not functioning effectively (or do not even exist). Viewed in this light the problems of demolition and urban renewal (or of urban and regional planning in general) can be seen as essentially problems of information and organisation: lack of technical documentation, poor co-ordination of activities of different departments and a shortage of qualified personnel. These constitute difficulties in any complex social system and are in fact inherent in them: overlapping administrative boundaries give rise to departmental rivalries and disputes; organisations differ in their ranking of priorities and in their access to the means of achieving these goals.

In a planned economy, planning is concerned both with overcoming contradictions between different schemes and with contradictions within planning organisations themselves. The definition of the Soviet Union as 'socialist', a society in which there are no antagonistic conflicts, virtually precludes any examination by the Soviets themselves of urban renewal (or any aspect of social structure or social change) except in terms of a natural progression of events which are conditioned by a level of development of the nation's material resources. As far as failures (*nedostatki*) are concerned, these are seen by Soviet authors (to a certain extent, justifiably) as being due to a lack of information and/or individual error and incompetence. Yet, as elsewhere, real disagreements over renewal policy do exist within the architectural profession. Some regard the rehabilitation of individual buildings in an area as a patchwork approach which should be abandoned, and in general oppose conservation policies, no matter how good the physical state of the buildings under review, on the grounds that they are of no architectural significance. This viewpoint is countered by those who contend that the pursuit of a wholesale demolition policy could have the unwanted effect of creating cities that are all alike, arguing instead that it is preferable to keep the face of old districts as they are and at the same time modernise their interiors to improve the living conditions of the tenants.[84]

Clearly, the housing strategy adopted in any town – to rehabilitate or to redevelop – will depend, among other things, on the nature of the housing stock, local terrain and on the Chief City Architect who at present will probably be influenced by the current trend towards rehabilitation. In keeping with this new direction of thinking, housing which at one time had been designated as obsolescent by Soviet officials is now being modernised.[85] The impact of the Chief City Architect in determining land use, though increasingly more effective, is still hampered by the procrastinatory tactics of enterprise executives. The Riga general development plan, drawn up in 1969, listed those institutions and enterprises that had to relocate outside the city centre in order to preserve the outward architectural form of the centre and to use the buildings for cultural and retail purposes. And yet, in early 1979 only 25 per cent of the directives issued had been acted upon; the rest had been ignored. Cases exist of enterprise executives using every conceivable pretext to avoid vacating their premises in the old part of Riga even after they had actually constructed new factories, workshops and warehouses in the earmarked industrial zone.[86] The centres of some cities seem to be valued locations whether for living or working. And this suggests the existence of a causal relationship between central city residence and social status.

URBAN RENEWAL AND SOCIAL STRUCTURE

In Western capitalist societies the introduction of the notion of 'social planning' has roughly coincided with the 'rediscovery of poverty', particularly in large cities. Physical or spatial planning, it is now argued, has failed precisely those people it ought to have helped most. American urban renewal programmes, for example, have simply displaced low-income residents from inner urban areas without providing alternative housing. Furthermore, the British New Town policy and the American Interstate Highway Programme have contributed to suburban dispersal of people and employment, with high-income residents and their associated services and jobs migrating to outer suburbs, leaving the older central districts increasingly separated from job opportunities. Whereas a certain hypocrisy underlies the Anglo–American 'discovery' of the effects of urban renewal on the poor, nevertheless sociological research has revealed, and governments have made a certain positive response to, the needs of social groups adversely affected by urban policies. Both research and response have above all demonstrated that the needs of social and spatially defined groups might be different from those which planners expected.

In the Soviet Union, despite the importance attached to urban renewal, little evidence can be found of any research having been conducted to examine the social consequences of reductions in the absolute population size (and relative population decline) of central districts, particularly of the larger cities, as urban renewal continues. It is generally held that no divisions of the city along class or ethnic lines exist, and whilst empirical evidence remains to be produced, the assumption made by Soviet authors appears to be that alcoholism and various officially designated forms of criminality or 'unlawful' or 'uncultured' behaviour are randomly distributed throughout the urban area. These authors would fiercely resist Louis Wirth's postulation that, 'The greater the number of individuals participating in a process of interaction, the greater is the *potential* differentiation between them. ... That such variations should give rise to the spatial segregation of individuals according to colour, ethnic heritage, economic and social status, tastes and preferences may readily be inferred'.[87] They contend that this phenomenon of the poor living in the central districts of capitalist cities is not new, nor do they find it surprising that today the poor fail to be the beneficiaries of urban planning.

A century earlier Engels had succinctly and accurately described the impact of urban renewal on this section of the population.[88] On the other hand, because the urban population in the USSR is, in social class terms, held to be randomly distributed throughout the city, the authors argue that urban renewal does not affect one social group more than another. Where decentralisation of population and jobs takes place in conjunction with urban renewal, no-one is seriously disadvantaged. Those who find that their previous jobs are too far removed from their old (or new) homes can always find work else-where in the city (or settlement system); or, since fares charged on public transport are very low, anyone willing to put up with the possible extra time spent travelling can easily afford the longer journey to work. Alternatively, those displaced may exchange their flat for another nearer their place of work, since the departmental housing sector still controls over 50 per cent of the total socialised housing stock. Therefore enterprises and institutions are in many cases in a position to offer their employees accommodation in their own build-ings close to their place of work. Alternatively, an individual can try to exchange his flat by placing an advertisement on a public notice-board (on the street or in a public building) or in a special publication issued monthly which is devoted solely to house exchanges (*Byulleten' po obmenu zhiloi ploschchadi*).[89] In fact local soviets are now being encouraged to allocate accommodation to people near to their place of work, and assist them to exchange their flats to the same end. The government regards this initiative as one way of reducing labour turnover.[90]

The problem remains, however, that in the absence of research there is no way of knowing whether planners are indeed representing the needs of those thousands of families displaced or rehoused in urban development programmes. For example, in recent years 90 000 people in Kiev and 70 000 in Dnepropetrovsk have been 'decanted' from the central districts to new housing estates on the city periphery. Yet there has been no published discussion of the implications of the change for the residents affected (see Table 8.12). Who will move out, who will remain and who might move in when the *Podol'*, the oldest district in Kiev, is redeveloped are important questions which are not even posed in the published press. There is certainly no *a priori* reason for assuming that the *gorsovet* is any more atuned to local requirements than is a town (or borough) council in the UK. Nor can it be assumed that the people being planned for constitute a socially homogenous mass with identical demands.

Sociology, urban planning and housing journals do not refer to any continuous debate on the impact urban renewal might be having on social groups, and offer little statistical data to show that certain social groups are disproportionately represented in particular areas of the city. But there are indications that Soviet sociologists are interested in these issues. One Soviet ethnographer in a study of ethnic segregation in Kazan' (1 011 000) and Al'met'evsk (113 000) in the Tatar Au-tonomous Republic, found that the rather pronounced group segrega-

TABLE 8.12 *The distribution of population and housing space in the centre of three large cities in 1970 and 1990 (est.)*

City	Housing space in central districts				Population residing in central district			
	1970		1990		1970		1990	
	mln m²	% of total city housing space	mln m²	% of total city housing space	thousands	% of total city popn.	thousands	% of total city popn.
Kiev	2.5	23.0	3.0	14.0	320	18.0	230	12.7
Dnepropetrovsk	1.25	21.8	1.36	10.7	185	22.0	115	11.5
Zaporozh'e	1.1	30.0	1.7	17.7	160	29.0	145	18.1

SOURCE G. I. Frumin, 'Tekhniko-ekonomicheskie voprosy rekonstruktsii tsentrov krupnykh gorodov', *Voprosy ekonomiki gradostroitel'stva i raionnoi planirovki*, Kiev, 1970, p. 35.

tion which existed prior to 1917 continues to persist in the older parts of these towns.[91] And in a recent essay two authors, in their outline of a programme of research, included as a necessary component 'a detailed analysis of the social structure of the city in order to establish the location of social groups in urban space'.[92] They noted that social differences in terms of size and source of income, housing provision, daily needs etc. created distinctive groups who engage in different recreational, cultural, and educational activities.

From this last observation it was a short step to insist on the need to identify 'those factors which affect social advancement and those social qualities which enable individuals to occupy different social positions'.[93] The Mertonian link between deviant behaviour and blocked access to highly valued societal goals[94] was clearly made when attention was drawn to the necessity of establishing 'the relationship between anti-social behaviour and the level of social opportunity'.[95] In the West, where criminology is a 'growth' area in sociology, a number of competing theories have been advanced to 'explain' deviancy in society.[96] Of those theories available to policy-inclined researchers it is likely that the ecological approach of the Chicago School of the 1920s and 1930s, with its research into the distribution of areas of work and residence, places of public interaction and urban concentrations of conformity and deviance, will be best received by the Party. The research methodology of the ecological school based on small scale, methodologically-detailed investigations encourages a focus on local problems.

The remedies normally recommended tend to be such that they do not generate hypotheses or policy suggestions critical of the structure of society, which might itself be systematically reproducing certain negatively-evaluated phenomena. In fact, despite the well-reasoned critiques of Western urban sociologists, Soviet sociologists are beginning to use the terminology and concepts which date from R. Park and the 1920s and refer, for instance, to large 'historically established cities as laboratories of scientific research',[97] and as a 'melting pot [*plavnyi kotel*']' for forming a new type of worker.'[98] One of the criticisms has been that instead of trying to identify links 'between the urban process and the concrete laws of development' in specific historical periods and in particular social formations, Western urban sociologists have been more interested in elucidating 'universal tendencies, characteristics and symbols inherent in cities in general'.[99] The subversive element inherent in the possibility of discovering forms and features in socialist cities that are common to all large cities is partially countered by pointing out the ideological basis and function of urban sociology in capitalist society. The argument takes the following form: if the causes of urban conflicts were not to be discovered in the basic contradictions of capitalist society but in the city itself, then it was completely natural to 'find' them in the conflict of interests occurring between different territorially-located groups comprising the urban organism.[100]

Thus, having unmasked the human ecologists (and Western urban sociologists in general) for what they really were (are) – mystifiers of the class struggle – Soviet sociologists are free to go ahead and use the ecologists' research methodology and concepts to analyse cities in socialist societies. The Soviet Union, regarded as a qualitatively different society, *ipso facto* renders criticisms of these methods inapplicable to the Soviet context. Indeed, it is now accepted by the Soviets that population density (a key variable in 'classical' urban ecological theory), intensified social interaction and the general tempo and rhythm of life in the city exert substantial influence on the behaviour, attitudes and psychic state of individuals. Yet Soviet sociologists complain that proper attention is still not being paid to their aggregate effect; particularly lacking are analyses of the 'ecological dimension of the urban way of life and of the reaction of different social and demographic groups to their local environments'.[101]

Soviet sociologists working within the Chicago school paradigm have adopted the view that urban anomie is a product of the impersonal, segmental and ephemeral nature of human relationships in the city, with the corollary that 'urbanism' acts as an independent variable to explain manifestations of social disorganisation.[102] In an article discussing the social–psychological consequences of urbanisation and their effect on crime, the author, a reader in law, in distinguishing between urban and rural communities pointed out that the city dweller has more contacts with other people than does the peasant, although they are more compartmentalised; furthermore, 'the urbanite interacts with his surroundings not with his whole personality but with only part of it. In the city the social control exerted by an individual's home environment is weakened, making it easier to commit crimes'.[103] The role and significance of a stable family background as an influential agent of socialisation and social control is afforded as much prominence by Soviet politicians as their Western counterparts.

One particularly appealing aspect of the ecologists' approach is that it stresses non-human environmental factors. A sociological study conducted in Nizhnii Tagil (404 000) to discover the reasons for the differential use of socio-cultural facilities in the city observed that

'Disproportions in cultural demand are based not only on the disproportions in the location of institutions. Of greater significance is the social composition of the district's population and the character of its buildings (does the state or private sector dominate). . . . The rank correlation coefficient characterising the link between the demand for cultural values and the character of buildings was 0.4'. The coefficient rose to 0.6 when the intelligentsia, as a social group, were included in the matrix.[104] Given the emphasis placed by Soviet criminologists on the persistence of normative behaviour patterns inherited from the past (e.g. 'money-grubbing', bribery, sponging, stealing),[105] there are good grounds for them to associate such anti-social acts with a distinctly individualistic form such as the privately owned home. With the gradual diminution in the size of this sector, attention will focus more on other social–physical factors. When certain issues and behaviour patterns become defined as deviant and a relevant object of social investigation, there will be a temptation for Soviet sociologists to regard them as expressions of individual or group pathologies, which are in turn a product of the built environment, and remedial through adjustments to that environment.

This potentially environmental–deterministic approach is well illustrated by the authors of one text who comment that:

> It is especially important today that action directed at changing conditions of life should be maximally effective and that architects possess an accurate image of how the environment, which they are instrumental in creating, influences people, their social and day-to-day contacts, and their physical and psychological states . . . Although sociological research in urban planning has begun in the USSR, recent housing projects demonstrate that research into the social problems of organising a new living environment has not yet percolated into the work of architects.[106]

According to this view, since urban renewal brings substantial improvements to the physical environment, it should have beneficial effects on human behaviour. However, in the UK and other West European states areas subject to urban renewal are often associated with immigrant labour and the latter with criminal activity.

In the Soviet Union there is no clear evidence of a link between urban renewal and immigrants (from the countryside). However, some migrants (as in the West) do rent accommodation from private house owners and it is often areas of low-rise, privately owned housing which are earmarked for demolition and renewal. Moreover, migrants are regarded as particularly susceptible to criminal behaviour ('the resort to socially disapproved methods of fulfilling aspirations') – partly because 'deformed or partly disintegrated family and kinship ties are more common among migrants than among people who have always lived in the city'. And, as in other countries, Soviet planners are urged to pay special attention to 'eliminating factors that could provoke conflicts between migrants and long term urban residents'.[107] The ingredients for an ecological explanation of a range of urban 'pathologies' and group conflicts are all present: Some areas of cities contain concentrations of migrants. Many of them are unskilled, single and uncontrolled by family and neighbourhood ties and live in grossly inadequate housing, in an environment that is not well maintained since it is probably destined for total renewal at a later date.

Again, it is possible that, as in Western societies, modernisation of inner city areas may be accompanied by the displacement of members of some social groups (who are rehoused on new estates away from the city centre) by individuals drawn from other social groups, leading to a Soviet form of 'gentrification'. Indeed, it seems probable that the decanting of the population, associated with urban renewal, and the renovation of older buildings will be accompanied by the concentration of a proportionately higher percentage of the intelligentsia (and other groups entitled to supplementary living space) in the central areas of the city near to its cultural and shopping centres – not least because 43 per cent of all cultural and social amenities are to be found there.[108] As a result of a 'centripetal tendency affecting the location of social and cultural activities', over 50 per cent of a sample survey of Muscovites interviewed in the central district of the capital considered the centrality of a location to be one of the most important factors which would determine their choice of residence.[109] Another survey of Muscovites living on three outlying housing estates revealed that over 73 per cent of those polled spent some time after work or study in the centre.[110]

Demographic evidence tends to support the hypothesis that those of higher socio-economic status gravitate towards the centre. For instance, there is an almost 30 per cent difference between the number of children living in the centre and the suburbs of Moscow.[111] Although this is partly explicable in terms of the concentration of an ageing population in the centre, another at least equally important factor is likely to be that higher socio-economic groups have fewer children. The explanation given is that this difference arises from the migration of larger families to the periphery, which basically means members of lower status socio-economic groups. The changing demographic structure of central and outlying areas 'exerts an influence on the planning of kindergartens and schools'. Another author, on the basis of an examination of birth registration certificates in Khar'kov and Kiev, has similarly suggested that fewer pre-school and school places need to be provided in central districts, allowing the additional space created to be used for building blocks of flats.[112]

Although social policy has to be responsive to changing demands, by reflecting them it also reinforces them; the provision of fewer school places in some areas already effectively determines the social composition of different parts of the city. Statistical data drawn from almost all large cities show that one of the reasons for the natural loss of accommodation in the central districts is the extreme difficulty of providing the population with schools, playgroup facilities and areas for physical recreation.[113] Research has further revealed that most families living there are childless or have only one or two children. One lobby opposing the allocation of too much valuable inner city land for accommodation, and yet at the same time wanting to prevent the centre being given over entirely to employment and recreational functions, recommends that accommodation should be provided mainly for people not requiring schools.[114] This recommendation is expressing an actual process.

CONCLUSION

Today, urban renewal, one of the central problematics of Soviet urban policy, is dominated by two factors: historically determined extensive, low-value housing development and (ergo) large scale demolition. The new lamps exchanged for Aladdin's old ones come in the shape of multi-storey blocks of flats: the exchange may have been for the better, but not without causing some discontent and frustration within the population and even within the architectural profession. The response to the complaints has been to build higher in order to break the uniformity of the sky-line, but thereby raising residential densities still further. This strategy brings an additional benefit, namely, land saving. Indeed, the need to conserve land (primarily for agricultural, but also for recreational and other, purposes) is used as a justification for a high-rise development policy.

Apart from the differences of opinion which exist on the subject of the form that the physical environment should take, another important facet of urban renewal programmes is their potential to affect the spatial segregation of social groups. Despite the various indications that certain social groups are probably disproportionately represented in particular areas in the city – primarily as a result of the local soviet allocating plots of land for house building in the centre of major cities to ministries, government departments and housing co-operatives – the term 'socially distinct areas' has to be used with caution. It normally means that a particular district does not contain a representative cross-section of the population, not that it is a single class area.[115] Moreover, it is not so much a neighbourhood or district that is so socially distinctive, as the block of flats or a small complex of blocks.

Generally speaking however, with singular exceptions, blocks of flats in the Soviet Union are characterised by social class heterogeneity – certainly by Anglo–American standards. It is impossible in Soviet cities to identify ghettos, whether rich or poor: there are only tendencies towards the congregation of social groups. The historical continuities in patterns of spatial segregation across the Rubicon of 1917 merit consideration. Suffice it to say here that it was a mixture of classes rather than segregation that characterised the fashionable areas of nineteenth-century St. Petersburg[116] – in contrast to nineteenth-century England, where urban growth witnessed increasing segregation of city dwellers into different streets and districts according to income and status.[117] What seems incontrovertible is the fact that the availability of shops, services and entertainment in the centre also restricts the amount of space that can be used to meet the needs of families with children. The status associated with the inner city flat, which is at least in part related to easy access to concert halls and theatres, almost certainly means that 'political' or 'administrative' contacts, bribery and key-money paid when exchanging flats help to determine who obtains accommodation in the centre.

The form urban renewal takes will influence existing tendencies to spatial social segregation, which are closely bound up with other aspects of urban development. The history of Soviet urban planning and practice may in fact be seen in terms of an attempt to arrive at a compromise between Ebenezer Howard and Le Corbusier, representatives of the Anglo–American and Continental traditions respectively. As far as Soviet elites are concerned, the combination of ownership of (or access to) a *dacha* on the city periphery or well outside the city boundaries, together with a flat in the centre, has generally been more attractive than the compromise of accommodation in the suburb or in a small town. Essentially, this is because those who live in the suburbs or small town will find themselves at some distance from the cultural centres with their wider range of amenities.

The tendencies referred to here, reflecting preferences and proclivities not just of elites but also large numbers of white and blue collar workers, are closely bound up with much broader aspects of urban development. Earlier chapters on housing tenures speculated on whether particular types of tenure (for instance, private and cooperative) might be associated with specific groups. This hypothesis, linked with suggestions put forward above that certain forces operating in Soviet cities are bringing about spatial patterns of social segregation, can be extended to a consideration of other key issues of urban policy: the formation of agglomerations, encouragement of small town growth and commuting. These issues form the substance of Part III.

Part III

Housing and Urban Growth

Introduction

The question of where housing should be erected, broached at the end of Chapter 8 in terms of whether residential areas should be sited on vacant or developed land, extends to the very kernel of Soviet urban policy, itself inseparable from the government's industrial location strategy. What constitutes an optimum sized town? The debate between the 'urbanists' and 'deurbanists' during the 1930s helped to highlight one of the fundamental ideological premises of urban policy – that not only must the size of cities be contained but, under socialism, the restriction of population growth in cities need not remain a utopian dream. The natural concomitant of such a policy has been the encouragement of the growth of small and medium sized towns. The next chapter examines the reality of urban development against this dual objective of restricting the growth of large cities and promoting small ones.

The issues discussed in Part I, on housing tenure, and in Part II, on the physical form and social content of housing policy, lead to questions on the relationship of housing to the much broader urban environment. Central to this section is the problematic of the degree to which the housing and urban policy aims of the Soviet state, expressing as they do ideological commitments, are compatible with objective economic constraints and reconcilable with the aspirations of the general population.

9 The Policy and Practice of Soviet Urbanisation

THE OPTIMUM SIZED CITY

In the 1930s the recommended optimum size for a city was 50 000 to 100 000 inhabitants. Writing in 1960, V. G. Davidovich concluded that the desirable size of towns varied from 50 000 to 200 000, but that it was admissible to plan for towns with populations ranging from 10 000 to 400 000 people. However, even the 'maximum' theoretical value for city size was not immutable and he regarded the figure of 400 000 as only a tentative maximum from which deviations were possible.[1] In a four-volume publication on *The Principles of Soviet Town Planning* prepared by the country's leading planners in the latter part of the 1960s, the optimum was defined as 'that size of town which, under given natural and economic circumstances, furnishes the best conditions for organising production and living with minimum outlays on construction and the running and maintenance of buildings, installations, public amenities and the environment'.[2] The authors concluded that in the main the optimum size fell between 20 000 and 300 000.[3] Furthermore, for any type of industrial complex, upper and lower population limits could be determined.[4] Evidence from the USA, France and Italy also shows that the cost of providing a new social infrastructure rises substantially in urban centres with populations of over 200 000. In capitalist societies the social costs are paralleled by the greater private costs borne by individuals in the form of higher accommodation charges, transport costs and local taxation levels.[5] However, in the controversy in Western academic circles on city size, some believe that it is impossible to demonstrate that large cities create net social costs. According to Richardson, many social costs found in large cities are more than offset by considerable, but difficult to measure, social benefits.[6]

Time–cost factors have figured in the debates on the optimum size

225

of cities and settlement networks, with leading Soviet authorities alleging that no individual should spend more than half an hour travelling to work, and that therefore the maximum size of a city should not exceed 250 000 people.[7] Survey findings do not, however, suggest that the very largest cities suffer any real disadvantage in this regard. For instance, in 1968 an investigation into the average time spent travelling to work in five of the country's largest cities found that the average journey times (including walking to the stop, waiting, travelling and then walking at the other end) was 34 minutes in Alma Ata (975 000), 31 minutes in Tashkent (1 858 000), 25 minutes in Karaganda (583 000) and 21 minutes in both Tbilisi (1 095 000) and Novokuznetsk (551 000). Much more time was lost during the peak travelling period; however, this is purportedly less a function of the size of the city than a consequence of the way in which the city's physical layout has evolved over time, of the low calibre of urban planners (who have failed to design city layouts or communications networks in such a fashion as to reduce travelling time), and of an inadequate transportation system (shortage of rolling stock, poor administration of the system).[8] In 1978 on average only 77 per cent of the country's trams and 74 per cent of buses and trolleybuses were actually in operation at one time.[9]

Yet even this exercise in establishing a relationship between city size and time spent travelling appears to have lost some of its significance now that the subject under study is not the isolated city but the system of settlements. Just as at an earlier date planners set themselves the task of defining the optimum size of a *city*, now the objective is to determine the optimum structure of a *system of settlements*.[10] Journey-to-work time none the less remains one of the main variables in defining the optimum system size. According to the normative guidelines (SNiP) operative until 1976, further industrial expansion was prohibited where it would have the effect of raising a city's population to over 300 000.[11] The updated Building Norms and Rules (1976) dropped the reference to a specific size limit and instead stipulated that further construction of industrial plant was to be restricted in 'large' and 'the largest' cities (that is, in cities with populations over 250 000) – in the majority of which all construction, beyond that directly servicing the city's population and providing housing and civic amenities, is expressly forbidden by government decrees.[12]

Some influential writers have criticised the whole idea of optimum city size, seeing no special advantages accruing to towns that have reached a 'magic optimum'.[13] Others even argue that there are no good reasons for preventing cities which have reached their theoretical or approved maximum from expanding further.[14] In reality, there are in some instances technological imperatives which require that the optimum far exceeds the planned limits specified in the Norms. In 1959 the city of Stavropol' had a population of 72 000. The decision to make it the site of the new Fiat plant (renaming the city Tol'yatti) led to the city's population rising to 251 000 in 1970 and to 523 000 by the beginning of 1981, with the anticipation that it will eventually stabilise at about 600 000.

But the issue is not whether this or that city should be contained within a 'magic optimum' but rather that the defining of an 'official' optimum (or maximum) represents a protest against the unrestricted growth of large cities. It is simultaneously a protest against those Soviet writers who tentatively question the general policy of restricting growth,[15] against theories predicting the ultimate formation of an 'ecumenopolis'[16] and lastly, against the growth of large cities actually taking place in the Soviet Union and other countries – such as, for example, the 800 mile 'megalopolis' stretching from Boston through New York to Washington. Of these debates one departmental head at Gosplan remarked: 'Neither in theory nor practice does any other question evoke such sharp disputes, such diametrically opposed opinions, as that on the fate of large cities. Yet the majority of Soviet specialists consider that in a planned economy it is both possible and essential to bring about a rational limitation on the growth of the largest cities'.[17] Although little is heard today of the 'optimum' as such, the principle of restricting the growth of large cities and encouraging the development of smaller ones has not disappeared, but is expressed in another form, namely, the policy to direct investment into small and medium sized towns.

In the Soviet Union, in order to plan the development of a town, the population is divided into three groups: (1) town-forming (*gradoobrazuyushchii*); (2) servicing (*obsluzhivayushchii*); (3) dependent (*nesamodeyatel'nyi*). The most important town-forming factor is manufacturing, to which are added seven other employment sectors whose catchment area extends beyond the city boundary – construction, transport, scientific research institutions, higher education establishments, the health system, the largest art and cultural institutes and administrative and political organisations. The city-servicing group comprises those working in spheres such as education, health, social security, catering, retail, administration, communications, finance and

municipal affairs which only affect the local population. The size of the
servicing population is determined on the basis of the existing and
planned level of provision of different types of services given in detail
in the Building Norms and Rules; the requirements of different age
groups for each category of services; and the size of the town and its
role within a system of settlements. The norms also provide a formula
for calculating a city's present and future size.

   In a society purporting to be socialist, it would be natural to expect to
find a system of planning – sufficient to meet the social, cultural and
material needs of the differing groups of people living in settlements of
varying size – based on a set of universally applicable norms, with due
allowance for divergences from the norm depending on the town's
special demographic characteristics. On the face of it, not only does the
delineation of a set of universally applicable norms underscore the
egalitarian nature of the government's social policy – thereby ensuring
for everyone equal access to what the government defines as basic
human material and social requirements – but it carries important cost
advantages. It permits accurate manpower planning in the service
sector and also enables economists to work out cost yardsticks for
erecting specialist buildings (shops, schools etc.) using standard building designs. From the point of view of social and economic planning,
concerned both with ensuring equal access by all to the same standard
of public facilities and with economic efficiency (which in a socialist
society should be to the benefit of all), there is much to recommend the
nation-wide use of these building norms.

   For many Soviet citizens, however, it is not these advantages or
disadvantages (such as architectural uniformity) which are the subjects
of discussion or contemplation, but the continuing widespread shortage of facilities. The abandonment of the concept of the optimum, the
difficulties encountered in containing city growth, and the failure to
adhere to the norms on infrastructure provision may be explained by
the operation of the same set of factors. The phasing out of the term
'the optimum city size' from the planners' vocabulary has to be seen in
the light of the continuing growth of very large cities and the gradual,
often reluctant, acceptance of the agglomeration as a fact of life.

LEGISLATIVE ATTEMPTS TO CONTROL LARGE CITY GROWTH

The first major governmental statement on restricting the growth of
large cities came in 1931 with the passing of a resolution by the Central

Committee of the CPSU to the effect that all building in Moscow and Leningrad was to cease after 1932.[18]

> Considering that further development of industrial building in the country should proceed in accordance with the idea of creating new industrial centres in agricultural regions, bringing closer the final elimination of differences between town and country, the Plenary Session of the Central Committee regards the further development of a large number of enterprises in existing large urban areas to be inexpedient and does not propose to build new industrial enterprises in these cities. All building in Moscow and Leningrad will stop as from 1932.

In March 1939 the ban on further industrial expansion was extended to Kiev, Khar'kov Rostov-on-Don, Gor'ky and Sverdlovsk.[19] Between these two dates, the government issued in 1933 a decree requiring that the creation of new towns and settlements and the redevelopment of existing ones had to be in accordance with a general layout plan, and in 1935 created the post of Chief City Architect, with responsibility for the compilation and implementation of these plans.[20] The role of this functionary was reaffirmed and expanded in 1940[21] and again in 1969.[22]

Such policies and some of the blueprints submitted during the 1930s indicated how the government and its advisers thought that cities should develop. But the country could neither wait for architects to be trained nor for chief city architects to draw up plans and supervise their strict observance. So, for instance, Gor'ky (a city with a population of 217 000 in 1926 and 644 000 in 1939) was without a development plan during the early five-year plan periods when 'manufacturing enterprises were located without any clearly thought out system of zoning and any comprehensive co-ordinated approach to transportation and amenity provision. As a rule, settlements consisting of flimsily constructed, barrack structures were errected in order to meet the urgent demand for accommodation. The construction of individual (detached) houses was encouraged and, as a result, many of the buildings had a temporary character'.[23] The XVI All-Russian Congress of Soviets held in January 1935 considered that many local soviets 'provided weak leadership in the various branches of the economy' and that they were responsible for, among other things, unfulfilled plans for housing and public amenity building and the poor organisation and management of urban planning.[24] The allegation that 'many local soviets do not feel themselves to be masters of all branches of the urban economy' was indeed true. The reason for this sense of impotence was well-founded since they were not the *de facto* masters of the territory under their nominal control. Real power over the development of the urban economy had passed into the hands of enterprises, ministries and central departments, in so far as resources for housing and public amenities were being channelled through them or they were using a proportion of their own generated surplus (see Chapter 3).

By the outbreak of World War II, the basic components of Soviet spatial policy and its associated institutional conflicts had been established: (1) the growth of large cities should be restricted; (2) all settlements should develop according to a general development plan; (3) an administrative system had been created to ensure the fulfillment of (1) and (2); (4) local soviets – 'the primary organs of Soviet power' – were being blamed by the central government for not using their powers to control changes within their juridically defined areas; (5) the local soviets were in conflict with (and much weaker than) departments and ministries.

In 1956 a further 41 cities (as well as all towns in the Moscow oblast') were added to the list of places where it was forbidden to construct new or expand existing industrial enterprises (see Table 9.1). Another list of 23 cities in which further industrial development was to be restricted was compiled at the same time (see Table 9.2). Because scientific research and planning institutes, laboratories and higher education establishments are regarded as 'town-forming agencies', no more were to be set up in Moscow or in Moscow oblast' after 1963, when the government reaffirmed the ban on industrial building in Ryazan', Tula and Kalinin.[25] By 1970 these lists were widely thought to be in need of revision and it was suggested[26] that a further 12 cities be added to those listed in Table 9.2: seven of them – Omsk, Krasnodar, Dneprodzerzhinsk, Makeevka, Alma-Ata, Vilnius and Frunze – had earlier been selected as centres of 'limited' expansion; the remaining five are shown in Table 9.3.

In spite of the government's declared policy of limiting the growth of the largest cities and encouraging the location of industry in small and medium-sized towns, according to one senior academic, 'the most salient feature of urbanisation at present remains the growth of cities with populations of over 100 000'.[27] Another author similarly noted that the large and very largest cities are continuing to grow – general development plans notwithstanding. Data produced by the Ukrainian Urban Planning Institute (*Giprograd*) shows that new enterprises and institutions are being located not in the small and medium sized towns, but in Kiev, Khar'kov and Dnepropetrovsk; between 1966 and 1970, for instance, the 460 new and reconstructed plants in the Ukraine's largest cities absorbed 347 000 more employees.[28] Table 9.4 illustrates only too vividly the growth in size and number of cities at the top of the population league; in 1982, 22 cities in the Soviet Union had over one million inhabitants, giving a total of 38.6 million – equivalent to 22.9 per cent of the total urban population. With another 27 cities having populations ranging between 500 000 and one million (10.0 per cent of the urban population),[29] the consensus among leading Soviet geographers and demographers is that by the year 2000 the number of 'millionaire' cities will have increased to thirty.[30]

The rate of population growth in small towns (those with up to 50 000 inhabitants) and medium-sized towns (50 000–100 000 people) during the intercensal period, 1959–1970, was 17.5 per cent and 18.8 per cent respectively. Measured in terms of population growth, the fortunes of small towns fell dramatically between 1970 and 1975, when they increased their total population by a mere 5 per cent, while towns in the medium-size category succeeded in maintaining an 18.5 per cent rise in their population. On the other hand, the considerably greater rate of growth in the largest cities helped them to increase their share of the total urban population (see Table 9.5), so that by 1981, 101.8 million people (60.3 per cent of the urban population) lived in cities with over 100 000 inhabitants, compared with 75.5 million (55.5 per cent) in 1970.

While the growth of large cities may well be linked to socio-economic imperatives corresponding to a particular stage of development, none the less this process of urban development is apparently 'taking place in the face of inadequately effective measures for limiting the growth of large and very large cities and in the absence of a purposeful elaboration of the problems involved in the development of an industrial, socio-cultural and transport infrastructure within an evolving system of settlements'.[31] For instance, between 1962 and 1972 the population of Alma-Ata increased annually by about 24 000 people, with immigration accounting for 72 per cent of the increase. This growth was a result, on the one hand, of the 'irrational' location in the city of industrial enterprises, scientific research institutes and other town-forming contingents and, on the other, the absence of economic and town planning measures to regulate and contain the growth.[32] As is discussed below, there is, however, nothing 'irrational' in the location decisions of enterprise managements.

TABLE 9.1 *Population growth in 47 cities in which further industrial expansion was prohibited after 1956*

City	Population (in thousands)				Annual average percentage change			
	1939	1959	1970	1976	1939–1959	1959–70	1970–76	1939–76
Moscow	4542	6044	7077	7734	1.44	1.44	1.49	1.45
Leningrad	3401	3340	3987	4372	−0.09	1.62	1.55	0.68
Kiev	851	1110	1632	2013	1.34	3.57	3.56	2.35
Gor'ky	644	941	1170	1305	1.91	2.00	1.84	1.93
Baku	733	968	1266	1406	1.40	2.47	1.76	1.78
Tashkent	556	927	1385	1643	2.59	3.72	2.87	2.97
Khar'kov	840	953	1223	1385	0.63	2.29	2.09	1.36
Novosibirsk	404	885	1161	1286	4.00	2.50	1.72	3.18
Kuibyshev	390	806	1045	1186	3.70	2.39	2.13	3.05
Sverdlovsk	423	779	1025	1171	3.10	3.53	2.24	2.79
Chelyabinsk	273	689	875	989	4.74	2.20	2.06	3.54
Kazan'	406	667	869	958	2.51	2.43	1.64	2.35
Perm'	306	629	850	957	3.67	2.78	2.00	3.13
Rostov-na-Don	510	600	789	907	0.82	2.52	2.35	1.57
Volgograd	445	591	817	918	1.43	3.00	1.94	1.98
Saratov	372	579	757	847	2.24	2.47	1.89	2.25
Ufa	258	547	771	923	3.83	3.17	3.04	3.51
Voronezh	344	447	660	764	1.32	3.61	2.47	2.18
Donetsk	474	708	879	967	1.98	1.99	1.60	1.95
Dnepropetrovsk	528	661	862	976	1.13	2.44	2.09	1.67
Odessa	599	664	892	1023	0.52	2.72	2.31	1.46
Zaporozh'e	289	449	658	760	2.23	3.54	2.43	1.43
Minsk	237	509	917	1189	3.90	5.50	4.42	4.46
Sumgait	6	51	124	168	11.18	8.41	5.19	9.42

City	Population (in thousands)				Annual average percentage change			
	1939	1959	1970	1976	1939–1959	1959–70	1970–76	1939–76
Riga	348	580	732	806	2.59	2.14	1.52	2.30
Yerevan	204	493	767	928	4.51	4.10	3.23	4.18
Yaroslavl'	309	407	517	577	1.39	2.20	1.83	1.70
Tula	285	351	462	506	1.05	2.53	1.53	1.56
L'vov	340	411	553	629	0.95	2.73	2.17	1.68
Irkutsk	250	366	451	519	1.92	1.92	2.57	1.99
Khabarovsk	207	323	436	513	2.25	2.76	2.75	2.48
Ivanova	285	335	420	438	0.81	2.08	1.45	1.29
Vladivostok	206	291	441	526	1.74	3.85	2.98	2.57
Penza	160	255	374	436	2.36	3.54	2.59	2.75
Kalinin	216	261	345	395	0.95	2.57	2.28	1.64
Grozny	172	250	341	381	1.89	2.86	1.87	2.17
Arkhangel'sk	251	258	343	383	0.14	2.62	1.86	1.15
Ryazan	95	214	350	432	4.14	4.57	3.57	4.18
Murmansk	119	222	309	369	3.17	3.05	3.00	3.11
Nikolaev	184	251	362	436	1.56	3.39	3.15	2.36
Voroshilovgrad	215	275	383	439	1.24	3.06	2.30	1.95
Tallinn	160	280	363	408	2.84	2.39	1.97	2.56
Taganrog	189	202	254	282	0.33	2.10	1.76	1.09
Kramatorsk	94	115	150	167	1.01	2.44	1.81	1.57
Komsomol'sk-na-Amur	71	177	218	246	4.67	1.91	2.03	3.42
Sevastopol'	114	148	239	290	1.31	4.45	3.28	2.56
Magnitogorsk	146	311	364	393	3.85	1.44	1.29	2.71

SOURCES   B. S. Khorev, *Problemy gorodov*, Moscow, 1975, p. 86; *Narodnoe khozyaistvo SSSR v 1975g.*, Moscow, 1976, pp. 22–31.

TABLE 9.2   *Population growth in 23 cities in which further industrial development was to be restricted after 1956*

City	Population (in thousands)				Average annual percentage change			
	1939	1959	1970	1976	1939–59	1959–70	1970–76	1939–76
Omsk	289	581	821	1002	3.55	3.19	3.38	3.42
Krasnoyarsk	190	412	648	758	3.95	4.20	2.65	3.81
Alma-Ata	222	456	730	851	3.66	4.37	2.59	3.70
Novokuznetsk	166	382	499	530	4.26	2.46	1.01	3.19
Krivoi Rog	192	401	573	634	3.75	3.30	1.70	3.28
Karaganda	154	383	523	570	4.66	2.87	1.44	3.60
Nizhnii Tagil	160	338	378	396	3.81	1.02	0.78	2.48
Krasnodar	193	313	464	543	2.45	3.64	2.66	2.84
Baranaul	148	303	439	574	3.65	3.43	2.66	3.42
Izhevsk	176	285	422	522	2.44	3.63	3.61	2.98
Kemerovo	137	289	385	446	3.80	2.64	2.48	3.24
Astrakhan'	259	305	410	458	0.82	2.73	1.86	1.55
Kirov	144	252	333	376	2.84	2.57	2.04	2.63
Tomsk	145	249	338	413	2.74	2.82	3.40	2.87
Makeeva	270	407	429	437	2.07	0.48	0.31	1.31
Zhdanov	222	284	417	467	1.24	3.55	1.16	2.03
Vilno	215	236	372	447	0.47	4.22	3.11	2.00
Kaunas	152	219	305	352	1.84	3.06	2.42	2.30
Frunze	93	220	431	498	4.40	6.30	2.44	4.64
Dushanbe	83	227	374	448	5.16	4.64	3.05	4.66
Dneprodzerzhinsk	148	194	227	248	1.36	1.44	1.49	1.40
Saransk	41	91	191	241	4.07	6.97	3.95	4.90
Angarsk	—	135	203	231	0	3.75	2.18	0

SOURCES B. S. Khorev. *Problemy gorodov*, Moscow, 1975, p. 86; *Narodnoe khozyaistvo SSSR v 1975g.*, Moscow, 1976, pp. 21–31.

That the government had not intended these cities to expand at this rate is evident both from statements by officials and population forecasts. The head of the house-building department of Stroibank noted that the general development plan for Leningrad, drawn up in 1962 and approved by the Council of Ministers in 1966, had forecast that the city's population would reach 3.2 million by 1980. In fact, in 1970 it was already approaching 4 million. Similarly in Kiev, the projected figure of 1.5 million to be reached some time after 1980 had, by 1970, been exceeded by 100 000[33], reaching 2.2 million in 1981. The discrepancies between the planned populations of 20 large cities and the actual populations in 1966 (and the continuing growth since then) shown in Table 9.6 are certain to have had a deleterious effect on infrastructural provision. Continued capital investment in large cities, necessitating an expansion in the labour force, has meant that despite a huge annual house-building programme in the Ukraine's six largest cities, the average amount of living space in the mid-1970s remained at 8.0–8.5 square metres per person.[34] The shortage of housing, retail outlets, public eating places and other social amenities could only have been partially alleviated by channelling additional resources through those ministries and departments building new or expanding existing plant in these towns.[35] This was not only because the funds would be insufficient to match demand, but also because of the reluctance of enterprises to part with these funds.

TABLE 9.3 *Cities in which it was suggested further industrial construction should be prohibited*

City	Population (000s)			Population increase (%)	
	1959	1970	1976	1959–70	1970–76
Dushanbe	227	374	448	65	20
Lipetsk	157	289	363	84	26
Ashkhabad	170	253	297	49	17
Volzhsky	67	142	195	112	37
Engels	91	130	159	43	18

SOURCE *Narodnoe khozyaistvo SSSR v 1975g.*, Moscow, 1976, pp. 22–31.

It is this which has led commentators to urge that enterprises granted permission to build in these cities should be strictly supervised to ensure that they pay their full share of the costs of providing housing and social amenities. Since on average, 'town-forming agents' in the 15 largest Ukrainian cities exceeded the planned limits by 12 per cent in the period 1970–1975, there is indeed a 'need for further improvements in spatial planning methods, a strengthening of the role both of local organs responsible for construction and architecture and of planning committees in resolving disputes over the location of new or the reconstruction of individual enterprises, educational, scientific and planning institutes. It is the growth of these which leads to increases in the workforce and thereby the total population of large cities'.[36] Notwithstanding statements such as this, populations in the largest cities will almost certainly continue to grow in the forseeable future.

236

TABLE 9.4   *Cities with populations exceeding one million*

				Population (in thousands)			
	1897 (9/11)	1917 (or nearest year)	1926 (17/12)	1939 (17/1)	1959 (15/1)	1970 (15/1)	1982 (1/1)
Moscow	1039	1854	2026 (2080)	4537 (4542)	6009 (6044)	6942 (7077)	8111(8302)
Leningrad	1265	(2500)	1614 (1739)	3119 (3401)	3003 (3340)	3550 (3987)	4202(4722)
Kiev	248	468	514	851	1110	1632	2297
Tashkent	156	257	314 (324)	556	927	1385	1902
Baku	112	(248)	(453)	544 (773)	643 (968)	852 (1266)	1066(1616)
Khar'kov	174	313	417	840	953	1223	1503
Gor'ky	90	127	185 (222)	644	941	1170	1373
Novosibirsk	12	70	120	404	885	1161	1357
Kuibyskev	91	249	176	390	806	1045	1243
Sverdlovsk	43	70	140	423	779	1025	1252
Minsk	91	(153)	(132)	237 (237)	509 (509)	907 (917)	1370
Tbilisi		231	294	519	703	889	1110
Odessa		466	418	599	664	892	1085
Omsk		80	162	289	581	821	1061

Population (in thousands)

	1897 (9/11)	1917 (or nearest year)	1926 (17/12)	1939 (17/1)	1959 (15/1)	1970 (15/1)	1982 (1/1)
Alma-Ata		35	44	222	456	730	1001
Dnepropetrovsk		217	237	528	661	862	1114
Donetsk		38	174	474	708	879	1047
Yerevan		34	65	204	493	767	1076
Kazan'		193	179	406	667	869	1023
Perm'		48	121	306	629	850	1028
Ufa		105	99	258	547	771	1023
Chelyabinsk		47	59	273	689	875	1066

The figures in parentheses refer to the population of the city including outlying settlements which fall within the central city's administrative boundaries. In the case of Moscow one of the settlements is Zelinograd, a satellite town created to take Moscow's overspill, with a population in 1976 of 121 000 (29.4% of the 'peripheral' population). Seven of Leningrad's satellites have an historical attachment: Kronstadt is a sea fortress. Petrodvorets, Pushkin and Pavlovsk have famous parks and palace-museums, Selenogorsk is a *dacha*-resort centre and Koplino and Sestroretsk are industrial suburbs. Taken together, Leningrad's 'subordinate' settlements have a population of 461 000.

SOURCES 1897: B.Ts Urlanis (ed.), *Narodo-naselenie mira*, Moscow, 1974, p. 431; 1917, 1926, 1939, 1959, 1970: *Narodnoe khozyaistvo SSSR 1922–72* Moscow, 1972, p. 19; 1981: *Narodnoe khozyaistvo SSSR 1922–82*, Moscow, 1982, pp. 21–6.

Writing in 1980, the country's leading urban development specialists could only reiterate that the continuing growth of large cities at rates far exceeding forecasts, with its attendant consequence of a labour shortage which in turn leads to further immigration, remains a major unresolved problem.[37]

TABLE 9.5   *Urban population by city size*

	Year							
	(million)				*1939 = 100*			
City Population	*1939*	*1959*	*1970*	*1975*	*1939*	*1959*	*1970*	*1975*
under 3000	0.9	1.6	2.1	2.0	100	177.8	233.3	222.2
3 000–5000	2.1	3.6	4.1	4.1	100	171.4	195.2	195.2
5000–10 000	5.3	9.2	10.1	10.7	100	173.6	190.6	201.9
10 000–20 000	6.9	11.2	12.7	13.7	100	162.3	184.1	198.6
20 000–50 000	9.7	14.8	18.5	19.5	100	152.6	190.7	201.0
50 000–100 000	7.0	11.0	13.0	15.4	100	157.1	185.7	220.0
100 000–500 000	15.7	24.4	38.2	43.1	100	155.4	243.3	274.5
over 500 000	12.8	24.2	37.3	44.6	100	189.1	291.4	348.4
Total urban population	60.4	100.0	136.0	153.1	100	165.6	225.2	253.5

SOURCE   *Narodnoe khozyaistvo SSSR v 1974g.*, p. 32.

Note: The annual statistical handbook no longer provides a table showing the number of cities in each size category. The figures cited in the text for 1981 are derived from data on cities with populations of over 50 000 in *Narodnoe khozyaistvo SSSR v 1980g.*, pp. 18–23.

THE CASE FOR SMALL AND MEDIUM SIZED TOWNS

The case for small and medium sized towns is to a significant extent based on their representing the antithesis of certain universally condemned features of the large city. Firstly, the problem of the growth of 'super cities' and the catastrophic violation of some natural cycles has come to be seen by many Soviet commentators as one of the primary problems of modern civilisation. The immense influence of the man-made environment on nature and the human race – on its biological and social processes – has been noted by many of the world's leading scientists.[38] Secondly, the distances between work and home means that people are spending an increasing amount of time travelling.

City	Actual population (thousands)			Population for 1966 as estimated in 1959	% difference between actual and projected	Annual percentage change		
	1959	1966	1976	1966		1959–66	1966–76	1959–76
* Perm'	629	785	957	680	+ 15.4	3.22	2.00	2.50
** Omsk	581	746	1002	630	+ 18.4	3.64	2.99	3.26
* Kuibyshev	806	969	1186	875	+ 10.7	2.67	2.04	2.30
** Krasnoyarsk	412	557	758	445	+ 25.2	4.40	3.13	3.65
* Gor'ky	941	1100	1305	1020	+ 7.8	2.26	1.72	1.94
* Penza	255	324	436	275	+ 17.8	3.48	3.01	3.21
* Murmansk	222	279	369	245	+ 13.9	3.32	2.84	3.03
** Izhevsk	285	360	522	310	+ 16.1	3.39	3.79	3.62
** Baranaul	303	395	574	350	+ 12.9	3.86	2.67	3.16
* Tula	351	371	506	375	– 1.1	0.79	3.15	2.17
** Ufa	547	683	923	600	+ 13.8	3.17	3.06	3.10
** Astrakhan	305	361	458	320	+ 12.8	2.44	2.41	2.42
* Kursk	205	249	363	220	+ 13.2	2.82	3.84	3.42
* Kalinin	261	311	395	285	+ 9.1	2.54	2.42	2.47
Orel	150	202	282	170	+ 18.8	4.34	3.39	3.78
Orenburg	267	316	435	280	+ 12.9	2.44	3.25	2.91
** Kirov	252	302	376	290	+ 4.1	2.62	2.22	2.38
** Kemerovo	279	358	446	300	+ 19.3	3.63	2.22	2.80
** Krasnodar	313	395	543	333	+ 18.6	3.38	3.23	3.29
** Tomsk	249	311	413	275	+ 13.1	3.23	2.88	3.02

* Further expansion prohibited after 1956.
** Further expansion prohibited after 1976.

SOURCES *Razmeshchenie zhilishchnogo stroitel'stva v gorodakh*, op. cit. p. 69; *Narodnoe khozyaistvo SSSR v 1965g.*, pp. 30–39; *Narodnoe khozyaistvo SSSR v 1975g.*, pp. 22–31.

Thirdly, distances between the periphery and the central shopping districts increase, as do distances between places of work and recreational facilities. Fourthly, these time–distance factors require vast outlays on improving the transportation system in terms of road widening, provision of more buses, trams and trolley-buses (and, in cities with over one million inhabitants, an underground railway system), and lead to increased transport running costs.[39]

The policy of restricting the growth of large cities, on the one hand, and encouraging industrial location and expansion in small towns on the other, has figured prominently in government speeches, resolutions and promulgations and in theoretical discussions over the past half century. The concept of the satellite city (*gorod-sputnik*) – introduced into the Soviet Union by Ernst May in the 1930s – was, in 1960, proclaimed as the 'radical socialist solution to the expansion of large cities'.[40] The satellite was principally intended to serve as overspill for the largest cities, with city-based industries and institutions being relocated there-in, so stabilising or even reducing the central city's population. The cornerstone of this policy was that the town-forming factors should be those which would lead to an 'unloading' of the city rather than the attraction into the suburban zone of new enterprises and organisations.[41] Satellite towns could have a population as low as 20 000 or, ideally, ranging between 80 000 and 100 000, using where possible the existing system of small towns and settlements within the suburban zone as their growth points. The new Building Norms and Rules (1976) have dropped the term 'satellite' and instead refer to 'new towns and settlements'.

So, to all intents and purposes, the notion of the 'gorod-sputnik' has been absorbed into the general discussion of expanding the role of small and medium sized towns, whose importance in the overall scheme of urban development has been mentioned at the last four Party Congresses. The XXIII Congress in 1966 emphasised the need, firstly, to study the processes involved in the formation of socialist settlement patterns and, secondly, to encourage the development of small and medium sized towns. The XXIV Congress (1971) referred to the need to pursue a 'steadfast course to contain the growth of large cities; to curtail, as a rule, the location in these cities of new industrial enterprises and to locate in small towns and workers' settlements specialist enterprises and subsidiaries of plants operating in the large cities'.[42] The wording of the relevant resolutions of the XXV and XXVI Congresses (1976 and 1981) remained in substance the same as that of the 1971 Congress.[43]

The policy to develop these small towns as local servicing and manufacturing centres recommends itself on a number of grounds. Firstly, it enables female labour to be drawn into social production. Secondly, it permits a more efficient use of the labour reserves which exist in many small towns,[44] including the provision of seasonal work for those employed in agriculture. Thirdly, by expanding the range of goods and services, the small towns will help to reduce the differences between town and country and between the large city and small town[45] – differences which remain considerable, especially as far as housing is concerned.[46] Compared with the inhabitants of small towns, residents of a large city of, say, over a quarter of a million people (of which there were 114 in 1981 with a total population of 77 406 000) are far better off. The least favourable working conditions, standard of living, service provision and opportunities for improving one's education and qualifications are to be found in small towns and settlements.[47]

In one sense, over the last decade the government has been consistent in pursuing its objective of bolstering the growth of small and medium sized towns. At the end of the 1960s up to 70 per cent of all capital investment in new projects costing more than 2.5 million roubles was allocated for developments in these settlements.[48] A map showing the location of factories built during the ninth five-year plan (1971–75) would indeed reveal that the majority of them had been erected in small and medium sized towns. In the RSFSR alone, over 1000 enterprises had been set up outside the main cities. But these very high figures lose some of their significance when it is realised that a large proportion of capital investment is being directed towards the technical re-equipment and reconstruction of existing enterprises,[49] on the grounds that 'experience has shown that, as a rule, it is economically advantageous to secure an increase in production by the reconstruction and technical modernisation of enterprises'.[50] The proportion of industrial investment directed to the modernisation and expansion of existing plant rose steadily throughout the 1970s, from 62 per cent in 1971 to 72 per cent in 1980. Although in 1980 the figure was 80 per cent for the machine-building and metal-working industry, it had been constantly high during the 1960s, reaching 78 per cent in 1966. Light industry witnessed the sharpest increase in the proportion of investment flowing into re-tooling and renovation, rising from 40 per cent in 1970 to 75 per cent in 1980.[51] In the Tula oblast', capital investment spent on reconstruction, expansion and technological re-tooling of existing plant as a proportion of capital investment in manufacturing rose from 79 per cent in 1966 to 91 per cent in 1971.[52]

Moreover, an examination of a graph indicating capital investment reveals that the lion's share has continued to flow into the republican and oblast' centres. In the three years 1971–73 alone, the three main construction ministries (*Ministroi, Minpromstroi, Mintyazhstroi* USSR) allocated over 50 per cent of their capital investment budget to projects in large cities in the RSFSR and only 16.6 per cent to small and medium sized towns. In other words the money was mainly spent not on new factories but on expansion and reconstruction.[53] A very similar situation holds with respect to the social infrastructure, with most of the budgetary allocation for some 'welfare services' being confined to maintenance and upkeep. In 1975, 93 per cent of resources assigned to education went on maintaining kindergartens, secondary schools, VUZy and vocational institutes, and 95 per cent of resources for health and physical culture were also devoted to the upkeep of existing buildings and facilities.[54]

It is not only chairmen of small town city soviets and other fairly low ranking officials who point to the neglect of their towns. The chairman of Gosplan of the Mordovian ASSR[55] spoke of the industrial development of the western parts of the republic as being 'severely hampered by the clear unwillingness of ministries and departments to build enterprises in small towns. This is the problem of problems'. He quoted the example of discussions with the Ministry of Light Industry about building a porcelain factory in Mordovia which had been going on over the past few years. A number of towns had been suggested as possible sites where there were manpower surpluses and water and electricity supplies, 'but, unfortunately, the ministry still has not made up its mind'. Furthermore of the 66 industrial projects agreed upon with Gosplan RSFSR to be situated in Mordovia in the period 1955–75, only ten had been completed by 1971[56]

The picture that emerges in one in which reconstruction in some cases exceeds severalfold the production capacity of the existing plant: the costs of rebuilding and re-equipping can be greater than building a new factory. Under the guise of reconstruction, what really takes place sometimes is no less than the erection of a new enterprise.[57] Indeed, some Soviet specialists accept that 'despite the decision to stop building new manufacturing enterprises in large cities, construction continues in the form of opening branches, general reconstruction, stock renewal etc'.[58]

This circumvention of the intention of industrial location policy may be compared with a similar phenomenon in British town planning. The Distribution of Industry Act passed in 1945 provided for comprehensive government controls over the distribution of industry. Any new industrial plant or any factory extension over a certain size had to obtain an industrial development certificate (IDC) from the Board of trade. However, any firm that was frustrated in its attempt to get an IDC in London or the Midlands could easily do one of two things. Either it could extend its existing plant by under 10 per cent a year (or 5 per cent, depending on the regulations at the time) thus increasing by 50 or 100 per cent in a decade. It could supplement this by moving out warehouse or office space into separate buildings, which did not need a certificate, and taking the space for factory production. Or it could simply buy a 'second-hand' vacated factory in the open market. One of the least mentioned negative aspects of this particular development in the Soviet Union is its creation of more jobs. A statistical analysis carried out in 1976 showed that the growth in the number of work-places was continuing to outstrip the overall increase in the labour force during the tenth five-year plan. 'In spite of instructions issued by the XXV Party Congress that existing production facilities should be developed without increasing the size of the workforce, technical re-equipping does create more jobs.'[59] And this, of course, as will be seen later, contributes to the further growth of existing large cities.

Some authors allege that a crucial factor in determining the functions and fate of small towns is the availability of transport.[60] Ensuring the provision of transportation links is, however, no guarantee that industry will be attracted to small towns. In the 1950s arterial roads were built joining the small Mordovian town of Krasnoslobodsk to the main Moscow–Kuibyshev highway and to other districts. These towns, including Krasnoslobsk and its surrounding area, were very under-developed with 'substantial labour reserves'. Moreover, they already possessed a manufacturing base, although the plants themselves were quite small. Despite these advantages, industry was by-passing this and other towns in the republic. The local residents who had written to press their case urged that 'from the point of view of efficiency, it is worth expanding and modernising these enterprises rather than building new ones in large cities'. The importance of this remark is its implied suggestion that ministries and enterprises are unwilling to incur the costs of setting up new branches in small towns because 'the location of enterprises in large industrial centres means that the time required to introduce new technology is less, workers can be trained more quickly and labour productivity is raised more quickly'. Further-more, ministries would appear to be content to see existing plants become obsolete and even, perhaps, watch their operations wound up in the long term. Krasnoslobsk is possibly one of the small towns to be passed by and destined never to be developed. It has been estimated that only one in ten (that is, about 500 small and medium sized towns has any potential for industrial development).[61] And yet, in the decade 1959–69 there was a 'substantial and unwarranted increase in the size of those small towns and urban-type settlements possessing limited scope for improving the standard and range of shops and other amenities they could supply'.[62] These are towns which, in Khorev's terms, lacking 'a clearly defined functional dominance', suffer population decline and demographic imbalance with high death rates, low birth rates and the highest proportion of the population of working age (predominantly women) not engaged in social production.[63]

These criticisms of unjustifiable expansion in 'towns without a future' do not however imply a refutation of the general policy of locating more enterprises in other small towns: for although many small towns have little potential, there are numerous others which, while possessing scarcely any industry at all, meet all the necessary preconditions for locating new manufacturing plants in them – an able-bodied work force not currently employed in useful, productive work, good building land, adequate water and energy resources and a favourable situation with regard to transport routes.[64]

Another serious problem associated with setting up a factory in a small town is the absence of a satisfactory construction industry for building factories and housing and providing the infrastructure. According to one estimate, over 70 per cent of these towns do not have a building industry capable of erecting industrial enterprises. As a result, when one of them is selected as a factory location, construction takes an inordinately long time and costs soar; for instance, an excavator manufacturing plant in Galicha (19 000 in 1967; 21 000 in 1974) was still under construction in 1974, having been started in 1962. The situation is not improved by the fact that the plans drawn up for these towns are completely unrealistic. Many of the plans inspected by the Leningrad Town Planning Institute (*Lengiprogor*) envisaged the demolition and replacement of low-rise detached homes, and yet the local construction industries were quite unable to undertake the tasks which the plans stipulated. The response to *Lengiprogor*'s findings was to reiterate what is, as has already been described, an important feature of current town planning theory, namely that: 'Reconstruction must approach the task flexibly, seeking to improve living conditions not solely by demolishing the existing housing stock but by maximalising its utilisation'.[65] Two reasons why plans sometimes appear so over-ambitious are that planners are too remote from the localities for which they are designing and that local officials have what might be called a 'Chamber of Commerce' mentality – that is to say, they tend to hold that a pleasant environment will be a means of attracting industry. However, neither the local officials nor planners should be blamed out of hand for devising ambitious projects for these small places. Nevertheless, given the system of allocating resources for town development, which favours those that already have better services and amenities, the wisdom and realism of the goals set by local officials and planners is surely open to question.

Soviet planners, politicians and academics often stress that 'much depends on local initiative' in developing small towns: responsibility for initiating proposals for hotel construction, for example, should not necessarily come from central government ministries or departments (Gosplan, Ministry of Finance etc.) but from the local level. Local government officials, like enterprise managers and building contractors, should operate on a self-financing basis and draw upon credit facilities to finance projects; they should also involve themselves more in the activities of enterprises newly arrived or expanding in their area. In fact, the director of a hydraulic factory in Odessa actually spoke of the need for local officials and enterprise managements to work hand-in-glove with one another.[66] Ideally no doubt, managers would like to exist in the same symbiotic relationship with the local soviet as can be found in some North American and West European small towns, such as one where 'the glass works and the town are in real partnership and are equally appreciative of each other. Whatever is done in the community they do together. From the beginning it has been company policy to encourage local independence and citizen initiative by giving in such a way that the gifts help the town to do its own growing'.[67] But in practice misunderstanding or lack of information often lead to a communication breakdown between the two groups. In the case of the Odessa factory, the director censured the local officials for occasionally demonstrating an unwarranted indifference to the construction of branch factories in their town and for being unwilling to meet newcomers. He explained their attitude as arising from an 'incorrect image of the social effects of industrialisation', which made them fear that industry would lure away skilled mechanics from the collective and state farms which constituted their primary responsibility.[68]

It is probably not uncommon for local officials to be indifferent and at best lukewarm to the import of manufacturing undertakings into their areas and sphere of influence. Indeed, the concern of officials in agricultural areas to which the factory director was referring is a very real one: in 1978 the average monthly wage of engineering and technical staff in agriculture was only 185.8 roubles compared with 208.4 roubles for their industrial counterparts, while workers earned 141.9 and 176.1 roubles in the agricultural and industrial sectors respectively.[69]

For the local authorities this is a serious matter, since in their view the drift from the land is now proceeding too rapidly – the increase in the mechanisation of agriculture is not fast enough to match the loss in manpower.[70] Of course, labour surpluses do exist in some agricultural regions. In general though, 'when the migration of labour from agricultural areas reaches a high level, there is a reduction in the rate of growth of agricultural output as a result of sowing taking place at the wrong time, protracted harvesting periods and underutilisation of agricultural equipment. An obvious additional consequence of these considerable outflows is the need to enlist city labour in agricultural work'.[71] Such has been the scale of migration from villages in some areas, that some Party officials have emphasised the need to prevent young people living in rural areas from leaving their villages for jobs in the cities. Teachers proffering advice should encourage school-leavers to take up agricultural occupations. And because some parents positively favour their children departing from the countryside, Party organisations and schools should 'exercise an influence on parents to change this attitude'.[72] The expression of these attitudes and interpretations and the very real wage differentials are further indications that the interchange between town and country, the contradictions between industry and agriculture consequent upon not only climatic vagaries and investment priorities, but also the careers and ambitions of local officials and managers, constitute important determinants of urban development.

Since the most rapidly developing manufacturing sectors are electronics, telecommunications and instrument making, it is in these fields that the advantages of locating in smaller towns are most evident, for they consume comparatively small amounts of energy, fuel and water, have a low freight-turnover and provide work for women. The major single setback is alleged by ministries and factory managements to be the provincial shortage of qualified workers. Although undoubtedly an important factor in some cases, its significance may well be exaggerated because much of the work carried out in certain fields of advanced technology tends to be of a routine and repetitive character; the level of training required to cope with the assemblage of parts on, for instance, a transistor radio assembly line is not very high. Moreover, there is no pool of skilled labour as such in large cities; in fact, in general, demand exceeds supply and any single enterprise is faced with a shortage of skilled workers which can only be overcome in the short run by 'pilfering' workers from other organisations.

Over a period of time, of course, the factory can train its own work-force in the local specialist educational establishments or recruit fresh graduates. Indeed, one advantage of the Soviet planned economy is that the enterprise or ministry can pass on its estimated future labour needs to a department which not only holds information on the annual 'output' of new graduates from specialist schools and institutes, but also has the right to direct them to specific plants and locations. In these circumstances, where enterprises manufacturing electronic equipment can use unskilled labour available in small towns and apply for young specialists to be 'allocated' to the enterprise, the argument that new plants in this sector must be located where there are supplies of skilled labour lacks cogency.

In other words, even when a small town possesses all the necessary prerequisites for building up an industrial base, it has to overcome resistance on the one hand from local officials who, rightly or wrongly, consider their interests to lie elsewhere, or who are reluctant to take on additional responsibilities (see Chapter 3), and, on the other hand, from those non-local officials who regard their interests as certainly not lying in small towns.

Specialists clearly disagree on whether the growth of the country's largest cities should be restricted and, the growth of small towns encouraged. It is equally clear that the spirit of government promulgations favours containment of the large and expansion of the small. In keeping with this spirit, most new manufacturing plant is being situated in small towns. But, having met this requirement formally, enterprise management and state planning bodies can – because a high proportion of capital equipment and factory buildings is old and in need of reconstruction and its obsolete technology replaced – invest in the large cities.

ECONOMIC AND DEMOGRAPHIC FACTORS STIMULATING CITY GROWTH

In seeking explanations for the fact that large cities continue to exceed their planned sizes, some Soviet authors have questioned the rationale behind attempts[73] 'artificially' to restrict their growth and have asked –

what social laws determine the growth of cities? Why do some cities grow more rapidly despite attempts to contain their growth? Why do others grow slowly and some even decline? Is it possible to predict – and if so, how accurately – the future of a city or of all cities in general? The answer to the first two questions is normally couched in terms of the operation of a set of 'objective factors' conducive to the concentration of production in existing large industrial centres – a process which is 'economically justified from the point of view of the general national economic interest of the republic and the nation at large'.[74]

The objective factors most commonly referred to are:[75]

(1) economies in construction and operation arise from the location in 'territorial–productive complexes' of enterprises which are united by a common productive process;

(2) where large scale building projects are in progress, the construction organisations can themselves specialise and this reduces the time taken to complete the buildings and also improves the workmanship;

(3) the presence in the large city of communication networks and public amenities means that the overall capital investment costs are lower and the construction time shorter;

(4) the advantages accruing from the reconstruction and re-tooling of existing enterprises instead of building new ones are (again) lower capital costs and a reduction in the time taken to bring the new capacity into production.[76] According to the Soviet Prime Minister, Mr Tikhonov, funds allocated for capital investment in technical modernisation are, on average, recouped three times more quickly than if invested in developing similar productive capacities by constructing new plant.[77] In fact, the pace of technological change means that every seven to ten years the largest enterprises undergo re-tooling and plant renewal which is accompanied not only by a rise in manufacturing output but also by an increase in the size of the workforce and the industrial area;

(5) the continuing influx of labour, especially commuters, means that industry and the building and servicing sectors can satisfy their manpower requirements;

(6) existing industrial centres not only have skilled and specialist workers but also schools and colleges for training new recruits. (It is at least worth commenting that in Britain the economic decline of the inner city is in part a consequence of the difficulties firms face in recruiting staff, particularly people with specialist skills.[78]

Thus, in both the USSR and the UK, the central districts of major metropolitan areas (agglomerations) suffer from shortages of skilled labour; however, this phenomenon occurs for quite different reasons in the two societies);

(7) labour productivity is higher in large cities. At the beginning of the 1960s, in manufacturing industry (measured in terms of gross output) it was 38 per cent higher in cities with over a million inhabitants than in all other urban settlements[79] – a finding corroborated by recent research in the United States which has shown a positive correlation between labour productivity and city size, with the former being on average 6 per cent higher with each doubling in city size;[80]

(8) recently, Soviet writers have viewed as an important cause of large city growth the expansion of scientific research. The centralisation of science, which to an even greater extent than manufacturing industry has been attracted to large cities, is closely linked with the concentration of institutes of higher education.[81] Kiev, for example, has over 150 institutes employing 123 000 people. Between 1964 and 1974 the number of scientific institute employees doubled in Zaporozh'e, L'vov, Dnepropetrovsk and Odessa and rose by a factor of between 1.2 and 1.6 in Kiev, Donetsk and Khar'kov, even though a number of institutes could easily have been located in other towns.[82] Explanations offered for this concentration include the following: science is closely related to industry and recent years have witnessed a growth in scientific–industrial associations (*ob'yedineniya*)[83]; the development of 'departmental' science (where each All-Union ministry or committee has its own scientific institutes and laboratories) is a product of a complex economy and so naturally these institutes should be situated near their respective ministries and state committees; scientific institutes engaged in fundamental research need the use of libraries, archives and specialist information services which it would be uneconomic to provide for individual institutes; and, direct face-to-face exchange of information between a narrow range of contacts is still very important.[84]

Apart from the effect the above factors have had on the choice of locations for new capital investment in manufacturing, educational and research establishments, other important determinants of urban growth are underlying demographic processes and labour mobility. Because of an ageing population in the nation's largest cities, a number of Soviet demographers argue that to restrict the population increase of these cities is to fail to understand the demographic changes which are occurring. In Moscow, Leningrad, Riga, Kiev, Khar'kov, Rostov-on-Don and Odessa, those in the retired age-group represent 13–15 per cent of the dependent population, whereas in other towns it avarages slightly more than 10 per cent.[85] In fact, if Leningrad is to maintain a 'progressive age structure' it needs an influx of 400 000 people under the age of nineteen;[86] in 1966 it was estimated that if Kiev relied solely on the natural growth rate, the proportion of the population of working age would fall from 64.8 per cent in 1961 to 60.4 per cent in 1980.[87] A commentary on the 1970 Census showed that in Moscow and Leningrad the proportion of the population of pensionable age was appreciably higher than in the surrounding oblast's, while the proportion of young workers was lower. The single most important explanation for this phenomenon is 'the relatively lower birth rate in these cities over a long period of time as a result of the passport system which has restrained the rate of population growth in these cities'.[88] In other words, because limiting population growth by 'administrative' methods creates labour shortages, the government is periodically compelled to relax these restrictions. This decline in natural population growth prompted Moscow's Party and city executive committees in 1977 to issue a special decree requiring the drawing up of a document on the present demographic situation in the capital and the suggesting of ways to stimulate the natural growth rate.[89]

Unfortunately, the movements of people from one town or region to another do not automatically coincide with what is most advantageous to the society as a whole or with what the government considers to be in the society's best interests. In other words, 'population movements do not always correspond to the national economic plan'.[90] Responsibility for the discrepancy between the supply and demand for labour in towns of different sizes, and in particular regions, is partly attributable to choices made by individual workers on where they want to live and work.[91] Although Leningrad and other large cities have to attract extra labour, 'the social importance of migration to Siberia and the Far East is often given a higher rating. But in so far as migrants are mainly oriented towards the very densely populated urban centres and the rural areas of the Ukraine and Moldavia, a conflict of interests is quite evident'.[92]

According to A. V. Topilin, who attempted to classify migration as 'rational' or 'irrational', the 'irrational' labour flows in the period 1959–1972 involved over one million people and cost the RSFSR two milliard rubles annually.[93] As a result of 'irrational' labour flows, some regions have labour surpluses and others deficits with, as the XXVI

Party Congress observed, many people preferring to move from north to south and from east to west, even though the rational location of productive forces requires movement in the opposite direction.[94] In Kazakhstan the effect of an underdeveloped manufacturing base in settlements outside the capital city, together with a high rural birth-rate and the 'irrational' concentration of industry and services in Alma Ata, has been a vast influx of people into areas surrounding the city, creating in them labour 'surpluses' which have to commute over 40 kilometres to jobs in the capital.[95] Where surpluses exist, employers have little incentive to introduce new technology, improve the organisation of labour or train workers. On the other hand, where labour is in short supply, capital equipment lies underutilised, labour turnover increases and a general decline in labour discipline is witnessed.[96] The government has tried to influence the direction of migration on different occasions in recent years by offering financial assistance, including credit for house construction to people willing to migrate to designated regions.[97] Although Soviet discussions on the subject mainly centre on regional and republic-wide manpower imbalances, almost identical problems of shortages and high labour turnover occur in the country's largest cities. For example, during the 1970s 15 000 workers and 10 000 engineers and office employees in Kaluga (276 000) changed their jobs each year, a fact closely tied to the city's manpower shortage.[98]

Whether the spatial object under study is the small town, large city, oblast', planning region or republic, an important determinant of labour mobility is the standard of housing provision. Cullingworth demonstrated that, in the case of Britain, few labour market studies have done more than make passing reference to non-labour factors such as housing market conditions or housing preferences.[99] Yet it seems probable that housing is becoming a more significant determinant of the rate, character and geographical pattern of labour mobility – a fact acknowledged by the British government in its 1980 Housing Act. An aspect of this relationship, of which Soviet social scientists have long been aware, is the correlation between, on the one hand, industrial (and agricultural) output, and on the other, the standard of living which includes the type of accommodation available.[100]

A survey conducted in 1976 in the Ukraine showed that the republic's 25 constituent oblast's could be placed in one of three categories depending on their per capita agricultural and industrial output: those with an output of up to 75 per cent of the republican average; those where output was 75–115 per cent of the average, and those with an output over 115 per cent (and averaging 133 per cent). Standard of living disparities reflected these output variations. For instance, the amount of dwelling space per urban resident for the three groups was, in percentage terms, 90.8, 95.4 and 106.6 of the republican average. In the industrialised and 'rich' Donetsk oblast', per capita earnings were one-third higher than in the Chernigov oblast' and retail sales 36 per cent higher. More importantly, the study revealed that reducing the difference in monetary earnings did not in itself equalise consumption levels for 'the distribution of public consumption resources plays a major part in perpetuating inequality'.[101] Regional variations in service provision are considerable: averaged for a whole range of services, the Baltic states are unquestionably best provided with 130 per cent compared with the central regions, while West Siberia with 70 per cent of the centre fares worst of all.[102] Labour mobility thus tends to be at least in part a reflection of differences in infrastructural provision. These differences are a product of decisions to locate new investment in large cities and therefore further manifestations of the determining significance of 'sector planning dominance'.

SECTOR AND SPATIAL PLANNING CONFLICTS

At various points so far, reference has been made to the infringement by ministries and enterprises of city plans. And this chapter has documented the growth of large towns and the relative failure of the government's small town policy. The factors responsible for this apparent lack of success are related to an issue never far from the fore in discussions at planning conferences (and a *leitmotiv* of this book) namely, the lack of co-ordination of industrial (branch) and spatial (territorial) planning.

A congress of the nation's leading architects held in 1960 drew attention to the fact that city layout plans frequently had to be regarded as 'fictional' since they were given hardly any consideration in the compilation of the national economic plan. In its selection of sites for new industrial enterprises, Gosplan could even disregard spatial layout plans, thus 'making it difficult to develop a rational settlement pattern'.[103] Matters have changed little, with writers now asserting that planning has taken on a special departmental (*vedomstvennyi*) character.[104] The benefits of comprehensive planning tend to be sacrificed whenever they are not to the sole advantage of one ministry.[105] It would be unjust though, to conclude from this that ministries are conspiring against the national interest, for it is hardly their brief to oversee all the activities taking place in an area in which they themselves are operating.

A long article by the chairman of the Kiev *gorispolkom* in 1969 described how the capital's long term development plan, covering the next 25 years, made no allowance for any industrial building in the city except that by enterprises supplying the building industry, food processing plants and consumer goods manufacturers. All other new factories were to be placed some 50–80 kilometres from the centre. 'Unfortunately, these plans have been violated on various occasions. Some Union ministries acting out of narrow departmental interests have succeeded in building in Kiev' and indeed, over the previous two years 140 plots of land had been developed by industrial enterprises.[106] The most important factor in the growth of the town-forming base of Kiev and other large cities is industrial construction undertaken by 'departments' of All-Union importance which are not covered by regulations enforceable by the republic. And, just as at the regional level, the intentions and actions of these departments do not necessarily coincide with the interests of the overall development of the city's economic and spatial structure. The extent to which the growth in the town-forming agents in the six largest cities in the Ukraine has exceeded their planned expansion is illustrated in Table 9.7. The increase in size of town-forming agents of different economic sectors during the period 1964–74 compared with changes envisaged in the general plans is shown in Table 9.8. The figures in this table illustrate the extent to which actual growth in numbers employed in capital construction exceeded the planned figures in six of the largest cities of the Ukraine in the period 1964–74. In the space of this decade, the number of workers in capital construction rose by 20 to 40 per cent in Kiev, Khar'kov, L'vov, Dnepropetrovsk and Zaporozh'e, despite the fact that the general development plans for these cities had anticipated an actual decrease in workers employed in this branch of the economy.

Although the construction of *new*, often large, enterprises, which bear little direct relationship to the existing industrial profiles of the largest Ukrainian cities, continues to take place, the obsolescence of the planning forcasts shown in the above tables may be attributed largely to the very high proportion of all new investment which is used for re-tooling and expansion of existing plant. Moreover, no change in policy is imminent; rather, the eleventh five-year plan expects an acceleration in the reconstruction of existing enterprises and a substantial increase in the proportion of capital investment being channelled into plant modernisation.[108] In these circumstances, the argument goes, proposals for enterprise reconstruction should be accepted only after it has been convincingly demonstrated, that technological improvements incorporated into the productive process will ensure production plan fulfillment by increases in labour productivity, not by the taking on of additional labour.[109] Now, after long experience of seeing forecasts on the population growth of large cities substantially exceeded in practice, Soviet planners are gradually becoming less assertive and more flexible in prognosticating city growth rates. It is now acknowledged that the exact details of a city's long-term growth cannot be known in advance; instead, growth must be predicted in terms of probabilities, so that deviations from initial forecasts do not lead to radical changes in the city's planned structure.[110] This change of attitude is closely associated with the revised view on the existence and nature of agglomerations.

TABLE 9.7   *Planned and actual growth in town-forming agents in six Ukrainian cities, 1964–74*

City	Growth in town-forming agents		Discrepancy between plan and actual (%)
	Projected figure (thousands) employees	Actual figure (thousands) employees	
Kiev	28.8	152.4	429.2
Khar'kov	32.2	71.4	121.7
Dnepropetrovsk	27.3	82.2	201.1
Odessa	33.3	76.1	128.5
Zaporozh'e	49.1	107.3	118.5
L'vov	30.3	90.9	200.0

SOURCE   L. Yu. Stolbun *et al.*, 'Osnovnye gradoobrazuyushchie faktory rosta chislennosti naseleniya krupnykh gorodov UkSSR,' in *Ekonomika razvitiya i rekonstruktsii gorodov*, Kiev, 1975, p. 28.

AGGLOMERATION FORMATION AS AN 'OBJECTIVE LAW OF SOCIAL DEVELOPMENT'

In the initial post-revolution period, the low level of development of the economy (and all that this implied for diverting resources into

TABLE 9.8 *Planned and actual growth in the number of employees in specific categories of town-forming agents, 1964–74 (thousands)*

City	Plan/actual	Capital construction	'External' transport	Higher and secondary education	Non-city administrative institutions	Research and design organisations
Kiev	general plan	− 2.3	+ 0.6	+ 16.3	− 4.9	+ 3.9
	actual	+ 40.0	− 6.9	+ 19.9	+ 11.1	+ 28.1
Khar'kov	general plan	− 3.2	+ 2.2	+ 16.4	− 7.0	+ 7.9
	actual	+ 6.4	+ 2.1	+ 17.2	− 3.5	+ 8.8
Dnepropetrovsk	general plan	+ 2.0	+ 3.9	+ 4.1	0	− 2.3
	actual	+ 6.9	− 12.8	+ 16.1	+ 10.1	+ 9.2
Odessa	general plan	− 7.1	+ 9.2	+ 2.5	− 0.4	+ 0.4
	actual	− 6.3	+ 9.2	+ 15.6	+ 8.1	+ 12.4
Zaporozh'e	general plan	− 4.6	+ 0.5	+ 1.0	0	+ 1.0
	actual	+ 12.2	+ 5.1	+ 10.5	+ 1.7	+ 6.2
L'vov	general plan	0	+ 0.4	+ 2.1	− 1.1	+ 0.9
	actual	+ 3.3	− 0.3	+ 7.8	+ 1.5	+ 9.8

SOURCE L. Yu. Stolbun *et al., op. cit.* p. 30.

devising methodologies for planning, data collection and training specialists) meant that it was difficult enough to construct elaborate planning models, let alone attempt to implement them. Nevertheless, serious and successful efforts were made both to construct and operationalise plans on a city–region scale. By the early 1930s the notion that a system of cities should be planned as a unitary whole had been enunciated; cities should not be planned in total isolation for 'each town plan formed a component part of a larger plan embracing the whole of the USSR'.[111] The idea of planning for groups of settlements was taken up again and given a position of prominence in the 1960s – with one urban economist, Davidovich, emphasising the necessity of 'struggling against voluntarism in the field of town planning, particularly against the fetishisation of the "ideal" single town rather than the group form'. He was later to reiterate the point that the object of study was not the isolated city but systems of towns, settlements and villages.[112] His data for the early 1960s on intra- and inter-urban commuting distances showed how spatially close settlements combining dozens or even over 100 towns and smaller settlements formed 'urban agglomerations'.

These he defined as: 'The aggregate of a considerable number of closely situated towns united by a complex system of economic, manpower and socio-cultural organisations, with travel from the periphery to the centre of the city taking no more than two hours'.[113] Using 1959 Census data, Davidovich identified 40 large agglomerations each with a population of over 400 000 inhabitants, of which ten had populations of over one million. This gave a total of 39 million people living in urban agglomerations, equivalent to 40 per cent of the urban population at that date.[114] Davidovich was but one among a number of Soviet academics who in the 1960s were seeking to define the term 'agglomeration' and to understand the forces responsible for its formation and development.[115] Yet in 1975 one researcher could still comment that: 'It is above all necessary to provide a definition of the concept of agglomeration and offer criteria for establishing boundaries. Finding answers to these questions is extremely important from both a theoretical and practical point of view'.[116] By this time there were 68 agglomerations, and if the trend over the past decades is maintained, then by 1990 about 70 per cent of the urban population will be living in 73 agglomerations.[117]

The reason why a definition has been so long forthcoming lies in the fact that urban agglomerations as such have hardly been studied at all in the Soviet Union; this is largely because 'they have not received official recognition by the state's statistical organisations'.[118] This non-recognition may be attributed to the fact that ideologically the agglomeration had for long been regarded as an undesirable phenomenon, an anomaly in socialist society. Consequently, few attempts were made to develop concepts for studying it.[119] Yet without concepts the phenomenon could not be investigated properly. An impediment to concept formation in this case was the lack of statistical data on the subject, which in turn came about because the state's statistical organisation's had not fully acknowledged the existence of agglomerations as a form of urban development. It was this state of affairs that led Davidovich to castigate those who preferred to study the 'ideal single town', and another author to call for the 'elimination of the existing discrepancy between literature dealing with methodological issues and statistical information'.[120]

This perplexing problem of a disjuncture between the development of theoretical models and the availability of data in a particular form is a major hindrance both to scientists seeking to understand patterns of urban growth and to planners faced with the task of determining optimal industrial location and land use policies. An important turning point in the process of recognising the agglomeration as a system rather than as a conglomeration of separate settlements was the Symposium on the Problems of Urbanisation (Moscow 1969), where contributors noted how 'the scientific technological revolution leads to a transgression of the historic limits imposed on the urban form'.

Such changes are seen primarily as arising from the rapid technological advances occurring in systems of communication, both of transport and information. These allow people greater freedom of choice in deciding where to live, so the concentration of activities no longer requires the concentration of the population in major cities.[121] The communications revolution can therefore be seen from two different perspectives. On the one hand, the overall manpower shortage makes the Soviet Union a highly mobile society in terms of occupational and geographical mobility. Thus, from the point of view of individual workers, the communications revolution – in granting them greater freedom to choose where they wish to live – introduces a voluntaristic element into planning models. This could mean that planners are now obliged to pay greater heed to people's preferences when selecting sites for new industrial complexes. On the other hand, improvements in transport and information systems mean that the high degree of physical concentration of people and production characteristic of earlier periods of industrial development is no longer 'objectively' necessary. As a result of the growth in the number of automated enterprises, improvements in transport etc., individual undertakings and whole industrial areas have relative freedom in the choice of location.[122] However, for reasons already mentioned, although changes in systems of communication could have a dispersal effect, enabling industry and individuals to leave the central city, this is not occurring.

A combination of social and economic forces has compelled Soviet planners and politicians to accept the formation of agglomerations as an 'objective law of modern settlement patterns'.[123] For this reason the traditional approach to working out general development plans for a city as a functionally and spatially independent object of regulation has come to be generally regarded as a pointless endeavour. The primary object of planning is no longer the individual city but the functionally and socially inter-related system of settlements in which the city appears as a subsystem.[124] Conceptually, the Soviet view of the 'agglomeration' bears a closer resemblance to the Western notion of 'metropolitan region' than it does to 'conurbation'. The latter, first coined by P. Geddes (*Cities in Evolution*, 1915) and then applied to contiguous local authorities comprising continuous built-up areas with more than 50 000 inhabitants, were characteristic of nineteenth century urbanisation. On the other hand, the 'metropolitan region' describes a larger, more open structure, which is one of interlacing arteries of roads and electrified railways uniting composite built-up areas with rural interstices. In reality, the 'agglomeration' combines features of both the conurbation and the metropolitan region, much depending on the town-forming base of the central city and its historical origins.

This tendency to view the agglomeration as a system of urban settlements is consistent with the tendency in modern science to cease isolating phenomena in narrowly confined contexts and to examine phenomena as complex patterns of interaction. However, the danger is that the agglomeration as a system of settlements may come to be regarded as a panacea for major contradictions in Soviet urban and regional development. One author considers it to be 'one of the most rational ways of solving one of the key problems facing our country namely, the socio-economic and cultural differences still existing between town and country',[125] and another writer describes it as 'a means of anticipating, averting and eliminating the shortcomings of larger cities'.[126] Their formation is even interpreted in dialectical terms: the very growth of settlements represents a quantitative phenomenon while the formation of agglomerations appears as a qualitative change in settlement formation. 'Towns with different sizes, when they enter into an agglomeration, take on new qualities; it enables them to use the advantages of large cities yet avoid their disadvantages, and to increase the range of cultural services provided to the residents of small settlements and create more favourable conditions for their development.'[127] The subject is not only a dialectical but also an ontological issue. Since it is not accidental but a phenomenon emerging according to social laws of development, a teleological purpose becomes imputed to urbanisation and the agglomeration (the latter being a manifestation of urbanisation at a particular level of development of the social formation): 'Urbanisation in its development strives to overcome the excessive overcrowding of population in relatively large cities. The conditions are created and the necessity is revealed in the formation of 'multi-polar' centres in grouped settlements which permits a more harmonious development of cities of different sizes and types'.[128]

Nothing said so far should be taken to mean that Soviet social scientists are unaware of the problems associated with the growth of agglomerations – the intermingling of industry, transport and residential areas, building on good agricultural land, pollution of the environment etc.[129] But, given the prevailing Soviet world-view which encourages a focus on the positive aspects of 'social laws' (in socialist societies), less is said of these negative features and attention is drawn instead towards the future, optimal state of a system (in this case the agglomeration) when the less desirable aspects will have disappeared. Hence, 'one of the central tasks of Soviet urban planners is to define the optimum structure of a system of settlements'. Yet some writers acknowledge that the definition of optimality cannot be absolute, and so is inapplicable outside a particular socio-economic and physical environment. Furthermore, since the system of settlements is in a state of evolution, there will be a series of stages in its development when a number of individual elements will not be optimalised. In fact, the most efficient state of a system may be achieved with some of its components not being optimalised.[130] This poses the question – which elements in the system do not reach an optimum state? The answer depends in the first instance on goal priorities. And according to most Soviet planners, 'one of the most important conditions for optimalising systems is the reduction in material and energy expenditures on intra-systemic communication; in other words, by making the system more compact'.[131] Whether one regards 'compactness' as the product of a teleological process or of human direction, the outcome is the same, with more resources being channelled into and concentrated in the large central city at the expense of the small towns which are probably destined to remain 'unoptimalised'.

COMMUTING

The social composition of the commuting population represents a significant unknown variable affecting the analysis of industrial location. Should it be composed of a large proportion of skilled workers, engineers and other specialists, then the argument for seeking a central city location on account of their shortage in small towns would to a certain extent be undermined. On the other hand, if statistics should show that commuters are mainly unskilled workers, then this would contribute to a picture of a non-random distribution of the population in terms of social class between the large city and outlying towns and smaller settlements. Furthermore, the implication would be that it is the concentration of skilled workers in the large city which is responsible for 'attracting new investment' and also that these workers do not want to move or to travel to jobs outside the city.

In Western industrialised nations, the growth of large cities and agglomerations has been accompanied almost universally by an increase in the proportion of the population commuting from their suburban residences outside the main city boundaries to jobs in the city. In the USSR, the proportion of people commuting to work is also on the increase. The issue of commuting as a basic form of population movement was first examined at an All-Union conference on problems of population migration held in Rostov-on-Don in May 1967. Yet the study of commuting is regarded as being seriously hampered by a lack of comprehensive and reliable data. The absence of systematic regional and nation-wide surveys notwithstanding, statistics confirm that 'daily commuting to work is on the increase everywhere'.[132] The only detailed data on commuting covering a period of years is that on rural dwellers travelling to towns for either work or study purposes. In 1970 over 4 million people made a daily journey to a town or smaller urban settlement; by 1975 this figure had risen to 5.5 million. By 1980, an estimated 10–15 per cent of the nation's rural population was commuting daily.[133] Unfortunately no accurate information exists on commuting from smaller towns to the larger cities or on reverse flows from towns to villages. Aggregated for the country at large, it has been estimated that no fewer than 10 million people, or about 12 per cent of the annual average number of manual and office workers and students in higher and secondary specialist education, commute.[134]

In 1964, Davidovich had observed that the average distance travelled by workers living in the suburbs and using railway transport was 25 km, while suburban and inter-urban 'bus trips averaged up to 20 km, resulting in a travelling time of 'no more than one hour'.[135] Other studies conducted in the mid-1960s in the Ukraine showed that the proportion of the workforce with jobs in Khar'kov and Kiev but living in the suburbs in 1965 was 18.5 per cent and 11.1 per cent respectively. Workers with jobs in Kiev were commuting over 50 km and those in Khar'kov up to 80 km. (50 km was regarded as the economic limit of commuting.) At the time of writing it was calculated that within ten to fifteen years the number of workers living outside the city boundaries with jobs in the central cities would be considerably reduced – in the case of Kiev by more than half, but in Khar'kov, because it is a mono-centred agglomeration, the reduction was expected to be only 25 per cent. These decreases were predicated on the location of additional manufacturing plant and offices in the outlying settlments.[136] The accuracy of these estimates may be judged from the fact that in 1971 the number of workers commuting from the suburban zone to jobs in Kiev stood at 100 000 (7.3 per cent of the workforce) and 150 000 (20 per cent) in Khar'kov.[137] Although the figures for Kiev reveal a proportionate decline (from 11.1 to 7.3 per cent), it is unlikely that the absolute figure fell by much if it fell at all. The lower percentage figure for 1971 is at least in part a result of the unanticipated rate of population growth of the capital city itself, which rose by 25.5 per cent between 1966 and 1971.

In 1970 another author noted that 'in the larger cities commuting to work takes 90 minutes or more', with the journey time of those commuting to work from the outlying areas of Moscow, Riga (850 000), Novokuznetsk (551 000), Kemerovo (486 000) and other large cities taking up to two hours in each direction.[138] Other studies have confirmed that commuting distances and the total flow of people into the centre of cities from surrounding towns have increased. For instance, the suburban zone of Minsk (embracing 1100 settlements, of which only nine had from 3000 to 6000 inhabitants and two with 10–15 000) covers an area with a 40 km radius from the city (that is, a radius drawn by two hour travelling time). During the period 1963–70, the size of the suburban population working in Minsk increased by a factor of 1.2 and the average travel time to work rose from 58 to 68 minutes.[139] No doubt a similar population flow takes place within the Leningrad agglomeration, for here, whereas the population of the central city grew by 18 per cent between 1959 and 1970, that of suburban towns falling within the administrative jurisdiction of the Leningrad soviet increased by 26 per cent and that of those further out, but still within the agglomeration, increased by 43 per cent.[140] According to calculations and forecasts up to 1990, made by the Central Town Planning Research Institute in Moscow (*TsNIIP gradostroitel'stvo*) on the basis of existing means of transport, the boundary of a city-region should be set at a $1\frac{1}{2}$–2 hour radius from the centre of a city, giving a distance of about 60 km. However, this distance will probably be extended to 80 km with the improvement in transport technology.

This tendency for journey time from home to place of work to increase has been one of the factors influencing Soviet town planning theory and policy, both with regard to curbing the growth of large cities and locating industry and state agencies in small towns in order to prevent the emergence of a network of dormitory suburbs. Most planners look upon commuting as a consequence of the 'irrational' location of workplaces in relation to housing, a fact that can be remedied by 'better' planning.[141] However, this view has been challenged not only on the grounds that it does not lead to 'a *rational* utilisation of labour resources between town and country', but also that it fails to pay sufficient attention to the 'social meaning of commuting' associated with increased geographical mobility and the gradual rise in the standard of living in small towns. Neither does it take into account the wishes of people who might prefer to commute. One survey conducted in the Sverdlovsk and Chelyabinsk agglomerations found that 40 per cent of their commuter respondents actually preferred to journey to work daily in the large city and live outside its limits in smaller settlements.[142] In many large industrial centres (for instance the *Donbas* and the *Pridnepr'*) some workers (for instance, those working in blast furnaces) prefer to live in suburbs because of the better environment and their desire to own a detached house with garden, which can only be built outside the city boundaries owing to the shortage of building land in the cities themselves.[143]

A variety of factors contribute to the increasing number of commuters: improvements in shopping facilities and the range of amenities and services provided outside the central city; better public transport; the reduction in the length of the working day (a stated objective of the government – people may now be willing to spend more time on travelling); and improvements in living standards (measured in terms of labour-saving devices and a greater assortment of consumer goods and food products, which may generate an increased interest in gardening, only feasible in small towns). Of particular importance for promoting the growth of small towns – if not the location of industry in them – is the fact that official housing policy is to give assistance to and encourage the construction of houses for owner-occupancy in small towns and workers' settlements.[144]

As a theoretical desideratum, compactness is not only at odds with reality but is even to a certain extent challenged by those who consider that commuting is a process which should not be arrested but, on the contrary, catered for and built into regional and city development plans. For example, one author notes that 'the diversification of employment in small towns and settlements, in itself a difficult task, cannot be reckoned to bring about a reduction in daily inter-settlement commuting, a phenomenon which is evident in most large agglomerations where many of the settlements have a diversified structure'.[145] Even when, in an attempt to decentralise, enterprises are located in small towns within an agglomeration, the number of people commuting to work does not necessarily diminish. In the opinion of some this is because what has become 'more and more important is the social demand for freedom of choice in the sphere of activity in which one is engaged'. And a person's choice is increasingly coming to depend upon 'qualitative differences between workplaces located in the central city and outlying towns'.[146] The city-based enterprise or plant will, as a rule, possess a stronger trade union branch, which will try to extract a variety of concessions from management in the form of better changing rooms, clothing and storage space, dining rooms, cleaner working conditions, up-to-date industrial safeguards etc. The management may itself be more efficient, or simply better placed to reap the benefits of economic externalities, which enables it to earn higher bonuses. It is also able to maintain contact with other organisations to obtain for the workforce tickets and coupons (*abonementy*) for a range of social and cultural activities. So, even 'when the supply and demand for labour in Novosibirsk's satellite towns was in equilibrium' no decline took place in the flow of workers into the central city from a number of these satellites.

The continuing location of industry and the creation of new jobs in the service sector in the central city constitute the main factors responsible for the rise in the number of commuters. The reason why at least some people do not move to be nearer to their workplace is that, as far as the country's larger cities are concerned, change of residence from an outlying settlement to the city itself is prevented by the operation of the passport system. In order to restrict the growth of larger cities, only under 'exceptional circumstances' does the government allow new workers to register as citizens of large cities and thereby become eligible to claim permanent residence there. A less directly administrative measure for controlling population movements is the availability of housing. Except for an infinitesimally small number of people, private house construction is forbidden in large towns. Therefore, apart from squeezing the existing housing stock in the short run by allowing city dwellers to rent out some of their own living space, the flow into the city is moderated by the city's housing policy. The available evidence does not justify the conclusion that, were these restrictions on mobility removed, people would flock into the city. What can be said however is that, despite improvements in housing and the provision of amenities in small towns, disparities in standards of living between large and small towns remain considerable. Thus, the removal of existing barriers to mobility would almost certainly result in a movement to the large city of a number of people at present commuting, as well as many workers from small towns. There may be exceptions to this general rule, depending on regional and more local conditions – particularly the existence of suburban railway line connections, the supply of housing and climatic factors. In the Kiev oblast', for example, with a particularly high level of private house ownership (78 per cent in 1966) people might prefer the benefits of a large garden with the possibility of more living space to living in the republican capital itself, to which they are in any case linked by a cheap, fast and frequent railway service.

What may be called the objective causes of commuting may be summarised thus: (1) the decisions taken to locate industry in large cities; (2) a passport system limiting the number of workers who can take up permanent residence in the city; (3) better working conditions and housing, shopping and recreational facilities in the large cities. But it is not only such 'objective' factors which give rise to commuting. Subjective factors also play an important contributory role. As in North America and England, suburban living is seen by some people as a way of achieving the virtues of both town and country; it enables them to benefit from the economic and recreational opportunities offered by the city and, at the same time, to enjoy the peacefulness of the more rural way of life. (A Gallup survey conducted in 1972 asked a representative American sample: 'If you could live anywhere you

wanted, would you prefer a city, suburban area, small town or farm?'
13 per cent opted for the city, 31 per cent for the suburbs, 32 per cent
for small towns and 23 per cent for farms.[147]

Environmental factors such as clean air and low noise levels and the
possibility of building one's own home – with the chance of more living
space than would be available in the city – and cultivating a garden,
may well be powerful motivating factors affecting preferences for
small town living. Whether by force or choice, socio-economic background is a factor influencing who actually lives outside the city. In
1975, of the 5.5 million rural inhabitants commuting to work and study
in towns and workers' settlements, a high proportion almost certainly
fall in the unskilled category,[148] many of whom, by virtue of their
cultural background and to a lesser extent their lower earnings, prefer
to own their own home and garden. There is also evidence that
migration from the countryside to the town progresses in stages: some
small towns, which are no more than local organisational centres for
the surrounding rural area, serve as 'transhipment bases' for those *en
route* to larger towns when the small town is unable to satisfy their
needs.[149] The passport system has the effect of blocking many migrants
from moving to the final stage, the large city, and preserves an army of
unskilled labour within the city's sphere of influence.[150] As one study
noted, 'the need to service the growing economy of the very large cities
gives rise to a continuous shortage of labour especially of unskilled
workers'.[151]

This demand for a low-paid, 'service population' is analogous to the
situation found in many North American and West European cities.
Explanations for the phenomenon in the West tend to refer to the
'functional need' for low status, low-income groups to perform essential tasks.[152] At present, the major urban centres in the Soviet Union
are still able to draw upon rural migrants to meet this particular
demand for labour. However, it is possible that, at a future date,
demographic imbalances created by differential birth-rates between
Slavonic and Asian peoples will occasion the migration of Asians to
cities in the non-Asian republics. It is also possible that these migrants,
for whom Russian is the second language, will find themselves per-
forming a whole range of low status occupational roles. Yet, to
speculate from this that the outcome will be racial conflict and residential segregation based on ethnicity, in a fashion akin to that found in
capital cities of the developed capitalist states,[153] would be pessimistic
in the extreme. However, in order to prevent such a situation developing, the government should now be initiating large scale sociological

and other academic research programmes to anticipate the (possible) consequences of a larger ethnic population in overwhelmingly Slavic cities. Since the Party in the past has not been wholly successful in overcoming prejudice in the population, it would be unwise for it to assume that hostility towards ethnic minority groups by the numerically dominant group, when living in close proximity to one another, is a feature solely of capitalist societies.

While one may only speculate on the possibility of such developments, it is true that the presence of a 'peripheral' population reduces the onus on the government to provide and maintain housing (since many own their own homes) and lowers the priority accorded to developing the infrastructure and supplying a better range of goods and services to the smaller settlements. Savings made in these areas can be diverted to improving housing and services in the main city; this is rationalised by asserting that 'the growing demand by the public for a broader assortment of goods and better services can only be met in large cities'.[154] In other words, those living in the city are indirectly 'exploiting' those living outside it – in so far as the former have better access to consumer goods and services paid for out of the general surplus product, and compel others to commute, thereby reducing their non-work time. This criticism could be countered by pointing to the fact that it is impossible to provide, on a universal basis, the whole range of services now available in large cities and further, that in the long run as the economy develops conditions in the small towns will improve. This argument is difficult to dispute, as is the logic behind industrial location. As an appeal it carries some force, but only when it rests on the acceptance of the existence of 'objective laws of social development'. However, factors operating to concentrate industry in large cities are subjective as well as objective. Factory managements, despite the absence in some cases of objective reasons, strive to justify a central city location for their undertakings in order to enhance their own kudos and be nearer the centres of decision-making, thereby enabling them to 'avoid a number of organisational difficulties which tend to arise during the construction stage'. They are assisted in their efforts by local government officials who seek to attract manufacturers in order to strengthen their own case for larger central budgetary allocations and to increase their revenues from the local taxes raised on undertakings operating within their jurisdiction. Above all, the standard of living, particularly of managers, is higher in the large cities.

The urban research centre in Moscow (*TsNIIP gradostroitel'stvo*) recognises that both rural–urban migration and the centripetal force drawing people from the suburbs into the centre are a consequence of individuals wanting to improve their standards of living.[155] And, according to the demographer and sociologist, Perevedentsev, there is every reason why we should expect both tendencies. For him the social advantages which the largest urban areas offer the individual are enormous: a choice of education, profession, speciality, job, friends, spouse and recreation. In this sense, the individual in the very large city is incomparably freer than one in the smaller and medium sized town. The large city creates new demands and offers the means for their satisfaction. Here the individual is released from the strict social control mechanisms characteristic of the village and small town.[156]

In a way that is reminiscent of Georg Simmel, the very diversity of the urban environment is seen as presenting a condition for 'the realisation of the freedom of the individual' and as being a 'mechanism for the crystallisation of the universal, the general and, in the final analysis, of the customary (*privychnyi*)'.[157] Furthermore, in the tradition of Robert Park, a founder of the Chicago School of sociology at the beginning of this century, 'the intensity and fullness of life in the large city forms a type of personality which is psychologically mobile and capable of orientating to complex and rapidly changing situations'.[158] The positive features of large city habitation are also available to the commuter, who is offered opportunities for social mobility through greater occupational choice and is also introduced and acclimatised to the urban way of life, its culture and psychology.[159] These 'gains' are partially negated by the adverse consequences of commuting such as 'higher morbidity rates, traumatism and lower levels of labour productivity which derive from long daily journeys and psychic overload'.[160]

In the theory of spatial planning, different ideas compete for the attention of policy makers. In general there is a tendency for one particular idea to dominate in a sphere of activity: in the case of spatial development it might be high-rise housing and demolition or, on the other hand, urban renewal; the agglomeration might be seen as an aberrant form to be condemned and avoided or a positive expression of social development to be encouraged; the idea of transplanting architectural forms and building technology from the towns into the villages has its champions, whilst others seek to preserve the traditional low-rise wooden houses, huddled together in a myriad of small communities linked together in an elaborate settlement system. Given the size of the country and the enormous physical and cultural variations encompassed within its borders, attempts universally and doctrinairely to apply a concept are more likely to hinder than to enhance the solution of problems. Since comprehensive planning must take into account uneven developments between sectors, between regions, between cities of different sizes and above all between town and country, the currently dominant idea of the 'grouped system of settlements' (see note 117) may prove to be a theoretical and methodological tool for helping to increase overall output in the society at large and possibly at every other spatial level – and also one for improving the geographical distribution of goods and services. And yet planners, who laboriously analyse and plot linkages between settlements as an integral part of a planned social and economic policy, are forced to accommodate to the choices and decisions made by rural officials, enterprise managers and millions of individuals who want to live and work elsewhere.

CONCLUSION

Having rejected a formal concept of the optimum sized city and having failed to contain the growth of the largest cities and stimulate the growth of small towns, Soviet social scientists are no longer able to ignore a phenomenon which exists in the USSR and in other countries, and have come to accept that a number of clusterings of settlements in a locality tend to merge to form continuous urban areas (agglomerations). Since, moreover, these are not accidental, amorphous assemblages of structures but complex entities with definite functional and spatial structures allegedly evolving according to specific laws of social development, Soviet planners are charged with understanding these laws and converting a spontaneous process into a planned and directed one, by identifying the linkages within the system.[161] The use of Soviet Marxist concepts such as 'concrete processes' and 'objective laws of development'[162] to explain the rise, acceptance and legitimation of, for example, the agglomeration, has the unfortunate effect of leading the student into the very teleological trap that marxists seek to avoid. The burgeoning literature on systems approaches to urban and regional planning, paralleling the popularity of systems theory among Western planners, has to be viewed and assessed in two ways: as a methodology for analysing and forecasting urban development corresponding to advances in the field of cybernetics and computer technology; and as an element in an argument designed to provide and *ex post facto* explanation of a social phenomenon, thereby creating an impression that 'all that is rational is real and all that is real is rational'.

A unanimous Soviet point of view cannot be said to exist on the desirability of allowing cities to grow without restraint or on the reasons for their growth – and, in a sense, unanimity should not be sought. However, differences notwithstanding, the prevailing Soviet view on the continuing process of resource concentration may be summarised as follows: although at first the location of productive forces is to a considerable extent determined by a coincidence of favourable environmental factors – river or sea port, good drainage, raw materials – at a later stage the very presence of a manufacturing base is sufficient to generate centripetal forces attracting other enterprises.[163] Then, at a particular level of development, cities acquire certain features which, in making them less reliant on factors external to the city, enable them to sustain a self-generating growth.[164] The city eventually assumes a certain autonomy – 'no longer playing a purely passive role in the process of industrial location but actually influencing the process'.[165]

The determinism in this interpretation of city development justifies a certain speculative prognostication. If patterns of urban settlement pass through definite stages related to a society's level of economic development, then one particular socio-technical factor, the private car, as yet relatively unimportant in the USSR (see Chapter 6), could in the future make a dramatic impact on the size of the commuting population, its socio-economic composition and the location of industry. In the USSR, people are rewarded with cars for saving hard and for their 'contribution to society'. Often these individuals will combine the qualities of parsimony, productivity and *partiinost'*. The potential demands made by this broad social group of car owners, as a latent interest group, may have been unanticipated by the government and yet may have to be met, at least in part. In time car ownership could lead to a situation similar to that found in the West, with higher status social groups preferring to 'leave the city', live in their privately owned homes and commute daily to the town for work. Eventually, if sufficient numbers of skilled workers, decision-makers and *apparatchiki* choose to live in the commuter belt, then the government's policy of industrial decentralisation might be achieved.

10 Conclusion

Soviet urban and regional policy has been influenced by two ideologically determined imperatives – namely, the elimination of differences between town and country and the uniform and proportional development of the nation's productive resources. It seems reasonable to assume that the level of development of the economy is the principal determinant of the extent to which the first goal can be achieved, for to raise the socio-cultural standards of living in the countryside requires firstly, an overall increase in the output of consumer goods, social facilities (libraries, cinemas) and public utilities (mains water and gas supplies) and secondly, a change in socio-economic relationships with the elimination of the personal plot of land.[1] But, consumer durables (furniture, domestic equipment, cars), social facilities and housing (bricks, cement, glass, steel), public utilities (sewerage and water supply systems requiring large investments in metal or plastic pipelines) and transportation systems (surfaced roads, railway lines and the means of transport) depend on the rate of growth of the means of production. Furthermore, the weaning away of peasants and others from the personal plot depends to a considerable extent on the mechanisation of agricultural production – the more widespread use of farm machinery and manufacture of spare parts.

The problem facing the government is how to produce these goods most efficiently. Apart from the technical issue of deciding on which technology to employ, there is the question of where the manufacturing units are to be located. The government's objective of eliminating differences between town and country would seem to be in contradiction to their other objective of achieving a more uniform distribution of the country's productive forces. In order to reach one goal, the other is perforce 'sacrificed', for to maximise output and reap the benefit of investment in the shortest period of time means expanding the manufacturing base in very large cities.

To speak of 'town' and 'village' may be regarded as a figurative way of expressing social, economic and cultural variations which exist between settlements of different sizes and/or which are located in different regions. Thus, urbanisation cannot be reduced to a 'simple' relationship of town and village *in senso strictu*; it refers to spatial development in its broadest sense – the type of housing, internal layout of towns, the spatial relationship of places of residence and work and inter-settlement spatial and functional linkages. Spatial development, though determined in the first instance by location decisions taken by industry, tends to become an expression of the level of infrastructural provision found in different places.

The present work has suggested, particularly in Chapter 3, that a systemic conflict has arisen between two institutional complexes – the local soviets on the one hand, and enterprises on the other. The former are principally concerned with spatial or physical planning, and the latter with economic planning. Furthermore, structural differentiation and specialisation, concomitants of industrialisation, have required the granting of greater functional autonomy to these two system elements or institutional complexes. Now, it may be postulated that two tendencies operate within social systems. The first tendency is for parts (institutions) already possessing some degree of functional autonomy to keep or enlarge their scope of independence. The second tendency, dealing with the system as a whole, attempts to limit the scope of the parts' independence, or even subordinate them to the system. Those elements which manage to acquire the largest scope of functional autonomy will become the foci of organised resistance to the integrating pressure of the system and may become the potential generators of change.[2] The struggle for functional autonomy on the part of two elements (for instance, local soviets and industrial sectors), leads one element (industrial sector) to seek to preserve its functional autonomy by reorganising the system as a whole in order to maintain its independent position. That is to say, it does not give up some things affecting its overall position (for example, housing) without ensuring a gain elsewhere. In the Soviet Union, this reorganisation means granting greater room for manoeuvre to enterprises in return for their surrender to the local soviets of resources they had hitherto controlled. The second tendency manifests itself in an 'alliance' of the two 'elements' (institutional complexes) representing local interests against the centre. In other words, there is a struggle between centralising and decentralising forces. Both tendencies operate simultaneously; decentralisation[3] and functional autonomy for institutional complexes represent different aspects of the same process.[4]

A contradiction exists when the satisfaction of one demand prevents the satisfaction of another. So, for example, contradictions exist between house-building co-operatives and state housing, between all four tenure-types, between locating industry in small or large cities, between pursuing a policy of urban renewal or rehabilitation and so on. One of Soviet Marxism's central tenets is that 'disequilibrium' is a natural state in any society; some elements are developed at different rates from others and, as a general rule, each element will be pursuing its interest at the expense of others. One author has been particularly explicit in his identification of the the problems arising from the pursuit of conflicting objectives. A characteristic feature of modern town planning, he reminds us, is the increase in the scale of the 'object' of study – from the city and its component parts to the large urban system embracing both rural and urban settlements. Each urban system contains 'socio-economic sub-systems' representing productive, scientific and cultural–educational activities. Since each subsystem (type of activity) has its own specific laws of territorial development, the whole territorial structure of settlements develops in a contradictory fashion. For instance, the 'overall progressive tendency' for production to become spatially concentrated is in some cases associated with, firstly, a 'worsening of the ecological situation in agglomerations' and, secondly, the maintenance of regional differences emanating from a 'lag in the development of an inter-settlement infrastructure which, in turn, limits the possibility of developing the peripheral area of the agglomeration'. Thus, 'generally speaking, it is possible to regard the optimisation of the regional settlement pattern as a process of inter-related contradictions in the development of the urban system'.[5] The task of the Soviet state is to mediate between these competing interests to ensure the achievement, by the 'best' means, of a set of objectives. The state must also (by virtue of the marxist definition of the state) mediate between competing interests in order to maintain the existing class relationships.

One of the questions posed in the Introduction was: for whom does housing constitute a 'problem'? The evidence suggests that a possible line of investigation to answer this question is through an exploration of the relationship between housing tenure and social class. Private housing is constantly being demolished in the cities where, in the main, further private construction is banned. This means that the owner-occupier is forced to live on the city periphery or in a small town. Typically, people living in the private sector will be rural–urban migrants and persons approaching retirement or already retired. They will be members of low status occupations and tend to fall into low wage categories, which will cause them to maintain a private plot in order to supplement their income. The poor provision of public utilities adds to the low status image of the private sector. This is not to say, however, that all privately owned housing is run down and completely lacking in basic amenities or is the preserve of a pariah caste, for new, well-provided and well-designed building for owner-occupation is taking place.

At the other end of the housing class spectrum stands the house-building co-operative. Although, legally, co-operatives are allowed to build in settlements of all sizes, they remain concentrated in the largest cities. The high monthly repayments required of the co-operative members and the buildings' frequently choice position within the city make them attractive to high status but not always the highest income groups. It is no mere accident that co-operatives came into being during NEP, and suffered a demise in the period of rapid industrialisation, or that their resuscitation coincides not only with the development of co-operatives in other East (and some West) European countries, but also with the economic reforms of the mid-1960s.

The state sector, housing three-quarters of the urban population, varies considerably in quality and, necessarily, caters for people from all social groups. Drawing a distinction between local soviet and departmental accommodation is akin to drawing a distinction between those who are given housing out of social need and those to whom it is offered as a reward. Again, in a very general sense, local soviets provide for those in the weak bargaining position in the job market and for the indigent (the role assigned by some Western commentators to the local authority in the UK). And the departmental sector caters for a wide range of occupational groups – from high status senior government officials and members of prestigious professions to less skilled, but socially necessary, labour such as railway employees. Since 'hostel' accommodation is included in the departmental sector statistics (but impossible to separate from them) some of the lower status groups are also accommodated in this sector. Undoubtedly the local soviets also own and control accommodation that is cramped, in serious need of repair and lacking in one or more basic amenities. Thus, we can expect to find poor living conditions in both private and state sectors. Furthermore, because housing can be treated as a reward, there is a tendency for a disproportionate number of those whose economic functions are looked upon as 'less important' to be less well housed. And, as Chapter 8 in particular indicated, it is not just the type of housing tenure or quality of the accommodation that is important for understanding the distribution of housing space among social groups. The spatial location of the property in which they live and, later, in which they are re-housed, has also to be taken into consideration. The people who find themselves in the worst accommodation and also low on the waiting list for re-housing are not, however, all members of unskilled manual occupational categories; doctors and teachers in primary, secondary and higher education may also rank low in the queue for a new flat. Each society has its own criteria for allocating individuals and social groups to positions in the status hierarchy and, as in any society, those on the lower rungs of the Soviet Union's status ladder are typically those with the poorest access to material goods and services and, thus, those for whom housing constitutes a 'problem'.

There is no reason to assume that the Soviet state did not hold as a basic premise of its existence the need to raise the standard of living of the population – which includes providing them with decent accommodation. Scarcity could be overcome by expanding either the private or the public sector. During the 1920s it was considered expedient to encourage individuals to provide housing for themselves. In the first place, resources did not exist on a scale sufficient to make state provision a realistic possibility; secondly, it used labour of the owner-occupier himself, which had a double benefit in a period of unemployment. With the introduction of the five-year plan in 1929, surplus labour was quickly absorbed into manufacturing industry. The new industrial workforce drawn into the towns from the countryside had to be housed. It was evident that the individual builder could not meet the demand – not that, as was discussed in Chapter 5, the government has always been unwilling to countenance this alternative. Consequently, the state found itself compelled to take over this function of principal provider of accommodation. It did not prove to be a commendable landlord: the average amount of living space per person fell during the 1930s, with people housed in hastily and flimsily constructed barracks and low-rise wooden dwellings. The harnessing of science and technology to meet social needs led inexorably towards the decision to industrialise the construction industry and the manufacture of dwellings. At the same time, a choice had to be made between directing the research effort into devising the mass production of low-rise or high-rise buildings. The cost of providing an infrastructure (including a transportation network) ensured that, at least in the long term, the socialist person of tomorrow would live in high-rise blocks of flats.

It could be argued, then, that what really determined the two choices – public instead of private forms of tenure and high-rise instead of low-rise building – were economic cost considerations. This is by no means to say that ideological, social and political factors played no part in formulating these outcomes. Remarkably perhaps, ideological pre-suppositions and economic necessity led to the same policy conclusions. On the one hand, the pervading scientific ethos within ruling circles relished and demanded the application of industrialised, assembly-line technology as a means to cater for a vital social need; they had a vision of units of accommodation supplied like any other mass produced commodity. On the other hand, since the city housed socialism and represented a radical break with the past – the 'idiocy' associated with the countryside, the conservative peasantry and the tsarist cities, which anyway were nothing more than 'overgrown villages' – its housing and architecture had to be distinguished from that past. Had research into the industrialisation of construction been geared to low-rise instead of high-rise residential development, then the suburbs of Moscow might now look more like those of Los Angeles and Novosibirsk's Akademgorodok like Levittown, New Jersey. Clearly though, the path of technological advancement (and the uses to which technology is put) is determined, to a considerable extent, by a wide range of social factors which rule out of court certain avenues of investigation and conduct. And when the Party turned its back on the *muzhik* and his wooden *izba*, low-rise development did not enter into consideration as part of a housing strategy for urban areas. The workers of tomorrow would be accommodated in high-rise, standardised blocks of flats. However, not only has reality presented a number of obstacles to the achievement of this goal, but the cartoon taken from *Krokodil* aptly illustrates popular feelings towards high-rise building.

In every generation there are individuals whose ideas may be said to run ahead of their time; what they seek to achieve is not congruous with the resources available. This minority – the nation's *avant garde* (such as Lissitsky and Sabsovich) – frequently finds itself out of tune with the ideas and demands of the majority. Milyutin realised, as did 'the Party' (especially through their gargantuan representative, Stalin) that each fundamental change in the ideas people hold requires an enormous length of time for its accomplishment. The 'revolutionaries' (with their 'hare-brained schemes') tended to speak of the changes they wished to inaugurate as though these covered no more than the space of a few years or, at most, decades. At the same time they acknowledged that the Reformation is the name of a movement in the minds of men in North Europe which went on for three centuries. As much as Stalin might have envisaged himself as a shaper of people's

They decided to build a block of flats,

but a whole settlement grew up!

Reproduced with kind permission from *Krokodil*, no. 25, September 1975, p. 7.

minds, he (the Party) could not help but be shaped by these minds – by the definition which millions of men and women had of their situation.[6] And the ideas which the leadership and the vast majority of the population held about existence derived directly from their life's experience – an experience characterised by fear, repression, hunger, material deprivation, patriarchism and authoritarianism. Changes can be (and were) brought about by legislative fiat, for instance, formal equality between the sexes. But, as Chapter 6 in particular sought to show, changes in people's sentiments require a much longer period of time: the *dom novogo byta* offering new freedom in personal relationships had to await the provision of 'material abundance'. Lenin the realist (as opposed to Lenin the idealist and propagandist who noted in his April Theses of 1917 that '. . . the ranks of the Party are ten times more revolutionary than the leaders and the masses outside are ten times more revolutionary than the ranks . . .') was aware of the fact that the form of intellectual activity most men engaged in most of the time did not merit applause, and even less emulation. 'Of course we shall not submit to everything the masses say, for the masses also yield to sentiments that are not in the least advanced.'[7] Stalin echoed this judgement, considering that the Party could not limit itself to registering what the masses of the working class felt and thought, 'drag at the tail of the spontaneous movement and fail to rise above the momentary interests of the proletariat'.[8]

In theory at least, there was a rejection of the strong strain of anti-urbanism in Western (especially Anglo-American, capitalist) culture in favour of 'urbanism'. The capitalist city could be accepted as being 'pestilential to the morals and health of man', the locale of the criminal and deviant, for at the same time its over-riding virtue lay in its being the home of the proletariat, the vanguard class of socialism. Under socialism the city is regarded as the fount of original ideas, innovations in production, behaviour and thought. Rejection of the 'village' is far from being total, however; it rather takes the form of a polemical repudiation not of the countryside as such but of the backwardness of the peasant with his attachment to his private home and plot of land, his individualism and the residual capitalism that his way of life entails. Since the gap between town and country remains to be bridged – the standard of living in rural areas raised – a premium is placed on central city habitation. Members of the various cultural, social, economic and political elites prefer to 'overcome' the separation of town and country – not by settling for the specifically Anglo-American suburban compromise, but by having as their permanent residence a flat in the city (the nearer the centre the better) and for recreation a villa (*dacha*) often a considerable distance outside the city.

At the same time, as Chapters 8 and 9 showed, suburban development and its corollary, commuting from the suburbs (and further afield) to the central city, are features of Soviet urban growth. However, in contrast to North American and British experience (particularly since the first quarter of the twentieth century), those living in suburbs, on city peripheries or in outlying settlements include low status workers newly arrived from the countryside and still closely wedded to home ownership. Whether or not the advent of the private car will begin to alter this pattern of social class distribution – as a result of pressure being put on the government to improve roads, utilities and social amenities outside the main urban centres – remains to be seen. Thus, in so far as *at present* people, if presented with a choice, move nearer the urban centres, and *in the future may* prefer to have as their permanent residence a home outside the main city, we are justified in saying that the laws of social development do push their way with 'iron necessity' and the urban spatial forms which characterised the industrially advanced capitalist societies at a particular stage in their development do represent a necessary pattern for settlements in the USSR.

There are evident disparities in the spatial distribution of consumer resources – both private and collective – between centre and periphery. Moreover, it would seem that some social groups are better placed (socially and *ergo* spatially) to enjoy the benefits of the nation's resources. The government is aware of such disparities, especially the spatial ones between town and village which it has made some attempt to reduce. If one of the criteria of success in reducing disparities is the industrial development of smaller settlements, then the government has had limited success. Moreover, differences in standards of living, measured in terms of infrastructure provision, also exist between regions and republics. The Soviet government has had two main urbanisation strategies from which to choose: (1) it can invest in the less developed regions as a means of raising the overall standard of living in those regions – because investment in manufacturing plant in an underdeveloped area requires development of the local social and technical infrastructure and the provision of jobs in the better paid manufacturing sector; (2) alternatively, investment can be concentrated in the already developed regions because the rate of return on capital will be greater and reaped in a shorter space of time and then these newly generated goods and services can be channelled into the less developed regions to raise their standard of living. Although in the main the former strategy, which is related to the notion of 'the even and proportional development of the country', has little support today (as testified by the high proportion of all investment used for the modernisation of plants, most of which are located in the European part of the country), Soviet industry does tend to be more dispersed than industry in Western economies. And, according to one recent (critical) commentator on the Soviet government's investment plan for 1981–86, dispersal will have to increase in the future.[9] The crucial question is, however, would any other spatial distribution of the productive forces at the present level of development improve the material life chances of the population as a whole?

'Mankind', wrote Marx, 'always sets itself only such tasks as it can solve; since ... it will always be found that the task itself arises only when the material conditions for its solution already exist or are at least in the process of formation.'[10] Yet, the Soviet government set itself goals it could not achieve, since the material conditions for their achievement did not exist. The environment in which planning was introduced was a constraint on the building of socialism and on planning itself. Despite the quantitative and qualitative changes that have taken place in the society, the constraints mentioned in the Introduction continue to exert their influence. In these circumstances, the political leadership compelled the adoption of an ideology affirming the existence of a social system which did not really exist. In doing so, theoreticians of the spatial environment (from housing to regional planning) were placed in a position where they were encouraged to design for a society that lacked the material wherewithal to realise their conceptions.

Today, in the eyes of many Soviet writers, the major problems of the economy have been resolved ('the problem is no longer one of quantity but quality'). Millennial expectations have declined and the impulse to create a radically different 'communist' society, though not moribund, lies quiescent. The Soviet leadership may with justification be said to be 'coming to live in a present which they hope to improve substantially but which they do not expect to undergo basic structural changes'.[11]

It is recognised by Soviet and non-Soviet marxists alike that social change in the USSR is determined not only by its internal contradictions (for instance, the uneven development of different regions and sectors of the economy) but also by its relationship to other nation states.[12] Thus, the privatisation of social life (associated with the mass production of domestic gadgetry and of cars for private ownership) owes at least as much to similar social arrangements found in Western societies as to the positive functions privatisation might have for the Soviet state. Above all else though, the Soviet Union's external contradictions manifest themselves in the relationship between manufacturers in the USSR and those in other countries; all are drawn into the global economic arena and subjected, in varying degrees, to its competitive logic.

Thus, as a consequence of the 'working out' of internal and external contradictions, it would appear that the Soviet Union and industrialised capitalist societies are converging along a number of paths,[13] notably in domestic life, sex-role stereotyping, urban growth and environmental protection. A telling testimony to convergence is found in the importance attached by the USSR and the UK to economic growth as a means for improving the standard of living compared with a priority of diverting resources to preserving the environment. By 1975, one Soviet economist records, environmental protection had become an integral part of annual, 5–7 year and long-range plans and it had become generally accepted that 'our concern with man's well-being' would mean that expenditure on environmental protection would increase at a faster rate than overall investment in production.[14] But, because the increase in investment in pollution control and conservation measures 'substantially reduces the return on assets', Loiter warned that the fact that environmental issues could not have been resolved at an earlier period should not be used now to justify a movement to the other extreme, with the immediate setting up of standards of 'absolute purity'. Indeed, 'the priority accorded to social goals of environmental protection in a developed socialist society must not be allowed to impede growth and hence postpone the achievement of the equally important goal of improving the general standard of living'. This view may be compared with that of a former Permanent Secretary at the UK Ministry of Housing and Local Government who phrased the same observation slightly differently: 'Economic policy is crucial to the Department of the Environment's priorities and in itself constitutes *the* priority, since prosperity matters more to people than anything else and anyway is the condition for improving the environment'.[15]

Appendix *A*

TABLE A.1   *Urban housing stock by union republic (mln. m² of overall (useful) living spac (at end of year)*

	1960	1961	1962	1963	1964	1965	1966	1967	1968	19
USSR	958.0	1017.0	1074.0	1130.0	1182.0	1238.0	1290.0	1350.0	1410.0	146
RSFSR	570.8	606.2	641.2	673.8	703.2	736.5	769.1	803.3	838.2	87
Ukraine	203.7	215.0	226.3	237.8	248.1	258.9	269.4	280.8	292.8	30
Belorussia	24.4	26.1	27.7	29.3	30.8	32.4	34.3	36.5	38.7	4
Uzbekistan	23.7	24.9	26.0	27.2	28.5	29.4	28.3	30.8	32.6	3
Kazakhstan	36.3	39.1	42.1	45.4	48.6	51.5	53.9	56.9	60.0	6
Georgia	17.9	19.2	20.3	21.1	22.0	22.8	23.8	24.9	25.9	2
Azerbaidzhan	15.8	16.6	17.5	18.6	19.5	20.4	21.3	22.2	23.1	2
Lithuania	10.6	11.1	11.7	12.4	13.1	13.8	14.6	15.4	16.2	1
Moldavia	6.1	6.5	7.0	7.5	8.0	9.0	9.4	10.1	10.7	1
Latvia	15.0	15.7	16.2	16.7	17.3	17.8	18.4	19.0	19.6	2
Kirghizia	5.7	6.4	6.8	7.1	7.5	7.8	8.2	8.6	9.1	
Tadzhikstan	5.7	6.0	6.3	6.7	7.1	7.5	8.0	8.5	9.0	
Armenia	7.7	8.4	9.0	9.8	10.5	11.2	11.8	12.5	13.0	1
Turkmenia	6.5	6.9	7.2	7.6	7.9	8.4	8.8	9.3	9.7	
Estonia	8.1	8.6	9.1	9.5	9.9	10.2	10.6	10.9	11.3	1

SOURCES   *Narodnoe khozyaistvo SSSR v 1975g.*, p. 577.
            Narodnoe khozyaistvo SSSR v 1969g., p. 568.
            Narodnoe khozyaistvo SSSR v 1968g., p. 580.
            Narodnoe khozyaistvo SSSR v 1967g., p. 682.
            Narodnoe khozyaistvo SSSR v 1964g., p. 610.

970	1971	1972	1973	1974	1975	1976	1977	1978	1979	1980	1981
29.0	1594.0	1661.0	1730.0	1800.0	1867.0	1932.0	2001.0	2070.0	2134.0	2202.0	2270.0
11.2	949.4	988.3	1028.8	1069.3	1109.2	1146.0	1185.8	1225.2	1261.2	1291.2	1324.7
13.3	325.3	337.9	350.1	363.1	375.8	389.0	402.1	415.4	428.2	440.7	456.2
43.5	46.1	48.9	52.0	54.9	57.6	6.3	63.3	66.4	69.5	71.2	74.4
35.9	37.8	40.3	42.8	46.8	48.8	51.2	53.8	56.9	59.4	64.0	68.0
65.3	68.4	71.6	74.8	77.8	80.7	83.8	86.9	90.0	92.8	97.3	100.9
27.7	28.6	29.6	31.0	32.1	33.3	34.4	35.4	36.5	37.5	38.0	39.3
24.4	25.3	25.8	26.6	27.5	28.5	29.4	30.2	31.1	32.0	35.9	38.3
18.4	19.4	20.6	21.7	22.8	23.9	25.0	26.1	27.3	28.3	30.6	31.9
11.8	12.4	13.1	14.1	14.8	15.5	16.2	16.9	17.6	18.3	19.4	20.4
20.9	21.5	22.2	22.9	23.7	24.5	25.1	25.8	26.4	27.2	27.2	27.7
9.9	10.4	10.9	11.3	11.7	12.2	12.6	13.0	13.5	13.8	15.4	15.9
9.8	10.3	10.7	11.2	11.6	11.9	12.0	12.2	12.6	13.1	14.4	15.0
14.7	15.7	16.4	17.3	17.9	18.7	19.5	20.3	21.0	21.9	25.8	26.4
10.4	10.7	11.2	11.7	12.2	12.4	12.9	13.3	13.8	14.1	13.8	14.0
12.3	12.8	13.3	13.8	14.2	14.5	15.0	15.6	16.1	16.6	16.7	17.4

Narodnoe khozyaistvo SSSR v 1962g., p. 499.
Narodnoe khozyaistvo SSSR v 1978g., p. 398.
Narodnoe khozyaistvo SSSR v 1979g., p. 418.
Narodnoe khozyaistvo SSSR v 1922–1982gg., p. 431.

TABLE A.2   *Urban population by union republic in thousands (at beginning of y*

	1961	1962	1963	1964	1965	1966	1967	1968	1969	19
USSR	108 273	111 884	115 088	118 531	121 673	123 751	126 900	130 935	134 177	135
RSFSR	66 195	68 207	70 039	71 974	73 559	74 698	76 744	78 113	79 738	80
Ukraine	20 823	21 334	21 859	22 495	23 093	23 358	24 330	24 951	25 612	25
Belorussia	2777	2911	3037	3146	3270	3403	3547	3692	3848	
Uzbekistan	3047	3185	3360	3476	3603	3741	3864	4054	4217	4
Kazakhstan	4622	4883	5096	5313	5576	5665	6022	6254	6479	6
Georgia	1818	1919	1968	2018	2085	2140	2201	2238	2292	2
Azerbaidzhan	1958	2031	2104	2186	2265	2309	2422	2486	2546	2
Lithuania	1123	1166	1203	1245	1289	1343	1381	1431	1486	1
Moldavia	727	752	783	819	858	949	986	1031	1077	1
Latvia	1233	1273	1303	1337	1367	1400	1428	1453	1484	1
Kirghizia	775	859	894	936	972	1020	1060	1102	1148	1
Tadzhikstan	723	756	778	820	865	921	970	1018	1049	1
Armenia	973	1030	1069	1124	1175	1209	1250	1288	1333	1
Turkmenia	771	807	844	874	908	924	970	995	1025	1
Estonia	706	731	751	768	788	804	816	830	844	

SOURCES   *Narodnoe khozyaistvo SSSR v 1922–1972gg.*, pp. 13–18.
Narodnoe khozyaistvo SSSR v 1959g., p. 10.
Narodnoe khozyaistvo SSSR v 1960g., p. 10.
Narodnoe khozyaistvo SSSR v 1961g., p. 10.
Narodnoe khozyaistvo SSSR v 1962g., p. 10.
Narodnoe khozyaistvo SSSR v 1963g., p. 10.
Narodnoe khozyaistvo SSSR v 1964g., p. 10.
Narodnoe khozyaistvo SSSR v 1967g., p. 10.
Narodnoe khozyaistvo SSSR v 1968g., p. 10.
Narodnoe khozyaistvo SSSR v 1969g., p. 10.
Narodnoe khozyaistvo SSSR v 1970g., p. 10.

*71	1972	1973	1974	1975	1976	1977	1978	1979	1980	1981	1982
023	142 541	146 099	149 589	153 100	156 590	159 593	162 492	163 586	166 210	168 919	171 731
576	84 406	86 297	88 231	90 172	92 101	93 715	95 275	95 374	96 796	98 153	99 569
282	26 993	27 633	28 195	28 751	29 341	29 844	30 349	30 512	30 972	31 423	31 850
054	4209	4378	4549	4715	4868	5012	5161	5263	5398	5550	5703
487	4599	4826	5030	5259	5484	5712	5914	6348	6500	6706	6955
685	6942	7151	7348	7550	7706	7880	8031	7920	8070	8267	8479
278	2322	2357	2398	2447	2507	2541	2572	2601	2629	2659	2694
624	2691	2752	2821	2879	2943	3007	3062	3200	3254	3313	3373
627	1686	1744	1796	1849	1903	1952	1968	2062	2106	2156	2207
172	1224	1289	1332	1379	1433	1474	1520	1551	1586	1635	1678
503	1530	1556	1584	1623	1650	1673	1700	1726	1745	1762	1781
131	1164	1195	1228	1261	1312	1344	1366	1366	1389	1418	1453
113	1165	1203	1242	1280	1300	1301	1301	1325	1349	1376	1405
527	1589	1644	1699	1754	1806	1859	1909	1993	2029	2069	2113
063	1101	1137	1182	1223	1254	1284	1322	1323	1354	1384	1411
901	920	937	954	968	982	995	1012	1022	1033	1047	1060

Narodnoe khozyaistvo SSSR v 1971g., p. 10.
Narodnoe khozyaistvo SSSR v 1972g., p. 10.
Narodnoe khozyaistvo SSSR v 1973g., p. 10.
Narodnoe khozyaistvo SSSR v 1974g., p. 10.
Narodnoe khozyaistvo SSSR v 1975g., p. 10.
Narodnoe khozyaistvo SSSR v 1977g., p. 11.
Narodnoe khozyaistvo SSSR v 1979g., p. 11.
Narodnoe khozyaistvo SSSR za 60 let, p. 43.
Narodnoe khozyaistvo SSSR v 1980g., p. 11.
Narodnoe khozyaistvo SSSR v 1922–72gg., p. 13.

TABLE A.3   *Per capita overall (useful) living space in urban areas by repub*
(beginning of year) (square metres)

	1961	1962	1963	1964	1965	1966	1967	1968	1969	197
USSR	8.8	9.1	9.3	9.5	9.7	10.0	10.2	10.3	10.5	10.
RSFSR	8.6	8.9	9.2	9.4	9.6	9.9	10.0	10.3	10.5	10.
Ukraine	9.8	10.1	10.4	10.6	10.7	11.1	11.1	11.3	11.4	11.
Belorussia	8.8	99.0	9.1	9.3	9.4	9.5	9.7	9.9	10.1	10.
Uzbekistan	7.8	7.8	7.7	7.8	7.9	7.9	7.3	7.6	7.7	7.
Kazakhstan	7.9	8.0	8.3	8.5	8.7	9.1	9.0	9.1	9.3	9.
Georgia	9.8	10.0	10.3	10.4	10.6	11.0	10.8	11.1	11.3	11.
Azerbiadzhan	8.1	8.2	8.3	8.5	8.6	8.9	8.8	8.9	9.1	9.
Lithuania	9.4	9.5	9.7	10.0	10.2	10.3	10.6	10.8	10.9	11.
Moldavia	8.4	8.6	8.9	9.2	9.3	9.5	9.5	9.8	9.9	9.
Latvia	12.2	12.3	12.4	12.5	12.7	13.0	12.9	13.1	13.2	13.
Kirghizia	7.4	7.5	7.6	7.6	7.7	8.1	7.7	7.8	7.9	8.
Tadzhikstan	7.9	7.9	8.1	8.2	8.2	8.1	8.2	8.3	8.6	8.
Armenia	7.9	8.2	8.4	8.7	8.9	8.9	9.4	9.7	9.8	9
Turkmenia	8.4	8.6	8.5	8.7	8.7	9.1	9.1	9.3	9.5	9.
Estonia	11.5	11.8	12.1	12.4	12.6	12.5	13.0	13.1	13.4	13.

SOURCE   Derived from Tables A.1 and A.2.

971	1972	1973	1974	1975	1976	1977	1978	1979	1980	1981	1982
1.0	11.2	11.4	11.6	11.8	11.9	12.1	12.3	12.7	12.8	13.0	13.2
1.0	11.2	11.5	11.7	11.9	12.0	12.2	12.4	12.8	13.0	13.1	13.3
1.9	12.5	12.3	12.4	12.6	12.8	13.0	13.2	13.6	13.8	14.0	14.3
0.7	11.0	11.2	11.4	11.6	11.8	12.0	12.3	12.6	12.8	12.8	13.0
8.1	8.2	8.4	8.5	8.9	8.9	9.0	9.1	9.0	9.1	9.5	9.8
9.7	9.9	10.0	10.2	10.3	10.5	10.6	10.8	11.3	11.5	11.8	11.9
2.1	12.3	12.6	12.9	13.1	13.3	13.5	13.8	14.0	14.3	14.3	14.6
9.3	9.4	9.4	9.4	9.5	9.7	9.8	9.9	9.7	9.8	10.8	11.4
1.3	11.5	11.8	12.1	12.3	12.6	12.8	13.2	13.2	13.4	14.1	14.5
0.1	10.1	10.2	10.6	10.7	10.8	11.0	11.1	11.3	11.5	11.9	12.2
3.9	14.1	14.3	14.5	14.6	14.8	15.0	15.1	15.2	15.6	15.4	15.6
8.8	8.9	9.1	9.3	9.3	9.3	9.4	9.5	9.9	9.9	10.9	10.9
8.8	8.8	8.9	9.0	9.1	9.2	9.2	9.2	9.5	9.7	10.5	10.7
9.6	9.9	10.0	10.2	10.2	10.4	10.5	10.6	10.5	10.8	12.5	12.5
9.8	9.7	9.9	9.9	10.0	9.9	10.0	10.1	10.4	10.4	10.0	9.9
3.7	13.9	14.2	14.7	14.7	14.8	15.1	15.4	15.7	16.0	16.0	16.4

TABLE A.4   *Absolute size of the socialised and private housing sectors in urban areas by ur‹ republic, 1960–81 (end of year) (mln. m^2 of overall (useful) dwelling space)*

Republic	Sector	1960	1965	1966	1967	1968	1969	197
USSR	Socialised	583	806	854	906	959	1014	1072
	Private	375	432	436	444	451	455	457
RSFSR	Socialised	385.4	526.7	557.2	589.3	622.5	657.6	694
	Private	185.4	209.8	211.9	214.0	215.7	216.3	217
Ukraine	Socialised	101.9	138.5	146.5	154.8	163.4	172.8	181
	Private	101.8	120.4	122.9	126.0	129.4	131.5	131
Belorussia	Socialised	12.7	18.9	20.5	22.3	24.2	26.3	28
	Private	11.7	13.5	13.8	14.2	14.5	14.7	1!
Uzbekistan	Socialised	8.6	13.5	13.8	16.0	17.6	19.1	2‹
	Private	15.1	16.1	14.5	14.8	15.0	15.3	1!
Kazakhstan	Socialised	17.9	29.7	32.0	34.7	37.4	39.7	4:
	Private	18.4	21.6	21.9	22.2	22.6	22.5	2:
Georgia	Socialised	8.2	11.2	11.8	12.5	13.2	13.8	1‹
	Private	9.7	11.6	12.0	12.4	12.7	12.9	1:
Azerbaidzhan	Socialised	9.8	13.5	14.2	14.9	15.6	16.1	1‹
	Private	6.0	6.9	7.1	7.3	7.5	7.6	
Lithuania	Socialised	6.6	9.2	9.9	10.6	11.3	12.2	1:
	Private	4.0	4.6	4.7	4.8	4.9	5.1	
Moldavia	Socialised	2.8	4.6	4.9	5.4	5.9	6.3	‹
	Private	3.3	4.4	4.5	4.7	4.8	4.8	‹
Latvia	Socialised	11.3	13.5	14.0	14.6	15.1	15.7	1‹
	Private	3.7	4.3	4.4	4.4	4.5	4.6	‹
Kirghizia	Socialised	2.4	3.8	4.2	4.5	4.9	5.2	!
	Private	3.3	4.0	4.0	4.1	4.2	4.3	‹
Tadzhikstan	Socialised	2.7	4.3	4.6	5.1	5.5	5.8	‹
	Private	3.0	3.2	3.4	3.4	3.5	3.6	:
Armenia	Socialised	3.1	6.0	6.5	7.2	7.7	8.4	‹
	Private	4.6	5.2	5.3	5.3	5.3	5.5	‹
Turkmenia	Socialised	3.5	5.2	5.6	6.0	6.3	6.6	‹
	Private	3.0	3.2	3.2	3.3	3.4	3.3	‹
Estonia	Socialised	6.1	7.5	7.8	8.1	8.5	8.9	‹
	Private	2.0	2.7	2.8	2.8	2.8	2.9	

Note: The statistical handbook published in 1982 (*Narodnoe khozyaistvo SS‹ 1922–1982*) raised many of the figures given in earlier handbooks on size of the urban housing stock and the relative contributions of socialised and private sectors for the years 1970, 1975 and 1980, while figures for 1965 remained the same.

In the tables calculated here, I have preserved the earlier series fr 1960 to 1979 and given the latest (1982) estimates for 1980 and 1981.

SOURCES   *Narodnoe khozyaistvo SSSR v 1968g.*, p. 580; *Narodnoe khozyaistvo SSS‹ 1969, p. 569.*
Narodnoe khozyaistvo SSSR v 1975g., p. 577; *Narodnoe Khozyaistro SS‹ 1922–1982gg.*, p. 432.
Narodnoe Khozyaistvo SSSR v 1979g., p. 419.

1971	1972	1973	1974	1975	1976	1977	1978	1979	1980	1981
132	1193	1257	1322	1385	1446	1510	1574	1634	1655	1715
462	468	473	478	482	486	491	496	500	547	555
731.5	770.0	809.6	849.7	889.4	926.5	966.4	1005.6	1041.7	1047.3	1081.3
217.9	218.3	219.2	219.6	219.8	219.5	219.4	219.6	219.5	243.9	243.4
190.9	201.1	211.1	221.5	231.6	242.1	252.8	263.3	273.6	283.4	295.0
134.4	136.8	139.0	141.6	144.2	146.9	149.3	152.1	154.6	157.3	161.2
30.9	33.5	36.3	38.9	41.4	43.8	46.7	49.5	52.4	54.2	57.1
15.2	15.4	15.7	16.0	16.2	16.5	16.6	16.9	17.1	17.0	17.3
22.3	24.3	26.1	29.5	31.2	33.0	35.0	37.0	38.9	38.7	40.7
15.5	16.0	16.7	17.3	17.6	18.2	18.8	19.9	20.5	25.3	27.3
45.1	47.9	51.0	53.7	56.5	59.5	62.5	65.5	68.3	69.3	72.5
23.3	23.7	23.8	24.1	24.2	24.3	24.4	24.5	24.5	28.0	28.4
15.3	16.0	17.1	18.0	19.0	19.9	20.8	21.7	22.6	21.6	22.5
13.3	13.6	13.9	14.1	14.3	14.5	14.6	14.8	16.4	16.4	16.8
17.5	17.9	18.5	19.3	20.1	20.9	21.5	22.3	23.1	22.9	23.9
7.8	7.9	8.1	8.2	8.4	8.5	8.7	8.8	8.9	13.0	14.4
14.1	15.1	16.1	17.0	18.0	18.9	19.9	20.9	21.7	23.5	24.6
5.3	5.5	5.6	5.8	5.9	6.1	6.2	6.4	6.6	7.1	7.3
7.4	8.0	8.7	9.4	9.9	10.5	11.1	11.7	12.3	13.2	14.2
5.0	5.1	5.4	5.4	5.6	5.7	5.8	5.9	6.0	6.2	6.2
16.8	17.5	18.2	18.9	19.5	20.1	20.7	21.3	22.0	22.6	23.0
4.7	4.7	4.7	4.8	5.0	5.0	5.1	5.1	5.2	4.6	4.7
6.0	6.4	6.7	7.1	7.4	7.7	8.0	8.4	8.7	8.4	9.0
4.4	4.5	4.6	4.6	4.8	4.9	5.0	5.1	5.1	7.0	6.9
6,7	7.0	7.5	7.9	8.2	8.4	8.5	9.0	9.4	9.6	10.2
3.6	3.7	3.7	3.7	3.7	3.6	3.7	3.6	3.7	4.8	4.8
10.1	10.7	11.5	12.2	13.0	13.8	14.6	15.3	16.1	17.1	17.6
5.6	5.7	5.8	5.7	5.7	5.7	5.7	5.7	5.8	8.7	8.8
7.3	7.7	8.1	8.5	8.8	9.2	9.6	10.0	10.2	9.7	9.8
3.4	3.5	3.6	3.7	3.6	3.7	3.7	3.8	3.9	4.1	4.2
9.8	10.2	10.6	11.0	11.3	11.7	12.2	12.7	13.1	13.3	14.0
3.0	3.1	3.2	3.2	3.2	3.3	3.4	3.4	3.5	3.4	3.4

TABLE A.5   *Proportion of the urban housing stock socialised and private by union republic (%)*

Republic	Sector	1960	1965	1966	1967	1968	1969	1
USSR	Socialised	60.9	65.1	66.2	67.1	68.0	69.0	7
	Private	39.1	34.9	33.8	32.9	32.0	31.0	2
RSFSR	Socialised	67.5	71.5	72.4	73.4	74.3	75.2	7
	Private	32.5	28.5	27.6	26.6	25.7	24.8	2
Ukraine	Socialised	50.0	53.5	54.4	55.1	55.8	56.8	5
	Private	50.0	46.5	45.6	44.9	44.2	43.2	4
Belorussia	Socialised	52.0	58.3	59.8	61.1	62.5	64.1	6
	Private	48.0	41.7	40.2	38.9	37.5	35.9	3
Uzbekistan	Socialised	36.3	45.6	48.8	51.9	54.0	55.5	5
	Private	63.7	54.4	51.2	48.1	46.0	44.5	4
Kazakhstan	Socialised	49.3	57.9	59.4	61.0	62.3	63.8	6
	Private	50.7	42.1	40.6	39.0	37.7	36.2	3
Georgia	Socialised	45.8	49.1	49.6	50.2	51.0	51.7	5
	Private	54.2	50.9	50.4	49.8	49.0	48.3	4
Azerbaidzhan	Socialised	62.0	66.2	66.7	67.1	67.5	67.9	6
	Private	38.0	33.8	33.3	32.9	32.5	32.1	3
Lithuania	Socialised	62.3	66.7	67.8	68.8	69.8	70.5	7
	Private	37.7	33.3	32.2	31.2	30.2	29.5	2
Moldavia	Socialised	45.9	51.1	52.1	53.5	55.1	56.8	5
	Private	54.1	48.9	47.9	46.5	44.9	43.2	4
Latvia	Socialised	75.3	75.8	76.1	76.8	77.0	77.3	7
	Private	24.7	24.1	23.9	23.2	23.0	22.7	2
Kirghizia	Socialised	42.1	48.7	48.8	52.3	53.8	54.7	5
	Private	57.9	51.3	51.2	47.7	46.2	45.3	4
Tadzhikstan	Socialised	47.4	57.3	57.4	60.0	61.1	61.7	6
	Private	52.6	42.7	42.5	40.0	38.2	38.3	3
Armenia	Socialised	40.3	53.6	55.1	57.6	59.2	60.4	6
	Private	59.7	46.4	44.9	42.4	40.8	39.6	3
Turkmenia	Socialised	53.8	61.9	63.6	64.5	64.9	66.7	6
	Private	46.2	38.1	36.4	35.5	35.1	33.3	3
Estonia	Socialised	75.3	73.5	73.6	74.3	75.2	75.4	7
	Private	24.7	26.5	26.4	25.7	24.8	24.6	2

SOURCE   Derived from Table A.4.

1971	1972	1973	1974	1975	1976	1977	1978	1979	1980	1981
71.0	71.8	72.7	73.4	74.2	74.8	75.5	76.0	76.6	75.2	75.6
29.0	28.2	27.3	26.6	25.8	25.2	24.5	24.0	23.4	24.8	24.4
77.1	77.9	78.7	79.5	80.2	80.8	81.5	82.1	82.6	81.1	81.6
23.0	22.1	21.3	20.5	19.8	19.2	18.5	17.9	17.4	18.9	18.4
58.7	59.5	60.3	61.0	61.6	62.2	62.9	63.4	63.9	64.3	64.7
41.3	40.5	39.7	39.0	38.4	37.8	37.1	36.6	36.1	35.7	35.3
67.0	68.5	69.8	70.9	71.9	72.6	73.8	74.5	75.4	76.1	76.7
33.0	31.5	30.2	29.1	28.1	27.4	26.2	25.5	24.6	23.9	23.3
59.0	60.3	61.0	63.0	63.9	64.4	65.0	65.0	65.5	60.5	60.0
41.0	39.7	39.0	37.0	36.1	35.6	35.0	35.0	34.5	39.5	40.0
65.9	66.9	68.2	69.0	70.0	71.0	71.9	72.8	73.6	71.2	71.9
34.1	33.1	31.8	31.0	30.0	29.0	28.1	27.2	26.4	28.8	28.1
53.5	54.1	55.2	56.1	57.1	57.8	58.8	59.5	60.3	56.9	57.3
46.5	45.9	44.8	43.9	42.9	42.2	41.2	40.5	39.7	43.1	42.7
69.2	69.4	69.6	70.2	70.5	71.0	71.2	71.7	72.2	63.4	62.4
30.8	30.6	30.5	29.8	29.5	29.0	28.8	28.3	27.8	36.6	37.6
72.7	73.3	74.2	74.6	75.3	75.6	76.2	76.6	76.7	76.8	77.1
27.3	26.7	25.8	25.4	24.7	24.4	23.8	23.4	23.3	23.2	22.9
59.7	61.1	61.7	63.5	63.9	64.8	65.7	66.5	67.2	68.0	69.6
40.3	38.9	38.3	36.5	36.1	35.2	34.3	33.5	32.7	32.0	30.4
78.1	78.8	79.5	79.8	79.6	80.1	80.2	80.7	80.9	83.1	83.0
21.9	21.2	20.5	20.3	20.4	19.9	19.8	19.3	19.1	16.9	17.0
57.7	58.7	59.3	60.7	60.7	61.1	61.5	62.2	63.0	54.5	56.6
42.3	41.3	40.7	39.3	39.3	38.9	38.5	37.8	37.0	45.5	43.4
65.1	65.4	67.0	68.1	68.9	70.0	69.7	71.4	71.8	67.7	68.0
35.0	34.6	33.0	31.9	31.1	30.0	30.3	28.6	28.2	32.3	32.0
64.3	65.2	66.5	68.2	69.5	70.8	71.9	72.9	73.5	66.3	66.7
35.7	34.8	33.5	31.8	30.5	29.2	28.1	27.1	26.5	33.7	33.3
68.2	68.8	69.2	69.7	71.0	71.3	72.2	72.5	72.3	70.3	70.0
31.8	31.3	30.8	30.3	29.0	28.7	27.8	27.5	27.7	29.7	30.0
76.6	76.7	76.8	77.5	77.9	78.0	78.2	78.9	78.9	79.6	80.5
23.4	23.3	23.2	22.5	22.1	22.0	21.8	21.1	21.1	20.4	19.5

Notes and References

PREFACE

1. I. Berlin, *Four Essays on Liberty* (Oxford University Press, 1969); E. H. Carr, *What is History* (London, Macmillan, 1961); E. H. Carr, *1917: Before and After* (London, Macmillan, 1969).
2. E. H. Carr, *The Soviet Impact on the Western World* (London, Macmillan, 1946); E. H. Carr, 'The Russian Revolution and the West', *New Left Review*, no. 111, 1978.
3. F. A. Hayek, *Law, Legislation and Liberty*, vol. I (London, Routledge & Kegan Paul, 1973), p. 12.
4. See: V. M. Perez-Diaz, *State, Bureaucracy and Civil Society: A Critical Discussion of the Political Theory of Karl Marx* (London, Macmillan, 1978).
5. W. Taubman, *Governing Soviet Cities* (London, Praeger, 1973), p. 18.
6. Ibid., p. 28.
7. *Materialy XXVI S"yezda KPSS* (Moscow, 1981), p. 50.
8. J. S. Adams, *Citizen Inspectors in the Soviet Union. The People's Control Committee* (London, Praeger, 1977).
9. *Materialy....* (1981).

INTRODUCTION

1. K. Marx and F. Engels, *The German Ideology* (London, Lawrence & Wishart, 1965), p. 39.
2. *Programma Kommunisticheskoi Partii Sovetskogo Soyuza* (Moscow, 1961), pp. 94–5.
3. *Materialy XXVI S"yezda KPSS* (Moscow, 1981), pp. 106, 181; *Osnovnye napravleniya razvitiya narodnogo khozyaistva SSSR na 1976–1980 gody* (Moscow, 1976), pp. 9, 72.
4. A. N. Kosygin, *Direktivy XXIV S"yezda KPSS po pyatiletnemu planu razvitiya narodnogo khozyaistva SSSR na 1971–75* (Moscow, 1972), pp. 10, 68.
5. *Materialy....* (1981), p. 60.
6. V. Vorontsov, *Sud'by kapitalizma v Rossii*, spb. (1882), p. 13.
7. K. Marx, *Capital*, vol. 1 (Moscow, 1965), p. 10.
8. Lest there be some misunderstanding, it should be made quite clear that the Marxist notion of objective historical laws is in no way teleological, as it is in the Hegelian system, for it does not imply a purpose or end to

which history is moving; there is no metaphysical or spiritual Reason underlying the process. These laws operate within the institutional framework which men have constructed in interaction with the prevailing natural and historical conditions. Thus, development proceeds through the actions of men who can choose between different alternatives. According to Soviet Marxism, 'a law is an essential and necessary, general and recurrent connection among the phenomena of the material world, which brings about a definite course of events.... Dialectical materialism proceeds from the recognition of the objective character of laws. This means that man is unable to make or change laws at will, he can only cognise, reflect them ... The objectivity of laws also implies that they operate independently of the will and desires of man and therefore any attempt to act contrary to the laws is foredoomed ... Nevertheless dialectical materialism opposes the idealist conception of laws and rejects fatalism i.e. the blind worship of laws, disbelief in the power of human reason and the ability of man to cognise laws and make use of them'. (V. A. Afanasyev, *Marxist Philosophy*, Moscow, Progress, 1965), p. 90.

The determination of these laws is itself a major problematic for Soviet Marxists; their occurrence, discovery and utilisation are not entirely the direct function of the internal development of the Soviet social structure. They have to be understood in terms of the interaction (dialectic) between Soviet and Western society. As Marcuse points out: 'Even the most cursory survey of Soviet Marxism is confronted with the fact that at almost every turn in its development Soviet theory (and Soviet policy) reacts to a corresponding Western development and vice versa'. (H. Marcuse, *Soviet Marxism*, London, Pelican Books, 1971, p. 12). Thus, any answer to the question posed above, involving as it does an assessment of alternative paths of housing and urban development, has to bear in mind the historical dynamic (the East–West dialectic) to which the leadership is subjected.

9. V. I. Lenin, *Polnoe sobranie sochinenii*, 5th edn (Moscow, 1962), vol. 23, p. 341; vol. 5, p. 151.

10. A. A. Nesterenko, *Zakonomernosti sotsial'no-ekonomicheskogo razvitiya gorodov i derevne i* (Kiev, 1975), p. 7.

Lenin on more than one occasion remarked on the leading socio-political role of cities – not only as the scenario for revolutionary activity, but also in connection with the spiritual development of the worker, his class consciousness and political maturity. It provided an environment for stimulating changes in the consciousness and psychology of rural migrants to the city. (O. N. Yanitskii, *Gorod, urbanizatsiya, chelovek. Kritika burzhuaznoi sotsiologii* Moscow, 1974), p. 5.

In contemporary Soviet writing on urban studies, the city tends to be referred to in the language of an organic or mechanistic metaphor. At the heart of such descriptions is the terminology of cyberneticians – itself a product of the communications revolution. For instance, 'The modern town resembles a powerful generator, transformer and accumulator of an enormous amount of varied information, the effective use of which depends on the improvement of urban structures. The search for the optimum-sized city must consider the social information aspect.' (L. B.

Kogan, V. I. Lotkev, 'Nekotorye sotsiologicheskie aspekty mod-elirovaniya gorodov', *Voprosy filosofii* no. 9, 1964), pp. 131–9.

11. Marx's ambivalence is most evident in his correspondence with Vera Zasulich in which he commented: 'The dualism within the commune permits an alternative: either the property element in it will overcome the collective element or the other way round. Everything depends on the historical environment in which it occurs'. See E. J. Hobsbawm (ed.) *Karl Marx: Pre-Capitalist Economic Formations* (London, Lawrence and Wishart, 1964), p. 145. In a similar vein, Marx wrote in the Preface to the Second Russian edition of the Communist Manifesto: 'If the Russian Revolution becomes the signal for a proletarian revolution in the West, so that both complement each other, the present Russian common ownership of land may serve as the starting point for a communist development'. (K. Marx and F. Engels, *Selected Works*, vol. 1, Moscow, 1962, p. 24).

12. As Lenin put it: 'The city inevitably leads the village. The village inevitably follows behind the city'. (Lenin, *op. cit.*, 1962, vol. 40, p. 5).

1 HISTORICAL BACKGROUND AND OVERVIEW

1. B. Ts. Urlanis, *Rost naseleniya v SSSR*, Moscow, 1966 pp. 23–27. Of 630 settlements officially defined as towns in 1811, 113 had fewer than 1000 inhabitants (K. Arsenyev, *Nachertanie statistiki Rossiskogo gosudarstva*, Spb., 1818), pp. 69–92.

2. *Narodnoe khozyaistvo SSSR, 1922–72* (Moscow, 1972).

3. J. Bater, *St. Petersburg. Industrialisation and Change* (London, Edward Arnold, 1976).

4. A. Weber, *The Growth of Cities in the 19th Century* (New York, 1899), pp. 43, 144; H. Perkin, *The Origins of Modern English Society, 1780–1880* (London, Routledge & Kegan Paul, 1969), p. 117.

5. A. Leroy-Beaulieu, *The Empire of the Tsars and Russians* (London, 1893), vol. I, p. 323.

6. *Goroda Rossii v 1910 gody. Statisticheskii sbornik* (Petersburg, 1914).

7. M. L. Tengborsky, *Commentaries on the Productive Forces of Russia* (London, 1855), vol. I, p. 102.

8. V. I. Lenin, *The Development of Capitalism in Russia* (Moscow, 1967), pp. 526–30.

9. N. P. Kozerenko, *Zhilishchnyi krizis i bor'ba s nim* (Moscow, 1928), p. 34.

10. Ibid. pp. 88–9.

11. Ibid. pp. 92–7.

12. D. L. Broner *et al. Ekonomika i statistika zhilishchnogo i kommun-al'nogo khozyaistva* (Moscow, 1972), p. 34.

13. E. Gauldie, *Cruel Habitations: A History of Working Class Housing 1780–1918* (London, George Allen and Unwin, 1974), p. 66.

14. V. Shmidt, *Rabochii klass SSSR i zhilishchnyi vopros* (Moscow, 1929), p. 11; see also, S. G. Strumilin, *Izbrannye proizvedeniya v pyati tomakh* vol. 3 (Moscow, 1964), pp. 356–8.

15. Kozerenko, *op. cit.* p. 33.
16. D. Broner, *Zhilishchnoe stroitel'stvo i demograficheskie protsessy* (Moscow, 1980), p. 7.
17. D. Broner *et al.* (1972), *op cit.* p. 35; D. L. Broner, *Zhilishchnyi vopros i statistika* (Moscow, 1966), p. 9. See footnote on p. 20.
18. Shmidt, *op. cit.* pp. 13–14.
19. Kozerenko, *op. cit.* p. 92.
20. D. L. Broner *et al.* (1972), *op. cit.* p. 15; A. I. Stanislavskii, *Planirovka i zastroika gorodov Ukraina* (Kiev, 1971), p. 82.
21. N. Astrov, 'The Effects of the War Upon Russian Municipal Government and the All-Russian Union of Towns', in P. Gronsky and N. Astrov, *The War and the Russian Government* (New Haven, Yale University Press, 1929), p. 132.
22. P. Miliukov, *History of Russia*, vol. 3, Reforms, Reactions and Revolutions (New York, Funk & Wagnalls, 1969), p. 31.
23. G. I. Schneyder, 'Gorod i gorodovoe polozhenie, 1870,' in *Istoriya Rossii v XIX veke*, vol. 4, Spb., n.d. pp. 1–29; W. Hanchett, 'Tsarist Statutory Regulation of Municipal Government in the 19th Century', in M. Hamm (ed.) *The City in Russian History* (University of Kentucky Press, 1976), pp. 91–114; N. Astrov, *op. cit.* p. 135.
24. G. I. Schneyder, 'Gorodskaya kontr-reforma 11th iyuna 1892', in *Istoriya . . . op. cit.* vol. 5, pp. 181–228; N. Astrov, *op. cit.* p. 134.
25. N. Astrov, Ibid.; J. Bater, *op. cit.* p. 357; W. Hanchett, *op. cit.* p. 111; D. Brower, 'Urban Russia on the Eve of World War One: A Social Profile', *Journal of Social History*, vol. 13, no. 3, Spring 1980.
26. *Sobranie Uzakonenii*, 1917, I, 2, No. 819 ('Temporary Statute on Municipal Administration') in R. Browder and A. Kerensky (Eds) *The Russian Provisional Government, 1917*, vol. I (Stanford University Press, 1961), p. 277.
27. For a recent and most important study of this question, see: T. Emmons and W. Vucinich (eds) *The Zemstvo in Russia: An Experiment in Local Self Government* (Cambridge University Press, 1982).
28. H. Cox, *Cities: The Public Dimension* (Harmondsworth, Penguin, 1976), p. 49.
29. International Labour Office, *European Housing Problems Since the War, Studies and Reports*, Series G., Housing and Welfare, (Geneva, 1924), pp. 452–453. It is instructive to note that the first rent control Act in the UK was also passed in 1915 (Rent Restriction Act). (See the Report of the Royal Commission on the Housing of the Industrial Population of Scotland, 1917–1918, Cmnd. 8731) Similarly in the USA rent controls were first imposed as a result of housing shortages during the First World War. M. R. Lett, *Rent Control Concepts, Realities and Mechanisms* (The State University, New Jersey, 1976), p. 1.
30. *European Housing Problems Since the War, op. cit.* p. 449.
31. R. Browder and A. Kerensky (eds) *op. cit.* p. 278.
32. Decree of the Second All-Russian Congress of Soviets, 26 October 1917, 'O zemle', *SU RSFSR*, 1917, no. 1, art. 3. See also: Decree of VTsIK, 29 December 1917, 'O zapreshchenii sdelok s nedvizhim-

ost'yu', *SU RSFSR*, 1917, no. 10, art. 154.

33. Decree of VTsIK, 20 August 1918, 'Ob otmene prava chastnoi sobstvennosti na nedvizhimosti v gorodakh', *SU RSFSR*, 1918, no. 62, art. 674. See also: 'Tezisy zakona o konfiskatsii domov s sdavaemymi v naem kvartirami', (20 November 1917) in V. Lenin, *Polnoe sobranie sochinenii*, 5th edn, vol. 35 (1962), p. 108; vol. 34, p. 314; I. P. Prokopchenko, *Zhilishchnoe i zhilishchno-stroitel'noe zakonodatel'stvo* (Moscow, 1977), p. 19.

34. *Leninskii sbornik*, vol. 21, 1933, p. 104.

35. Postanovlenie NKVD, 30 October 1917, 'O pravakh gorodskikh samoupravlenii v dele regulirovaniya zhilishchnogo voprosa', *SU RSFSR*, 1917, no. 1. art. 14. See also: D. Broner, 'Zhilishchnaya problema v trudakh i gosudarstvennoi deyatel'nosti V. I. Lenina', *Vestnik statistika*, no. 3, (1970), pp. 3–12.

36. *KPSS v resolyutsiyakh s"ezdov, konferentsii i plenumov TsK*, part 1 (Moscow, 1953), pp. 427–28.

37. Ibid.

38. N. Bukharin, E. Preobrazhensky, *The ABC of Communism*, E. H. Carr (ed.), (Harmondsworth, Penguin, 1969), p. 402 (First published *AZBUKA Kommunizma*, Peterburg, 1920).
For detailed references covering the period 1917–1920 on housing legislation and the housing stock in different regions, see the bibliographical guide: E. V. Bazhanova (Sostav) *Narodnoe khozyaistvo SSSR v 1917–1920* (Moscow, 1967), pp. 484–85.

39. Kozerenko, *op. cit.* pp. 258–261.

40. In 1919, the Commissariat for Health (*Narkomzdrav*) set the minimum space requirement at 8.25 m² of actual dwelling space per person and 30 cubic metres of air space for each adult and 20 cubic metres for children under 14 years of age. As from 1926 the minimum dwelling area norm was raised to 9 m², which is still used as the basis for allocating accommodation in most of the country's fifteen republics. (See: D. Broner (1980), *op. cit.* p. 23).

41. Postanovlenie NKVD, 30 October 1917, 'O zhilishchnom moratorii', *SU RSFSR* (1917), no. 1, art. 13.

42. Dekret SNK, 10 July 1919, 'O kvartirnoi pribavke k zarabotke rabochikh i sluzhashchikh v gorodakh Moskve i Petrograde i o zapreshchenii povysheniya platy za zhilye pomeshcheniya', *SU RSFSR* (1919), no. 35, art. 351.

43. Dekret SNK, 27 January 1921, 'Ob otmene vzivaniya platy za zhilye pomescheniya s rabochikh i sluzhashchikh . . .' *SU RSFSR* (1921), no. 6, art. 47.

44. Dekret SNK, 20 April 1922, 'Ob oplate za pol'zovanie zhilymi pomeshcheniyami', *SU RSFSR* (1922), no. 30, art. 349.

45. Postanovlenie SNK, 23 May 1921, 'O merakh uluchcheniya zhilishchnykh uslovii trudyashchegosya naseleniya i o merakh bor'by a razrusheniem zhilishch', *SU RSFSR* (1921), no. 49, art. 253.

46. Dekret SNK, 18 July 1921, 'O privlechenii naseleniya k remontu vodoprovoda, kanalizatsii, gazovogo i tsentral'nogo otopleniya v munit-

sipalizirovannykh domakh', *SU RSFSR* (1921), no. 56, art. 355.

47. N. Kozerenko, *op. cit.* p. 262.
48. V. Shmidt, *op. cit.* p. 15. By 1919 in Omsk, over 7000 people (about 10 per cent of the city's population) were living in dugouts; 40 per cent of these had less than 1 square metre of living space per person. *Narodnoe khozyaistvo Omskoi oblasti*, (Omsk, 1969), p. 158.
49. The standard unit of account for calculating housing (standards) in the USSR is the amount of 'overall (useful) living space' (*obshchaya (poleznaya) ploshchad' zhilishch*) in square metres. This includes living rooms, bedrooms, kitchens, corridors and bathrooms. To calculate actual 'dwelling area' (*zhilaya ploshchad'*) i.e. just living- and bed-rooms, the larger figure is multiplied by a factor of 0.7. Following Soviet practice, the figures cited in this book refer to the 'overall (useful) living space'. However, for simplicity's sake and following convention, it is translated as '*living space*'. On the few occasions when '*zhilaya ploshchad*'' is referred to, it will be translated as '*actual dwelling area*'.
50. V. Shmidt, *op. cit.* p. 23. See also: *Sovetskoe stroitel'stvo* December 1926, no. 5, p. 116; *Vestnik finansov*, June 1925, no. 6, p. 226.
51. D. Broner (1980) *op. cit.* p. 15.
52. E. H. Carr, R. W. Davies, *Foundations of a Planned Economy, 1926–29* (London, Macmillan, 1969), p. 614.
53. Average urban per capita living space in 1926 in six republics: Uzbek SSR – 4.6 square metres; Belorussian SSR – 5.3 square metres; Ukrainian SSR – 5.6 square metres; Turkmen SSR – 6.1 square metres; RSFSR – 6.5 square metres; Caucasian SSR – 6.7 square metres (V. Shmidt, *op. cit.* p. 25).
54. The 1926 Census showed that in the RSFSR out of 126 towns:

    4 had 8–10 square metres of living space per person
    8 had 7– 8 square metres of living space per person
    28 had 6– 7 square metres of living space per person
    45 had 5– 6 square metres of living space per person
    34 had 4– 5 square metres of living space per person
    7 had 3– 4 square metres of living space per person
    V. Schmidt, *op. cit.* pp. 25–26

55. V. Shmidt, *op. cit.* p. 31.
56. *Vestnik truda*, no. 7, July 1924.
57. *Trud*, 6 February 1925. Although such vivid descriptions rarely coloured the pages of the daily and periodical press in the 1930s, the situation itself did not alter. See, for instance, *Trud* 12 September 1933.
58. V. Shmidt, *op. cit.* pp. 52, 60.
59. *Vsesoyuznoe soveshchanie po gradostroitel'stvu*, 7–10 June, 1960, (Sokrashchennyi stenograficheskii otchet) (Moscow, 1960), p. 11; *Narodnoe khozyaistvo 1922–1972. Yubileiniyi statisticheskii sbornik* (Moscow), p. 55; O. O. Litvinov *et al. Vosstanovlenie mnogoetazhnykh domov* (Kiev, 1947), p. 4; V. L. Vol'fson *et al. Organizatsiya kapital'nogo remonta zhilogo fonda* (Leningrad, 1968); N. Grigoryev, *Zhilishchnaya problema budet reshena* (Moscow, 1963), p. 30.
60. In the early 1970s, individual builders were still responsible for 65–70

per cent of new construction in the countryside, whilst over 85 per cent of the rural housing stock was privately owned. (*Perspektivy razvitiya zhilishchya v SSSR*, Moscow, 1975, pp. 96–7). By 1981, 76.3 per cent of housing in the countryside was in 'owner-occupation' (*N. Kh. SSSR 1922–1982*, p. 431).

61. For a comment on these republican differences, see: H. Morton, 'What Have Soviet Leaders Done about the Housing Crisis?' in H. Morton and R. Tökes (eds), *Soviet Politics and Society in the 1970s* (New York, The Free Press, 1974).

62. L. M. Volodarskii, 'Nash sovetskii narod', *Ekonomicheskaya gazeta*, no. 7 (Feb. 1980), pp. 12–13.

PART I INTRODUCTION

1. Postanovlenie TsIK i SNK, 10 June 1926, 'O kvartirnoi plate i merakh k uregulirovanyu pol'zovaniya zhilishchami v gorodskikh poseleniyakh', *SZ SSSR*, 1926, no. 44, art. 312.

2. Postanovlenie TsIK i SNK, 4 January 1928, 'O zhilishchnoi politike', in *Resheniya partii i pravitel'stva po khozyaistvennym vopraosam*, vol. 1 (Moscow, 1967), pp. 696–703.

3. Postanovlenie VTsIK i SNK RSFSR, 14 May 1928, 'Ob oplate zhilykh pomeshenii v gorodakh i rabochikh poselkakh', *SU RSFSR*, 1928, no. 53, art. 402.

4. V. I. Rotkov, Yu. E. Grif, *Planirovanie zhilishchno-kommunal'nogo khozyaistva stroitel'no-montazhnykh organizatsii* (Moscow, 1968), pp. 42–53.

5. M. Sidirov (Departmental head Gosplan USSR) 'Nekotorye voprosy razvitiya zhilishchnogo stroitel'stva na perspektivu,' *Zhilishchnoe stroitel'stvo* no. 4, April 1979, p. 13. But even this low rate of payment is only a temporary phenomenon. The Programme of the CPSU adopted in 1961 envisaged the termination of all payments for rent and basic services by 1981. This goal has still not been attained.

In 1976 two professional artists and their daughter paid 16 roubles 22 kopeks per month for their two-roomed flat (24 square metres, excluding kitchen and bathroom). This total sum comprised the following charges:

	Roubles	Kopeks
Rent	4	08
Water & Sewerage disposal	1	50
Central heating	4	02
Gas	0	69
Electricity	3	78
Television aerial	0	15
Telephone	2	0
	16	22

A typical rent bill for a family of three (two of whom are working) occupying a 2-roomed flat in the centre of Moscow has been drawn up by two Soviet authors:

Service	Roubles	Kopeks
Rent	4	0
Heating	1	21
Water & sewerage	1	50
Relay radio	0	50
Hot water	1	11
Television aerial	0	15
Electricity	2	80
Gas	0	48
Telephone	2	0
	13	75

Source: K. Zhukov, V. Fyodorov, *Housing Construction in the Soviet Union* (Moscow, 1974), p. 8.

6. TsSU, *Narodnoe khozyaistvo SSSR v 1980g.* (Moscow, 1981), p. 392.
7. 'Zhilishchnoe stroitel'stvo,' *Ekonomicheskaya gazeta*, no. 20, May 1976, p. 1; *Politicheskoe samoobrazovanie*, no. 9 (1977), p. 128.
8. Writing in 1965, one senior commentator on housing and architecture observed that 'since rents by no means cover the outlay on housing, some officials advocate raising rents'. (B. Svetlichnyi, 'Sovetskym lyudyam – blagoustroennye zhilishcha', *Kommunist*, no. 6 1965.) There is no reason to suspect that this policy alternative as a way of increasing housing revenue has not been debated in government circles.

2 THE DEVELOPMENT OF THE FOUR HOUSING
   TENURES, 1917–41

1. Dekret VTsIK, 28 December 1917, 'O zapreshchenii sdelok s nedvizhemst'yu', *SU RSFSR*, 1917, no. 10, art. 154.
2. D. L. Broner (1980) *op. cit.* p. 12.
3. *SU RSFSR*, 1918, no. 62, art. 674.
4. Dekret SNK, 8 August 1921, 'O peresmotre Kommunal'nymi otdelami spiskov munitsipalizirovannykh domov', *SU RSFSR*, 1921, no. 60, art. 409.
   According to B. B. Veselovskii, this decree re-established payments for communal services. The rates charged, however, did not cover costs 'because Soviet power approached extremely carefully the burdening of workers with payments'. (B. B. Veselovskii, *Kurs ekonomiki planirovaniya Kommunal'nogo khozyaistva* (Moscow, 1945), p. 144.
5. Postanovlenie SNK, 27 April 1922, 'O nevyselenii v administrativnom poryadke grazhdan iz zanimaemykh imi zhilishch', in *Izvestiya VTsIK*, 30 April 1922.
6. Postanovlenie VTsIK, 22 May 1922, 'Ob osnovnykh chastnykh imushchestvennykh pravakh ...' in *Izvestiya VTsIK*, 18 June 1922.
7. *SU RSFSR*, 1923, no. 44, art. 465.

8. For details, see: articles: 30, 33, 69–70, 80–82, 147, 149, 159, 322, 402, 417, 419, 434, *Grazhdanskii Kodeks*, 1922.
9. *SU RSFSR*, 1924, no. 7, art. 40; no. 73, art. 719.
10. *Zhilishchnye usloviya gorodov po perepisi 1923 goda, po SSSR v tselom. Statisticheskii ezhegodnik 1922–1923 g.g.* (Moscow n.d.), pp. 182–3; N. Kozerenko, *op. cit.* p. 257.
11. B. B. Veselovskii, *Kurs ekonomiki i planirovaniya kommunal'nogo khozyaistva* (Moscow, 1945), p. 139, footnote 1.
12. *SU RSFSR*, 1925, no. 91, art. 662.
13. Dekret VTsIK i SNK RSFSR, 30 November 1925, 'O poryadke raspredeleniya natsionalizirovannykh i munitsipalizirovannykh stroenii i o poryadke pol'zovaniya takovymi', *SU RSFSR 1925*, no. 86, art. 638
14. *Vsesoyuznaya perepis' naseleniya 1926 goda* (Moscow, 1932), vol. *LVI*, p. 130.
15. *SU RSFSR*, 1927, no. 76, art. 522.
16. Postanovlenie TsIK i SNK SSSR, 4 January 1928, 'O zhilishchnoi politike', in *Resheniya partii i pravitel'stva po khozyaistvennym voprosam*, vol. 5 (Moscow, 1967), pp. 696–703 (*SZ SSSR*, 1928, no. 6, art. 49).
17. *SZ SSSR*, 1936, no. 20, art. 169. If an enterprise fulfils its planned production programme using fewer resources than budgeted for, it will be left with a margin greater than the planned profit. Part of this is paid into a 'Director's Fund' to be used at the discretion of the enterprise for a range of specified purposes.
18. Postanovlenie TsIK i SNK SSSR, 17 October 1937, 'O sokhranenii zhilishchnogo fonda i uluchshenii zhilishchnogo khozyaistva v gorodakh', *SZ SSSR*, 1937, no. 69, art. 314; B. B. Veselovskii. *Kurs ekonomiki i organizatsii gorodskogo khozyaistva* (Moscow, 1951), p. 160.
19. *Byulleten' NKVD*, 1922, no. 27.
20. *SU RSFSR*, 1925, no. 86, art. 638.
21. V. Shmidt, *op. cit.* p. 55.
22. *SU RSFSR*, 1932, no. 67, art. 302; *SU RSFSR*, 1936, no. 12, art. 72; *SU RSFSR*, 1938, no. 12, art. 363.
23. *SZ SSSR*, 1931, no. 1, art. 1. This revised a decree of September 1929 (*SZ SSSR*, 1929, no. 60, art. 551) 'O peredache trestami obshchesoyuznogo znacheniya v Donetskom basseine i Krivoirozh'e sovetam rabochikh poselkov zemel'nykh uchastkov, zhilikh domov i kommunal'nykh predpriyatii'.
24. T. Sosnovy, *The Housing Problem in the Soviet Union* (New York, Research Program on the USSR, 1954), p. 24.
25. Dekret VTsIK i SNK RSFSR, 14 June 1926, 'Ob usloviyakh i poryadke administrativnogo vyseleniya grazhdan iz zanimaemykh imi pomeshchenii', *SU RSFSR*, 1926, no. 35, art. 282.
26. *SZ SSSR*, 1931, no. 10, art. 110. In October 1931, this ruling was extended to the Central Administration of Roads and Automobile Transport (*SZ SSSR*, 1931, no. 58, art. 376) See also: *SU SSSR 1933*, no. 10, art. 30; no. 50, art. 216; *SU SSSR*, 1935, no. 13, art. 15; no. 4, art. 31; no. 6, art. 63; no. 11, art. 116.

27. Postanovlenie SNK SSSR, 1 July 1943, 'O poryadke administrativnogo vyseleniya lits, samoupravno zanyavshikh zhiluyu ploshchad', *SP SSSR*, 1943, no. 10, art. 165.
28. Postanovlenie VTsIK i SNK RSFSR, 28 February 1930, 'O prave pol'zovaniya dopolnitel'noi zhiloi ploshchadi', *SU RSFSR*, 1930, no. 14, art. 181. For details on this and subsequent additions and amendments, see *Sbornik zhilishchnogo zakonodatel'stva* (Moscow, 1963), pp. 297–301.
29. *SZ SSSR*, 1933, no. 5, art. 128.
30. Similar privileges were accorded to the Union of Writers and Unions of Artists and Sculptors. (*SZ SSSR*, 1933, no. 43, art. 252; *SU SSSR*, 1933, no. 12, art. 123). March 1935 saw the setting up of the 'Architects fund for the Union of Soviet Architects' (*SZ SSSR*, 1935, no. 4, art. 27). A further decree extended to 'inventors all those housing privileges laid down for scientific workers'. (*SU SSSR*, 1935, no. 17, art. 172).
31. *SZ SSSR*, 1937, no. 74, art. 360. According to this decree tenants of the liquidated co-operatives were not subject to eviction except in those cases where the accommodation was transferred to organisations which provided accommodation as part of the labour contract.
32. *SZ SSSR*, 1937, no. 75, art. 370.
33. *SP SSSR*, 1939, no. 28, art. 188.
34. G. Stepanov, *Potrebitel'skoe obshchestvo i rabochii klass* (Moscow, 1920), p. 30.
35. *Programma i ustav RKP (b)*, p. 139, *et passim*.
36. V. I. Lenin, 'O kooperatsii', *Polnoe sobranie sochinenii* 5th edn, vol. 45, pp. 369–77.
37. *SU RSFSR*, 1924, no. 63, art. 636; *KPSS v resolyutsiyakh i resheniyakh s"ezdov, konferentsii i plenumov TsK*, vol. 3, (Moscow, 1970), p. 74.
38. *SZ RSFSR*, 1924, no. 5, art. 60.
39. *Resheniya partii i pravitel'stva po khozyaistvennym voprosam*, vol. 1, (1967), pp. 494–97.
40. *Entsiklopediya mestnogo upravleniya i khozyaistva* (Moscow, 1927), p. 662.
41. *Vsesoyuznaya perepis' ... op. cit.*
42. B. B. Veselovskii, *Kurs ekonomiki i organizatsii gorodskogo khozyaistva* (Moscow, 1951), p. 141.
43. V. Ya. Belousov, *Kul'turnye zadachi zhilishchnoi kooperatsii* (Moscow, 1926), p. 7.
44. V. I. Lenin, *Collected Works*, vol. 26, (Moscow, Progress, 1964), p. 409. See also Lenin's reference to 'The living, creative activity of the masses is the principal factor in the new public life ... Living, creative Socialism is the work of the masses themselves ... Socialism cannot come into being through orders from above'. (Cited by R. Garaudy, *The Turning Point of Socialism*, Fontana, 1970, p. 83).
45. Ts. G. Ryss, *Zhilishchnaya kooperatsiya SSSR, 1924–25: statistiko – ekonomicheskii obzor* (Moscow, 1926), p. 44.
46. A. Ya Vyshinskii, *S"ezdy Sovetov RSFSR* (Moscow, 1939), p. 463.
47. I. P. Prokopchenko, *Upravlenie i pol'zovanie zhilishchnom fondom v SSSR* (Moscow, 1972), p. 52.
48. Sh. D. Chikvashvili, *Zhilishchno-stroitel'naya kooperatsiya v SSSR*

(Moscow, 1965), p. 4.

49. International Labour Office, *The Housing Problem in Soviet Russia*, vol. 12, no. 2 (Geneva, 1925), p. 258.
50. V. Ya. Belousov, *op. cit.* p. 9.
51. *Ekonomicheskaya zhizn'* 24 March 1925.
52. *SZ SSSR*, 1928, no. 6, art. 49.
53. A. Vyshinskii, *op. cit.*, p. 463.
54. V. Belousov, *op. cit.*, pp. 31–2.
55. *Sovietskoe stroitel'stvo*, nos 5–6, 1931, p. 150.
56. *SU RSFSR*, 1921, no. 44, art. 253.
57. *SU RSFSR*, 1921, no. 60, art. 408; *SU RSFSR*, 1922, no. 21, art. 645.
58. *SU RSFSR*, 1921, no. 60, art. 409; no. 60, art. 411.
59. *Narodnoe Khozyaistvo*, August–September, 1921.
60. For 1923–28, see: *Narodnoe khozyaistvo SSSR: statisticheskii spravochnik* (Moscow, 1932), p. 301.
61. *Voprosy truda*, no. 12, 1924.
62. *SU RSFSR*, 1924, no. 90, art. 914.
63. B. B. Veselovskii, (1945), *op. cit.*, p. 148.
64. B. B. Veselovskii, (1951), *op. cit.*, p. 140.
65. *SP SSSR*, 1939, no. 28, art. 188.
66. *KPSS v rezolyutsiyakh, s"yezdov, Konferentsii i plenumov TsK*, 8th edn, vol. 4, (1970), pp. 439–40, 545.
67. This decree is translated in: J. Hazard, *Soviet Housing Law* (New Haven, Yale University Press, 1939), pp. 130–141.
68. I. P. Prokopchenko, *Zhilishchnoe i zhilishchno – stroitel'noe zakonodatel'stvo* (Moscow, 1977), p. 29.

3   THE STATE HOUSING SECTOR

1. P. Obraztsov (chairman of the Zaporozh'e *oblast'* planning committee), 'O edinom rukovodstve gorodskom khozyaistve', *Izvestiya*, 5 April 1951, p. 2. In some instances the government issued special decrees criticising the Executive Committees of specific cities for not doing everything possible to improve the functioning of the urban economy. See for instance, Postanovlenie Soveta Ministrov SSSR, January 1947, 'O rabote Kolomenskogo gorispolkoma'. (*SP SSSR*, 1947, no. 3, art. 6); 'O rabote Voronezhskogo gorispolkoma' (*SP SSSR*, 1947, no. 3, art. 7).
2. Obraztsov, Ibid.
3. There are three different kinds of ministry in the Soviet Union; (1) the *all-union ministries*, which directly run from Moscow the activities of their subordinate units within the republic; (2) *union–republican ministries*, which exist both at the centre and in the republics; (3) *republican ministries*, which have no direct superior in Moscow. Some enterprises are directly subordinate to all-union ministries, while at the other end of the scale, those of local significance fall under republican ministries or even under the local soviet.
4. I. Grishmanov, 'O kompleksnom razvitii gorodskogo khozyaistva', *Izvestiya*, 3 June 1951, p. 2.

5. K. Dlugoshevskii, 'V zashchitu kooperirovaniya zhilishchnogo stroitel'stva', *Izvestiya*, 18 September 1951, p. 2.
6. Postanovlenie TsK KPSS i Soveta Ministrov SSSR, 31 July 1957, 'O razvitii zhilishchnogo stroitel'stva v SSSR', *SP SSSR*, 1957, no. 9, art. 102.
7. Postanovlenie Soveta Ministrov SSSR, 26 August 1967, 'O merakh po uluchsheniyu eksploatatsii zhilishchnogo fonda i ob"ektov kommunal'nogo khozyaistva', *SP SSSR*, 1967, no. 22, art. 56.
8. M. Georgadze, 'Demokratiya dlya vsekh', *Sovety Deputatov trudyashchikhsya*, 1967, no. 10, p. 16.
9. *Planirovanie khozyaistva mestnogo podchineniya* (Moscow, 1970), p. 110.
10. N. Ushpik, 'O chem dumaet gorod', *Izvestiya*, 30 June 1970, p. 3.
11. P. N. Lebedev (ed.) *Sistema organov gorodskogo upravleniya* (Leningrad, 1980), p. 49.
12. A. Bukhtiyarov, 'Gorod i zavod', *Izvestiya*, 1 March 1972, p. 3.
13. Some writers prefer to see the local soviets using their 'initiative' rather than 'power'/'rights'. See 'The effective utilisation of the material resources of enterprises depends on the initiative of local soviets,' *Planirovanie khozyaistva mestnogo podchineniya* (Moscow, 1970), p. 109.
14. TsK KPSS, 'Ob uluchshenii deyatel'nosti mestnykh Sovetov i usilenii ikh svyazi s massami', in *Spravochnik*, 1957, p. 459.
15. Postanovlenie TsK KPSS i Soveta Ministrov SSSR, 3 February 1970, 'O seryozhnikh narusheniyakh gosudarstvennoi ditsipliny v gorodskom stroitel'stve i zhilishchnom khozyaistve', *SP SSSR*, 1970, no. 4, art. 25.
16. Ibid.
17. G. Mil'ner, E. Gilinskaya; 'Mezhraionn'oe regulirovanie urovnya zhizni naseleniya', *Planovoe khozyaistvo*, no. 1, 1975, p. 61.
18. *Materialy XXVI S"yezda KPSS* (Moscow, 1981), p. 106.
19. R. S. Pavlovskii, *Zakonodatel'stvo o mestnykh sovetakh deputatov trudyashchikhsya* (Khar'kov, 1975), p. 35.
20. Ibid.
21. Ibid., pp. 35–36.
22. P. N. Lebedev. *op. cit.* pp. 73, 75.
23. Postanovlenie Soveta Ministrov SSSR of 1 March 1978, 'O merakh po rasshireniyu v gorodakh praktiki kompleksnogo potochnogo stroitel'stva zhilykh domov, ob"ektov kul'turno-bytovogo naznacheniya i kommunal'nogo khozyaistva', *SP SSSR* 1978, no. 6, art. 36.
24. D. G. Khodzhaev 'O nekotorykh problemakh razvitiya novykh gorodov', *Planovoe khozyaistvo*, no. 2, 1979, p. 74.
25. Postanovlenie TsK KPSS, 14 March 1971, 'O merakh po dalneishemu uluchsheniyu raboty raionnykh i gorodskikh Sovetov deputatov trudyashchikhsya', *Pravda*, 14 March 1971.
26. *Vedomsti Verkhovnogo Soveta SSSR*, 'Ob osnovnykh pravakh i obyazannostyakh gorodskikh i raionnykh v gorodakh Sovetov deputatov trudyashchikhsya', 1971, no. 12, art. 132.
27. *Konstitutsiya SSSR* (Moscow, 1977).
28. Postanovlenie Soveta Ministrov SSSR, 'Ob osnovnykh pravakh i

obyazannostyakh gorodskikh i raionnykh v gorodakh Sovetov deputatov trudyashchikhshya', *Izvestiya*, 20 March 1971.

29. In the Ukraine, the transfer of a portion of profits made by enterprises of republican significance began in 1962 (R. S. Pavlovskii, *op. cit.* p. 47.)
30. *Sovety za 50 let*, (Moscow, 1967), p. 441; *Zasedaniya Verkhovnogo Soveta SSSR. Stenog. otchot 3-i sessii VIII sozyva* (Moscow, 1972), p. 71; G. B. Polyak, *General'nyi plan i byudzhet Moskvy* (Moscow, 1973), pp. 24–25; R. S. Pavlovskii *op. cit.* p. 47.
31. Whereas the workforce in the economy as a whole rose by 46 per cent between 1965 and 1980, and 34 per cent in industry, the number employed in the housing and municipal economy and in daily service provision rose by 89 per cent (from 2.4 million to 4.5 million employees). *Narodnoe khozyaistvo SSSR v 1980g.*, 1981, p. 358.
32. P. N. Lebedev, *op. cit.* pp. 47, 81; D. D. Butakov, *Mestnye byudzhety stran-chlenov SEV* (Moscow, 1980), p. 148.
33. Butakov, *op. cit.*, p. 149.
34. Ibid.
35. *Narodnoe khozyaistvo RSFSR. Statisticheskii sbornik* (Moscow, 1957), p. 359.
36. B. M. Kolotilkin, *Dolgovechnost' zhilykh zdanii* (Moscow, 1965), p. 22.
37. S. A. Alekseev, *Ekonomika zhilishchnogo khozyaistva* (Moscow, 1966), p. 24.
38. F. A. Shevelev, 'Zhilishchno-kommunal'noe khozyaistvo: osnovnye napravleniya tekhnicheskoi politiki na 1976–80 gody', *Zhilishchnoe i kommunal'noe khozyaistvo*, no. 10, 1976, p. 4.
39. Postanovlenie Soveta Ministrov SSSR, 4 September 1978, 'O merakh po dal'neishemu uluchsheniya eksploatatsii i remonta zhilishchnogo fonda', *SP SSSR*, 1978, no. 22, art. 137.
40. T. Fetisov, 'Zaboty ne tol'ko Saratovskie', *Sovety narodnykh deputatov*, 1, 1980, p. 56. In the Ukraine, the corresponding increase in the local soviet stock was from 44 to 46 per cent; in Kazakhstan, 31 to 34 per cent; and, in Tadzhikstan, 48 to 52 per cent.
41. P. Lebedev *op. cit.* p. 80. (49 per cent of the urban housing stock was classified as 'departmental', 4 per cent as co-operative, and 23 per cent as 'private'.)
42. Fetisov, Ibid., and Table 1.5.
43. Before the Second World War, house building by local soviets was mainly concentrated in these cities. (See B. B. Veselovskii, *Kurs ekonomiki i planirovaniya kommunal'nogo khozyaistva*, Moscow, 1945, p. 174.)
44. *Sovershenstvovat' raboty Sovety deputatov trudyashchikhsya* (Moscow, 1970); B. Gryazov, N. Vinogradov, *Partiinaya organizatsiya stolitsy i Sovety* (Moscow, 1974), pp. 16–17. In an attempt to rationalise the process of planning Moscow itself, in June 1968, state capital investment for the construction of housing and municipal facilities was transferred from ministries and enterprises to the Moscow city soviet.
45. Whether the amount controlled by the local soviets as a percentage of the total stock will be larger or smaller is determined by the size of the private sector; thus, the more important statistic, as far as this section is

concerned, is the one showing the local soviet share as a percentage of the public sector.

46. V. K. Isupov, 'Segodnya v Kemerove', *Zhilishchnoe i kommunal'noe khozyaistvo*, no. 3, 1979, p. 22.
47. *Narodnoe khozyaistvo Permskoi oblasti v 9-i pyatiletke* (Perm', 1974), p. 153.
48. B. Rudden 'Soviet Housing Law', *The International and Comparative Law Quarterly*, vol. 12, part 2, 4th Series (April 1963), p. 594.
49. G. Churchward, *Contemporary Soviet Government* (London, Routledge & Kegan Paul, revised 2nd edn, 1975), p. 179.
50. I. P. Prokopchenko, *Upravlenie i pol'zovanie zhilishchnym fondom v SSSR* (Moscow, 1970), p. 38. See also F. A. Shevelev *op. cit.*
51. *SP SSSR*, 1959, no. 8, art. 72.
52. The term 'housing management' is used to translate what authors variously refer to as 'domoupravlenie', 'upravlenie domani' and 'zhilishchnoe upravlenie'. The ZhEK, though serving the same function, relates to agencies normally found only in large cities. Model statutes for the housing management of local soviets were approved by the RSFSR Ministry of Communal Economy in July 1963.
53. V. G. Savchenko-Bel'skii *et al., Ekspluatatsiya zhilykh massivov* (Kiev, 1980), pp. 9–20.
54. Yu M. Safronov, *Organizatiya zhilishchnogo khozyaistva* (Moscow, 1972), p. 65.
55. S. A. Alekseev, *Ekonomika zhilishchnogo khozyaistva* (Moscow, 1966), p. 25.
56. A. Balayants, 'Zhilym domam – odin khozyain', *Izvestiya*, 15 December 1964, p. 2.
57. Fetisov, *op. cit.*, p. 57.
58. D. L. Broner, *Sovremennye problemy zhilishchnogo khozyaistva* (Moscow, 1961), p. 19.
59. 'Gorod – kompleks edinyi', *Pravda*, 13 November 1976, p. 3.
60. 'Zhilishchno-kommunal'noe khozyaistvo', *Ekonomicheskaya gazeta*, no. 31, July 1975, p. 2.
61. V. L. Vol'fson *et al., Organizatsiya kapital'nogo remonta zhilogo fonda* (Leningrad, 1968), p. 5.
62. G. B. Polyak 'Ekonomika zhilishchnogo khozyaistva – povsednevnoe vnimanie', *Zhilishchnoe i kommunal'noe khozyaistvo*, no. 7, 1976, p. 23.
63. S. K. Ovchinnikova, 'Kak izmerit' effekt kapital'nogo remonta', *Zhilishchnoe i kommunal'noe khozyaistvo*, no. 3, 1979, p. 20. See also *Zhilishchnoe i kommunal'noe stroitel'stvo*, no. 1, 1979, p. 2; no. 4, 1977, p. 15.
64. T. Fetisov, *op. cit.* p. 56.
65. M. Matthews, 'Social Dimensions in Soviet Urban Housing', in R. A. French and F. E. Hamilton (eds), *The Socialist City* (John Wiley, Chichester, 1979), p. 107.
66. *SP SSSR* 1978, no. 22, art. 137. The ten page long decree dealt with issues ranging from the planning, financing (including, for example, the handing over to housing maintenance departments the whole of the rent charged on non-residential premises belonging to the local soviet) and

organisation of repair work (the creation of an Administration for Repairs to the Housing Stock within the framework of the State Committee for Civil Construction – (*Gosgrazhdanstroi*) to specifying which ministries are to undertake the development of new materials, electrical appliances and other equipment to be used mainly for housing interiors.

67. The following account is taken from T. Fetisov 'Zaboty ne tol'ko Saratovskie', *Sovety narodnykh deputatov*, no. 1, 1980, pp. 56–62.
68. G. Petrov, 'Zhil'yu – odnogo khozyaina', *Sovet narodnykh deputatov*, no. 3, 1980, p. 58.
69. Ibid., p. 59.
70. Ibid., p. 60.
71. P. N. Lebedev *op. cit.*, p. 25.
72. Ibid., p. 26.
73. The following figures are based on a personal communication from an official in the research department at the Greater London Council.
74. *The Guardian*, 21 September, 1981.
75. 'Esli videt' perspektivu', *Pravda*, 6 December 1971, p. 2.
76. A. Bukhtiyarov, 'Gorod i zavod', *Izvestiya*, 1 March 1972, p. 3.
77. B. Lentsov, 'V interesakh naseleniya', *Izvestiya*, 7 February 1976.
78. The region is almost six times larger than the United Kingdom. (The Tyumen' *oblast'* covers 1 435 400 square kilometres and the UK 244 021 sq. km).
79. A. Protozanov, 'Goroda zaural'ya', *Izvestiya*, 4 December 1966, p. 3.
80. In the early 1970s, the planning norms in the country at large were only being partially met: retail outlets by 63 per cent, pre-school places by 60 per cent, public dining rooms and daily service needs by 56 per cent and cinemas by 42 per cent. (A. Kochetkov, 'Sotsial'no-ekonomicheskie aspekty gradostroitel'stva', *Voprosy ekonomiki*, no. 10, 1975. p. 26).
81. 'Zhil'e dlya severa', *Pravda*, 19 June 1976, p. 2. see also M. Vershinin (Divisional Head of the Construction Department of the Central Committee of the CPSU), 'Povysit' uroven' gradostroitel'stva', *Ekonomicheskaya gazeta*, no. 39, September 1976, p. 9.
82. *Materialy XXVI S"yezda KPSS* (Moscow, 1981), p. 54. See also S. N. Zhelezko, 'Faktory stabilizatsii kadrov na stroitel'stve BAM', *Sotsiologicheskie issledovaniya*, no. 1, 1980, pp. 84–87.
83. *Sotsiologicheskie issledovaniya*, no. 2, 1976, p. 63.
84. R. I. Kuzovatkin, 'Front i tyl Samotlora', *Ekonomkia i organizatsiya promyshlennogo proizvodstva*, no. 6, Nov–Dec 1976, p. 84. The average age in Nizhnevartovsk is 26 which helps to explain the fact that the birth-rate in the town is twice the national average and the proportion of children under the age of four is 40 per cent higher than the average for the country as a whole. Nevertheless, only 50 per cent of the money allocated for pre-school facilities was taken up and used for this purpose. See also 'Zhil'e dlya Tyumentsev' *Sotsialisticheskaya industriya*, 4 April 1978, p. 3. By 1981, the population of Nizhnevartovsk was 134 000.
85. F. G. Arzhanov, 'Vokrug burovoi', *Ekonomika i organizatsiya promyshlennogo proizvodstva*, no. 2 February 1979, pp. 23–31.
86. *Materialy* ... (1981), *op. cit.* p. 149.
87. R. I. Kuzovatkin, *op. cit.* p. 86.

88. P. Kraznikov, 'Gorodu-stabil'nye kadry', *Sotsialisticheskaya industriya*, 25 January 1977, no. 20, p. 3. See also *SP SSSR*, 1979, no. 5, art. 27.
89. A. Elokhin, 'Bratsk segodnya i zavtra', *Izvestiya*, 6 March 1979, p. 3.
90. *SP SSSR*, 1980, no. 3, art. 17.
91. *Vestnik statistiki*, no. 2, 1973, p. 85.
92. A. Kocherga, 'Problemy territorial'nogo planirovaniya narodnogo blagosostoyaniya', *Planovoe khozyaistvo*, no. 2, February 1979, p. 96.
93. A. V. Topilin, *Territorial'noe pereraspredelenie trudovykh resursov v SSSR* (Moscow, 1975), p. 14.
94. V. V. Onikienko, V. A. Polovkin, *Kompleksnoe issledovanie migratsion-nykh protsessov* (Moscow, 1973), p. 3. In fact, according to an official governmental study, of all persons seeking work in the RSFSR in 1975, only 25 per cent went through a 'labour exchange' (*sluzhba trudoustroist-vo*). (Gosudarstvennyi komitet Soveta Ministrov RSFSR po ispol'zon-vaniyu trudovykh resursov, *Trudovye resursy* (Moscow, 1973), p. 3).
95. Compare for example, the article by V. A. Glazov *et al.* 'Osobennosti mezhraionnoi migratsii naseleniya v RSFSR', with V. D. Zaitsev 'Prob-lemy modelirovaniya migratsii naseleniya', in A. S. Maikov *Migratsiya naseleniya RSFSR* (Moscow, 1973), p. 3.
96. A. Kocherga, *op. cit.* p. 96.
97. Postanovlenie Soveta Ministrov SSSR, 4 October 1965, 'Ob utver-zhdenii Polozheniya o sotsialisticheskom, gosudarstvennom proizvod-stvennom predpriyatii', (*SP SSSR*, 1965, no. 19–20, art. 155). A few years earlier the Council of Ministers had ruled that ministries and central state organisations could allow their subordinate undertakings to use a sum not exceeding 30 per cent of the revenues earned from above-plan economies for housing construction. Postanovlenie Soveta Ministrov SSSR, 24 March 1958, 'Ob ispol'zovanii sredstv sverkh-planovoi ekonomiki dlya zhilishchnogo stroitel'stva', (*SP SSSR*, 1958, no. 5, art. 58). In 1969 the privileges of erecting and controlling housing and cultural facilities which applies to productive enterprises was ex-tended to design, surveying and scientific research institutes engaged in capital construction. (*SP SSSR*, 1969, no. 15, art. 83).
98. Despite the considerable funds so far allocated to providing crèches and kindergartens and the high proportion of children attending such institu-tions, the 1970s witnessed the publication of numerous letters and articles on the negative effects the shortfall in playschool places was having on 'the drawing of women into productive employment'. See, for example, *Izvestiya*, 28 April 1976 ('Detskie sady dlya 52 845 rebyat') and the editorial comment in *Izvestiya*, 4 May 1976. The role of industri-al enterprises in meeting their employees' basic needs has been further extended by the XXVI Party Congress which urged that 'maximum support should be given to farms run by industrial enterprises to supply their workforce'. *Materialy . . .* (1981) *op. cit.* p. 48.
99. *SP SSSR*, 1980, no. 3, art. 17.
100. *Sbornik zhilishchnogo zakonodatel'stva* (Moscow, 1963), pp. 210–211. At present the 10 per cent transferred is only for two of the four categories of people – invalids of the 1941–45 war and families of dead soldiers. See: *Zakonodatel'stvo o zhilishchno-kommunal'nom khozyaist-ve* (Moscow, 1972)., vol. 1, p. 529.

101. E.g. *SP RSFSR*, 1960, no. 8, art. 37; *SP RSFSR*, 1962, no. 17, art. 91; *SP SSSR*, 1966, no. 23, art. 207.

102. Postanovlenie Soveta Ministrov, 7 September 1970, 'O uporyadochenii uderzhaniya Sovetami deputatov trudyashchikhsya zhiloi ploshchadi v domakh, postroennykh dlya predpriyatii i organizatsii', *SP SSSR*, 1970, no. 16, art. 128.

103. Yu. K. Tolstoi, *Sovetskoe zhilishchnoe pravo* (Leningrad, 1967), p. 13; V. F. Maslov, *Zashchita zhilishchnykh prav grazhdan* (Khar'kov, 1970), p. 10.

104. *Radya'nske pravo* 1959, no. 4, p. 141, A. M. Fel'dman, S. N. Landkof, T. N. Lisnichenko, *Zhilishchnoe i zhilishchno-stroitel'noe zakonodatel'-stvo* (Kiev, 1971), p. 37.

105. *Byulleten' Verkhovnogo Suda RSFSR*, 1971, no. 9, pp. 3–4.

106. Yu. M. Safronov, *Organizatsiya zhilishchnogo khozyaistva* (Moscow, 1972), p. 67.

107. V. Kurasov, 'Novosel v nagruzku', *Izvestiya*, 16 May 1979.

108. *SP SSSR*, 1978, no 6, art 36.

109. 'Gorod raduet cheloveka', *Pravda*, 21 May 1976.

110. *Planirovanie khozyaistva mestnogo podchineniya* (Moscow, 1970), p. 112. In 1968, 58.8 per cent of central capital investment funds for housing in the RSFSR were allocated to agencies subordinate to Union and Republican ministries and departments. (V. Solomin, 'Metodologiya planirovaniya zhilishchnogo stroitel'stva', *Voprosy ekonomiki*, Nov. 1969, no. 11, p. 131.)

111. N. G. Dmitriev, *Vazhnaya sotsial'naya problema* (Moscow, 1970), p. 115.

112. *Pravda*, 14 March 1957.

113. G. Makarov, *Uchyot nuzhdayushchikhsya v zhiloi ploshchadi i poryadok yego rasprede leniya* (Moscow, 1967), p. 3.

114. V. Bodyrev, 'Pochemu chelovek uvol'nyaetsya', *Pravda*, 20 January 1971.

115. 'Kto khozyain zhilogo doma?', *Izvestiya*, 24 November 1964, p. 3.

116. *Programma Kommunisticheskoi Partii Sovetskogo Soyuza* (Moscow, 1961), p. 94.

117. 'Kak upravlyat' domami', *Pravda*, 17 November 1976.

118. 'Novoselii stanet bol'she', *Pravda*, 2 October 1976, p. 1.

119. 'Goroda i poselki stanut krashe', *Izvestiya*, 30 November 1975, p. 1.

120. 'Gorod raduet cheloveka', *Pravda*, 21 May 1976.

121. 'Zhil'e dlya severyan' *Pravda*, 19 June 1976. p. 2. See the detailed considerations given to this in a decree of 4 December 1963 in *Resheniya partii i pravitel'stva po khozyaistvennym vosprosam*, vol. 5 (Moscow, 1968), pp. 427–433.

122. L. Sivov, 'Vokrug kompleksa', *Pravda*, 7 January 1977.

123. A. A. Ponomarev, 'Putevoe khozyaistvo i perspektivy ego razitiya', *Zhilishchnoe i kommunal'noe khozyaistvo*, no. 1, 1976. p. 29.

124. M. M. Mezhevich, 'Kompleksnoe planirovanie krupnykh gorodov', *Planovoe khozyaistvo*, no. 3, 1978.

125. 'Gorod kompleks edinyi', *Pravda*, 13 March 1976, p. 3.

126. V. T. Chemodurov (Chairman of the Crimea *oblast'* Executive Committee), 'Krug polnomochii', *Izvestiya*, 20 January 1977, p. 5. See also:

Yu. Tikhomirov, 'Poisk novykh resursov', *Izvestiya*, 19 June 1977, p. 4. The article outlines the widening powers of local soviets over industrial enterprises and organisations in their area as specified in the new constitution (1977).

127. *Materialy* ... (1981) *op. cit.* p. 65.
128. E. Patsevich, 'Zhilishchno-kommunal'noe khozyaistvo i mestnye organy vlasti', *Zhilishchnoe i kommunal'noe khozyaistvo*, no. 10, 1976, pp. 12–13.
129. Ibid.
130. 'Prichiny disproportsii', *Gorodskoe khozyaistvo Moskvy*, no. 2, 1978, p. 15. See also: 'Vvstupaya v chetvertyi god pyatiletki', *Gorodskoe khozyaistvo Moskvy*, no. 1, 1979, p. 2. See also: *Materialy* ... (1981), *op. cit.* p. 58.
131. *Sixth Annual Report of the Commission for the New Towns* (London, HMSO, 1968), p. 12.
132. *Materialy XXIV S"yezda KPSS* (Moscow, 1971), p. 174.
133. Lebedev, *op. cit.* p. 48.
134. Ibid., p. 49.
135. Ibid., pp. 50–52.
136. V. A. Pertsik, *Osnovy ratsional'noi organizatsii truda v mestnykh Sovetakh* (Moscow, 1975).
137. B. A. Pavlovich, 'Analiz reshenii ispolkomov kak sposob izucheniya sistemy upravleniya v krupnom gorode', *Chelovek i obshchestvo* (Leningrad, 1977), vyp. 16, p. 67.
138. G. B. Barabashev, K. F. Sheremet, *Sovetskoe stroitel'stvo* (Moscow, 1974; L. Churchward, *Contemporary Soviet Government* (London, Routledge & Kegan Paul, 2nd revised edn 1975).
139. V. Andrle, *Managerial Power in the Soviet Union* (London, Saxon House, 1976).
140. *Materialy* ... (1981), *op. cit.* p. 71.
141. See: C. Lewis and S. Sternheimer, *Soviet Urban Management: with Comparisons to the United States* (New York, Praeger, 1979).
142. Fetisov, *op. cit.* p. 62.

4   THE HOUSE-BUILDING CO-OPERATIVE

1. Postanovlenie TsK KPSS i Soveta Ministrov SSSR, 31 July 1957, 'O razvitii zhilishchn ogo stroitel'stva v SSSR', *SP SSSR*, 1957, no. 9, art. 102.
2. See: Article 25 of the *Principles of the Civil Code, RSFSR*; 'Polozhenie o zhilishchno-stroitel'nykh kollektivakh i individual'nykh zastroish-chikakh v gorodakh i poselkakh gorodskogo tipa Ukrainskoi SSR, utverzhdennoe postanovleniem Soveta Ministrov UkSSR ot 30 aprelya 1958', *ZP URSR*, 1958. no. 4, art. 83. Bernard Rudden uses the term 'co-operative' and 'collective' interchangeably. (B. Rudden, 'Soviet Housing and the New Civil Code', *The International and Comparative Law Quarterly*, vol. 15, January 1966, pp. 252 *et passim*.); A. DiMaio has confused the house-building co-operative and the collective. The

1957 decree did not speak of 'organising individual builders into housing co-operatives' as he states in A. J. DiMaio, *Soviet Urban Housing. Problems and Policies* (New York, Praeger, 1974), p. 180.

3. Postanovlenie Soveta Ministrov SSSR, 20 March 1958, 'O zhilishchnykh i dachynkh stroitel'nykh kooperativakh', *SP SSSR*, 1958, no. 5, art. 47.

4. See, for example, T. N. Lisnichenko, 'Chto sderzhivaet kooperativnoe zhilishchnoe stroitel'stvo?' *Sovety deputatov trudyashchikhsya*, 1960, no. 10, pp. 70 *et passim*; Ya. F. Mikolemko, *Pravo kooperativnoi sobstvennosti v SSSR* (Moscow, 1961), p. 84.

5. *Materialy XXII S"ezda KPSS* (Moscow, 1962), p. 390.

6. *SP SSSR*, 1962, no. 12, art. 93.

7. *SP SSSR*, 1964, no. 25, art. 147.

8. The improved credit arrangements did not go far enough for some people. The following month, a letter from a worker in Chita in E. Siberia complained that he and his family had moved to a timber-framed house, lacking in basic amenities, lying on the city outskirts, because they did not have enough money for the down payment necessary to join a co-operative. ('Pust' budet bol'she novoselii', *Pravda*, 28 December 1964, p. 2).

9. V. B. Kolotilkin, *Dolgovechnost' zhilikh domov* (Moscow, 1965), p. 150.

10. Postanovlenie Soveta Minstrov SSSR, 19 August 1982, 'O zhilishchno-stroitel'noi kooperatsii', *SP SSSR*, 1982, no. 23, art. 120.

11. *SP SSSR*, 1965, no. 23, art. 144. In rural areas, a co-operative must have at least twelve members.

12. I. P. Prokopchenko, *Zhilishchnoe i zhilishchno-stroitel'noe zakonodatel'stvo* (Moscow, 1977), p. 151.

13. Prokopchenko (1977) *op. cit.* p. 254.

14. I. S. Budzilovich *et al.*, *Tipovoi ustav zhilishchno–stroitel'nogo kooperativa* (Kiev, 1975), p. 175.

15. *Zhilishchnoe i kommunal'noe khozyaistvo*, no. 10, 1977, p. 46.

16. In contrast with the 1920s, today, house-building co-operatives have no formal links with one another through a central co-ordinating agency. Each *ZhSK* is an independent organisation whose activities are supervised by the local *gorispolkom*, with the Republican Ministry of Municipal Economy acting as overseer of the activities of all *ZhSKs* within the Republic.

17. See: J. B. Cullingworth, *Essays on Housing Policy* (London, George Allen and Unwin, 1979), ch. 7; J. Hamdi, B. Greenstreet (eds), *Participation in Housing*, Working Paper nos. 57, 58 (Oxford Polytechnic 1981).

18. *Sbornik postanovlenii plenuma Verkhovnogo Suda SSSR 1924–1970* (Moscow, 1970), p. 97; I. P. Prokopchenko, (1977), *op. cit.* pp. 251–2.

19. I. S. Budzilovich *et al.*, *op. cit.* p. 48. Not only must everyone over the age of 15 possess a passport but in order to live in a town a person must have a residence permit (*propiska*) which when entered in the passport by a police department entitles the holder to reside in that particular town on a permanent or temporary basis.

20. *SP SSSR,* 1966, no. 18, art. 162.

21. *SP UkSSR*, 1968, no. 3, art. 42.

22. *SP UkSSR,* 1969, no. 8, art. 97.
23. *SP SSSR,* 1965, no. 4, art. 22.
24. *SP SSSR,* 1967, no. 29, art. 203.
25. On the administrative difficulties involved in providing workers in the Far North with places in house-building co-operatives, see: V. N. Litovkin, '*ZhSK* dlya rabotnikov Krainego Severa', *Zhilishchnoe i kommunal 'noe khozyaistvo.* no. 9, 1976.
26. D. S. Meerson, D. G. Tonskii, *Zhilishchnoe stroitel 'stvo v SSSR v desatoi pyatiletke* (Moscow, 1977), p. 4.
27. Calculated from: D. Broner (1980), *op. cit.* p. 41, and *Pravda,* 20 September 1977.
28. *Narodnoe khozyaistvo RSFSR v 1980g* (Moscow, 1981), pp. 230, 236, *N. Kh. RSFSR v 1981g* (Moscow, 1982), p. 223.
29. S. A. Grant (ed.), *Soviet Housing and Urban Design* (US Dept. of Housing and Urban Development, Washington, 1980).
30. See, for instance, *Narodnoe khozyaistvo Tyumenskoi oblasti za gody vos'moi pyatiletki* (1971), p. 170; *N.Kh. Kirovskoi oblasti* (1971). p. 129; *Sverdlovskaya oblast' v tsifrakh 1966–70,* (1971), p. 89; *Ivanovskaya oblast' v vos' moi pyatiletke* (1971), pp. 261–2.
31. *Narodnoe khozyaistvo RSFSR v 1975g.* (1976), p. 343.
32. *Yerevan v tsifrakh* (1972), p. 66.
33. *N.Kh. Permskoi oblasti v 9-i pyatiletke* (1974), pp. 153–4.
34. K. I. Nikulin, 'Problemy kooperativnogo khozyaistva', *Gorodskoe Khozyaistvo Moskvy,* no. 2, 1979, p. 22.
35. *Narodnoe khozyaistvo RSFSR v 1975g. op. cit.* pp.343–4.
36. Prokopchenko (1977), *op. cit.* pp. 103, 114; E. P. Lavygin, 'Kooperativnoe stroitel'stvo na sele', *Zhilishchnoe stroitel'stvo,* no, 11, 1978, p. 7; 'Novoe v kooperativnom stroitel'stve', *Ekonomicheskaya gazeta,* no. 5, January 1978, p. 16.
37. H. Morton, 'Who Gets What, When and How? Housing in the Soviet Union', *Soviet Studies,* vol. XXII, no. 2, April 1980, p. 243; S. A. Grant, *op. cit.* p. 25; G. D. Andrusz, 'Some Aspects of Housing and Urban Development in the U.S.S.R', unpub. Ph.D. thesis. (Birmingham University), pp. 125–6.
38. I. S. Budzilovich, *op. cit.,* pp. 88–100.
39. If a co-operative member has gained the consent of the governing body, he may lease out his own flat if he and his family are going to be away for a length of time. This right to sublet is not forfeited even when a member has been 'deprived of freedom' and/or deported – regardless of the duration of the punishment. But the shareholder is prohibited from sub-letting if this would mean that there is less than 6 square metres of living space per person. (N. Shevchenko, M, Nechetskyi, 'Sokhranenie zhiloi ploshchada za paishchikom ZhSK i chelam evo sem'i', *Sovetskaya yustitsiya,* 1972, no. 8, p. 7).
40. I. P. Prokopchenko, (1977), *op. cit.,* p. 253.
41. O. A. Beyul, 'Goroda rastut vverkh', *Izvestiya,* 7 March 1971, p.1.
42. D. Cattell, *Leningrad: A Case Study of Soviet Urban Government,* (London, Praeger, 1968), p. 137.
43. D. Broner (1980) *op. cit.* p. 35; Prokopchenko (1977) *op. cit.* p. 106.

44. This partly explains why one commentator, soon after the legislation setting up the co-operatives, urged that: 'it is necessary to adopt measures to attract into the ZhSKs wider strata of the population' ('Direktivy XXIII S'yezda KPSS', *Izvestiya*, 20 February 1966).
45. 'Novoe v kooperativnom stroitel'stve', *Ekonomicheskaya gazeta*, no. 5, January 1978, p. 16.
46. K. I. Nikulin, *op. cit.* pp. 22–3.
47. I. Prokopchenko (1977), *op. cit.* p.106.
48. Central Statistical Office, *Social Trends* (London, HMSO, 1981) p. 146.
49. Cited by T. Friedgut, *Political Participation in the USSR* (Princeton University Press, 1979).
50. Prokopchenko (1977) *op. cit.* p. 156.
51. B. Svetlichnyi, 'Sovetskim lyudyam – blagoustroennye zhilishcha,' *Kommunist*, April 1965, no. 6, p. 47.

5 THE PRIVATE HOUSING SECTOR

1. Postanovlenie SNK SSSR of 29 May 1944, 'O meropriyatiyakh po vosstanovleniyu individual'nogo zhilishchnogo fonda v osvobozhdennykh raionakh i usileniya individual'nogo stroitel'stva v gorodakh i rabochikh poselkakh SSSR', *SP SSSR*, 1944, no. 7, art. 109. This decree permitted the Central Municipal and Housing Bank (*Tsekombank*) to grant loans to individual builders to erect houses, costing up to 10 000 roubles, the sum being repayable over a seven-year period.
   A decree of 1946 projected that 84 per cent of housing space erected in the Urals, Siberia and the Far East in 1947 should be in 'individual houses' to be sold off to workers and engineers working in these regions. (Postanovlenie Soveta Ministrov SSSR, 14 October 1946, 'O povyshenii zarabotnoi platy i stroitel'stve zhilishch dlya rabochikh i inzhenerno-tekhnicheskikh rabotnikov predpriyatii i stroek, raspolozhennykh na Urale, v Sibire i na Dal'nem Vostoke', *SP SSSR*, 1946, no. 12, art. 226).
2. Ukaz Presidiuma Verkhovnogo Soveta SSSR, 26 August 1948, 'O prave grazhdan na pokupku i stroitel'stvo individual'nykh zhilykh domov', *SP SSSR*, 1948, no. 5, art. 62.
3. A. I. Stanislavskii, *Planirovka i zastroika gorodov Ukrainy* (Kiev, 1971), p. 134.
4. *Stroitel'naya gazeta*, 20 January 1957.
5. D. Cattel, (1968) *op. cit.* p. 134.
6. Postanovlenie TsK KPSS i Soveta Ministrov SSSR, 31 July 1957, 'O razvitii zhilishchnogo stroitel'stva v SSSR', *SP SSSR*, 1957, no. 9. art. 102.
7. Postanovlenie TsK KPSS i Soveta Ministrov SSSR, 1 June 1962, 'Ob individual'nom i kooperativnom zhilishchnom stroitel'stve', *SP SSSR*, 1962, no. 12, art. 93.
8. A. S. Bodyrev (Chairman of Gosstroi RSFSR), 'Stroitel'noi kooperatsii – novye prostory', *Izvestiya*, 20 September 1963.
   Two years earlier, the government acted on another, related front when it forbade 'the allocation of land to citizens to build *dachas* everywhere

(*povsemestna*)' and considered it 'necessary to curtail sales of dachas to citizens by state, co-operative and public organisations'. Postanovlenie Soveta Ministrov SSSR, 30 December 1960, 'Ob individual'nom stroitel'stve dach'. *SP SSSR*, 1961 no. 1, art. 2. The building norms and rules published in 1976 state that one- and two-storey houses may be erected in the suburbs (*prigorodnaya zona*) of the largest cities (i.e. those with populations exceeding 500 000) and in cities with under 250 000 on 'special plots of land set aside for such construction'. However, as is discussed in Chapter 8, care has to be taken in interpreting these statements for low-rise development is by no means synonymous with private building. (*Stroitel'nye normy i pravila. Normy proektirovaniya* (Moscow, 1976), p. 17, para. 5.5.

9. A. G. Potyukov, *Zhilishchnoe pravo* (Leningrad, 1973), p. 6.

10. F. T. Dobrynin, R. V. Lukina, *Ekonomika, organizatsya i planirovanie stroitel'stva* (Moscow, 1971), p. 15.

11. 'Doma – Pasynki', *Izvestiya*, 17 January 1965.

12. Postanovlenie Soveta Ministrov SSSR, 28 August 1967, 'O merakh po uluchsheniyu eksploatatsii zhilishchnogo fonda i ob'yektov kommunal'nogo khozyaistva', *SP SSSR*, 1967, no. 22, art. 156.

13. *Vedomosti Verkhovnogo Soveta SSSR*, 1958, no. 16, art. 284.

14. *SP SSSR*, 1957, no. 2, art. 8; S. N. Landkof *et al., op. cit.* p. 281.

15. Ukas Presidium Verkhovnogo Soveta SSSR, 6 September 1967, 'Ob ustanovlenii dopolnitel'nykh l'got Geroyam Sovetskogo Soyuza, Geroyam Sotsialisticheskogo truda i litsam, nagrazhdennom orderami Slavy trekh stepenei', *Vedomosti Verkhovnogo Soveta SSSR*, 1967, no. 36, art. 496.

16. *SZ SSSR* 1933, no. 23, art. 128; Point 19 Polozhenie o pensionnom obespechenii rabotnikov nauki, utverzhdennogo postanovleniem Soveta Ministrov SSSR, 28 September 1949, *Sbornik zakonodatel'nykh aktov o trude* (Moscow, 1965), p. 778); *SZ SSSR*, 1933, no. 62. art. 393; *SSSR*, 1935, no. 10, art. 79.

17. Article 141 Polozhenie ob otkrytiyakh, izobreteniyakh i ratsionalizatorskikh predlozheniyakh, utverzhdennoe postanovleniem Soveta Ministrov SSSR, 21 August 1973. *SP SSSR*, 1973, no. 19, art 109.

18. *Vedomosti Verkhovnogo Soveta SSSR*, 1964, no. 24, art. 416.

19. B. Svetlichnyi, *op. cit.* p. 47.

20. A. Koryagin, 'Stroitel'stvo kommunizma i zhilishchnyi vopros', *Voprosy ekonomiki*, no. 6, June 1962, p. 37. In view of the continuing problem of agricultural production failing to meet targets, the official Party line is now to encourage subsidiary individual holdings. (*Materialy . . .* (1981), *op. cit.*, p. 48). See: Postanovlenie TsK KPSS i Soveta Ministrov SSSR, 8 January 1981, 'O dopolnitel'nykh merakh po uvelicheniyu proizvodstva sel'skokhozyaistvennou productsu v lichnykh podsobnykh khozyaistvakh grazhdan," *SP SSSR*, 1981, no. 6, art. 37

21. *Osnovy grazhdanskogo zakonodatel'stva*, art. 58, part 2. *Grazhdanskii kodeks RSFSR*, art. 328, parts 2, 3, 4.

22. Postanovlenie Soveta Ministrov RSFSR, 9 August 1963, 'O predel'nykh stavkakh platy za sdavaemie v naem zhilye i dachnye pomeshcheniya v

domakh i dachakh, prinadlezhashchikh grazhdanam na prave lichnoi sobstvennosti', *SP RSFSR*, 1963, no. 15, art. 102.

23. N. S. Nozdrin, L. A. Furman, *Osnovy zhilishchnogo i trudovogo prava*, (Moscow, 1975), p. 75.

24. Whilst the house may be personal property and transferable, Article 238 of the Civil Code does not allow an owner to sell more than one house every three years – although Article 107 of the Code provides for the following exceptions: if an individual or his wife or children receive a house as a gift or as part of an inheritance, then he/she has to dispose of the second dwelling within twelve months of receiving it. If the person does not dispose of it, then the house becomes subject to compulsory sale. The sum of money derived from the sale, after a deduction for costs incurred in its disposal, is handed over to the former owner. In the absence of a buyer for the property, it is transferred by a decision of the Executive Committee of the district or city soviet – without compensation – to the state. Those owning more than one property before 1 October 1964 were exempted from this regulation prohibiting possession of multiple properties so long as they were not a source of unearned income (see *Vedomosti Verkhovnogo Soveta RSFSR*, 1964, no. 24, art. 416). Inheriting a house may not, however, be to a persons's advantage. In response to a reader's enquiry that since his brother had made a present of his house to him, could he now be evicted from his local soviet owned house, the editor replied that: 'the lessor has the right to demand the cancellation of the agreement and evict the leaseholder and his family without offering alternative accommodation in those cases where the leaseholder has a right of personal ownership to a house which is fit for permanent habitation and is in that same locality', (*Zhilishchnoe i kommunal'noe khozyaistvo*, 1977, no. 5, p. 46).

25. M. G. Markova, 'Ponyatie i osushestvlenie prava lichnoi sobstvennosti', *Vestnik Leningradskogo Universiteta (Seriya ekonomiki)*, 1957. no. 5, pp. 103–115.

26. 'O sudebnoi praktike po delam o prave lichnoi sobstvennosti na stroeniya', in *Sbornik postanovlenii plenuma Verkhovnogo Suda SSSR 1924–1970* (Moscow, 1970), pp. 73–78.

27. 'O sudebnoi praktike po delam o bezvozmezdnom iz"yatii domov, dach i drugikh stroenii, vozvedennykh ili priobretennykh grazhdanami na netrudovye dokhody', in *Sbornik postanovlenii . . . op. cit.* pp. 78–82; S. N. Landkof *et al., Zhilishchnoe i zhilishchno–stroitel'noe zakonodatel'stvo* (Kiev, 1975), p. 132.

28. V. P. Gribanov, A. Yu. Kabalkin, *Zhilishchnye prava sovetskikh grazhdan* (Moscow, 1964), p. 17.

29. 'Na chastnoi kvartire', *Pravda*, 9 June 1979, p. 3.

30. N. Gladkov, 'Bumazhnye krugi', *Pravda*, 21 September 1975.

31. *Byulleten' Verkhovnogo Suda RSFSR*, 1975, no. 6.

32. *Byulleten' Verkhovnogo Suda RSFSR*, 1976, no. 3.

33. T. V. Ryabushkin *et al.*, *Sotsiologiya i problemy sotsial'nogo razvitiya* (Moscow, 1978), pp. 191–2, 197.

34. Ibid.

35. *Problemy rasseleniya v SSSR* (Moscow, 1980), pp. 220–1.

36. Postanovlenie Soveta Ministrov SSSR, 20 December 1976, 'O kreditovanii individual'nogo zhilishchnogo stroitel'stva v sel'skoi mestnosti', *SP SSSR 1977* no. 3, art. 17.

37. Postanovlenie TsK KPSS i Soveta Ministrov SSSR, 19 June 1978, 'O dal'neishem razvitii stroitel'stva individual'nykh zhilikh domov i zakreplenii kadrov na sele', *SP SSSR*, 1978, no. 17, art. 102.

38. R. V. Ryvkina, 'Zhilishchnye usloviya i obraz zhizni sel'skogo naseleniya', *Sotsiologicheskie issledovaniya*, 1975, no. 4. See also: I. Filiorenko, 'Dom s sadom', *Pravda*, 17 November 1977, p. 3.

39. Postanovlenie Soveta Ministrov SSSR, 14 April 1979, 'O kreditovanii individual'nogo zhilishchnogo stroitel'stva v gorodakh i poselkakh gorodskogo tipa', *SP SSSR*, 1979, no. 12, art. 74.

40. *SP SSSR,* 1980, no. 3, art. 17.

41. *Byulleten' Verkhovnogo Suda SSSR*, 1975. no. 6.

PART II   INTRODUCTION

1. The interconnectness of housing and town planning is indicated in one criticism levelled at press sensationalisation of discussions on urban planning: 'Under the pretext of a debate on the socialist cities, the soviet public is being invited to discuss problems of the construction of modern housing in the USSR', *Sovremennaya arkhitektura*, nos. 1–2, 1930.

2. As Marx observed: 'The very essence of the city as such is distinguished from a simple aggregation of individual houses. Here the whole is not simply the sum of its parts. It is itself an independent organism'. K. Marx and F. Engels, *Sochineniya*, 2nd edn, vol. 46, part I, p. 470.

3. For instance: 'The city is itself a system which organically enters into much a larger and more complex social formation'. P. N. Lebedev, *Sistema organov gorodskogo upravleniya* (Leningrad, 1980), p. 14.

6   THE SOCIAL AND SPATIAL DIMENSIONS OF SOVIET HOUSING POLICY

1. *KPSS v resolyutsiakh i resheniyakh s"ezdov, konferentsii i plenumov TsK, (1897–1970)*, 8th edn, vol. 2 (Moscow, 1970), pp. 43, 38. The phrase 'liberating women from the shackles of the domestic economy' can be found in conferences and resolutions ever since. See for example, the June 1931 Plenum of the Central Committee of the RKP(b), 'O moskovskom gorodskom khozyaistve i o razvitii gorodskogo khozyaistva SSSR', in *Resheniya partii i pravitel'stva po khozyaistvennym voprosam*, vol. 2, 1929–40 (Moscow, 1967), p. 322.

2. V. I. Lenin, 'O zadachakh zhenskogo rabochego dvizheniya v sovetskom republike', (Rech' na IV moskovskoi obshchegorodskoi bezpartiinoi konferentsii rabotnits, 23 September 1919, in *Pol'noe sobranie sochinenii*, vol. 39, 5th edn. (Moscow 1963), p. 201.

3. *Iz istorii Sovetskoi arkhitektury 1917–1925gg. Dokumenty i materialy* (Moscow, 1963), pp. 63–64.

4. *Perspektivy razvitiya zhilishcha v SSSR* (Moscow, 1975), Appendix A.
5. A. V. Lunacharskii, 'Arkhitekturnoe oformlenie gorodov: kul'tura v sotsialisticheskikh gorodakh', *Revolyutsia i kul'tura*, 1930, no. 1.
6. S. G. Strumlin, *Izbrannie proizvedenniya*, vol. 4 (Moscow, 1964), p. 13. Even as an octogenarian in the 1960s, Strumlin continued to advance these ideas. See, for instance, *Novy Mir,* July 1960, no. 7; *Oktyabr'* March 1960, no. 3, and a longer discussion in: *Nash mir cherez 20 let* (Moscow, 1964).
7. N. A. Milyutin, *Problema stroitel'stva sotsialisticheskikh gorodov* (Moscow, 1930).
8. V. Ya. Belousov, *Kul'turnye zadachi zhilishchnoi kooperatsii* (Moscow, 1926), p. 25.
9. N. I. Kozerenko, *Zhilishchnyi krizis i bor'ba s nim* (Moscow, 1928), p. 262.
10. L. M. Sabsovich, *Goroda budushchego i organizatsiya sotsialisticheskogo byta* (Moscow, 1929).
11. L. M. Sabsovich, *SSSR cherez 10 let: gipoteza general'nogo plana kak plana postroenia sotsializma v SSSR* (Moscow, 1929), p. 128.
12. L. M. Sabsovich, 'O proektirovanii zhilykh kombinatov', *Sovremennaya arkhitektura*, no. 3, 1930, p. 7.
13. M. A. Milyutin, 'Osnovnye voprosy zhilishchno-bytovogo stroitel'stva SSSR', *Sovremennaya arkhitektura*, no. 1, 1931, pp. 2–4.
14. N. G. Chernyshevsky, *What is to be done?* (trans. B. Tucker), (New York, Vintage Books, 1961) (First published in Russian in 1864). The 'new Soviet woman', strikingly similar to Vera Pavlovna, is well depicted in the novel by F. Gladkov, *Cement* (trans. A. Arthur and C. Ashleigh), London, 1929 (First published in Russian in 1925).
15. N. A. Milyutin, *Problema stroitel'stva sotsialisticheskikh gorodov* (Moscow, 1930), trans. A. Spague as *Sotsgorod: The Problem of Building Socialist Cities*, (London, MIT Press, 1974), p. 81.
16. Unquestionably the best book in the English language on the debates and experiments in architecture, designs for living and urban planning in the Soviet Union in the pre-war years is: A. Kopp, *Town and Revolution. Soviet Architecture and City Planning 1917–1935* trans. from the French by T. E. Burton (New York, George Braziller, 1970).
17. L.Ya. Vygodskii, 'Osnovy gradostroitel'stva i planirovki v usloviyakh sotsialisticheskogo stroya', *Planovoe khozyaistvo*, 1927, no. 2.
18. M. A. Okhitovich, 'Ne gorod – a novyi tip rasseleniya', in *Goroda sotsialisma* (Moscow, 1930).
19. A. Pasternak, 'Spory o budushchem goroda', *Sovremennaya arkhitektura*, nos. 1–2, 1930, p. 60.
20. *Sovremennaya arkhitektura*, nos 1–2, 1930. pp. 4–6.
21. A. Pasternak, *op. cit.*
22. I. Lermak, 'K probleme sotsialisticheskogo goroda', *Kommunal'noe delo*, no. 1, 1930.
23. See, for instance, G. M. Krzhizhanovskii, *Problemy postroeniya General'nogo plana* (Moscow, 1930).
24. United Nations, Dept. of Economic and Social Affairs, *Growth of the World's Urban and Rural Population, 1920–2000* (New York, 1969), pp. 31, 58.

25. Postanovlenie SNK SSSR, 23 April 1934, 'Ob uluchshenii zhilishchnogo stroitel'stva', *SZ SSSR,* 1934, no. 23, art. 180. The Sixteenth All-Russian Congress of Soviets held on 15–23 January 1935 reiterated that four- and five-storey houses (with all amenities) should be built in towns and workers' settlements. *SU RSFSR,* 1935, no. 9, art. 97.

26. For a discussion of these two 'traditions', see P. Hall, *Urban and Regional Planning,* (Harmondsworth, Penguin, 1974), ch 3.

27. El Lissitzky, *Russia: Architecture for World Revolution* (London, Lund Humphries, 1970), p. 35.

28. *Pravda,* 29 May 1930.

29. Postanovlenie SNK SSSR, 11 March 1931, 'O vypolnenii direktiva Soveta narodnykh komissarov Soyuza SSR i TsK VKP(b) ob uluchshenii i udeshevlenii rabochego zhilishchnogo stroitel'stva', *SZ SSSR,* 1931, no. 4, art. 143.

30. *KPSS v resolyutsiakh i resheniyakh s"ezdov, konferentsii i plenumov TsK,* 8th edn. vol. 4 (Moscow, 1970), pp. 557–558.

31. *Stroitel'stvo Moskvy,* nos. 8–9, August–September 1932.

32. V. Nekrasov, 'O proshlom, nastoyashchem i chut' – chut' o budushchem', *Literaturnaya gazeta,* 20 February 1960.

33. O. Shvidovsky, *Le Korbyusier: tvorcheskii put'* (Moscow, 1970), p. 22.

34. As Engels explained in his letter to Bloch: 'The economic situation is the basis, but the various elements of the superstructure ... also exercise their influence upon the course of historical struggle and in many cases preponderate in determining their form', K. Marx and F. Engels, *Selected Works,* vol. 2 (Moscow, 1962), p. 488.

35. Cf. D. Bell, *The Coming of Post-Industrial Society,* London, Heinemann, 1973), pp. 159–160: The vast increase in participation by individuals and groups in city life in America at present 'leads to a paradox – the greater the number of groups, each seeking diverse or competing ends, the more likelihood that these groups will veto one another's interests ... Thus the problem of how to achieve consensus on political questions will become more difficult. Without consensus there is only conflict and persistent conflict simply tears a society apart, leaving the way open to repression by one sizeable force or another'.

36. V. I. Lenin, 'O nashei revolyutsii', *Polnoe sobranie sochinenii,* vol. 45, 5th ed. (Moscow) p. 381.

37. B. B. Veselovskii, *Kurs ekonomiki i planirovaniya kommunal'nogo khozyaistva* (Moscow, 1945), p. 154.

38. Cited by R. Nisbet, in *The Sociological Tradition* (London, Heinemann, 1970), p. 40.

39. See, for instance, C. Buci-Glucksmann, *Gramsci and the State* (London, Lawrence & Wishart, 1980).

40. A. Ya. Vyshinskii, *S"ezdy Sovetov RSFSR* (Moscow, 1939), p. 463; *SU RSFSR,* 1935, no. 9, art. 97.

41. On efforts to improve the manpower situation, see: *Spravochinik partiinogo rabotnika,* vypusk 8 (Moscow, 1934), pp. 446–7; Postanovlenie SNK RSFSR, 2 March 1935, 'Ob utverzhdenii Polozheniya ob institute rukovodyashchikh kadrov kommunal'nogo khozyaistva', *SU RSFSR,* 1935, no. 7, art. 75; Postanovlenie SNK SSSR i TsK VKP(b), 11 Feb-

ruary 1936: 'Ob uluchschenii stroitel'nogo dela i ob udeshevlenii stroitel'stva', in *Resheniya partii i pravitel'stva ...* vol. 2 (Moscow, 1967), p. 577. This last decree set up schools and encouraged the formation of correspondence courses for training building-trades craftsmen and improving the earnings of building workers.

42. Postanovlenie SNK SSSR, 23 April, 1934, 'Ob uluchshenii zhilishchnogo stroitel'stva', *SZ SSSR*, 1934, no. 23, art. 180.

43. As one Soviet planner writing in the 1960s observed: By the end of the 1930s, a compromise had been reached between 'the creative devices of architects and the real possibilities of construction'. *Arkhitektura zhilogo kompleksa* (Moscow, 1969), p. 36.

44. The best documented source on this subject for the 1930s in English remains, T. Sosnovy, *The Housing Problem in the Soviet Union* (New York, 1954).

45. V. A. Gradov, the director of the Central Scientific Research and Design Institute for Standard and Experimental Designs for Educational Establishments (*TsNIIEP uchebnykh zdanii*), is the most important spokesman and representative of what might be called a 'visionary' or left-wing tendency in the urban planning profession. See, for example, his book, *Gorod i byt* (Moscow, 1968) and his contributions in: *Napravlenie formirovaniya sistemy i tipov obshchestvennykh zdanii* (Moscow, 1971); *Obshchestvennye zdaniya* (Moscow, 1973).

46. B. V. Sazonov, 'Sotsial'nyi smysl' gradstroitel'nykh kontseptsii obshchestvennogo obsluzhivaniya gorodskogo naseleniya', in O. I. Shkaratan, A. N. Alekseev, *Planirovanie sotsial'nogo razvitiya gorodov* (Moscow, 1973), p. 172.

47. Postanovlenie TsK KPSS i Soveta Ministrov SSSR, 20 February 1959, 'O dal'neishem razvitii i uluchshenii obshchestvennogo pitaniya', *SP SSR*, 1959, no. 4, art. 24.

48. B. V. Sazonov, *op. cit.* p. 174.

49. S. G. Strumlin, *Izbrannye proizvodeniya*, vol. 5 (Moscow, 1960), p. 424.

50. *Rekomendatsii po proektirovaniyu obshchestvennykh tsentrov mikroraionov* (Moscow, 1974); *Perspektivy razvitiya zhilishcha v SSSR* (Moscow, 1975).

51. B. V. Sazonov, *op. cit.* p. 174.

52. L. Kogan, V. Lokter 'Nekotorye sotsiologicheskie aspekty modelirovaniya gorodov', *Voprosy folosofii*, no. 4, 1964.

53. V. A. Kamenskii, V. I. Vasilevskii, 'Puti resheniya problemy rasseleniya krupnogo goroda na primere Leningrade', *Trudy VI Sessii Akademii Stroitel'stva i Arkhitektury po voprosam gradostroitel'stva* (Moscow, 1961), pp. 74–75.

54. *Narodnoe khozyaistvo SSR v1980g.*, p. 171.

55. A. M. Yakshin, *Perspektivy razvitiya seti gorodskikh magistraelei* (Moscow, 1975), p. 34.

56. T. V. Ryabushkin *et al. Sotsiologiya i problemy sotsial'nogo razvitiya* (Moscow, 1978) p. 190.

57. V. T. Efimov, G. I. Mikerin, 'Avtomobilizatsiya v razvitom sotsialisticheskom obshchestve', *Sotsiologicheskie issledovaniya*, no. 1, 1976, pp. 128–138.

58. Efimov and Mikerin, Ibid.
59. In 1975, the USA had 495 cars per 1000 people, Sweden – 323, France – 288 and Italy – 257. *Basic Statistics of the Community. Comparisons with Some European Countries, Canada, USA, Japan and the USSR, 1975–76* (Luxemburg, Eurostat, 1977), p. 169.
60. A. M. Bazilevich *et al.* 'O general'nom plane g. Tol'yatti', in *Voprosy gradostroitel'stva* (Kiev, 1968), pp. 12–18; B. V. Cherepanov, 'Organizatsiya dvizheniya transports v predzavodskikh zonakh gorodov s krupnymi promyshlennymi uzlami', in *Perspektivy gradostroitel'nogo proektirovaniya na osnove nauchnykh issledovanii*, (Moscow, 1975), p. 81.
61. V. I. Perevedentsev, *Goroda i vremya* (Moscow, 1975), p. 45.
62. A. G. Kharchev, V. G. Alekseeva, 'Sotsial'naya sreda i vospitanie', *Vestnik Moskovskogo universiteta. Nauchnyi Kommunizm*, no. 6, 1973, p. 46.
63. In 1982, three years after the last population census held in January 1979, not a single volume of censal data has been published, hence the references here to the 1970 census.
64. K. Marx, *Capital*, vol. 1 (London, Lawrence & Wishart, 1970), p. 352.
65. M. M. Rutkevitch, 'O sotsial'nom razlichii mezhdu gorodom i derevnei v sovremennyi period', in *Problemy razvitiya Sotsialisticheskikh obshchestvennykh otnoshenii. Materialy gorodskoi nauchnoi konferentsii obshchestvennykh nauk*, (Sverdlovsk, 1970), p. 3.
66. *Ekonomicheskaya gazeta*, no. 4. January, 1978, p. 22. The CPSU Programme states that: 'Only when the public sector can completely replace the private plot and when the collective farmers are convinced that it is not to their advantage to maintain the private plot will they of their own free will abandon it'. *Programma KPSS*, Politizdat, 1961, 1975, p. 83).
67. A. V. Topilin, *Territorial'noe pereraspredelenie trudovykh resursov v SSSR* (Moscow, 1975), p. 94.
68. See, for instance, *Kratkii ekonomicheskii slovar'* (Moscow, 1968), pp. 157–58.
69. R. G. Vartanov, 'Klassy ili osnovnye sloi?' in *Problemy izmeneniya sotsial'noi struktury sovetskogo obshchestva'* (Moscow, 1968).
70. A. G. Pyrin, 'Lichnoe podsobnoe khozyaistvo kak faktor sotsial'nkh razlichii sredi gorodskogo naseleniya', in M. N. Rutkevitch (ed). *Sotsial'nye razlichiya i ikh preodolenie: sotsiologicheskie issledovaniya*, vypusk 3 (Sverdlovsk, 1969), p. 93. Also, M. I. Gigashvili, 'O sootnoshenii sushestvennykh razlichii mezhdu gorodom i derevnei i klassovykh razlichii', in *Problemy izmeneniya . . . op. cit.*
71. I. P. Trufanov, *Problemy byta gorodskogo naseleniya* (Leningrad 1973), p. 106. In Latvia, the average working day of a working mother (including household chores) is 2 to 3 hours longer than that of a working man. (R. Galetskaya, 'Demograficheskaya politika: ee napravleniya', *Voprosy ekonomiki*, August 1975, no. 8, pp. 149–152.
72. T. V. Ryabushkin *et al. op. cit.* p. 245.
73. *Demograficheskie problemy zanyatosti*, (Moscow, 1969), p. 108.
74. L. A. Gordon, E. V. Klopov, *Chelovek posle raboty: Sotsial'nye problemy byta i vnerabochego vremeni* (Moscow, 1972), p. 126.

75. *Trud*, 16 July 1982, p. 4. The author of the article made a number of 'interesting' observations: 'Another important duty of the husband is childrearing. However, our children's upbringing often leaves much to be desired, largely because in many families only the mother deals with the children. But the mother's tender heart and the father's sensible mind are equally necessary in forming a child's character'. For further discussion on this and related topics on women in Soviet society, see: J. Brine et al., *Home, School and Leisure in the Soviet Union* (London, Allen and Unwin, 1980); G. W. Lapidus, *Women in Soviet Society* (Berkeley, University of California Press, 1978).

76. As one correspondent noted, many enterprises ignore the construction of nurseries of their workers' children because it has no bearing on the plant's performance-evaluation indicators. (D. Novplyanskii, 'Otkaz', *Pravda*, 14 November 1976, p. 3). A recent report prepared by the Kursk *oblast'* Soviet Committee on Education rebuked factories and institutions for failing to put pressure on builders in view of 'the lack of nurseries has caused a great shortage of female labour (4000 in the city of Kursk alone) and has turned at least one factory into a chronically poor performer'. (V. Novikov, 'Nesostoyavshiesya novosel'ya', *Izvestiya*, 4 January 1977, p. 2). At present, in 'many' republics (for example, the RSFSR and Moldavia) over half of the children of pre-school age attend nurseries. ('Detskim sadam – zabotu i vnimanie', *Izvestiya*, 7 February 1978.). In comparison, in 1979 in England and Wales, the number of full-day care places for pre-school children was 121 500 – equivalent to 40 places per 1000 children under the age of five. 57 per cent of these children were cared for by registered child-minders, 23 per cent in local authority nurseries, 18 per cent in other nurseries and just 2 per cent in employer-provided nurseries. Even when day care places provided for under-fives on a sessional (mainly play group) basis are included, the total number of children catered for amounts to only 140 places per 1000 children in the age group. *Central Statistical Office, Social Trends* (London, HMSO, 1981), p. 43.

77. *Narodnoe khozyaistvo SSSR v 1980g.*, p. 31.

78. V. Perevedentsev, *Literaturnaya gazeta*, no. 33, 13 August 1975.

79. *Voprosy narodonaseleniya i demograficheskoi statistiki* (Moscow, 1966), p. 254.

80. B. Ts. Urlanis, *Problemy dinamiki naseleniya SSSR* (Moscow, 1974), pp. 117–119.

81. V. I. Perevedentsev, *Goroda i vremya* (Moscow, 1975), pp. 57–59; see also: Yu. Ryurikov, 'Pochemu detei stanovitsa men'she', *Literaturnaya gazeta*, no. 46, November 1976, p. 13.

82. P. Grossman (Central Intelligence Agency) 'Labour Supply Constraints and Responses', in H. Hunter (ed.), *The Future of the Soviet Economy: 1978–1985* (Boulder, Colorado, Westview Press, 1978), p. 155.

83. M. Feshbach, S. Rapawy, 'Labour Constraints in the USSR', US Congress, Joint Economic Committee, *Soviet Economic Prospects for the Seventies* (Washington, DC, US Government Printing Office, 1973), pp. 485–563.

84. T. V. Ryabushkin, *op. cit.* p. 216.

85. *Materialy ...* (1981), *op. cit.* p. 55.
86. V. Belova, *Chislo detei v sem'e* (Moscow, 1975), p. 109; M. Feshbach, 'Between the lines of the 1979 Soviet Census', *Problems of Communism*, Jan–Feb 1982, p. 36.
87. M. Feshbach, Ibid.
88. V. Barsis, *Sotsial'nye problemy svobodnogo vremeni trudyashchikhsya* (Vilnius, 1974), p. 82.
89. *Sotsiologicheskie issledovaniya*, no. 2, April–June 1979, pp. 90–92.
90. *Literaturnaya gazeta*, 16 May 1979, p. 13.
91. *Materialy XXV S''ezda KPSS* (Moscow, 1976), p. 126.
92. *Politicheskoe samoobrazovanie*, no. 7, 1976, p. 125.
93. *Osnovnye napravleniya razvitiya narodnogo khozyaistva SSSR na 1976–1980 gody* (Moscow, 1976), p. 70. According to Urlanis, an increase in the number of pre-school places will only be important insofar as it might, to a certain extent, influence the woman's decision to have a second child. B. Ts. Urlanis, *Problemy dinamiki naseleniya SSSR* (Moscow, 1974), p. 112. One of the most significant demographic changes which has occurred in recent years is the dramatic drop in the proportion of children born to mothers with three or more children from 38 per cent in 1965 to 26 per cent in 1975. *Narodnoe khozyaistvo SSSR v 1975* (Moscow, 1976), p. 41.
94. *Sovetskaya Rossiya*, 17 May 1979, p. 4.
95. *Perspektivy razvitiya zhilishcha v SSSR* (Moscow, 1975), p. 14.
96. *Materialy ...* (1981), *op. cit.*, pp. 105, 178.
97. Postanovlenie TsK KPSS i Soveta Minstrov SSSR, 22 January 1981, 'O merakh po usileniyu gosudarstvennoi pomoshchi sem'yam, imeyushchim detyei,' *SP SSSR*, 1981, no. 13, art. 75; Postanovlenie Soveta Ministrov SSSR i VTsSPS, 2 September 1981, 'O poryadke vvedeniya chastichno oplathivaemogo otpuska po ukhody za rebenkom do dostizheniya im vozrasta odnogo goda i drugikh meropriyatii po usileniyu gosudarstvennoi pomoshchi sem'yam, imeyushchim detei,' *SP SSSR*, 1981, no. 24, art. 141.
98. *Perspektivy razvitiya zhilishcha v SSSR*, *op. cit.* pp. 22–3.
99. O. N. Yanitskii, 'Simposium po problemam urbanizatsii', *Voprosy filosofii*, no. 10, 1969, p. 143.
100. D. L. Broner, (1980), *op. cit.* p. 55.
101. B. Brandenburg, 'Novyi tip gorodskogo zhilishcha dlya semei iz trekh pokolenii,' *Arkhitektura SSSR*, no. 9, 1979, pp. 44–49.
102. *Voprosy demografii* (Moscow, 1970), pp. 253–4.
103. I. P. Katkova, *Demograficheskoe povedenie molodykh semei* (Moscow, 1970), pp. 4–5.
104. D. L. Broner, *op. cit.* p. 49.
105. J. Chinn, *Manipulating Soviet Population Resources* (London, Macmillan, 1977), pp. 126–130. See also, H. Desfosses (ed.), *Soviet Population Policy* (Oxford, Pergamon Press, 1981).
106. e.g. B. Ts. Urlanis, *Problemy dinamiki naseleniya SSSR* (Moscow, 1976); A. Kvasha, *Demograficheskaya politika v SSSR* (Moscow, 1981).
107. T. V. Ryabushkin, *op. cit.* pp. 208–16, 240.

108. N. Dimitriev, *Zhilishchnyi vopros* (Moscow, 1973), p. 150.
109. For detailed discussion of the Dom novogo byta see: 'Dom, v kotorom budem zhit', *Literaturnaya gazeta*, no. 45, 6 November 1968; Yu. Polukhin, 'Mnogoe viditsya po-inomu', *Literaturnaya gazeta*, no. 52, 25 December 1968; Ya. Zhuchok, 'Dom s privilegiyami?...' *Literaturnaya gazeta*, no. 2, 8 January 1969; N. Osterman, 'Razvedka budushchego', *Literaturnaya gazeta*, no. 10, 5 March 1969; P. Bronnikov, 'Doma, podobnye derev'yam', *Literaturnaya gazeta*, no. 35, 30 August 1972.
110. M. A. Sidorov, 'Nekotorye voprosy razvitiya zhilshchnogo stroitel'stva na perspektivu', *Zhilishchnoe stroitel'stvo*, no. 4, April 1979, p. 13.
111. *Materialy XXII S"ezda KPSS* (Moscow, 1962), p. 390.
112. Ya. E. Dikhter, 'Dom novogo byta', *Gorodskoe khozyaistvo Moskvy*, no. 1, 1979, p. 11.
113. D. Broner (1980) *op. cit.* p. 31.
114. Women represent 51 per cent of the total labour force and 49 per cent of workers in industry. In 1959, 27.4 per cent of women of working age stayed at home; in 1970, only 10.3 per cent did not go out to work. International Labour Office, *Work and Family Life. The Role of the Social Infrastructure in East European Countries* (Geneva, 1980), pp. 61–3.
115. D. Broner (1980) *op. cit.* pp. 55–6.
116. See, for example, N. Spulber, *Socialist Management and Planning* (Indiana University Press, 1971); I. Jeffries (ed.), *The Industrial Enterprise in Eastern Europe* (New York, Praeger, 1981).

7 THE HOUSING PROBLEM: ECONOMIC AND TECHNOLOGICAL ASPECTS

1. 'If the railway had reached Surgut in 1967 instead of 1974, the Tyumen' complex would have been spared many of the transportation problems it has today. If planning agencies had possessed sufficient foresight, the Tyumen' *oblast'* would now have its own pipe mill instead of having to transship pipe right across the country. If a power line had been built from Surgut to Urengoi four or five years ago, Urengoi would today have its own power supply and not have to rely on undependable temporary sources. It is clear that had money been invested in capital construction just 3 or 4 years earlier, the resultant economic efforts would have been enormous.' *Ekonomika i organizatsiya promyshlennogo proizvodstva*, no. 2, 1979, pp. 5–11.
2. *Materialy ...* (1981), *op. cit.*, pp. 36–7.
3. H. Kissinger, *White House Years* (New York, Little, Brown, 1979).
4. Postanovlenie SNK SSSR, 11 March 1931: 'O vypolnenii direktiva Soveta narodnykh komissarov Soyuza SSR i TsK VKP(b) o uluchshenii i udeshevlenii rabochego zhilishchnogo stroitel'stva', *SZ SSSR*, 1931, no. 4, art. 143.
5. V. Shmidt, *Rabochii klass SSSR i zhilishchnyi vopros* (Moscow, 1929), p. 73.
6. Postanovlenie SNK SSSR, 1 January 1930: 'O merakh uluchsheniyu

raboty stroitel'nykh organizatsii', *SZ SSSR*, 1930, no. 2, art. 22; *SZ SSSR*, 1933, no. 24, art. 142; *SZ SSSR*, 1936, no. 9, art. 9, ('Ob uluchshenii stroitel'nogo dela i ob udeshevlenii stroitel'stva'); *SU SSSR*, 1938, no. 9, art. 58, ('Ob uluchshenii proektnogo i smetnogo dela i ob uporyadochenii finansirovaniya stroitel'stva').

7. *SP SSSR*, 1938, no. 9, art. 57.

8. Postanovlenie SNK RSFSR, 5 June 1939, 'O typovikh proektakh zhilishchnogo stroitel'stva', *SZ SSSR*, 1939, no. 33, art. 232.

9. *SZ SSSR*, 1931, no. 14, art. 143, *op. cit.*

10. Postanovlenie Soveta Ministrov SSSR, 6 April 1951, 'Ob ukreplenii proektnykh organizatsii i likvidatsii melkikh proektnykh kontor', in *Resheniya partii i pravitel'stva po khozyaistvennym voprosam*, vol. 3, (Moscow, 1968), pp. 656–659.

11. This committee was set up by a decree of 1943. See: Postanovlenie SNK SSSR, 29 September 1943, 'Ob obrazovanii komiteta po delam arkhitektury pri Sovnarkome SSSR', *SP SSSR*, 1943, no. 13, art. 231.

12. Postanovlenie Soveta Ministrov SSSR, 24 August 1955, 'O merakh po uluchsheniyu raboty proektnykh organizatsii', in *Direktivy KPSS i Sovetskogo pravitel'stva po khozyaistvennym voprosam*, vol. 4 (Moscow, 1958), pp. 497–500.

13. Postanovlenie TsK KPSS i Soveta Ministrov SSSR, 4 November 1955: 'Ob ustranenii izlishchestv v proektirovanii i stroitel'stve', in *Direktivy KPSS i Sovetskogo pravitel'stva . . .*, *op. cit.* pp. 515–525.

14. Postanovlenie Soveta Ministrov SSSR, 20 February 1959 'Ob uluchshenii proektnogo dela v stroitel'stve', *SP SSSR*, 1959, no. 3, art. 18. The government could not have expressed itself more clearly or forcefully and yet four years later another decree, after acknowledging that 'design organisations have made considerable progress in recent years', went on to add that 'the most advanced technological processes are still not being employed'. *SP SSSR*, 1963, no. 16, art. 160.

15. Postanovlenie VTsIK i SNK RSFSR, 4 October 1926, 'Ob ob''yazannosti dlya gorodskikh poselenii i poselkov imet' plany i proekty planirovki', *SN RSFSR* (1926), no. 65, art. 512.

16. A. V. Vlasov, 'Stroitel'stvo i zadachi arkhitektorov', *Pravda*, 19 May 1961, p. 2.

17. 'Planirovku malykh gorodov nuzhno uprosit' i uskorit'', *Pravda*, 3 February 1960, p. 3.

18. Postanovlenie Soveta Ministrov SSSR, 21 August 1963, 'Ob uluchshenii proektnogo dela v oblasti grazhdanskogo stroitel'stva i zastroiki gorodov', *SP SSSR*, 1963, no. 16, art. 170. By 1981, 'almost all towns and 75 per cent of urban-type settlements' had *genplans*. But 'these quickly become obsolete because of the rapid pace of change in the economy at large.' B. Ya. Ionas, G. G. Starostina, *Ekonomika stroitel'stva* (Moscow, 1981), p. 128.

19. All these cities with the exception of Volgograd, Riga and Rostov-on-Don, today have populations in excess of one million. The remaining three will have joined the millionaire set by 1990.

20. The actual ratification of plans depends on the size and function of the city: (a) general plans for Moscow and Leningrad are examined by

Gosgrazhdanstroi and then presented to *Gosplan* USSR, *Gosstroi* USSR and the Council of Ministers USSR for their acceptance; (b) general plans for capitals of Union Republics and for a number of other cities and all new towns are ratified by the Union Republic Council of Ministers in agreement with *Gosgrazhdanstroi*; (c) cities with populations of over 500 000 require the further consent of *Gosstroi* USSR and *Gosplan* USSR; (d) *Gosgrazhdanstroi* was also charged with working out in conjunction with Union Republican Councils of Ministers a system for ratifying development plans for all remaining towns.

21. Postanovlenie TsK KPSS i Soveta Ministrov SSSR, 28 May 1969, 'Ob uluchshenii proektno-smetnogo dela', *SP SSSR*, 1969, no. 15, art. 83.

22. These institutes conduct research into and design, among other things: housing; educational, cultural and recreational complexes, health centres and sanatoria.

23. P. N. Lebedev, *Sistema organov gorodskogo upravleniya* (Leningrad, 1980), p. 89.

24. Ibid.

25. *Perspektivnoe planirovanie ekonomicheskogo i sotsial'nogo razvitiya goroda: Metodticheskie rekomendatsii* (Moscow, 1977).

26. For instance, *SP RSFSR*, 1974, no. 11, art. 51; *Konstitutsiya SSSR*, (1977), art. 147; see also, Chapter 3, this volume.

27. P. Lebedev, *op. cit.* p. 94.

28. Postanovlenie TsK KPSS i Soveta Ministrov SSSR, 12 July 1979, 'Ob uluchshenii planirovaniya i usilenii vozdeistviya khozyaistvennogo mekhanizma na povyshenie effektivnosti proizvodstva i kachestva raboty,' *SP SSSR*, 1979, no. 18, art. 118.

29. Lebedev, *op. cit.* p. 96.

30. In these circumstances it is unwise, when Soviet researchers and officials themselves do not find it easy to understand the relationship between organisations, to attribute the absence of organisational charts, classificatory systems indicating command hierarchies and responsibilities of institutions, ministries and various agencies to deviousness or secrecy on the part of Soviet officials. They simply do not exist.

31. Lebedev, *op. cit.* p. 100.

32. I. Dmitriev (Head of the Construction department of the Central Committee of the CPSU), 'Stroit' bystro, ekonomichno, na sovremennoi tekhnicheskoi osnove', *Ekonomicheskaya gazeta*, no. 46, 1976, p. 6. See also, L. Eidinova, 'Finansirovanie zhilishchnogo khozyaistva i osobennosti ego vzaimootnoshenii s byudzhetom', *Zhilishchnoe i kommunal'noe khozyaistvo*, no. 3, 1977, p. 15.

33. Postanovlenie TsK KPSS i Soveta Ministrov SSSR, 30 March 1981, 'O merakh po dal'neishemu uluchsheniyu proektno-smetnogo dela', *SP SSSR*, 1981, no. 14, art. 84.

34. *Materialy . . .* (1981), *op. cit.* pp. 174–5.

35. *SP SSSR*, 1964, no. 8, art. 54. Gosgrazhdanstroi has become the most important organisation in the field of housing and civic design and urban planning. It is assisted by a number of organisations notably the Central Scientific Institute for Town Planning (*TsNIIP gradostroitel'stva*) which 'provides methodological guidance in the working out of designs of

general city plans, draws up the rules and norms for urban planning and (when called upon as consultant) works out lay-out plans for individual cities'.

36. *SP SSSR*, 1968, no. 3, art. 14.
37. D. S. Meerson, D. G. Tonskii, *Zhilishchnoe stroitel'stvo v SSSR v desyatoi pyatiletke* (Moscow, 1977), pp. 23ff.
38. Postanovlenie TsK KPSS i Soveta Ministrov SSSR, 28 May 1969, 'O merakh po uluchsheniyu kachestva zhilishchno-grazhdanskogo stroitel'stva', *SP SSSR*, 1969, no. 15, art. 84.
39. A strikingly similar barrage of criticisms had been raised by a report on housing in England and Wales published in 1961. 'Homes are being built at the present time which are not only too small to provide adequately for the family but are also too small to hold the possessions in which so much of the new affluence is being expressed. In the present consumer oriented industrial societies, storage place for gadgets and consumer durables is a central concern for planners. The "private domain" then expands in order to provide not so much more space for people as for things.' The authors of the report added sombrely that such expansion is at the expense of the community of individuals. (*Central Housing Advisory Committee, Homes for Today and Tomorrow*) The Parker Morris *Report* (London, HMSO, 1961), pp. 2–3.
40. *Materialy ...* (1981), *op. cit.*, p. 63. Mr Brezhnev repeated the much quoted quip that 'we should avoid cases such as that of the film character who found himself in another town and was unable to distinguish either the house or the flat he entered from his own'.
41. S. A. Grant, *op. cit.* p. 35.
42. *Pravda*, 28 March 1979, p. 3.
43. The Supreme Soviet passed resolutions in 1928, 1934, 1939 and 1946 forbidding the construction of new residential estates if there were no design drawings and cost estimates. See: T. Sosnovy (1954), *op. cit.* p. 79.
44. Yu. Sokolov, L. Avdot'kin, 'Arkhitekturnoe obrazovanie i nauchno-tekhnicheskii progress', *Arkhitektura SSSR*, no. 7, 1971, pp. 50–1; V. N. Belousov, 'Im prodolzhat' nashe delo', *Arkhitektura SSSR*, no. 13, 1978.
45. According to Soviet accounts, a preliminary step towards industrial construction was taken in 1944 with the issuing of a decree which envisaged that by July 1945, 3.6 million square metres of living space would be erected annually from factory-assembled units. In 1946, the first blocks of flats using large, factory-produced concrete panels were erected. See: Postanovlenie Gosudarstvennogo komiteta Oborony, 23 May 1944, 'O sozdanii industrial'noi bazy dlya massovogo zhilishchnogo stroitel'stva', in *Resheniya partii i pravitel'stva po khozyaistvennym voprosam*, vol. 3 (Moscow, 1963), pp. 200–5; *Industrializatsiya zhilishchnogo stroitel'stva v SSSR* (Moscow, 1965), p. 26.
46. Yu. Safronov, *Organizatsiya zhilishchnogo stroitel'stva* (Moscow, 1972), pp. 28–31.
47. G. Kochetkov, 'Paradoksy gorodskikh informatsionnykh sistem SShA', *Gorodskoe khozyaistvo Moskvy*, no. 4, 1979, pp. 33–4.
48. B. Ya. Ionas, G. G. Starostina, *op. cit.* p. 34.
49. Postanovlenie Soveta Ministrov SSSR, 9 May 1950, 'O snizhenii

stoimosti stroitel'stva', in *Resheniya partii. . . op. cit.*, vol. 3, pp. 603–14. See also, *Resheniya partii. . .* vol. 4, 1968, pp. 250–68.

50. B. Ya. Ionas, M. F. Yasneva, *Ekonomicheskie problemy razvitiya domos-troitel'nykh kombinatov* (Moscow, 1972), p. 8.

51. *Stroitel'nye normy i pravila. Glava 1. Zhilye zdaniya. Normy proek-tirovaniya.* (SNiP 11–L. 1–71) (Moscow, 1971).

52. S. V. Smirnova, 'Predlozheniya po snizheniyu smetnoi stoimosti zhilishchno-grazhdanskogo stroitel'stva', *Zhilishchnoe stroitel'stvo*, no. 1, 1978, pp. 27–29.

53. D. S. Meerson, D. G. Tonskii, *op. cit.* p. 8; *Zhilishchnoe stroitel'stvo*, no. 11, 1967, p. 16; 'Zhilishchnoe stroitel'stvo', *Ekonomicheskaya gaze-ta*, no. 8, February 1975, p. 2.

54. B. Ya. Ionas, G. G. Starostina, *op. cit.* p. 137.

55. Ibid.

56. Ibid. p. 43.

57. D. Meerson, D. G. Tonskii, *op. cit.* p. 8.

58. In Czechoslovakia the large panel method constitutes 80 per cent of all state and co-operative construction and in the GDR, Hungary, Bulgaria and Poland from 50 to 60 per cent.

59. I. P. Prokopchenko, *Upravlenie i pol'zovanie zhilishchnom fondom v SSSR* (Moscow, 1970), p. 22; A. Tomsen, 'Zhilishchnaya problema i ee reshenie na sovremennom etape', *Politicheskoe samoobrazovanie*, no. 5, 1972, p. 100.

60. B. Ionas, G. Starostina, *op. cit.* pp. 42–4.

61. V. F. Promyslov, *Industrializatsiya zhilishchnogo stroitel'stva Moskvy* (Moscow, 1959), p. 212.

62. Postanovlenie Plenuma TsK KPSS, 13–14 February 1957, 'O dal'neishem sovershenstvovanii organizatsii upravleniya promyshlen-nost'yu i stroitel'stvom', in *KPSS v rezolyutsiyakh, s"yezdov, konferentsii i plenumov TsK*, vol. 7, 1955–9 (Moscow, 1971), pp. 249–56.

63. L. P. Lukaev, N. A. Godlevskii, *Organizatsiya i planirovanie stroitel'stva* (Moscow, 1964), p. 13.

64. *KPSS v rezolyutsiyakh . . .* vol. 8, 1959–65 (Moscow, 1972), pp. 516–22. See also: A. Nove, *The Soviet Economic System* (London, 1977), pp. 70–5.

65. Postanovlenie TsK KPSS i Soveta Ministrov SSSR, 21 January 1967, 'Ob uluchshenii organizatsiya upravleniya stroitel'stvom', *SP SSSR*, 1967, no. 5, art. 19. (See also: *SP SSSR*, 1969, no. 21, art. 214; art. 214; *SP SSSR*, 1969, no. 26, art. 141; *SP SSSR*, 1970, no. 3, art. 18).

66. In the USSR, the number of primary building organisations stood at 4000 in 1940. This figure had doubled by 1955 (8240) and doubled again by 1968 (16 125). By the end of 1980, it had reached 26 944. This growth has been, in part, accompanied by a reversal in the ratio of general to specialist building contractors. In 1940 the ratio was 73 to 27 and in 1980, 45 to 55. (*Narodnoe khozyaistvo SSSR v 1980 g.*, p. 349).

67. *Industrializatsiya zhilishchnogo stroitel'stva SSSR* (Moscow, 1965), pp. 20–30.

68. B. Ya. Ionas, G. G. Starostina, *op. cit.* p. 58.

69. Postanovlenie TsK KPSS i Soveta Ministrov SSSR, 15 February 1960,

'O novom metode organizatsii stroitel'stva krupnopanel'nykh zhilykh domov domostroitel'nymi kombinatami v gorode Leningrade'.
70. B. Ya. Ionas, G. G. Starostina, *op. cit.* p. 59.
71. B. Ya. Ionas, M. F. Yasneva, *op. cit.* pp. 16–19.
72. B. Ya. Ionas, G. G. Starostina, *op. cit.* p. 43.
73. D. L. Broner (1980) *op. cit.* p. 37.
74. The combined heat and power station in Kiev supplies the electrical and heating needs of over one million people (half the city's population). In 1980, 44.6 per cent of the overall urban consumption of energy was met by combined heat and power plants. (A. M. Nekrasov, A. A. Troitskii, *Energetika SSSR v 1981–1985 godakh*, Moscow, 1981) The government is now proposing to initiate a fundamentally new trend in centralised heating supply for large cities – the building of several nuclear power stations, each of which will be able to ensure dependable heat supplies to a large city (without polluting the atmosphere). *Materialy . . .* (1981), *op. cit.*, p. 114.
75. *Narodnoe khozyaistvo SSSR v 1980 g.* p. 347.
76. P. Lebedev, *op. cit.* p. 72.
77. V. G. Savchenko-Bel'skii *et al. Eksploatatsiya zhilykh massivov* (Kiev, 1980), p. 7.
78. P. Zibov, 'Novym gorodam – kompleksnuyu zastroiku', *Zhilishchnoe stroitel'stvo*, no. 3, 1978.
79. Postanovlenie Soveta Ministrov SSSR, 19 March 1970, 'O poryadke planirovaniya i finansirovaniya stroitel'stva ob"yektov obshchikh dlya gruppy predpriyatii', *SP SSSR*, 1970, no. 5, art. 36.
80. N. S. Koval', *Planirovanie narodnogo khozyaistva* (Moscow, 1973), p. 273; 'Zhilishchnoe stroitel'stvo', *Ekonomicheskaya gazeta*, no. 8, 1975, p. 2.
81. For a detailed list of Stroibank's functions, see: Postanovlenie Soveta Ministrov SSSR, 15 October 1981, 'Ob utverzhdenii ustava Vsesoyuznogo banka finansirovaniya kapital'nogo vozheniya (Stroibank SSSR)', *SP SSSR*, 1981, no. 30, art. 176. See also the earliier decrees: *SP SSSR*, 1964, no. 19, art. 122; *SP SSSR*, 1965, no. 21, art. 156.
82. M. Zotov (Chairman of the Board of Stroibank SSSR), 'Effektivnost' kapital'nykh vlozhenii i kreditnye otnosheniya v stroitel'stve', *Voprosy ekonomiki*, no. 4, April 1977, p. 55.
83. *SP SSSR*, 1981, no. 30, art. 176. See also: *SP SSSR*, 1969, no. 15, art. 82; P. Podshivalenki, 'Povyshenie roli kredita v stroitel'stve', *Ekonomicheskaya gazeta*, no. 43, 1972, p. 4; Podshivalenki, 'Puti povysheniya effektivnosti kreditovaniya stroitel'stva', *Ekonomicheskaya gazeta*, no. 21, 1973, p. 9; *Osnovnye napravleniya razvitiya narodnogo khozyaistva SSSR, 1976–1980 g.*, p. 18.
84. *SP SSSR*, 1969, no. 15, art. 82. See also, for example, the editorials in *Pravda*, 24 February 1970, 23 July 1980.
85. *SP SSSR*, 1979, no. 18, art. 118.
86. P. Bunich, 'Resurs upravleniya', *Izvestiya*, 10 March 1979; V. Rybin, A. Khachaturyan, 'Sovershenstvovanie kreditovaniya kapital'nykh vlozhenii', *Planovoe khozyaistvo*, no. 3, 1980, p. 58.
87. M. Zotov, *op. cit.* p. 49.

88. See also: S. Merrett, *State Housing in Britain* (London, Routledge & Kegan Paul, 1979), ch. 4.

89. V. Rybin, A. Khachaturyan, Ibid.

90. A. Kolesnikov, 'Vvod ob"yektov i finansirovanie', *Ekonomicheskaya gazeta*, no. 5, 1978, p. 9.

91. M. Zotov, *op. cit.* pp. 53, 56.

92. V. Rybin, A. Khachaturyan, *op. cit.* p. 60.

93. V. Ya. Ionas, G. G. Starostina, *op. cit.* pp. 29–31.

94. See the preamble to the May 1969 decree (*SP SSSR*, 1969, no. 15, art. 82). See also: E. Kozlov, M. Makhlin, 'Chto sokratit 'Nezaver-shenku'?' *Ekonomicheskaya gazeta*, no. 34, 1975, p. 9.

95. Up to 1 January 1984 construction cost estimates were based on a set of norms, prices and tariffs introduced on 1 July 1967. *Zhilishchnoe stroitel'stvo*, no. 1, 1978, p. 28. As from 1 January 1984, the estimated cost of capital construction has to be based on the new estimated norms for building and assembly work which were introduced on that date. Other determinants of the new estimates include: the new wholesale prices for industrial products and tariffs for electricity and lighting introduced on 1 January 1982, and the norms and tariff rates for labour in the building industry adopted on 1 January 1980. See: Postanovlenie Soveta Ministrov SSSR, 4 January 1981, 'O perekhode na novye smet-nye normy i tseny v stroitel'stve', *SP SSSR*, 1981, no. 4, art. 14.

96. *SP SSSR*, 1969, no. 15, art. 82. See also: 'Uluchshat' delo proek-tirovaniya', *Izvestiya*, 19 September 1975.

97. B. M. Litvin, *Sovershenstvovanie planirovaniya stroitel'nogo proizvodstva* (Kiev, 1980), p. 11.

98. T. Fetisov, 'Zaboty ne tol'ko Saratovskie', *Sovety narodnykh deputatov*, no. 1, 1980, p. 61.

99. *New Statesman*, 24 October 1980.

100. E. Z. Maiminas, *Protsessy planirovaniya v ekonomike* (Moscow, 1971), p. 318.

101. A senior official in Gosplan's Economic Research Institute in reviewing employment trends has outlined the consequences of limited labour resources and pointed to the need to raise productivity, increase the capital–labour ratio, employ a better quality workforce, improve working conditions, use better manpower planning techniques, improve project-design work and pay higher wages or give other forms of material incentive. (V. Kostakov, 'Ratsional'noe ispol'zovanie trudovykh resursov', *Ekonomicheskaya gazeta*, January 1977, p. 10).

102. *Ekonomika i organizatsiya promyshlennogo proizvodstva* (Novosibirsk), no. 1, 1972, pp. 75–7.

103. G. Zelenskii, E. Voronin, 'Luchshe ispol'zovat' trudovye resursy strany', *Planovoe khozyaistvo*, no. 6, 1968, p. 1.

104. Osnovnye napravleniya... (1976) *op. cit.* p. 64. See also: Dmitriev, (Head of the Construction Department of the Central Committee of the CPSU), 'Stroit' bystro, ekonomichno, na sovremennom etape', *Ekonomicheskaya gazeta*, no. 46, 1976, pp. 5–6.

105. B. Ya. Ionas, G. G. Starostina, *op. cit.* p. 233.

106. *Materialy...* (1981) *op. cit.* p. 108.

107. B. Ya. Ionas, G. G. Starostina, *op. cit.* p. 226; *Narodnoe khozyaistvo SSSR v 1980 g.*, pp. 357–8.

108. Postanovlenie Soveta Ministrov SSSR, 20 December 1962, 'O merakh po uluchsheniyu podgotovki kvalifitsirovannykh rabochikh i obespechenii imi predpriyatii i stroek', *SP SSSR*, 1962, no. 12, art. 181.

109. Postanovlenie TsK KPSS i Soveta Ministrov SSSR, 28 May 1969, 'O merakh po uluchsheniyu kachestva zhilishchno-grazhdanskogo stroitel'stva', *SP SSSR*, 1969, no. 15, art. 84.

110. Postanovlenie TsK KPSS i Soveta Ministrov SSSR, 'O merakh po dalneishemu uluchsheniyu podgotovki kvalifitsirovannykh kadrov i zakrepleniyu ikh v stroitel'stve', *Izvestiya*, 13 February 1979, p. 1.

111. 'V Tsentral'nom komitete KPSS', *Ekonomicheskaya gazeta*, no. 13, 1978, p. 3.

112. Postanovlenie TsK KPSS i Soveta Ministrov SSSR, 12 January 1968, 'O merakh po obespecheniya kapital'nogo stroitel'stva kadrami', in *Resheniya partii... op. cit.* vol. 6, 1968, pp. 655–9.

113. 'Ostaet sooruzhenie', *Ekonomicheskaya gazeta*, no. 19, 1978, p. 9.

114. B. Ya. Ionas, G. G. Starostina, *op. cit.* pp. 226–7. Women form a smaller proportion of all construction workers, although they predominate in certain occupations, e.g. plastering and painting.

115. More workers in the construction industry than in any other branch of the economy live in hostels. V. Rotkov, *Planirovanie zhilishchno-kommunal'nogo khozyaistva stroitel'no-montazhnykh organizatsii* (Moscow, 1968), p. 4.

116. It is mainly those in the 20–30 year old age group, lacking qualifications and unmarried who, attracted by the social and recreational facilities, migrate from the villages to the towns (and to urban construction sites). T. N. Dubina, O. V. Romashov, 'Sotsial'nye aspekty migratsii molodyozhi v Moskovskoi oblasti', *Sotsiologicheskie issledovaniya*, no. 2, 1980, p. 159. Over half of all building workers are under thirty years of age. B. Ya. Ionas, G. G. Starostina, *op. cit.* p. 224.

117. Postanovlenie Soveta Ministrov SSSR, 21 May 1967, 'O peredache zakazchikami podryadnym stroitel'nym organizatsiyam desyati protsentov vvodimoi v ekspluatatsiyu zhiloi ploshchadi'. *Izvestiya*, 21 May 1967.

118. On the new system of bonuses and awards see: 'Premii stroitel'stva', *Ekonomicheskaya gazeta*, no. 23, June 1978, p. 16. A decree in 1962 specified new systems of remuneration in the construction industry involving the establishment of new wage-differentials, bonuses and other kinds of monetary rewards. See: Postanovlenie Soveta Ministrov, 10 August 1962 'Ob uluchshenii planirovaniya kapital'nogo stroitel'stva i ob izmenenii uslovii oplaty truda i sistemy premirovaniya rabotnikov stroitel'o-montazhnykh i proektnykh organizatsii' *SP SSSR*, 1962, no. 16, art. 127. See also an earlier decree whose objective was 'to strengthen the initiative and responsibility of the building and assembly organisations for carrying out their output plans, cutting costs and increasing profits'. Postanovlenie Soveta Ministrov SSSR, 8 June 1947, 'O fonde nachalnika stroitel'no-montazhnykh organizatsii', *SP SSSR*, 1947, no. 3, art. 62. For a still earlier attempt to influence output in the

construction industry see: Postanovlenie Sovnarkoma SSSR, 16 May 1931, 'Ob uvelichenii nachislenii na zarabotnuyu platu rabochikh i sluzhashchikh zanyatykh na stroitel'stve', *SP SSSR*, 1931, no. 28, art. 220.

119. Y. Zabortsev, 'Na okraine', *Trud*, 18 November 1977, p. 2.
120. *Grazhdanskii kodeks RSFSR* (Moscow, 1976), arts. 331–41, pp. 85–88.
121. Ibid. Commentary to article 334 (pp. 223–5). Also, I, P. Prokopchenko (1977) *op. cit.* pp. 230–44.
122. 'Vyselenie iz vedomstvennykh domov (obzor sudebnoi praktiki)', *Byulleten' Verkhovnogo Suda SSSR*, no. 5, 1974, pp. 37–43.
123. US Congress (Senate), Government Operations Subcommittee, 'Federal Role in Urban Affairs', Hearings, 1966, 89th Congress, Second Session, 1966.
124. *Housing and Construction Stastics*, 1971–1981, GSS, 1982, Table 103, p. 116. *Narodnoe khozyaistvo SSSR v 1967 g.* p. 684; *N. Kh. SSSR v 1980 g.*, pp. 392, 394.
125. I. Prokopchenko, (1977), *op. cit.* p. 191.
126. D. S. Meerson, D. G. Tonskii, *op. cit.* p. 13.
127. Ibid. p. 14.
128. *Materialy...* (1981) *op. cit.* p. 134.
129. A. I. Gyul'-Akhmedov, 'Struktura semei–struktura kvartira', *Zhilishchnoe stroitel'stvo*', no. 7, 1978; S. F. Legornev, 'Zhilishchno-kommunal'noe khozyaistvo: tsifry rosta', *Zhilishchnoe i kommunal'noe khozyaistvo*, no. 3, 1979, p. 13.
130. *Perspektiva razvitiya zhilishcha v SSSR* (Moscow, 1975), p. 96.
131. *Vsesoyuznaya perepis' naseleniya 1970 g.* (Moscow, 1976), p. 262. Family sizes tend to be higher in republics in Central Asia and the Caucasus: the highest average is Armenia (4.7 persons), followed by Turkmenia (4.6); Tadzhikstan (4.5), Uzbekistan (4.5). In Tashkent, 14 per cent of all families consisted of six or more persons. In the UK, the average household size fell from 2.89 persons in 1971 to 2.67 in 1979. 72 per cent of all households consisted of 1–3 people. (Central Statistical Office, *Social Trends*, 1981, pp. 28–30).
132. D. S. Meerson, D. G. Tonskii, *op. cit.* p. 29. These statistics represent not only a change in the indices used to calculate the growth in living space but also an increase in the range of statistics available. In 1974, Morton noted that information was still lacking on, inter alia, the average number of rooms per flat, density of occupancy per room and the proportion of the population living in separate flats. H. Morton in H. Morton & R. Tokes (eds) *Soviet Politics and Society in the 1970s* (New York, The Free Press, 1974).
133. D. L. Broner, *Zhilishchnoe stroitel'stvo i demograficheskie protsessy* (Moscow, 1980), p. 58. According to H. Morton, there is a 9.6 million deficit of housing units in towns in relation to the number of households. Such a figure has to be used with circumspection: since a household can consist of a 'single person living by him/herself', hypothetically there could be almost as many households as there are adults. Indeed, it could be suggested that the growth of single person households in the UK,

USA and other industrialised societies is in part a function of the increased size and changing structure of the housing stock. H. Morton, 'Who gets what, when and how? Housing in the Soviet Union' *Soviet Studies*, vol. XXXII, no. 2, April 1980, p. 236.

134. V. Dobrotov, 'Kvartira dlya molodyozhenov', *Sovetskaya Rossiya*, 14 February 1979, p. 3. In 1978, the Karaganda local soviet set up a 'Social Institute of Marriage' attached to the main *oblast'* hospital (!). Its primary function is to serve as a marriage guidance council to 'promote the stabilisation of families'. (*Sotsiologicheskie issledovaniya*, no. 1, 1980, p. 228). One in every three marriages now ends in divorce; one-third of all divorces are of couples who have been married for less than 1 year and a further one-third after 1–5 years of marriage; c.50 per cent of couples who divorce are childless. (See: *Literaturnaya gazeta*, 15 February 1978, p. 13.).

8 LOW RISE HOUSING, URBAN MORPHOLOGY AND SOCIAL STRUCTURE

1. During the 1920s almost all housing built was of wood. The proportion of all newly erected *housing space* in towns with stone or brick walls rose from 10.5 per cent in 1923 to 21.0 per cent in 1926. (V. Shmidt, *Rabochii klass... op. cit.* p. 61). By 1938 urban dwelling space in the public sector was 56.4 per cent brick, 32.2 per cent wood and 11.4 per cent 'other materials'. (I. Prokopchenko, 1970, *op. cit.* p. 12.).

2. *Razmeshchenie zhilishchnogo stroitel'stva v gorodakh* (Moscow, 1960), pp. 16–17. This form of development, though most common in mining regions, also took place in industrial centres such as the Avtozavodsk district of Gor'ky, and the Metallurgicheskii zavod district of Chelyabinsk.

3. A. D. Ivanova, *Gorodskie raiony usadebnoi zastroiki* (Kiev, 1952), pp. 5–22.

4. Ibid. pp. 6, 9.

5. V. G. Davidovich, *Rasselenie v promyshlennykh uzlakh* (Moscow, 1960), p. 64.

6. Ibid. p. 65.

7. *SP SSSR*, 1957, no. 9, art. 102.

8. Postanovlenie TsK KPSS i Soveta Ministrov SSSR, 12 August 1965, 'Ob etazhnosti zhilikh domov stroyashchikhsya v gorodakh i poselkakh', *SP SSSR*, 1965, no. 17, art. 102.

9. *Pravda*, 19 November 1969.

10. The city of Birmingham (England) with a population double the size of that in Karaganda in 1975 covered less than a third of the area (20 900 hectares).

11. *Razmeshchenie...* (1960), *op. cit.* p. 6.

12. A. O. Kudryavtsev, *Ratsional'noe ispol'zovanie territorii pri planirovke i zastroike gorodov SSSR* (Moscow, 1971), pp. 23–4.

13. B. Svetlichnyi, 'Nekotorye voprosy perspektivnogo razvitiya gorodov', *Voprosy ekonomiki*, no. 3, 1962, pp. 57–69.

14. O. P. Litovka, 'Aktual'nye problemy prostranstvennogo razvitiya

gorodskikh poselenii', in O. I. Shkaratan, A. N. Alekseev, *Planirovanie sotsial'nogo razvitiya gorodov* (Moscow, 1973), p. 162.

15. Yu. Bocharov, V. Lyubovnyi, 'Kompleksnoe razvitie krupnykh gorodov', *Planovoe khozyaistvo*, no. 12, 1976, pp. 78–86.

16. In 1956, in Kishinev (the capital of Moldavia) 72.3 per cent of new housing was of one and two storey units, whilst in Kirov (1959 – 252 000; 1981 – 396 000) the figure for 1958/9 was 50 per cent and for Astrakhan (1959 – 305 000; 1981 – 470 000) and Khabarovsk (1959 – 323 000; 1981 – 545 000) 40–45 per cent. See: A. S. Konstantinov, *Kishinev* (Kishinev, 1966), p. 117.

17. A. A. Voinov, 'Novye gorody v Belorussii', *Stroitel'stvo i arkhitektura*, no. 7, 1966.

18. V. M. Orekhov, A. D. Ivanova, *Rekonstruktsiya i razvitie krupnykh gorodov UkSSR* (Kiev, 1974), p. 8.

19. A. O. Kudryavtsev, *op. cit.* p. 35.

20. D. S. Meerson, D. G. Tonskii, *Zhilishchnoe stroitel'stvo v SSSR v desyatoi pyatiletke* (Moscow, 1977), pp. 9–10; E. V. Kaznin, 'Dlya zhilishchnogo khozyaistva', *Zhilishchnoe i kommunal'noe khozyaistvo*, no. 2, 1976, p. 12.

21. Meerson and Tonskii Ibid., p. 38.

22. I. G. Karanaukhov, 'Novyi oblik Podmoskov'ya', *Zhilishchnoe stroitel'stvo*, no. 5, 1978, pp. 6–9.

23. V. Orekhov, *op. cit.* pp. 87–8.

24. E. Yu. Peresvetov, 'Maloetazhnyi dom s dvorikom dlya gorodskoi zatroiki', *Zhilishchnoe stroitel'stvo*, no. 5, 1978, pp. 22–4.

25. S. V. Smirnova, 'Predlozheniya po snizheniyu smetnoi stoimosti zhilishchno-grazhdanskogo stroitel'stva', *Zhilishchnoe stroitel'stvo*, no. 1, 1978, pp. 27–9.

26. A. Kochetkov, 'Sotsial'no-ekonomicheskie aspekty gradostroitel'stva,' *Voprosy ekonomiki*, no. 10, 1975, p. 25.

27. One, for instance, asserted in 1968 that 'house building in cities and urban-type settlements prior to 1963 had consisted mainly of five storey blocks of flats'. G. Mishchenko, 'Zastroika gorodov na sovremennom etape', *Planirovka i zastroika gorodov* (Kiev, 1968), p. 3.

28. V. G. Savchenko-Belskii et al. *Ekspluatatsiya zhilykh massivov* (Kiev, 1980), p. 3.

29. A. O. Kudryavtsev, *op. cit.* pp. 8–9.

30. A. Kochetkov, Ibid.

31. R. H. Best, 'Agricultural land loss: myth or reality', *The Planner*, January 1977, vol. 63, no. 1, p. 15; A. O. Kudryavtsev, *op. cit.* p. 8.

32. A. Ya. Khorkhot, *Arkhitektura i blagoustroistvo promyshlennykh predpriyatii* (Kiev, 1953), pp. 39, 76, 79, 223, 233.

33. Postanovlenie SNK RSFSR, 26 February 1938, 'Ob uluchshenii proektnogo i smetnogo dela i ob uporyadochenii finansirovaniya stroitel'stva', *SP RSFSR*, 1938, no. 9, art. 58.

34. Postanovlenie Soveta Minstrov SSSR, 9 May 1950, 'Ob snizhenii stoimosti stroitel'stva', in *Resheniya partii i pravitel'stva po khozyaistvennym voprosam*, vol. 3 (Moscow, 1968), pp. 603–614.

35. *Trudy VI Sessii Akademii Stroitel'stva Arkhitektury po voprosam gradostroitel'stva* (Moscow, 1961), p. 8.

36. V. G. Perekhin, *Ratsional'noe ispol'zovanie gorodkikh territorii pri raz-meshchenii zhilishchnogo stroitel'stva v usloviyakh slozhivsheishya zas-troiki* (Novosibirsk, 1965).
37. See, for example, *Izvestiya*, 10 February 1960.
38. *Stroitel'nye Normy i Pravila*, (SNiP) 11-K.2-62 (Moscow, 1962), point 5.
39. *Stroitel'nye Normy i Pravila*, (SNiP) 11-60-75 (Moscow, 1976), points 1.10, 2.4.
40. Karanaukhov, *op. cit.*
41. Postanovlenie Plenuma TsK KPSS, 25–27 May 1966, 'O shirokom razvitii meliorizatsii zemel' dlya porucheniya vysokikh i ustochivykh urozhaev i drugikh sel'skokhozyaistvennykh kul'tur', in *KPSS v rezolyut-siyakh i resheniya s"yezdov, konferentsii i plenumov TsK*, vol. 9 (Moscow, 1972), pp. 106–111.
42. E. Ya. Kipper, 'Ob ekonomicheskom obosnovanii rekonstruktsii zhilykh raionov gorodov s uchetom gradostroitel'nykh porogov', in *Rekonstrukt-siay gorodov* (Kiev, 1968), pp. 10–14; A. I. Stanislavskii, *Planirovka i zastroika gorodov Ukrainy* (Kiev, 1971), pp. 166–7.
43. 'Deputat i zemlya', *Izvestiya*, 20 January 1976.
44. O. P. Litovka, *op. cit.* p. 161.
45. A. O. Kudryavtsev, *op. cit.* p. 16.
46. *Report of the Expert Committee on Compensation and Betterment* (Uthwatt Report), Cmnd 6386) (London, HMSO, 1942), para. 17.
47. V. Vashanov, 'Planirovanie ispol'zovaniya zemel' pod stroitel'stve', *Voprosy ekonomiki*, no. 8, 1972.
48. A. A. Nesterenko, *Zakonomernosti sotsial'no-ekonomicheskogo raz-vitiya goroda i derevni* (Kiev, 1975), p. 12.
49. For discussions on compensation paid to agricultural users and optimum land use, see: Postanovlenie Soveta Ministrov SSSR, 9 August 1974, 'O vozmeshchenii ubytov zemlepol'zovatelyam i potere sel'skokhozyaist-vennogo proizvodstva pri otvode zemel'dlya gosudarstvennykh ili ob-shchestvennykh nuzhd', *SP SSSR, 1974, no. 17, art. 97, N. B. Ermolin, Razmeshchenie zhilishchnogo stroitel'stva v krupnykh gorodakh* (Moscow, 1971), pp. 32–3; L. V. Motorina, V. A. Ovchinikov, *Prom-yshlennost' i rekul'tivatsiya zemel'* (Moscow, 1975).
50. Kh. K. Aben, 'Ob uchete tsennosti gorodskoi territorii', in *Problemy ekonomiki gradostroitel'stva* (Kiev, 1974), pp. 7–18.
51. L. Leont'ev, 'O tovarnom proizvodstve pri sotsializme', *Pravda*, 31 August 1966.
52. R. I. Khametskii, 'Razmeshchenie zhiloi zastroiki v tsentrakh krupnykh gorodov', in *Planirovka i zastroika gorodov* (Kiev, 1968), p. 10.
53. See, for example, J. Ratcliffe, 'Planning gain is not the answer', *Built Environment*, vol. 3 no. 3, 1974, pp. 148–9.
54. For a discussion of the bargaining process in England, which could be of relevance to Soviet policy makers, see: J. Jowell, 'Bargaining in De-velopment Control', *Journal of Planning Law*, June 1977, pp. 414–33.
55. See, especially, A. V. Ikonnikov, *Arkhitektura goroda: Esteticheski problemy kompozitsii* (Moscow, 1972), p. 4.
56. See, for instance, I. G. Romm, 'O vremmenykh stroitel'nykh rezhimakh v general'nykh planakh gorodov', *Voprosy ekonomiki gradostroitel'stva i*

raionnoi planirovki, vypusk 4, (Kiev, 1970), p. 60. The author cites data published by the Leningrad Housing Design Institute (*Lenzhilproekt*) which demonstrates that it is cheaper to renovate some of the housing stock consisting of buildings of 2–5 storeys, than carry out wholesale demolition and erect in their place 5–9 storey blocks. On the other hand, in 1980, four- and five-storey blocks were being demolished in Moscow to make way for tower blocks of 16 and more storeys.

57. From a purely economic point of view, in capitalist societies, whether it is cheaper to renovate or replace will depend on three factors: the rate of interest; the expected future length of life of the renovated property; and the difference in maintenance costs between improved and rebuilt dwellings. (L. Needleman, *The Economics of Housing*, London, Staples, 1965.) The calculations made by British and Soviet planners when deciding on a policy of renovation or replacement on comparable projects would make an interesting case study.

58. V. Lavrov, *Rekonstruktsiya krupnykh gorodov* (Moscow, 1972), p. 141.

59. A. A. Dolonin, *et al.*, 'O sotsial'nom raionirovanii v SSSR', in O. I. Shkaratan, A. N. Alekseev, *Planirovanie sotsial'nogo razvitiya gorodov* (Moscow, 1973), p. 101.

60. 'Zachem snosit' dom?' *Pravda*, 19 December, 1969, p. 3.

61. *SP SSSR* 1961, no. 20, art. 146; *SP SSSR* 1966, no. 18, art. 162; *SP SSSR*, 1974, no. 17, art. 97; see also: I. D. Chevskii, *Garantii i kompensatsii grazhdanam pri iz"yatii zemel'*, (Moscow, 1971), pp. 25–26; 'Kompensatsii pri snose domovladenii', *Trud*, 12 November 1975, p. 4.

62. On the conflicts in the UK between planners and the public, see: N. Dennis, *People and Planning* (London, Faber, 1970).

63. 'Berech' zhil'e', *Pravda*, 22 November 1969, p. 1.

64. 'Zachem snosit' dom?' *Pravda*, 19 December 1969.

65. Ibid.

66. *Pravda*, 17 December 1969, p. 3.

67. A. O. Kudryavtsev, *op. cit.* p. 46.

68. Postanovlenie TsK KPSS i Soveta Ministrov SSSR, 3 February 1970, 'O serezhykh narusheniyakh gosudarstvennoi distsipliny v gorodskom stroitel'stve i zhilishchnom khozyaistve', *SP SSSR*, 1970, no. 4, art. 25. The loss of living space associated with increasing housing densities (*razuplotnenie*) can be as high as 30–35 per cent of the total housing stock in the central districts of cities. Between 1966 and 1968, housing demolition exceeded the planned target figure in Kiev, Dnepropetrovsk, Khar'kov, Rovno, Cherkassy and Chernovtsy. G. S. Krutenko 'Nasushchnye zadachi gradostroitelei Ukrainy', in *Raionnaya planirovka i problemy rasseleniya*, vypusk 2 (Kiev, 1970), p. 6.

69. *SP SSSR*, 1970, no. 4, art. 25.

70. *Housing Policy (Technical Volume, Part 1)* (London, HMSO, 1977), p. 23, Table 1.12; Central Statistical Office, *Social Trends*, 11, 1981, p. 152.

71. V. G. Davidovich, 'Raschet ekonomicheski opravdannykh razmerov snosa zastroiki pri rekonstruktsii goroda', *Planirovka i zastroika goroda* (Kiev, 1968), p. 4.

72. *Perspektivy razvitiya zhilishcha v SSSR* (1975), p. 97.

73. For details of these categories of obsolescence, see: V. Kolotilkin, *Dolgovechnost' zhilykh zdanii* (Moscow, 1965), ch.2. 2.
74. V. Orekhov, A. Ivanova, *op. cit.* p. 84.
75. 'Zakon SSSR ob okhrane ispol'zovanii pamyatnikov istorii i kul'tury', *Pravda*, 31 October 1976.
76. V. G. Savchenko-Bel'skii *et al. Ekspluatatisya zhilykh massivov*, (Kiev, 1980), p. 3.
77. E. Poltoratskii, 'I ploshchadei gromada, i ugolochek tishina', *Literaturnaya gazeta*, no. 34, August 1975, p. 10; V. Davitskaya, 'A zodchemu – tol'ko mechta' *Literaturnaya gazeta*, no. 30, July 1975, p. 11.
78. See, for instance, N. Sokolov, 'Obratnaya svyaz'zodchevo', *Literaturanaya gazeta*, no. 26, June 1977, p. 13.
79. *SP SSSR*, 1970, no. 13, art. 104. See also, notes 7 and 8 above.
80. A. O. Kudryavtsev, *op. cit.* pp. 37, 45.
81. S. V. Smirnova, *op. cit.* p. 25.
82. Postanovlenie Soveta Ministrov SSSR, 5 October 1981, 'O merakh po povysheniyu effektivnosti kapital'nykh vlozhenii, vydelyaemykh na zhilishchnoe stroitel'stvo', *SP SSSR*, 1981, no. 29, art. 169.
83. A. Stanislavskii, *Planirovka i zastroika gorodov Ukrainy* (Kiev, 1971), p. 165.
84. Yu. M. Safronov, *Organizatsiya zhilishchnogo khozyaistva* (Moscow, 1972), pp. 156–7.
85. E. G. Kozlov, 'Ne 8 chasov, a 480 minut!', *Zhilishchnoe i kommunal'noe khozyaistvo*, no. 4, 1977, p. 4.
86. G. Asaris, 'Panorama goroda,' *Pravda*, 28 March 1979, p. 3.
87. L. Wirth, 'Urbanism as a Way of Life', *American Journal of Sociology*, vol. XLIV, July 1938.
88. 'Little Ireland .... for years the disgrace of Manchester .... has long ago disappeared and on its site there now stands a railway built on a high foundation. The bourgeoisie pointed with pride to the happy and final abolition of Little Ireland as to a great triumph. Now last summer a great inundation took place. And it was then revealed that Little Ireland had not been abolished at all, but had simply been shifted from the south side of Exford Road to the north side, and that it still continues to flourish ... This is a striking example of how the bourgeoisie settles the housing question in practice. The breeding places of disease ... are not abolished; they are merely shifted elsewhere.' F. Engels, 'The Housing Question', in K. Marx and F. Engels, *Selected Works*, Vol. 1 (Moscow, 1962), pp. 608–618.
89. N. Rumyantsev, 'Vsegda slozhnyi variant', *Literaturnaya gazeta*, No. 11, March 1977, p. 12; V. Belkin, 'Vygody bez zatrat, ili obmen zhil'ya glazami ekonomistov', *Izvestiya*, 6 July 1976; M. I. Alekseev, 'Vam nuzhno obmenyat' zhil'e ...', *Zhilishchnoe i kommunal'noe khozyaistvo*, no. 1, 1977, p. 15.
    Because there are no standardised exchange procedures, each city sets its own regulations and this makes inter-city exchanging 'complicated and troublesome'.
90. *SP SSSR*, 1980, no. 3, art. 17.
91. *Sovetskaya etnografiya*, no. 1, 1978, p. 87. See also: R. French, F. Ian Hamilton (eds) *The Socialist City* (Chichester, John Wiley, 1979).
92. M. N. Mezhevich, L. I. Spiridonov, 'Kompleksnoe issledovanie sotsi-

al'nykh problem razvitiya gorodov', in O. I. Shkaratan, A. N. Alekseev, *op. cit.* p. 91.
93. Ibid.
94. R. K. Merton, *Social Theory and Social Structure* (New York, The Free Press, 1957), ch. 4.
95. M. N. Mezhevich, L. I. Spiridonov, *op. cit.* pp. 94–95.
96. For a comprehensive summary of current Soviet thought on this topic, see: *Kriminologiya*, 3rd edn (Moscow 1976), especially ch. 7 (Prichiny prestupnosti v SSSR) and ch. 9 (Prichiny i usloviya soversheniya konkretnogo prestupleniya). And for a Western interpretation of Soviet criminology, see W. D. Connor, *Deviance in Soviet Society: Crime, Delinquency and Alcoholism* (New York, Columbia University Press, 1972).
97. A. Kogan, 'Sovremennyi gorod: Kak on funksioniruet', *Arkhitektura (Prilozhenie k Stroitel'naya gazeta*,) 4 April 1976, no. 7, pp. 6–7.
98. The term 'melting pot' is specifically referred to, in: T. V. Ryabushkin (ed.) *Sotsiologiya i problemy sotsial'nogo razvitiya* (Moscow, 1978), p. 183.
99. O. N. Yanitskii, *Gorod, urbanizatsiya, chelovek. Kritika burzhuaznoi sotsiologii* (Moscow, 1974), p. 9.
100. Ibid. p. 11.
101. T. V. Ryabushkin, *op. cit.* p. 186.
102. The methodology and concepts associated with the human ecologists have also found a place in the work of academic sociologists in other socialist societies. Czech sociologists, for example, consider that 'ecological analysis can be a significant help in throwing light on the problems of interrelations between social and spatial structure', P. Mateju *et al.* 'Social Structure, Spatial Structure and Problems of Urban Research', *International Journal of Urban and Regional Research*, vol. 3, no. 2, 1979, p. 181.
103. Yu. M. Antonyan, 'Sotsial'no-psikhologicheskie posledstviya urbanizatsii i ikh vliyanie na prestupnost', *Sovetskoe gosudarstvo i pravo*, no. 8, 1975, pp. 65–73.
104. V. L. Barsuk, A. F. Sharova, 'Izuchenie i planirovanie razvitiya dukhovnoi kul'tury v sotsialisticheskom gorode', in O. I. aratan, A. N. Alekseev, *op. cit.* p. 77.
105. See, *Kriminologiya, op. cit.* pp. 127–133; *Materialy XXIV S"ezda KPSS* (Moscow, 1971), p. 84.
106. *Arkhitektura zhilogo kompleska* (Moscow, 1969), p. 5.
107. Antonyan, *op. cit.*
108. I. M. Smolyar, *Novye goroda: Planirovochnaya struktura gorodov promyshlennogo i nauchno-proizvodstvennogo profilya* (Moscow, 1972), p. 66. Some Polish sociologists have acknowledged that 'as a result of spontaneously working ecological forces, there are internal migrations in the city that bring about concentrations of people in particular social categories'. I. Z. Pioro, 'Comment', *Journal of the American Institute of Planners*, February, 1965, p. 33. The allegation that the formation of such social areas is associated with parity in the provision of housing, services and transportation in all districts is not strictly true and never can be, at least not between the central area and all other city districts.
109. A. Kogan, *op. cit.*

110. V. G. Vardosanidze, 'K probleme vklyucheniya novykh zhilykh raionov v strukturu sovremennogo krupnogo goroda', in *Arkhitekturno-planirovchnye problemy goroda* (Moscow, 1976), pp. 61–62.

111. M. N. Silant'eva, B. K. Smoilovskaya, 'Nekotorye voprosy normironiya uchrezhdenii kul'turno-bytovogo obsluzhivaniya pri rekonstruktsii zhiloi zastroiky Moskvy', in *Planirovka i zastroika gorodov* (Kiev 1968), p. 20.

112. I. E. Polubotko, 'Povyshenie effektivnosti ispol'zovaniya territorii v zhilykh raionakh s preimushchestvennoi pyatietazhnoi zastroikoi' in *Ekonomika razvitiya i rekonstruktsii gorodov. Sbornik nauchnykh trudov* (Kiev, 1975), pp. 72–77. In one *mikroraion* in Khar'kov there were 19.2 per cent fewer children in 1974 than in 1966.

113. R. I. Khamenskii, 'Rameshchenie zhiloi zastroiki v tsentrakh krupnykh gorodov', in *Planirovka i zastroika gorodov* (Kiev, 1968), pp. 10–13.

114. Ibid.

115. The social imbalance can sometimes be very considerable. The already cited Nizhnii Tagil study revealed that the intelligentsia fluctuated between 5 and 23 per cent of the total population in a *mikroraion*. V. L. Barsuk, A. F. Sharova, *op. cit.* p. 78.

116. J. H. Bater, *St. Petersburg, Industrialisation and Change*, (London, Edward Arnold, 1976), pp. 79–80, 377.

117. See, for example, H. Perkin, *The Origins of Modern English Society, 1780–1880* (London, Routledge & Kegan Paul, 1959), pp. 172–4.

9   THE POLICY AND PRACTICE OF SOVIET URBANISATION

1. V. G. Davidovich, *Rasselenie v promyshlennykh uzlakh* (Moscow, 1960), p. 159. Other writers defined the optimum as ranging from 180 000–250 000 (Yu. Bocharov, 'K probleme "optimal'nogo goroda",' *Arkhitektura SSSR*, 1960, no. 5), 100 000–200 000 (A. Skortsov, 'Nazervzhye voprosy organizatsii i planirovaniya gorodskogo khozyaistva SSSR', *Voprosy ekonomiki*, 1958, no. 4), 50 000–100 000 (K. F. Knyazev, 'K probleme optimal'noi velichiny i struktury novykh gorodov', *Problemy sovetskogo gradostroitel'stva*, 1960, no. 13).

2. *Osnovy sovetskogo gradostroitel'stva* (Moscow, 1966), p. 77.

3. Ibid. p. 81.
   So, for example, according to research conducted in the early 1960s, the savings in capital expenditure achieved by developing four cities of 200 000–250 000 inhabitants instead of one with 800 000–1 million people would amount to 360 million roubles. *Opyt proektirovaniya gorodov Ukrainy i Moldavii*, (Kiev, 1965), p. 11.

4. *Osnovy sovetskogo gradostroitel'stva*, *op. cit.* pp. 77–8.

5. See S. Holland, *The Regional Problem* (London, Macmillan, 1976), p. 27.

6. H. Richardson, 'The Arguments for Very Large Cities Reconsidered: A Comment', *Urban Studies*, 13, 1976, p. 307.

7. Western economists have similarly estimated that a population of 200 000–250 000 is necessary for a community to provide a comprehen-

sive range of services. See, for example, H. Richardson, *The Economics of City Size* (London, 1973).

8. B. I. Dobrer, 'Raspredelenie summarnykh zatrat vremeni na peredvizheniya k mestam raboty', in *Rasselenie v gorodakh* (Moscow, 1968), p. 190.

9. M. Buzhkevich, 'Po puti na rabotu', *Pravda*, 11 June 1979, p. 2.

10. G. I. Fil'varov, 'K voprosu optimizatsii reshenii raionnoi planirovki', in *Raionnaya planirovka i problemy rasseleniya* (Kiev, 1974), p. 42.

11. *Stroitel'nye Normiy i Pravily* (SNiP) 11-K.2-62 (Moscow, 1962), point 1.4.

12. *Stroitel'nye Normy i Pravily* (SNiP 11-60-75) (Moscow, 1976), point 1.5.

13. e.g. O. S. Pchelintsev, 'Problemy razvitiya bol'shikh gorodov', in *Sotsiologiya v SSSR*, vol. 2 (Moscow, 1965), p. 275; O. M. Yanitskii, 'Simposium po problemam urbanizatsii', *Voprosy filosofii*, no. 10, 1969, p. 144.

14. e.g. V. I. Perevedentsev, *Problemy sovremennoi urbanizatsii* (Moscow, 1972).

15. O. S. Pchelintsev, 'Formy rasseleniya i razmeshcheniya proizvodietel'nykh sil', in *Urbanizatsiya, nauchno-tekhnicheskaya revolyutsiya i rabochii klass* (Moscow, 1972), p. 131.

16. C. A. Doxiadis, *Ekistiks. An Introduction to the Science of Human Settlements* (London, 1968).

17. D. G. Khodzhaev, 'Nekotorye problemy regulirovaniya rosta i razvitiya naselennykh mest', in *Problemy gradostroitel'stva*, vypusk 1 (Kiev, 1970), p. 16.

18. Rezolyutsiya po dokladu tov. Kaganovicha L., prinyataya Plenumom TsK VKP (b), 15 June 1931: 'O Moskovskom gorodskom khozyaistve i razvitii gorodskogo khozyaistva SSSR', Irkutsk, 1931, p. 44.

19. *XVIII S"yezd VKP (b), 10–21 marta, 1939: stenograficheskii ochet,* (Moscow, 1939), p. 660.

20. Postanovlenie SNK RSFSR, 26 July 1935, 'Ob utverzhdenii dolzhnosti glavnogo gorodskogo arkhitektora v gorodskikh otdelakh kommunal'nykh kozyaistv', *SU RSFSR*, 1935, no. 19, art. 184.

21. Postanovlenie SNK RSFSR, 4 September 1940, 'Ob utverzhdenii polozheniya o glavnom gorodskom arkhitektore', *SP RSFSR*, 1940, no. 16, art. 67.

22. Postanovlenie TsK KPSS i Soveta Ministrov SSSR, 28 May 1969, 'O merakh po uluchsheniyu kachestva zhilishchno-grazhdanskogo stroitel'stva', *SP SSSR*, 1969, no. 15, art. 84.

23. V. V. Voronikov, *Rasskaz o general'nom plane* (Gor'ky, 1971), p. 7.

24. Postanovlenie XVI Vserossiiskogo S"yezda sovetov po dokladu Narodnogo Kommissara kommunal'nogo khozyaistva, 'O sostoyanii i razvitii kommunal'nogo khozyaistva RSFSR', *SU RSFSR*, 1935, no. 9, art. 97.

25. B. S. Khorev, *Problemy gorodov* (Moscow, 1975), p. 86. There are no ostensible reasons to explain why these cites were singled out for special mention.

26. D. G. Khodzhaev, 'Nekotorye problemy regulirovaniya rosta i razvitiya naselennykh mest', *Problemy gradostroitel'stva* (Kiev, 1970), p. 22.

27. N. A. Solofnenko, 'Sistemnyi podkhod k resheniyu problemy rasseleniya', in *Raionnaya planirovka i problemy rasseleniya* (Kiev, 1974), p. 5.

28. A. I. Stanislavskii *et al.* 'Tempy razvitiya krupneishchikh gorodov UkSSR i zadachi regulirovaniya ikh rosta', in *Problemy ekonomiki gradostroitel'stva* (Kiev, 1974), p. 48.
29. Calculated from: *Narodnoe khozyaistvo SSSR 1922–1982* (Moscow, 1982), pp. 21–26.
30. 'Rod lyudskoi: skol'ko nas budet?', *Literaturnaya gazeta*, no. 4, 28 January 1976.
31. A. S. Khokhlov, 'Osobennosti proektirovaniya zon vliyaniya krupneishchikh gorodov (na primere g. Alma-Ata),' in *Praktika gradostroitel'nogo proektirovaniya na osnove nauchnykh issledovanii* (Moscow, 1975), p. 61.
32. Ibid.
33. O. A. Beyul, 'Goroda rastut vverkh', *Izvestiya*, 7 March 1971.
34. L. Yu. Stolbun *et al.* 'Osnovnye gradoobrazuyushchie faktory rosta chislennosti naseleniya krupnykh gorodov UkSSR', in *Ekonomika razvitiya i rekonstruktsii gorodov* (Kiev, 1975), p. 28.
35. Ibid. pp. 31, 34.
36. V. M. Orekhov, A. D. Ivanova, *op. cit.* p. 79.
37. *Problemy rasseleniya v SSSR* (Moscow, 1980), p. 203.
38. See, e.g. E. K. Fedorov, *Vzaimodeistvie cheloveka i prirody* (Moscow, 1972); O. Yanitskii, 'The Urban Way of Life and Ecology', *Social Sciences*, vol. 10, no. 4, 1979.
39. There are good social and economic reasons for focusing on the time factor as a major problem of large cities. The theoretical underpinning is provided by Marx who, on a number of occasions, referred to the saving of work-time as being equivalent to increasing the amount of free-time available to the individual – that is, time for his all-round development. K. Marx and F. Engels, *Sochineniya*, vol. 46, part 2 (Moscow, 1969), p. 21.
40. V. Shkvarikov, *Razmeshchenie zhilishchnogo stroitel'stva v gorodakh* (Moscow, 1960).
41. *Osnovy Sovetskogo gradotroitel'stva*, vol. 1, *op. cit.*, p. 90.
42. *Materialy XXIV S''yezda KPSS* (Moscow, 1971), p. 279.
43. *Materialy XXV S''yezda KPSS* (Moscow, 1976), p. 223; *Materialy XXVI S''yezda KPSS* (Moscow, 1981), p. 138.
44. According to one estimate, surplus labour rarely exceeds 500–700 people. Given that about 40 per cent of the population in a town of 50 000 inhabitants would belong to the 'town-forming group', floating labour (the unemployed) would amount to $2\frac{1}{2}$–$3\frac{1}{2}$ per cent of the town's work force. See B. R. Parlchinskii, G. S. Ronkin, 'Problemy razvitiya malykh i srednykh gorodov', in *Voprosy ekonomiki gradostroitel'stva i raionnoi planirovki*, vypusk 4 (Kiev, 1970), p. 39.
45. As a policy goal this may be preferable to that suggested by Richardson who holds that 'the way to improve the distribution of welfare is to redistribute income not to change the settlement pattern'. H. W. Richardson, (1976) *op. cit.*
46. A. A. Nesterenko, *Zakonomernosti sotsial'no – ekonomicheskogo razvitiya goroda i derevni* (Kiev, 1975), p. 59.
47. A. V. Kochetkov, 'Sotsial'noe planirovanie i regional'noe razvitie', in A. N. Alekseev, O. I. Shkaratan (eds) *Planirovanie sotsial'nogo razvitiya*

gorodov (Moscow, 1973), p. 46. The per capita consumption of services in the Ukraine as a whole, in 1974 amounted to 25 roubles 13 kopeks; in rural areas the figure was 16R 11K. Even allowing for the fact that Kiev is the capital and many people from the countryside will make purchases there, the per capital expenditure in Kiev of 44R 94K none the less acts as an indicator of the higher standard of living in large cities. *Narodnoe khozyaistvo Ukrainskoi SSR v 1974* (Kiev, 1975), p. 45; V. Baranov, 'Problemy razvitiya malykh gorodov', *Ekonomicheskaya gazeta*, October 1974, no. 40, p. 9.

48. G. Zelensky, E. Voronin, 'Luchshe ispol'zovat' trudovye resursy', *Planovoe khozyaistvo*, June 1968, no. 6. A list of towns had been drawn up by *Gosplan* USSR at the beginning of the eighth five-year plan (1966–70); in 1966–68 work started on 155 new enterprises in the towns listed. By the end of 1968, this list had to be revised since the towns had expanded to a point where further industrial investment would be 'inexpedient'. So, in 1969, work began on compiling a new list of towns for the ninth five-year plan (1971–75). D. G. Khodzhaev, 1970, *op. cit.*, p. 23.

49. *Materialy XXV S"yezda KPSS, op. cit.* p. 125.

50. 'Vygody rekonstruktsii,' *Izvestiya*, 12 November 1975 p. 1.

51. *Narodnoe khozyaistvo SSSR v 1967g.*, p. 622; *N.Kh. SSSR v 1975g.*, p. 509; *N.Kh. SSSR v 1980g.*, p. 339.
   See also: V. Isaev, 'Provyshenie effektivnosti kapital'nogo stroitel'stva', *Voprosy ekonomiki*, no. 2, February 1977, p. 7.

52. *Narodnoe khozyaistvo Tul'skoi oblasti: statisticheskii sbornik* (Tula, 1973), p. 169. The actual figures were:

Year	1966	1967	1968	1969	1970	1971
%	79	83	81	78	86	91

53. V. Beketov, 'Zavod v raitsentre', *Pravda*, 9 September 1975.

54. *Problemy razvitiya sotsialisticheskikh finansov* (Moscow, 1977), p. 162.

55. The republic is situated to the south-east of Moscow and its capital, Saransk, is 400 miles from Moscow. Although its population has declined over the past decade (1966–76) from 1 009 000 to 985 000 this has been at the expense of the rural population. Its urban population increased from 297 000 (29 per cent) to 436 000 (44 per cent), of which 55 per cent live in Saransk.

56. S. Esin, 'Bol'shie problemy malykh gorodov', *Sotsialisticheskaya industriya*, 11 May 1971.

57. D. G. Khodzhaev, *op. cit.*, p. 20.

58. *Migratsionnaya podvizhnost' naseleniya v SSSR* (Moscow, 1974), p. 5.

59. A. Tsygichko, 'Tekhnicheskoe perevooruzhenie truda i effektivnosti obshchestvennogo proizvodstva', *Planovoe khozyaistvo*, no. 3, 1979, pp. 75–83. Mr Tikhonov, the Prime Minister, in his address to the XXVI Party Congress, contradicted this view by stating that by investing in retooling 'labour requirements are also reduced'. *Materialy . . .* (1981) *op. cit.* p. 110.

60. A. Nesterenko, *op. cit.* pp. 59–60.

61. V. Perevedentsev, *Goroda i vremya* (Moscow, 1975), p. 81.
62. N. Solofnenko, 'Sistemnyi podkhod k resheniyu problemy rasseleniya', in *Raionnaya planirovka i problemy rasseleniya* (Kiev, 1974), p. 4.
63. *Problemy rasseleniya v SSSR*, 1980, *op. cit.* p. 201.
64. B. Svetlichnyi, 'Bol'shie sud'by malykh gorodov', *Arkhitektura SSSR* no. 5, 1974, p. 22.
65. V. Baranov, 'Problemy razvitiya malykh gorodov', *Ekonomicheskaya gazeta*, no. 40, October 1974, p. 9.
66. L. Lugovskii, 'Gde byt' filialy', *Sotsialisticheskaya industriya*, 1 October 1975.
67. M. Mead, 'The Crucial Role of the Small City in Meeting the Urban Crisis', in R. Eells and C. Walton, *Man in the City of the Future: a Symposium of Urban Philosophers* (London, Macmillan, 1968), p. 52.
68. L. Lugovskii, *op. cit.*
69. *Narodnoe khozyaistvo SSSR v 1978g.*, p. 372. In 1975, the average monthly wage of a state farm worker was 80 per cent of that of a worker in industry, while the wage of a collective farmer was 20 per cent less than that of a state farm worker, thus making him much more dependent on the private plot to supplement his income.
70. I. Pereverzev, 'Sotsial'noe razvitie sela', *Voprosy ekonomiki*, no. 2, February 1977, p. 3.
71. V. A. Glazov *et al.* 'Osobennosti mezhraionnoi migratsii naseleniya v RSFSR', in A. Z. Maikov (ed.), *Migratsiya naseleniya RSFSR* (Moscow, 1973), p. 32.
72. S. Grivashevskii, 'Chtob sel molodelo', *Pravda*, 10 May 1977. The reasons for this out-migration are not solely connected with 'better' infrastructural provision outside the village. The *General Plan for Settlements in the USSR* envisages that only about 120 000 out of almost 470 000 rural settlements enumerated in the 1970 Census should be preserved, the remainder to be abandoned or consolidated into larger units. In some *oblasts* in the RSFSR, 70–80 per cent of the rural settlements were defined as being 'without a future'. (TsNIIP gradostroitel'stvo, *Regional'noe rasselenie i raionnaya planirovka*, Moscow, 1976, p. 30.) According to one senior official the out-migration of the rural population, especially of skilled workers, may be attributed to the consolidation of rural places taking place in virtual disregard of villagers' preferences. The rationale behind this policy of consolidation is evident and, on the face of it, well justified. However, as already noted in earlier chapters, not everyone accepts as axiomatic any more that 'all that is urban is good'. Of the 5642 rural communities in the Perm' *oblast'* 5170 (92 per cent) have been classified as 'futureless'. Just over one-third of these were to be 'eliminated' during the period 1976–80; yet, by 1979 less than one quarter of the families affected had moved out, which suggests that people do not want to move to 'central, consolidated villages'. In the whole of this *oblast'*, where almost half a million square metres of housing have been erected in recent years in villages scheduled for development, not one unit has been planned to include outbuildings for farm purposes. (M. L. Strongina, 'Razvitie i regulirovanie sistem rasseleniya', *Voprosy ekonomiki*, no. 12, December 1978, p. 63.) One sociologist recommended that measures to regulate migration should be

applied differentially depending on the type of village, the intensity of migration, the proportion emigrating and the need to ensure 'the demographic and social reproduction of the population'. In order to curtail the high outflow, a whole complex of factors will have to be influenced; most importantly, working conditions must be improved, opportunities for female work expanded, wages increased and a system for providing professional education developed. (A. Zubanov, 'Motivy migratsii sel'skogo naseleniya i ikh regulirovaniya', *Sotsiologicheskie issledovaniya*, no. 1, 1980, p. 95).

73. V. Perevedentsev, (1975), *op. cit.*, pp. 12, 30.

74. V. Orekhov, A. D. Ivanova, *op. cit.*, p. 74.

75. A. Stanislavskii *et. al.* 'Tempy razvitiya krupneishchikh gorodov UkSSR i zadachi regulirovaniya ikh rosta', in *Problemy ekonomiki gradostroitel'stva* (Kiev, 1974), p. 49.

76. For instance, between 1966 and 1970, output in the tractor industry was mainly increased by doubling the capacity of existing factories in Khar'kov, Minsk, Omsk and Volgograd (all cities where further industrial construction is prohibited) – even though subsidiaries could have been set up in nearby small and medium-sized towns.

77. *Materialy.* . . . (1981), *op. cit.* p. 110.

78. Department of the Environment, *Change or Decay?* Final Report of the Liverpool Inner Area Study (London, HMSO, 1977).

79. *Puti razvitiya malykh i srednykh gorodov* (Moscow, 1967), p. 14. At a conference held at the Institute for the International Workers' Movement in 1969, it was pointed out that the productivity of labour in industry in large cities was about 25–40 per cent higher than in the country at large. 'Urbanizatsiya: nastoyashchee i budushchee', *Voprosy ekonomiki*, no. 11, 1969. For further details, see: Yu. Pivovarov, *Sovremennaya urbanizatsiya* (Moscow, 1976), pp. 113–119, who refers to Alonso's observations on the tendency of per capita income to grow with increases in city size.

80. L. Sveikauskas, 'The Productivity of Cities', *Quarterly Journal of Economics*, vol. 89, 1975, pp. 393–413.

81. V. I. Perevedentsev, *Migratsiya naseleniya i trudovye problemy Sibiri*, (Novosibirsk, 1966), pp. 17–18; Yu. P. Bocharov, 'Razmeshchenie nauchnykh uchrezhdenii v gorodakh i aglomeratsiyakh', in *Problemy Sovestskogo gradostroitel'stva*, vypusk 2 (Kiev, 1971), p. 7.

82. L. Yu. Stolbun *et al.* 'Osnovnye gradoobrazuyushchie faktory rosta chislennosti naseleniya krupnykh gorodov UkSSR', in *Ekonomika razvitiya i rekonstruktsii gorodov* (Kiev, 1975), p. 32.

83. Because of a tendency of certain industries – particularly precision engineering, electronics, radiotechnology, computer and automated systems – to form such scientific–productive associations, whereas the total number of people employed in manufacturing in Novosibirsk increased by 34 per cent over the decade 1963–73, in electronics the figure was 69 per cent, in radiotechnology – 52 per cent and in general engineering – 39 per cent. G. S. Ronkin, 'Voprosy formirovaniya ekonomicheskoi bazy gruppovykh sistem naselennykh mest', in *Problemy ekonomiki gradostroitel'stva*, (Kiev, 1974), pp. 42–43.

84. V. I. Perevedentsev, (1975), *op. cit.* pp. 25–30.

344 Notes and References to pp. 250–2

85. F. M. Listengurt, 'O perspektivakh formirovaniya naseleniya krup-
neishikh gorodov', in *Voprosy ekonomiki gradostroitel'stva i raionnoi
planirovki*, vypusk 4 (Kiev, 1970).

86. I. V. Polyakov, 'Vosproizvodstvo naseleniya Leningrada', in *Sovetskoe
zdravookhranenie*, 1973, no. 8, p. 45.

87. I. P. Bronshtein, 'K voprosam metodiki opredeleniya proektnoi chislennosti naseleniya gorodov', in *Zastroika gorodov i razmeshchenie
uchrezhdenii obsluzhivaniya* (Kiev, 1966). See also: I. P. Polyakov, N. S.
Sokolovna, 'Kharakteristiki tendentsii rozhdaemosti v Leningrade',
Sovetskoe zdravookhranenie, 1972, no. 10, p. 32; *Raionnye osobennosti
vosproizvodstva naseleniya SSSR* (Cheboksary, 1970), pp. 10–12.

88. G. M. Maksimov (ed.) *Vsesoyuznaya perepis' naseleniya 1970 goda.
Sbornik statei* (Moscow, 1976), pp. 176–7.

89. *Byulleten' ispolkoma Moskovskogo gorodskogo Soveta*, no. 21, 1977.

90. *Migratsionnaya podvizhnost' naselenii v SSSR* (Moscow, 1974), p. 11.

91. A. Z. Maikov (ed.) *Migratsiya naseleniya RSFSR* (Moscow, 1973), p. 5.

92. A. N. Yushchenko, *Molodyozh' rabochikh obshchezhitii: problemy i
resheniya* (Leningrad, 1976), p. 10.

93. A. V. Topilin, *Territorial'noe pereraspredelenie trudovykh resursov v
SSSR* (Moscow, 1975), pp. 44–47.

94. *Materialy . . .* (1981), *op. cit.* p. 54.

95. A. S. Khokhlov, 'Osobennosti proektirovaniya zon vlyaniya krupneishchikh gorodov (na primere g. Alma-Ata)', in *Praktika gradostroitel'nogo proektirovaniya na osnove nauchnykh issledovanii* (Moscow, 1975), p. 63.

96. V. A. Glazov *et al.* 'Osobennosti mezhraionnoi migratsii naseleniya v
RSFSR', in A. Z. Maikov, *op. cit.* p. 32.

97. Postanovlenie Soveta Ministrov SSSR, 31 May 1973, 'O l'gotakh po
pereseleniyu', *SP SSSR* 1973, no. 13, art. 70; Postanovlenie Soveta
Ministrov SSSR, 23 July 1977; 'Ob uvelechenii razmera kredita na
stroitel'stvo zhilykh domov dlya pereselentsev', *SP SSSR*, 1977, no. 20,
art. 125; Postanovlenie TsK KPSS, Soveta Ministrov SSSR i Vsesoyuznogo tsentral'nogo soveta professional'nykh soyuzov, 13 December
1979, 'O dal'neishem ukreplenii trudovoi distsipliny i sokrashchenii
tekuchesti kadrov v narodnom khozyaistve', *SP SSSR*, 1980, no. 3,
art. 17.

98. 'Rekomenduet byuro trudoustroistva', *Ekonomicheskaya gazeta*,
no. 46, November 1976, p. 10.

99. A. Murie *et al. Housing Policy and the Housing System* (London, George
Allen & Unwin, 1976), pp. 66–67.

100. A. V. Topilin, *op. cit.* pp. 101–117.

101. A. Kocherga, 'Problemy territorial'nogo planirovaniya narodnogo
blagosostoyaniya', *Planovoe khozyaistvo*, no. 2, February 1979,
pp. 92–99.

102. R. Vitebskii, 'Regional'nye razlichii v zatratakh na infrastrukture',
Voprosy ekonomiki, no. 9, 1978, p. 50.

103. N. V. Baranov, 'Sostoyanie i perspektivy razvitiya gradostroitel'stva',
in *Trudy VI sessii ASiA SSSR* (Moscow, 1961), p. 7.

104. V. V. Vladimirov, 'O povyshenii kompleksnosti raionnoi planirovki', in
Raionnaya planirovka i problemy rasseleniya (Kiev, 1974), p. 15.

105. E. E. Leizerovich, 'O proektirovanii territorial'no-proizvodstvennykh kompleksov v raionnoi planirovke', in *Raionnaya planirovka ... op. cit.* pp. 28–9; V. Dementyev, 'Otraslevoi i territorial'nyi aspekty upravleniya', *Planovoe khozyaistvo*, no. 11, November 1975, pp. 152–4.
106. *Pravda*, 19 November 1969.
107. A. Stanislavskii *et al.* (1974), *op. cit.* p. 48.
108. *Materialy ...* (1981), *op. cit.* p. 110.
109. L.Yu. Stolbun *et al. op. cit.* p. 31.
110. D. G. Khodzhaev, 'O nekotorykh problemakh razvitiya novykh gorodov', *Planovoe khozyaistvo*, no. 2, 1979, pp. 68–76.
111. V. Davidovich, *Voprosy planirovki novykh gorodov* (Leningrad, 1934), pp. 68–9. The notion of a group of settlements forming an integrated spatial structure is not new. Sakulin in the early 1920s and a government decree of 1933 established that towns could not be planned in isolation. In December 1918, B. V. Sakulin, a member of the Department of Town Planning for Urban and Rural Reconstruction (*Ugorsel'stroi*), presented a report on *The Replanning of Moscow as a City for Tomorrow* in which he proposed the creation of a large city–region complex, consisting of a series of satellite towns located in three concentric zones surrounding the capital. (*Vooruzhenii narod*, no. 4, 10 December 1918; *Tekhnika, stroitel'stvo i promyshlennost'*, no. 1, 1922.) His layout plan for Moscow and its satellites bore a resemblance to plans for the 'ideal' city which were gaining support in western Europe at the turn of the twentieth century. But in condemning to failure attempts to create optimum-sized cities of the order of 60 000 inhabitants, Sakulin anticipated later debates which were to occur in the Soviet Union on the subject of an optimum. In his view the city had to be understood and planned for as a link in the organisation of large industrial regions; thus, his plan for Moscow and its zone of influence with its provisions for a transportation – network to link the various towns in the agglomeration with one another and with the central city, was the country's first regional layout plan. Far-sighted planners in Western Europe were also aware, at this time, of the need to compile urban plans which would include a large central city and its adjacent region. But whereas the plan for the Ruhr, for instance, covered an area of 3500 sq. km., Sakulin's plan for Moscow embraced 90 000 sq. km. – although the region which, he calculated, came under the direct economic influence of Moscow was only a quarter of this (i.e. 22 500 sq. km.). He also drew up a plan for an area covering one million square km., ranging from Kostroma in the North to Belgorod in the South and from Minsk in the West to Tambov in the East. (*Tekhnika, stroitel'stvo i promyshlennost'*, 1922, no. 3, pp. 13–16.) The 1933 decree, regarded by some authors as laying the official foundations for regional planning in the USSR (I. P. Savchenko, A. F. Lipyavkin, *Osnovy raionnoi planirovki*, Moscow, 1970, p. 33), reaffirmed that both the creation of new towns and settlements and the redevelopment of existing ones should be in accordance with a general layout plan. (Postanovlenie TsIK i SNK SSR, 27 June 1933, 'O sostavlenii i utverzhdenii proektov planirovki i sotsialisticheskoi rekonstruktsii gorodov i drugikh naselennykh mest SSSR', *SZ SSSR*, 1933, no. 41, art. 243.)

These early policy decisions were instrumental in establishing the principle that short and long term planning policies should be compiled on both a 'branch' and a 'territorial' basis, the first indicating what is to be produced by the different sectors of the economy and the other showing the spatial location of enterprises and industrial complexes in cities, groups of settlements and over large regions.

112 V. G. Davidovich, *Rasselenie v promyshlennykh uzlakh* (Moscow, 1960), p. 292; V. Davidovich, 'Gorodskie aglomeratsii v SSSR', in *Voprosy gorodskogo rasseleniya* (Kiev, 1964), p. 16.

113. Davidovich (1964), *op. cit.* pp. 16–17.

114. Ibid, p. 21.

115. A. G. Vishnevskii, 'Ponyatie i granitsy gorodskikh aglomeratsii', in *Gradostroitel'stvo. Voprosy rasseleniya* (Kiev, 1966), pp. 26–37; D. I. Bogograd, 'Zadachi izucheniya i regulirovaniya rosta gorodskikh aglomeratsii', in *Nauchnye problemy geografii naseleniya*, 1967, p. 101.

116. *Sotsial'nye osnovy razvitiya gorodov* (Moscow, 1975), p. 95.

117. *General'naya skhema rasseleniya na territorii SSSR na 1970,* cited by A. V. Allakhverdiev, 'Voprosy kolichestvennoi otsenki formy planirovochnoi struktury gorodskikh aglomeratsii', in *Arkhitekturno-planirovochnye problemy goroda* (Moscow, 1975), p. 15. The agglomeration must not be confused with the concept of the 'grouped system of settlements' which refers to a spatial unit in which the whole population in the system is within 4–5 hours travel time by a developed public transport system of a major regional centre 'with national level status as regards economic, technical, cultural and educational facilities'. The radius of the grouped system centred on Moscow is expected to be c. 150 kilometres. D. G. Khodzhaev *et al.*, *Sistema rasseleniya v SSSR: Voprosy kompleksnogo planirovaniya* (Moscow, 1977), pp. 76–8.

118. M. L. Strongina, *Sotsial'no-ekonomicheskie problemy razvitiya bol'shikh gorodov v SSSR* (Moscow, 1970), p. 46.

119. For instance, Lenin had written on the need and possibility for the Soviet state to guide the development of the nation's resources at the same time avoiding the growth of huge conurbations characteristic of capitalist industrial cities. See: A. O. Kudryavtsev, 'V. I. Lenin i problemy Sovetskogo gradostroitel'stva', in *Problemy gradostroitel'stva*; and Yu. P. Bocharov, 'V. I. Lenin ob osnovakh novogo rasseleniya', in *op. cit.*

120. L. M. Kopetskii, 'Metologicheskie voprosy proizvodstva i raionnaya planirovka', in *Voprosy ekonomiki gradostroitel'stva i raionnoi planirovki*, vypusk 4 (Kiev, 1970), p. 7.

121. O. N. Yanitskii, 'Symposium po problemam urbanizatsii', *Voprosy filosofii*, 1969, no. 10, 141–2.

122. N. N. Sheverdyaeva, 'Osobennosti razmeshcheniya promyshlennykh raionov v gorodskikh aglomeratsiyakh', in *Arkhitekturno-planirovochnye problemy gorodov*, (Moscow, 1975), p. 11.

123. D. G. Khodzhaev, 'Nekotory problemy regulirovaniya rosta i razvitiya naselennykh mest', in *Problemy gradostroitel'stva*, vypusk 1, (Kiev, 1970). As another author expressed it: 'The spatial concentration of populations in agglomerations is an objective consequence of the operation of socio-economic laws'. V. I. Nudel'man, 'Vzaimosvyaz' skhem

raionnoi planirovki s narodnokhozyaistvennymi planami i prognozami', in *Raionnaya planirovka i problemy rasseleniya* (Kiev, 1974), p. 25.

124. G. I. Lavrik, N. M. Demin, *Metodologicheskie osnovy raionnoi planirovki* (Moscow, 1975), pp. 3–4. M. L. Strongina, *op. cit.* pp. 30, 36, 76.

125. O. P. Litovka, 'Aktual'nye problemy prostranstvennogo razvitiya gorodskikh poselenii', in O. I. Shkaratan, A. N. Alekseev, *op. cit.*

126. V. I. Perevedentsev, (1975) *op. cit.* p. 74.

127. V. A. Lavrov, (1972), *op. cit.* p. 24.

128. G. V. Osipov, 'Sotsiologicheskie aspekty urbanizatsii', *Problemy Sovetskogo gradostroitel'stva,* vypusk 2 (Kiev, 1971), p. 4.

129. A. S. Khokhlov, *op. cit.* p. 64; V. M. Orekhov, A. D. Ivanova, *op. cit.* p. 12.

130. G. Fil'varov, 'K voprosu optimizatsii reshenii raionnoi planirovki', in *Raionnaya planirovka i problemy rasseleniya* (Kiev, 1974). pp. 42–3.

131. G. I. Lavrik, I. M. Demin, *Prognozirovanie sistemy naselennykh mest. Metodologicheskie rekomendatsii* (Kiev, 1972).

132. V. G. Davidovich, 'Metod raschyota rasseleniya v predelakh gruppy gorodov', in *Raionnaya planirovka* (Kiev, 1969), p. 10.

133. B. S. Khorev, *Problemy gorodov* (Moscow, 1975), p. 331; *Problemy rasseleniya v SSSR*, (1980), *op. cit.* pp. 222, 227.

134. B. Khorev (1975), Ibid.

135. V. G. Davidovich, 'Gorodskie aglomeratsii v SSSR' in *Voprosy gorodoskogo rasseleniya* (Kiev, 1964), p. 16.

136. *Gradostroitel'stvo. Voprosy rasseleniya* (Kiev, 1966), pp. 51–2.

137. V. M. Orekhov, A. D. Ivanova, *op. cit.* p. 83.

138 *Rasselenie v prigorodnykh zonakh: voprosy geografii. Sbornik vosem'desyat sed' moi* (Moscow, 1971), p. 7. In 1976, the average work-to-home travelling time for all large cities, including intra-city travel, was 53 minutes. (A. Bolshak, Head of the Chief Passenger Administration of the RSFSR Ministry of Motor Transport, 'Gorod, transport, passazhir', *Izvestiya*, 17 January 1976).

139. F. G. Glink, 'Formirovanie trudovykh svyazei prigorodnogo raiona Minska', in *Proektirovanie setei gorodskogo transporta*, (Kiev, 1972), pp. 55–56. Another study revealed how, when a research institute in Moscow moved some 10 km. from old to new premises, the proportion of the 300 employees spending 60–90 minutes on the journey to work rose from 12.5 to 55.2 per cent immediately after the transfer. This figure fell to 48.2 per cent after two years as people either changed their jobs or moved closer to the institute. Yu. A. Fedutunov, 'Dinamika svyazei mest truda i zhil'ya', *Rasselenie v gorodakh* (Moscow, 1968), pp. 205–209.

140. O. P. Litovka, *Problemy prostranstvennogo razvitiya urbanizatsii* (Leningrad, 1976), p. 47.

141. I. A. Fomin, 'Formirovanie planirovochnoi struktury sistem rasseleniya v raionnoi planirovki', *Raionnaya planirovka* ... (1974) *op. cit.*

142. V. A. Taratynov, 'Odin iz metodov prognozov urovnya trudovoi mayatnikoi migratsii v zone vliyaniya krupnogo goroda', *Raionnaya planirovka* ... (1974) *op. cit.* p. 47.

143. V. Orekhov, A. Ivanova, *op. cit.* p. 84. See also Chapter 8.

144. *Materialy* ... (1976), *op. cit.* p. 220; *Materialy* ... (1981), *op. cit.* p. 181.

145. V. Taratynov, *op. cit.* pp. 47–50.
146. G. S. Ronkin, 'Voprosy formirovaniya ekonomicheskoi bazy gruppovykh sistem naselennykh mest', in *Problemy ekonomiki gradostroitel'stva* (Kiev, 1974), p. 46.
147. C. Fischer, *The Urban Experience* (New York, Harcourt Brace, 1976), p. 21.
148. M. V. Kurman, I. V. Lebedinskii, *Naselenie bol'shogo sotsialisticheskogo goroda* (Moscow, 1968), p. 95. The occupational and social class background of commuters in the Soviet Union contrasts with that of commuters in the United States or UK, where in the main they are drawn from the higher status, non-manual occupations.
149. *Problemy resseleniya v SSSR* (Moscow, 1980), p. 201.
150. This is not to say that migration into large cities has ceased – this is, as we have seen, far from being the case. For the USSR as a whole, the share of migrants in swelling the size of the urban population between 1959 and 1970 was 45.5 per cent (see Table 6.2). In other cities their share was much greater:

The share of net immigration in urban population growth, 1959–68*

City	Proportion (%)
Krasnodar	78.3
Odessa	73.2
Voronezh	72.0
Rostov-on-Don	71.7
Zaporozh'e	69.8
Gor'ky	69.4
Kiev	68.7
Riga	68.2
Saratov	67.8

*D. G. Khodzhaev (1970) *op. cit.* p. 18.

151. *Migratsionnaya podvizhnost' naseleniya v SSSR, op. cit.*, pp. 18–19.
152. See for example, H. Gans, *People and Plans* (New York, Basic Books, 1968); R. Pahl, *Whose City?* Harmondsworth Penguin, 1975), ch. 8.
153. See, for example, R. Lewis, R. Rowland, *Population Redistribution in the USSR. Its Impact on Society 1897–1977* (New York, Praeger, 1979).
154. E. B. Alaev, 'Nekotorye voprosy povysheniya effektivnosti stroitel'stva v malykh i srednykh gorodakh', in *Puti razvitiya malikh . . .* (1967) *op. cit.* p. 122.
155. B. Ts. Urlanis, *Problemy dinamiki naseleniya SSSR* (Moscow, 1974), p. 258. ('The striving by people to live in large cities will continue into the future. The striving derives from a number of economic and social advantages accruing to the large city.')
156. V. Perevedenstev, *Kontsentratsiya gorodskogo naseleniya SSSR i kriterii optimal'nogo razmera goroda* (Moscow, 1970), p. 8.
157. T. V. Ryabushkin (1978), *op. cit.* p. 181.
158. L. B. Kogan, 'Urbanizatsiya i nekotorye voprosy gorodskoi kul'tury', in

Urbanizatsiya, nauchno-tekhnicheskaya revolyutsiya i rabochii klass (Moscow, 1972), p. 105.

159. *Problemy rasseleniya v SSSR* (1980) *op. cit.* p. 233.
160. Ibid.
161. A. V. Kochetkov, 'Sotsial'naya i ekonomicheskaya effektivnost' planomernogo formirovaniya sistem rasseleniya', in *Raionnaya planirovka* ... (1974) *op. cit.* pp. 9, 11.
162. It is possible that with the more widespread adoption of systems theory with its concepts of feed-back, cybernetic control etc., Soviet applied social scientists will refer less frequently to objective laws which, as part of the 19th century scientific vocabulary, was as central to Herbert Spencer (for whom the discovery of 'the laws of social life' was a matter of supreme urgency*) and Durkheim (who considered that 'if we know in what sense the law of property evolves as societies become larger and denser ... we shall be able to foresee them, and foreseeing them, will them beforehand'**) as for Marx (for whom cognition gives access to universal truths***).
    *H. Spencer, *Social Statistics* (London, 1968), p. 56.
    **E. Durkheim, *The Division of Labour in Society* (New York, The Free Press, 1964), p. 34.
    ***G. Lichtheim, *The Concept of Ideology* (New York, Vintage Books, 1967), pp. 18, 32.
163. V. Perevedentsev (1975) *op. cit.* p. 40.
164. Ibid. p. 16.
165. V. Nudel'man, 'Modelirovanie vozmozhnykh urovnei perspektivnogo razvitiya promyshlennosti v gorodakh', in *Raionnaya planirovka* (Kiev, 1969), p. 17.

10 CONCLUSION

1. The private household plot represents a mode of production which more than anything else may be said to perpetuate a psychology of private ownership. (See, e.g. V. Staroverov, 'Preodolenie sushchestvennykh razlichii mezhdu gorodom i derevnei kak sostavnaya chast' zadachi postroeniya sotsial'no odnorodnogo obshchestva', *Sotsiologichestie issledovaniya*, no. 4, 1975). Despite serious differences of opinion within the higher echelons of the Party and state apparatus, the XXVI Party Congress has now come out firmly in support of the private plot. (See *Materialy* ... (1981) *op. cit.* p. 48.)
2. P. Sztompka, *System and Function. Towards a Theory of Society* (London, Academic Press, 1974).
3. L. Tivey has provided a useful difinition of this term: 'Properly understood, decentralisation means that each level specifies the powers to be exercised by the level below, and leaves it free to exercise them; it does not mean that superior-level policies can be ignored'. (L. Tivey, *Nationalisation in British Industry* (London, Jonathan Cape, 1966), p. 112.
4. Whether or not they represent aspects of *the* dominant struggle in the Soviet Union, viz. greater autonomy for enterprise managers (*vis à vis* central planning authorities), has been fully discussed elsewhere. See: V.

Andrle, *Managerial Power in the Soviet Union* (London, Saxon House, 1976).

5. G. S. Yusin, 'Nekotorye voprosy optimizatsii regional'nogo rasseleniya', in I. M. Smolyar, *Arkhitekturno-planirovochnye problemy goroda* (Moscow, 1975).

6. 'Each man', as Gramsci observed, 'carries on some form of intellectual activity, that is, he is a 'philosopher, an artist, a man of taste, he participates in a particular conception of the world, has a conscious line of moral conduct and therefore contributes to sustain a world or modify it.' (Q. Hoare, G. Nowell Smith (eds) *Selections from the Prison Notebooks of Antonio Gramsci* (London, Lawrence & Wishart, 1971), p. 9.

7. V. Lenin, *Selected Works*, vol. IX (New York, 1943), pp. 253–4.

8. J. Stalin, *Problems of Leninism* (Moscow, FLPH, 1954), pp. 96–8.

9. B. Rumer, 'Soviet Investment Policy: Unresolved Problems', *Problems of Communism*, September–October 1982 p. 68.

10. K. Marx & F. Engels, *Selected Works*, vol. 1 (Moscow, FLPH, 1962), p. 363.

11. A. Gouldner, *The Coming Crisis of Western Sociology* (London, Heinemann, 1971), ch. 12.

12. According to Soviet philosophers: 'There is no whole existing in itself, in isolation. Each whole has a particular relationship with the external environment . . . The given whole is characterised not only by the specific composition of its elements and specific structure but by the form of its interrelationship with the environment', (V. Afanasyev, *Nauchnoe upravlenie obshchestva* (Moscow, 1968), p. 54. See also, note 8 to the Introduction.

13. The notion of societal convergence achieved popularity for a short period in the 1960s. More recently, D. Lane has defined it as 'a process by which heterogeneous cultures, characterising different societies, develop and change in the direction of greater likeness to one another until eventually they adopt similar arrangements for the performance of important social functions' (D. Lane, *The Socialist Industrial State* (London, George Allen & Unwin, 1976), p. 54).

14. M. Loiter, 'Effektivnost' kapital'nykh vlozhenii v okhrane prirodnoi sredy', *Voprosy ekonomiki*, no. 1 1976, pp. 28–38.

15. E. Sharp, 'Super Ministry. The First Steps', *Built Environment*, vol. 1, no. 1, 1972.

Index